THE LOEB CLASSICAL LIBRARY

FOUNDED BY JAMES LOEB, LL.D.

EDITED BY

E. H. WARMINGTON, M.A., F.R.HIST.SOC.

PREVIOUS EDITORS

† T. E. PAGE, C.H., LITT.D.　　　† E. CAPPS, PH.D., LL.D.

† W. H. D. ROUSE, LITT.D.　　　L. A. POST, L.H.D.

PHILO

X

PHILO

IN TEN VOLUMES
(AND TWO SUPPLEMENTARY VOLUMES)

X

THE EMBASSY TO GAIUS

WITH AN ENGLISH TRANSLATION BY

F. H. COLSON, M.A.
LATE FELLOW OF ST. JOHN'S COLLEGE, CAMBRIDGE

INDICES TO VOLUMES I–X
J. W. EARP

CAMBRIDGE, MASSACHUSETTS
HARVARD UNIVERSITY PRESS
LONDON
WILLIAM HEINEMANN LTD
MCMLXXI

American
ISBN 0-674-99417-5

British
ISBN 0 434 99379 4

First printed 1962
Reprinted 1971

Printed in Great Britain

CONTENTS OF VOLUME X

PREFACE TO VOLUME X

Mr. Colson lived long enough to correct his last proofs, but not to complete his notes and index. What he left is here given. This translation is really his work, although other names are associated with the early part; but I have gone through the whole in ms. with him, so I know that the work is Colson's monument, and I believe it will last. A translator more careful and more competent I never worked with.

W. H. D. Rouse

November 1943

For compilation of the indices we are indebted to the Rev. J. W. Earp.

E. H. W.

INTRODUCTION TO THE
DE LEGATIONE

THE treatise generally known by this somewhat mis-
leading name is a very lively and powerful invective
against the Emperor Gaius.   One part of it, in which
he gives an account of the ineffectual design of Gaius
to introduce his statue into the temple of Jerusalem,
supplementing and in many places differing from
Josephus's account of the same incident, is of considerable value in the history of Judaism.   Otherwise
it adds little or nothing to our knowledge of the reign
of Gaius or to the accounts given in the regular
historians of his follies and vices.   It does not repel
by its vindictiveness to the same extent as the *Flaccus*,
though perhaps if we possessed the " Palinode "
which is promised at the end, this opinion would have
to be modified.   It has some difficult problems peculiar to itself which are discussed later in this introduction.   Meanwhile I give the following analysis
of its contents.

It opens with a few introductory remarks, on which
see p. xx (1-7), and then proceeds to describe the
splendid prospects with which Gaius's reign opened
and the world-wide delight and hope which his accession aroused (8-13), then the deep disappointment
and sorrow which his serious illness caused, followed

ix

by renewed rejoicing for his recovery (14-21). From this recovery dates the revelation of Gaius's true character: and there follows a full account of the compulsory suicide of Tiberius Gemellus (22-31) and of Macro, prefaced by a long description of the services he had rendered to Gaius before his accession and his attempts to keep him in the straight path after his accession and the resentment felt by him at his admonitions (32-64); also the murder of his father-in-law Silanus (62-65). Public opinion indeed was shocked by these atrocities; yet it still clung to the hope that Gaius was not really depraved, and found some measure of justification for them (66-73).

Having thus freed himself from all rivalry and restraint Gaius proceeded to his crowning wickedness, his claim to divinity. This occupies the next forty sections and is developed with very powerful rhetoric. He held that he was as far above other men as a shepherd is above his sheep (74-76); so he assumed the insignia of the demigods Heracles, the Dioscuri and Dionysus, but his actions were the complete reverse of the beneficent labours of the first, the brotherly affection of the second and the gift of wine bestowed by the third (77-92). Worse still, he assumed the part of the full-blown deities Hermes, Apollo, Ares. What a contrast was his life to the pacific mission of the herald's staff of Hermes, to the work of Apollo as physician and prophet, and to the function of the true Ares which is to protect the weak! (93-113).

Hitherto the treatise has dealt entirely with the general depravity of Gaius culminating in his assumption of godship, and the Jews have not been mentioned since the introductory sections. From this point onwards it is his hostility to the Jews and their sufferings traceable to it which occupy the treatise. The connecting link between the two is that this hostility is supposed to be due to the Jews alone refusing to acknowledge his godship (114-119). The Alexandrians knew his resentment of this, and made it an opportunity for the great pogrom of A.D. 38 which is described in 120-131. In this description we traverse much the same ground as in the *Flaccus*, though there there is no suggestion that Gaius's resentment had anything to do with it, while on the other hand the active connivance of Flaccus, which was there a leading feature, is only just hinted here. There are many differences but no substantial contradiction between the two accounts. But in this treatise the pogrom is followed by the attack made upon the synagogues by introducing the images of Gaius (132-136) and here the differences are numerous. In the *Flaccus*, the violation of the synagogues precedes the pogrom and nothing is heard of the wholesale destruction by fire or demolition nor of the effective resistance by the Jews in neighbourhoods where they were in considerable force. That the motive of the Alexandrians was not really loyalty to the emperor is shown because no such attempt was made by them during the reigns of previous sovereigns, neither of the Ptolemies nor yet of Tiberius nor Augustus, though if Gaius deserved such honours, how much more did they, and this is followed by a glowing and possibly sincere panegyric on Augustus (137-151). Why then did the Alexandrians make no attempt during these two reigns to force the Jews to admit their images into the synagogues? It was because they knew that Augustus would tolerate no such violation and that in fact in various ways he showed his careful consideration and respect for Jewish institutions (152-158). The same in general may be said of Tiberius in spite of certain troubles which were entirely due to Sejanus's evil influence (159-161).

Gaius however was so deluded as to believe that the adoration of the Alexandrians was genuine, and their influence helped to excite him against the Jews (162-165). Others who worked in the same direction were the Egyptian courtiers headed by Helicon, who was particularly intimate with the emperor and employed his gift of satire to prejudice him against the Jews in the way which Philo describes at length (166-177). At first the Jewish Embassy hoped to conciliate him, but when they found this impossible they determined to address the emperor directly, but it was in vain (178-180). Gaius indeed greeted the envoys in a friendly manner, but this was hypocrisy as Philo suspected at the time (181-183), and this was proved when while waiting for the summons they heard the terrible news of the proposed violation of the temple at Jerusalem (184-188). The horror caused by the news and the perplexity of the envoys as to what should be their next step are fully described (189-196), and we pass on to the full story of the proposed introduction of the statue into the temple, which occupies two-fifths of the treatise. The first part of this is supposed to be told by the persons who brought the tidings, but it glides imperceptibly into a narrative by Philo himself. There are five main stages : (1) the Jamneian incident, the destruction by the Jews of the rude altar set up by the Jamneians, the anger of Gaius when this was reported to him by Capito, and his consequent order to

Petronius the governor of Syria that a colossal statue of himself should be introduced into the Temple (197-206) ; (2) Petronius while seeing the danger of the proposal makes an unsuccessful attempt to reconcile the Jewish authorities to the inevitable (207-224) ; (3) a vast assembly of Jews from all parts comes to supplicate Petronius saying that they would rather die than live to see such sacrilege. Meanwhile they demand to be allowed to send an embassy to the emperor (225-242) ; (4) Petronius though much moved by their appeal cannot accept this demand but sends a diplomatic letter to the emperor pleading for or rather apologizing for delay (243-253). Gaius though much enraged postponed taking any measures against Petronius, but merely bade him get the statue made and set up as soon as possible (250-260) ; (5) meanwhile Agrippa appears on the scene and hears from Gaius the story of what has happened. He collapses utterly and remains in this state for some days (261-275). On his recovery he writes a long epistle to Gaius, appealing for consideration for the Jewish nation, the city of Jerusalem and the Temple, and with regard to this last he expatiates on the honour which has been paid to it by Gaius's ancestors and predecessors (276-329). The emperor yields to this appeal and countermands his orders for the time, but Philo declares that he not only nullified the concession by threatening to punish any Jews who did violence to any altar or statue dedicated to himself outside Jerusalem, but really intended to carry out his previous intention in the course of the coasting voyage which he proposed to make to Egypt (330-338). To this story is appended some denunciations of his treachery, capriciousness, and cruelty in

other matters, stressing especially his hatred of the
Jews and the sin of intending to violate the Temple
itself (339-348). The rest of the treatise is an account
of the scene in which the ambassadors were summoned to Gaius's presence to lay before him their
political claims whatever they were. It is one continuous scene, in the first part of which they are
carried about in the company of the emperor who is
engaged in inspecting some houses, and have a few
contemptuous remarks flung at them not bearing on
the subject (349-362). In the second part they are
treated a little more seriously and are actually invited
to state their case, but no real hearing is given to
them and they are finally dismissed with the verdict
that they are not so much knaves as fools (363-367).
The sense of hopelessness with which they depart is
described (368-372) and the treatise breaks off with
the promise of the Palinode (373).

The title Περὶ ἀρετῶν is mysterious. It is given in
all the mss. used by Reiter save one, and the majority
have the addition of αʹ. It is vouched for as the title
assigned by Philo himself in two passages of Eusebius,
in one of which he says that the name was given by
Philo to his description of Gaius's blasphemous
impiety (θεοστυγία) " facetiously (or whimsically) and
ironically " (μετὰ ἤθους καὶ εἰρωνείας), *i.e.* it really
means " On the wickedness of Gaius and his gang."

No one I think has ever taken this explanation of
Eusebius seriously, yet perhaps we should note that
in this treatise we do find ironical phrases which do
not appear elsewhere as well as I can remember in
his writings, *e.g.*, his description of Gaius's " wise and
excellent advisers," and the " aristocratic " Helicon
(203), his application of σεμνός to the animal worship

suffered under those two persons. Is it really necessary to look beyond the passage about Sejanus in
Legatio 154 f. and the story of Pilate bringing images
into Jerusalem in *Legatio* 299 ff. ? These scholars all
ignore the obvious fact that Eusebius is not here
concerned to give an account of Philo's writings,
which he does somewhat confusedly in the eighteenth
chapter, but to support his conviction that the troubles
of the Jews date from the Crucifixion, and were a
retribution for it.

The passage about Sejanus is very short but it is
good enough to prove that Philo supports this view
and Eusebius here follows his words pretty closely,
while his entry in the *Chronicle* to judge from Jerome's
version is closer still. As to Pilate, if we had this
passage alone it might well be argued that the reference is to something outside our existing *Legatio*, for
the attempted outrage is said to be against the
temple, whereas in *Legatio* 299 ff. not only is there no
such suggestion but the point is made that unlike
Gaius's proposed sacrilege it was not against the
temple (302). But in the *Demonstratio Evangelica*
viii. p. 403 Eusebius cites Josephus as stating that
Pilate brought the images of Caesar by night into the
temple and continues : " to this Philo testifies saying
that Pilate set up by night the royal ensigns of Caesar
in the temple, which was the beginning of factions."
Now I think there can be no reasonable doubt in
spite of the discrepancy between shields and ensigns [a]
that the incident here mentioned as being described
by Josephus and testified to by Philo is the same as

[a] It should be added that Philo in *Legatio* does not say
that the shields were brought in by night, though he does
not deny it.

that described by Agrippa in *Legatio* 299.[a] But
Eusebius states that both Josephus and Philo made
the temple the scene of the outrage.[b] Now we know
that Josephus does not do so in either of the two
accounts [c] which he has written and that Philo does
not in the account which has come down to us. Which
is the more natural supposition ? That Philo in some
other version of the incident lost to us contradicted
himself or that Eusebius made the same mistake
about Philo as he did about Josephus ? If we say the
latter, the natural conclusion is, that when he speaks
in the *History* of an attempt on the temple mentioned
by Philo he refers to the same incident. And in
view of this there seems to me to be no more necessity
to postulate a fuller account now lost of Pilate's
activities than of those of Sejanus.

In addition to this supposed necessity Cohn and
Massebieau rely on the number of lacunas which they
think are evident in the existing treatise. The first
of these lies between the first and second chapters.
The γάρ with which the second opens has, they say,
no logical connexion with the preceding chapter. I
think this is a misapprehension of Philo's regular
method. The essence of the introductory chapter is
in the first three or four sections. Men judge blindly
by the present (1, 2) and yet the events which have
happened should convince them of the reality of
providence, especially its care for Israel (3, 4). At
this point he goes off into a thoroughly Philonic

[a] I observe that Reiter, though he accepts the mutilation
theory, gives on *Legatio* 299 a reference to Dem. p. 403, and
that Heikel on Dem. p. 403 gives a reference to *Legatio* 299.

[b] He ascribes the same statement to Josephus in the
Chronicle. See citation, p. xviii.

[c] *Ant.* xviii. 3. 1, *Bell. Jud.* ii. 9. 2.

ramble : (a) Israel means he who sees God, (b) to see
God is the highest gift, (c) for reason in itself cannot
apprehend God nor even His powers, (d) the powers
mean His punitive as well as His beneficial powers.
Now I confess I am surprised that in introducing the
treatise Philo has allowed himself to ramble into a
train of ideas which belong to the Commentary,
where all four frequently reappear, particularly as he
keeps clear of anything of the kind in the rest of the
book. But I am not surprised, that when after the
introduction he starts to work, he harks back to what
is the essence of the introduction. It is quite in his
way to go back to the main point after a rambling
parenthesis, often as here with a logical connexion
which ignores the parenthesis.[a] And if this is understood what better proof of the blindness of men could
be found than the joy and hopefulness which greeted
Gaius's accession and recovery ?[b] Though indeed
the γάρ goes further than this. It suggests that
the story which begins with this blind rejoicing
will also illustrate the belief expressed in § 4 that
providence watches over Israel and overthrows the
oppressor. Should we expect him to put this into
words at this point and anticipate the Palinode by
mentioning the fate of Gaius, an event presumably
quite recent and common knowledge to all his
readers ?

Of the other three lacunas registered in Reiter's

[a] For such resumptive conjunctions after a longer or
shorter parenthesis see, *e.g.*, (γάρ) *Spec. Leg.* i. 6, iv. 101, (οὖν)
Leg. All. i. 77 and iii. 211, (ὥστε) *De Fug.* 64, (οὕτως) *De
Cong.* 135. The resumption of Gaius's vices in § 339 of this
treatise, after the parenthetical disquisition on Alexandria,
is much the same, though μέντοι does not imply the same
causal connexion, *cf.* also note on § 292.   [b] *Cf.* § 21.

text two are discussed in the notes on §§ 180 and 292.
Before we come to the fourth we have Cohn's complaint that the Embassy is suddenly introduced in
§ 174 without any account of how it came to be sent,
which therefore must have dropped out. This seems
to me to mistake entirely the nature and object of
the treatise. It has acquired the title of the *Embassy*
naturally enough because all that Philo tells us about
himself is connected with the Embassy, but there is
no sign that Philo himself gave it that title. In fact
throughout it is a " Philippic," [a] an invective against
Gaius and to a minor extent his satellites, and nothing
else. Hardly anything [b] is mentioned which does not
reflect on these, either directly or indirectly by
extolling his predecessors or his honest servants like
Petronius. The Embassy only appears in the story
when Philo gives us his personal experiences of the
enemy. It first appears when the machinations of
Helicon in fostering Gaius's hostility are described.
Then comes the first meeting with Gaius and Philo's
conviction that his friendly greeting was only hypocrisy. There follows the scene in which they hear of
the proposed outrage. In his long story of this
attempt Philo is throughout at pains to emphasize
the Jewish feeling of horror and he inevitably begins

---

[a] Though the analogy is of course very rough, one cannot
help observing how Cicero in the *Second Philippic* leaves a
vast number of less relevant matters unexplained. Philo is
not likely to have read Cicero, but he did read Demosthenes,
and may have got something of the same lesson from his
attacks on Aeschines. The story in Eus. ii. 18, that he read
the Περὶ ἀρετῶν or part of it to the whole senate in Rome
does not sound very probable but does represent a feeling
that the treatise was of the epideictic Oration type.

[b] The one thing which strikes me as irrelevant to the
invective is the mention of the memorial in § 179.

with the sensations and perplexities of his own party. At this point the story passes on to scenes and personages far away from the ambassadors and while it is proceeding we hear no more of them. Then comes the actual interview. Surely, says Delaunay, he must have described how this interview came to be conceded. Possibly if his subject was the Embassy, not if it is Gaius. I cannot feel that there is any strong reason for placing a lacuna at § 311.

Cohn and Delaunay might possibly have replied that my view that the treatise is essentially a Philippic and not a sober history of the Embassy is not only unacceptable to them, but is contradicted by Eusebius when he says that Philo gives a carefully detailed account of what he did at that time. Different opinions may be held about this, but it seems to me that what we have in the treatise would be felt by Eusebius to justify his statement. For the scenes in which the ambassadors appear, particularly the last, are described with the vividness of detail which deserves the epithets τὰ κατὰ μέρος ἀκριβῶς and I do not think he would have troubled himself about the abruptness of the introduction. Moreover the phrase " the things done by him " is used with a loosenes; which forbids taking it very seriously. For he says that of these " doings " he will omit most and cite— what ? the troubles caused by Sejanus and Pilate, which on no supposition can be parts of his doings.

So far then I can find no sign that apart from the Palinode the *Legatio* ever extended beyond what we still have. But what about the Five Books ? Can we pack them or even four of them into the existing 372 sections ? If not, it may reasonably create a suspicion that something has been lost.

INTRODUCTION TO *DE LEGATIONE*

The description given by Eusebius of the scope of the five books agrees quite closely with what we have. It may suggest that more was said about the Embassy, but as it confines itself to the events of Gaius's reign it certainly does not support the idea that events of Tiberius's reign like the persecutions of Sejanus and Pilate were given at any length. As no titles are given we cannot rule out the possibility that the *Flaccus* was one of the five, since it certainly describes one of the matters mentioned in the list. But the phrase πέντε βιβλίοις does not fit in very well with a five made up of four books of *Legatio* plus a totally distinct work like the *Flaccus*. The *Legatio*, if judged by the sense, naturally splits up into four parts: (1) 1-113, where Gaius's degeneration and his three murders of Gemellus, Macro and Silanus and his blasphemous assumption of godship are the subject, and the Jews are never once mentioned after the introductory sections ; (2) 114-161, giving the troubles of the Jews in Alexandria and the contrast of their treatment under former emperors, and it is significant that the two matters mentioned by Eusebius as belonging to the second book of the *Embassy* or *Virtues* both fall within these limits [a] ; (3) 162-348, events outside Egypt and the whole story of Gaius's proposed outrage on the temple ; (4) 349 to the end, the interview, and if we add as all the others do the Palinode we get the required number. I indeed feel very doubtful whether Eusebius included this among the Five or knew of its existence, for surely he would have added such a leading matter as the

---

[a] *i.e.* the sufferings of the Alexandrian Jews " in the second of the books which he entitled *On the Virtues* " ; Sejanus " in the second book of the *Legation* " (*Chronicle*).

retribution on the blasphemer to his list of subjects.
I should prefer to get a five-fold division rather than
a four-fold from the 372 sections, but I do not find
it easy. A good break indeed is made at § 73, but
this would bring the two matters definitely stated as
being in the second book into the third. Possibly
the inordinately long third division might have been
re-divided at the appearance of Agrippa at § 261, but
such an arrangement would not be very logical as the
story of the statue is a continuous whole which does
not admit of any real break. But let us take the
easier course, and assume that the 372 sections made
up four books. Can it be objected that βιβλίον is
too big a word for such divisions ? I do not know of
any grounds for thinking so. Or that the mss. tradition has no knowledge of such divisions as separate
books except the inscription Περὶ ἀρετῶν α′ at the
beginning which may have held on when β′ and
γ′ and δ′ were lost ? The argument may have some
force, but surely will apply with much more force
to the schemes of the advocates of the mutilation
theory. Or that the length of the third division
and the brevity of the fourth are objections ? I
think that the first may have some weight but not
the second. The *De Specialibus Legibus* i. with 350
sections is divided in the mss. into six separate
treatises, the first of which is only eleven sections
and the other, *De Virtutibus*, includes one separate
heading *On repentance* which is only twelve.

Altogether, even if the statement about the five
books creates some difficulty, the possibilities [a] con-

---

[a] Among these may perhaps be included the possibility
that a single letter ε′ was put by mistake for some other
numeral letter.

nected with it are so many, that we cannot build on it without that support from internal evidence which to my mind is entirely wanting. However I quite feel the weight of the body of opinion which asserts the contrary, and do not forget the Cromwellian adjuration " to believe that it is possible that I may be mistaken."

The Embassy is not the subject of the treatise, but we have to consider what we learn about it from incidental hints.

It had two distinct objects, and was sent to plead two distinct causes (ὑποθέσεις). These two are vaguely indicated in describing the memorandum (179) as our sufferings or experiences (ὧν ἐπάθομεν) and our claims (ὧν τυχεῖν ἠξιοῦμεν). But they are more clearly defined in §§ 191 ff. where it appears that one was concerned with the synagogues (προσευχαί) and the other with their πολιτεία. As to the first, the envoys remark that if Gaius does not shrink from desecrating the Temple he will not listen to any appeal against the desecration of the synagogues. As to the other, we learn that it consists in " showing that we are Alexandrians." When we come to the actual reception (349 ff.), how many months after we do not know, the envoys are invited to state their claims as to πολιτεία, this only, and the other is not mentioned.[a] For the opening passage of arms, in which Gaius reproaches the Jews for refusing to admit his deity and is backed up by Isidorus's state-

[a] This is curious. Had there been meanwhile a change of conditions in Alexandria, which made the plea unnecessary? or was it thought more politic not to start a question which by its similarity might stir up Gaius's resentment at having been driven to make the concession to Jerusalem, which I assume him to have made before the interview?

ment that they neglected to sacrifice, a charge which the envoys indignantly deny, has really nothing to do with the complaint that the synagogues have been desecrated. The claim which they are invited to discuss is represented (350) as a plea to retain rights which have never been questioned in the four centuries during which Alexandria has existed, and it is alleged (371) that an adverse decision would be a disastrous blow to the whole of the Dispersion and would put the Jewish population in every city at the mercy of the hostile Gentiles, who would destroy the synagogues and take away the privileges which they had enjoyed. Whether this claim was one for full Alexandrian citizenship, as the phrase " showing that we are Alexandrians " suggests, or to specific rights to independence asserted by the Jews and denied by the others,[a] is a question which I do not feel competent to answer, and I doubt whether in the absence of other evidence it can be answered with any certainty.

A further very difficult question is the chronological. Did this Embassy, of which are we only told that it set out in mid-winter, arrive in Italy in A.D. 39 or 40 ?

We have the following certain data to work upon : we know that the troubles at Alexandria which gave rise to the Embassy took place in the summer of A.D. 38, that Gaius was away from Italy in Gaul and Germany from September 39 to at least May 40,[b]

---

[a] That is to say, $\pi o\lambda\iota\tau\epsilon\iota a = \pi o\lambda\iota\tau\epsilon\upsilon\mu a$ or membership of a $\pi o\lambda\iota\tau\epsilon\upsilon\mu a$, *i.e.* of a " corporation formed by membership of race or community domiciled in a foreign state." This perhaps would give more body to the prophecies of the disasters to be anticipated from an adverse decision.

[b] See Balsdon, *Journal of Roman Studies*, vol. xxiv. pp. 17 and 21.

and that he was killed on 24th January 41. Now clearly Gaius was in Rome when the ambassadors first met him, and in the south of Italy when they first heard of the proposed violation of the Temple, and in Rome when they had their interview with him. We have therefore to place each of these incidents either before September 39 or after May 40.

Now if we took Josephus's (*Ant.* xviii. 261-308) account, we should place them all at the later date. According to him Gaius had written to Petronius cancelling the order for the statue before he received Petronius's apologetic letter, but this enraged him so much that he sent a violent reprimand which being delayed on the way did not reach Petronius till two months after the assassination, *i.e.* in March 41. Mr. Balsdon [a] arguing for the arrival of the ambassadors in 40 gives careful calculations to show, that if we accept this story, the whole of the correspondence from the first report to Gaius of the Jamneian incident to the final letter to Petronius can be got in after his return in May 40, though this perhaps is unnecessary for his purpose, since part of it might have been carried on while Gaius was in the north, though it only became known to Philo after his return.[b] Is there anything in Philo's account which conflicts with the view that the Embassy arrived in 40? Apart from the general probability that it would be undertaken as soon as possible after Flaccus's arrest in September 38 and not be postponed for more than a

[a] *Journal of Roman Studies*, vol. xxiv. p. 19.
[b] Mr. Balsdon assumes that the order had just been given, when Philo heard of it at Puteoli. It seems to me more natural to suppose that the news travelled to him from Palestine, and that the matter may have been far advanced before he heard of it.

year, there is only one serious fact to be reckoned
with.   While Josephus speaks of the recalcitrant
Jews as neglecting their tilling though it was the
season for sowing, Philo says that Petronius, after
receiving the order and spending some considerable
time in trying to talk over the chief Jews and in
meeting the great body of the people, proceeded to
write his letter recommending postponement of the
installation of the statue and gave as one of his
reasons that the sown crops were now ripe and he
feared that the Jews might ravage them as well as
the fruit trees later.   That is to say this letter was
written between April and June.   Mr Balsdon meets
this by suggesting that the crops are the spring sown
crops.   I do not know whether this is agriculturally
sound, but I think that anyone who reads through
the second book of the *Special Laws* with its account
of the ripening of the crops and fruits and their
adjustment to the various feasts will find it difficult
to believe that Philo meant by what he calls τὰ θέρη
anything but the autumn sown crops.   At any rate
this is what his readers would inevitably infer.   If
this is so, and if Petronius's letter was written not
later than June,[a] the order must have been given
some time earlier while Gaius was still in the north.
This does not prove that the ambassadors did not
arrive in the spring of 40, but at any rate the suggestion that the whole of the affair can be concentrated
into the eight months between Gaius's return and
his death must be given up.

[a] Philo is, I think, the better authority.   He need not have
had any authentic knowledge of Petronius's correspondence,
but he would hardly put into his mouth a statement conflicting
with dates which were known to him by personal experience.

I suggest as an alternative the following scheme
for consideration. The ambassadors sailed in the
winter of 38–39, arrived at Rome in the spring, and
after looking about them for some time were met and
greeted by Gaius and later heard the story of the
proposed outrage before he left Italy. Meanwhile
he had heard of the Jamneian incident, had sent his
first order to Petronius but was not aware of the
opposition till he got the letter pleading for delay.
He replied to this acquiescing in some delay though
maintaining his purpose. When was it that Agrippa
intervened? If Josephus is to be believed, it would
be before Gaius left Italy, since he says that Agrippa
was then staying at Rome, though as far as Philo's
story is concerned it might have been while he was
at Lyons at the end of the year.[a] It was after his
return in the next May or later that he granted the
interview to the ambassadors.[b]

For it seems to me that the most certain point in
the controversy is that the interview occurred after
the whole of the affair of the statue had died down.
If we are to give any weight to Philo's account I
cannot conceive that the conference should have
taken the form described and that Gaius should
have merely censured the Jews for their refusal to
acknowledge his deity and their offering sacrifices

---

[a] The statement of Dio lix. 24. 1 that people at Rome were
disturbed to hear that Agrippa was in Gaius's company
(συνεῖναι) seems to apply to the time of his absence from Italy.

[b] The statement about the sacrifices (356) points, I think,
to the same. If they were carried out at Jerusalem (see
note to § 356), this would most likely be when the expedition
was well afoot. And even if it was somewhat earlier, time
must be allowed for the ambassadors to know that they had
been offered.

for him and not to him, if he was boiling with rage
at the threat of a national insurrection, or that he
should have dismissed them with the comparatively
kindly remark that they were more fools than knaves.
And if so we can hardly find time for the interview
before Gaius's departure in September 39. That
there should have been a delay of many months
was natural in any case, since the Jews at any rate
would not during the crisis press their case, in which,
as Philo himself says, §§ 190 ff., they would be at a
hopeless disadvantage, but it became inevitable from
the simple reason that Gaius was inaccessible.

Of course this scheme involves throwing Josephus
over. If it is right, he was mistaken, not only in
placing the crisis at seed time instead of harvest, but
also in bringing the events into so close a connexion
with the death of Gaius. This is certainly a serious
and some may think a fatal objection and therefore I
only put it forward for consideration ; the question is
one, I think, on which certainty is unobtainable.

INTRODUCTION TO INDICES

I HAVE tried to make it as easy as possible for the reader to find what he wants. In this the Editors and the Printer have given me every assistance. Some of the abbreviations used for Philo's treatises are confusing for those not familiar with his works, and so I have adopted ones which will, I hope, be readily understood. It is likely that many will wish to use the Index who do not possess a set of the Loeb edition of Philo, and so I have given the references to chapters, rather than to pages. Roman numerals indicate the Loeb volume, the " n " or " nn " stands for " footnote(s)," the capital " N " or " NN " for the additional notes given by the Translators at the end of the volume. To give an example :

V. *Mut.* 63f, *Som.* i. 192, ii. 70 & N, **VI.** *Abr.* 12 & n, 57, 73nn

means Loeb Philo volume V, *De Mutatione Nominum*, chapters 63 and 64, *De Somniis*, First Treatise, chapter 192, Second Treatise, chapter 70 and the Additional Note thereto, Volume VI, *De Abrahamo*, chapter 12 and the footnote thereto, chapter 57, and the footnotes to chapter 73. I have avoided " ff " as much as possible, since in Philo that might stand for two chapters or twenty. Occasionally round brackets have been placed round a reference to indicate that there is no direct allusion in those chapters or that it is too trivial to be studied.

In the Scripture Index the alignment of chapters and verses has been designed to help the reader's eye. Where there is a divergence in numeration between the Septuagint and the English Versions, this has been indicated ; the reader is warned, however, that the Translators were not consistent and that there will sometimes be a discrepancy between their references and mine.

In compiling the Index to Names and Places in Philo's text I have had in mind the reader who recalls a passage without remembering where it occurs. To trace some such recollections in an author like Philo might take hours, even days ; I have therefore given a summary of what Philo has to say about the commoner figures or places. Sometimes this may contribute something new to the understanding of Philo's interpretations, but the summaries are deliberately concerned with Philo's language more than with the philosophical background of his thought, and I hope that scholars will not expect more from them than that.

In the Index to the Translators' Notes I have marked with an asterisk those names that also occur in the text of Philo and therefore in the Index of Names. There is no need to distinguish them there, since references to notes are included. I had thought of compiling a fourth index to comprise all notes concerned only with the text adopted ; but I have decided to include this in this third index. The reader who wishes to study textual readings will find that these have been included under the names of the several previous editors of Philo—Yonge, Mangey,

INTRODUCTION TO INDICES

Cohn and Wendland, Heinemann, etc.—and, for the Loeb edition, *s.v.* Translators. Mr Colson himself listed the Translators' own readings in Supplements at the end of vols. V (for I-V) and VI ; for subsequent volumes the reader is referred to what I have listed, but my list includes not only new readings adopted by the Translators but also the many more tentative suggestions made by them in the footnotes or Additional Notes.

Finally, I know very well that these indices cannot be exhaustive, and I should welcome notice of any mistakes or omissions, so that these may be corrected in any later edition.

ABBREVIATIONS

Abr. = *De Abrahamo*
Aet. = *De Aeternitate Mundi*
Agr. = *De Agricultura*
Cher. = *De Cherubim*
Conf. = *De Confusione Linguarum*
Congr. = *De Congressu Eruditionis gratia*
Decal. = *De Decalogo*
Det. = *Quod Deterius Potiori insidiari soleat*
Ebr. = *De Ebrietate*
Flacc. = *In Flaccum*
Fug. = *De Fuga et Inventione*
Gig. = *De Gigantibus*
Hyp. = *Hypothetica*
Jos. = *De Josepho*
Leg. = *De Legatione ad Gaium*
Leg. All. i, ii, iii = *Legum Allegoriarum*
Mig. = *De Migratione Abrahami*
Mos. i, ii = *De Vita Mosis*
Mut. = *De Mutatione Nominum*

INTRODUCTION TO INDICES

LIST OF PHILO'S WORKS

SHOWING THEIR DIVISION INTO VOLUMES IN THIS EDITION

LIST OF PHILO'S WORKS

[1] Only two fragments extant.
[2] Extant only in an Armenian version.

ON THE EMBASSY TO GAIUS

(THE FIRST PART OF THE TREATISE ON VIRTUES)

(DE VIRTUTIBUS PRIMA PARS, QUOD EST DE LEGATIONE AD GAIUM)

ΦΙΛΩΝΟΣ ΑΡΕΤΩΝ ΠΡΩΤΟΝ Ο ΕΣΤΙ
ΤΗΣ ΑΥΤΟΥ ΠΡΕΣΒΕΙΑΣ ΠΡΟΣ ΓΑΙΟΝ

[545] I. | ῎Αχρι τίνος ἡμεῖς οἱ γέροντες ἔτι παῖδές
1 ἐσμεν, τὰ μὲν σώματα χρόνου μήκει πολιοί, τὰς
δὲ ψυχὰς ὑπ᾽ ἀναισθησίας κομιδῇ νήπιοι, νομίζοντες τὸ μὲν ἀσταθμητότατον, τὴν τύχην, ἀκλι-
νέστατον, τὸ δὲ παγιώτατον, τὴν φύσιν, ἀβεβαιό-
τατον; ὑπαλλαττόμεθα γὰρ καθάπερ ἐν ταῖς
πεττείαις τὰς πράξεις μετατιθέντες, οἰόμενοι τὰ
μὲν τυχηρὰ μονιμώτερα εἶναι τῶν φύσει, τὰ δὲ
2 κατὰ φύσιν ἀβεβαιότερα τῶν τυχηρῶν. αἴτιον δὲ
τὸ τὰ παρόντα βραβεύειν[1] ἀπροοράτως τῶν μελλόντων ἔχοντας, αἰσθήσει πεπλανημένῃ χρωμένους
πρὸ διανοίας ἀπλανοῦς· ὀφθαλμοῖς μὲν γὰρ τὰ ἐν
φανερῷ καὶ ἐν χερσὶ καταλαμβάνεται, λογισμὸς
[546] δὲ φθάνει καὶ πρὸς τὰ | ἀόρατα καὶ μέλλοντα, οὗ
τὴν ὄψιν ὀξυωπεστέραν οὖσαν τῆς δι᾽ ὀμμάτων
σώματος ἀμαυροῦμεν, οἱ μὲν ἀκράτῳ καὶ πλη-
σμοναῖς ὑποσυγχέοντες, οἱ δὲ τῷ μεγίστῳ τῶν
3 κακῶν, ἀμαθίᾳ.   πλὴν ὁ παρὼν καιρὸς
καὶ αἱ κατ᾽ αὐτὸν κριθεῖσαι πολλαὶ καὶ μεγάλαι
ὑποθέσεις, κἂν εἰ ἄπιστοι γεγόνασί τινες τοῦ προ-

[1] Perhaps read θεραπεύειν as Mangey suggests. See note a.

2

ON THE EMBASSY TO GAIUS

(THE FIRST PART OF THE TREATISE ON VIRTUES)

I. How long shall we the aged continue to be 1
children grown grey in our bodies through length of
years, but infants in our souls through want of sense,
holding fortune, the most unstable of things, to be
the most unchangeable, nature, the most constant, to
be the most insecure? For we change our actions
about from place to place as on a draught board, and
fortune's gifts seem to us more permanent than
nature's, nature's more insecure than fortune's.
The reason is that, having no forethought for the 2
future, we are ruled[a] by the present, following erratic
sense-perception rather than unerring intelligence.
For the eyes of the body discern what is manifest
and close at hand, but reason reaches to the unseen
and the future. Reason's vision, which is keener than
the vision of the bodily eyes, we bedim and confuse,
some with strong drink and surfeiting, others with
that worst of evils, ignorance. And yet 3
the present time and the many important questions
decided in it are strong enough to carry conviction
even if some have come to disbelieve that the Deity

---

[a] This use of βραβεύειν is doubtful, since when transitive
it is usually applied to contests, suits and the like. If θεραπεύειν is read ἔχοντας is of course the subject.

νοεῖν τὸ θεῖον ἀνθρώπων, καὶ μάλιστα τοῦ ἱκετικοῦ
γένους, ὃ τῷ πατρὶ καὶ βασιλεῖ τῶν ὅλων καὶ
πάντων αἰτίῳ προσκεκλήρωται, ἱκαναὶ [τοῦ] πεῖσαι
4 αὐτούς. τοῦτο δὲ τὸ γένος Χαλδαϊστὶ μὲν Ἰσραὴλ
καλεῖται, Ἑλληνιστὶ δὲ ἑρμηνευθέντος τοῦ ὀνόματος
" ὁρῶν θεόν," ὅ μοι δοκεῖ πάντων χρημάτων ἰδίων
5 τε καὶ κοινῶν εἶναι τιμιώτατον. εἰ γὰρ πρεσβυ-
τέρων ἢ ὑφηγητῶν ἢ ἀρχόντων ἢ γονέων ὄψις κινεῖ
τοὺς βλέποντας πρὸς αἰδῶ καὶ εὐκοσμίαν καὶ σώ-
φρονος βίου ζῆλον, πόσον τι νομίζομεν ἀρετῆς ἔρμα
καὶ καλοκαγαθίας ἀνευρήσειν[1] ἐν ψυχαῖς, αἳ τὸ
γενητὸν πᾶν ὑπερκύψασαι τὸ ἀγένητον καὶ θεῖον
ὁρᾶν πεπαίδευνται, τὸ πρῶτον ἀγαθὸν καὶ καλὸν
καὶ εὔδαιμον καὶ μακάριον, εἰ ⟨δὲ⟩ δεῖ τἀληθὲς
εἰπεῖν, τὸ κρεῖττον μὲν ἀγαθοῦ, κάλλιον δὲ καλοῦ,
καὶ μακαριότητος μὲν μακαριώτερον, εὐδαιμονίας
δὲ αὐτῆς εὐδαιμονέστερον, καὶ εἰ δή τι τῶν εἰρη-
6 μένων τελειότερον. οὐ γὰρ φθάνει προσαναβαίνειν
ὁ λόγος ἐπὶ τὸν ἄψαυστον καὶ ἀναφῆ πάντῃ θεόν,
ἀλλ' ὑπονοστεῖ καὶ ὑπορρεῖ κυρίοις ὀνόμασιν ἀδυνα-
τῶν ἐπιβάθρᾳ χρῆσθαι πρὸς δήλωσιν, οὐ λέγω τοῦ
ὄντος—οὐδὲ γὰρ ὁ σύμπας οὐρανὸς ἔναρθρος φωνῇ
γενόμενος εὐθυβόλων καὶ εὐσκόπων εἰς τοῦτο ἂν
εὐποροίη ῥημάτων—ἀλλὰ τῶν δορυφόρων αὐτοῦ
δυνάμεων, κοσμοποιητικῆς τε καὶ βασιλικῆς καὶ
προνοητικῆς καὶ τῶν ἄλλων ὅσαι εὐεργέτιδές τε

[1] mss. ἀνεύρεσιν.

takes thought for men, and particularly for the suppliants' race which the Father and King of the Universe and the Source of all things has taken for his portion. Now this race is called in the Hebrew 4 tongue Israel, but, expressed in our tongue, the word is " he that sees God " and to see Him seems to me of all possessions, public or private, the most precious. For if the sight of seniors or instructors or 5 rulers or parents stirs the beholders to respect for them and decent behaviour and the desire to live a life of self-control, how firmly based is the virtue and nobility of conduct which we may expect to find in souls whose vision has soared above all created things and schooled itself to behold the uncreated and divine, the primal good, the excellent, the happy, the blessed, which may truly be called better than the good, more excellent than the excellent, more blessed than blessedness, more happy than happiness itself, and any perfection there may be greater than these. For reason[a] cannot attain to 6 ascend to God, who nowhere can be touched or handled, but subsides and ebbs away unable to find the proper words by which it may approach to expound, I do not say the God who is, for if the whole Heaven should become an articulate voice, it would lack the apt and appropriate terms needed for this, but even for God's attendant powers. Such are the creative, the kingly, the providential, and of the others all that are both beneficial and punitive,

[a] *i.e.* those who infer the existence of God and His Powers from His created works have an apprehension inferior to the higher intuition of the Israel-soul. *Cf. De Praem.* 40-46 and *Leg. All.* iii. 97-99. Mangey understands λόγος as language (*sermo*), which is perhaps more in accordance with the words that follow, but not so Philonic in thought.

7 καὶ κολαστήριοι, εἰ[1] καὶ τὰς κολαστηρίους ἐν εὐερ-
γέτισι τακτέον, οὐ μόνον ἐπειδὴ νόμων καὶ θεσμῶν
εἰσι μοῖραι—νόμος γὰρ ἐκ δυοῖν συμπληροῦσθαι
πέφυκε, τιμῆς ἀγαθῶν καὶ πονηρῶν κολάσεως,—
ἀλλ' ὅτι καὶ ἡ κόλασις νουθετεῖ καὶ σωφρονίζει
πολλάκις μὲν καὶ τοὺς ἁμαρτάνοντας, εἰ δὲ μή,
πάντως γοῦν τοὺς πλησιάζοντας· αἱ γὰρ ἑτέρων
τιμωρίαι βελτιοῦσι τοὺς πολλοὺς φόβῳ τοῦ μὴ
παραπλήσια παθεῖν.[2]

8 II. Τίς γὰρ ἰδὼν Γάιον μετὰ τὴν Τιβερίου Καίσαρος τελευτὴν παρειληφότα τὴν ἡγεμονίαν πάσης
γῆς καὶ θαλάσσης ἀστασίαστον καὶ εὔνομον καὶ
πᾶσι τοῖς μέρεσιν ἡρμοσμένην εἰς τὸ σύμφωνον,
ἑῴοις, ἑσπερίοις, μεσημβρινοῖς, ἀρκτικοῖς—τοῦ
[547] μὲν βαρβαρικοῦ γένους τῷ | Ἑλληνικῷ, τοῦ δ' Ἑλ-
ληνικοῦ τῷ βαρβαρικῷ, καὶ τοῦ μὲν στρατιωτικοῦ
τῷ κατὰ πόλεις, τοῦ δὲ πολιτικοῦ τῷ στρατευο-
μένῳ συμφρονήσαντος εἰς μετουσίαν καὶ ἀπόλαυσιν
εἰρήνης—οὐκ ἐθαύμασε καὶ κατεπλάγη τῆς ὑπερ-
9 φυοῦς καὶ παντὸς λόγου κρείττονος εὐπραγίας, ἐξ
ἑτοίμου τἀγαθὰ ἀθρόα σωρηδὸν κεκληρονομηκότα,
παμπληθεῖς θησαυροὺς χρημάτων, ἄργυρον καὶ
χρυσόν, τὸν μὲν ὡς ὕλην, τὸν δὲ ὡς νόμισμα, τὸν
δὲ ὡς προκόσμημα[3] δι' ἐκπωμάτων καί τινων
ἑτέρων ἃ πρὸς ἐπίδειξιν τεχνιτεύεται, παμπληθεῖς
δυνάμεις, πεζάς, ἱππικάς, ναυτικάς, προσόδους
ὥσπερ ἐκ πηγῶν ἀενάῳ τινὶ φορᾷ χορηγουμένας,

---

[1] A has εἰ μὴ (so Mangey), but as ὅσαι . . . τε has already
identified the two, the doubt expressed in εἰ μὴ is out of place.
Cf. note *a*.
[2] Reiter here notes a lacuna. See Introd. pp. xxii.

assuming that [a] the punitive are to be classed among 7
the beneficial, not only on the ground that they are
a part of laws and statutes, since no law can be
complete unless it includes two provisions—honours
for things good and punishment for things evil, but
because the punishment of others often admonishes
offenders and calls them to wisdom, or, certainly at
any rate, their neighbours. For penalties are good
for the morals of the multitude, who fear to suffer
the like.

II. For who that saw Gaius when after the death 8
of Tiberius he succeeded to the sovereignty of the
whole earth and sea, gained not by faction but established by law, with all parts, east, west, south, north,
harmoniously adjusted, the Greek in full agreement
with the barbarian, the civil with the military, to
enjoy and participate in peace—who I say was not
filled with admiration and astonishment at his pro-
digious and indescribable prosperity ? He found 9
ready in hand a mass of accumulated goods, gold and
silver, which he had inherited, some in bullion, some
in specie, some as ornaments in the form of drinking-
cups and other things which craftmanship produces
for display ; vast forces of infantry, cavalry, ships,
revenues supplied like a perennial stream flowing
from a fountain ; a dominion not confined to the 10

----

[a] *Cf. De Conf.* 171 δυνάμεις ἀρωγοὺς καὶ σωτηρίους τοῦ γε-
νομένου πάσας, αἷς ἐμφέρονται καὶ αἱ κολαστήριοι· ἔστι δὲ καὶ ἡ
κόλασις οὐκ ἐπιζήμιον, ἁμαρτημάτων οὖσα κώλυσις καὶ ἐπαν-
όρθωσις.

----

[3] mss. προβόσκημα.

10 ἀρχὴν οὐχὶ τῶν πλείστων καὶ ἀναγκαιοτάτων
μερῶν τῆς οἰκουμένης, ἃ δὴ καὶ κυρίως ἄν τις
οἰκουμένην εἴποι, δυσὶ ποταμοῖς ὁριζομένην, Εὐφράτῃ τε καὶ Ῥήνῳ, τῷ μὲν ἀποτεμνομένῳ Γερ-
μανίαν καὶ ὅσα θηριωδέστερα ἔθνη, Εὐφράτῃ δὲ
Παρθυηνὴν καὶ τὰ Σαρματῶν γένη καὶ Σκυθῶν,
ἅπερ οὐχ ἧττον ἐξηγρίωται τῶν Γερμανικῶν, ἀλλ᾽,
ὡς εἶπον ἤδη, τὴν ἀφ᾽ ἡλίου ἀνιόντος ἄχρι δυομένου
τήν τε ἐντὸς ὠκεανοῦ καὶ ὑπερωκεάνιον; ἐφ᾽ οἷς
ὅ τε Ῥωμαίων δῆμος ἐγεγήθει καὶ πᾶσα Ἰταλία
11 τά τε Ἀσιανὰ καὶ Εὐρωπαῖα ἔθνη. ὡς γὰρ ἐπ᾽
οὐδενὶ τῶν πώποτε γενομένων αὐτοκρατόρων ἅπαντες ἠγάσθησαν, κτῆσιν καὶ χρῆσιν ἰδίων τε καὶ
κοινῶν ἀγαθῶν οὐκ ἐλπίζοντες ἕξειν, ἀλλ᾽ ἔχειν
ἤδη νομίζοντες πλήρωμά τινος εὐτυχίας, ἐφεδρευ-
12 ούσης εὐδαιμονίας. οὐδὲν γοῦν ἦν ἰδεῖν ἕτερον
κατὰ πόλεις ἢ βωμούς, ἱερεῖα, θυσίας, λευχειμο-
νοῦντας, ἐστεφανωμένους, φαιδρούς, εὐμένειαν ἐξ
ἱλαρᾶς τῆς ὄψεως προφαίνοντας, ἑορτάς, πανηγύ-
ρεις, μουσικοὺς ἀγῶνας, ἱπποδρομίας, κώμους,
παννυχίδας μετ᾽ αὐλῶν καὶ κιθάρας, τέρψεις, ἀνέσεις, ἐκεχειρίας, παντοίας ἡδονὰς διὰ πάσης αἰ-
13 σθήσεως. τότε οὐ πλούσιοι πενήτων προύφερον
οὐκ ἔνδοξοι ἀδόξων, οὐ δανεισταὶ χρεωστῶν, οὐ
δεσπόται δούλων περιῆσαν, ἰσονομίαν τοῦ καιροῦ
διδόντος, ὡς τὸν παρὰ ποιηταῖς ἀναγραφέντα
Κρονικὸν βίον μηκέτι νομίζεσθαι πλάσμα μύθου
διά τε τὴν εὐθηνίαν καὶ εὐετηρίαν τό τε ἄλυπον
καὶ ἄφοβον καὶ τὰς πανοικίας ὁμοῦ καὶ πανδήμους

ᵃ Lit. "the most and most necessary." For this frequent
coupling of πλεῖστα with another superlative see note on
Flaccus 46 (vol. ix. p. 326).

8

really vital parts which make up most^a of the inhabited world, and indeed may properly bear that name, the world, that is, which is bounded by the two rivers, the Euphrates and the Rhine, the one dissevering us from the Germans and all the more brutish nations, the Euphrates from the Parthians and from the Sarmatians and Scythians, races which are no less savage than the Germans, but a dominion extending, as I said above, from the rising to the setting sun both within the ocean and beyond it. All these things were a joy to the Roman people and all Italy and the nations of Europe and Asia; not so much had they all exulted over any of his im- 11 perial predecessors. It was not now a matter of hoping that they would have the possession and use of good things public and private ; they considered that they had already the plenitude as it were of good fortune with happiness waiting in its train. Thus nothing was to be seen throughout the 12 cities but altars, oblations, sacrifices, men in white robes and crowned with garlands, bright and smart, their cheery faces beaming with goodwill, feasts, assemblages, musical contests, horse races, revels, nightlong frolics with harp and flutes, jollification, unrestraint, holiday-keeping, every kind of pleasure ministered by every sense. In these days the rich 13 had no precedence over the poor, nor the distinguished over the obscure, creditors were not above debtors, nor masters above slaves, the times giving equality before the law. Indeed, the life under Saturn, pictured by the poets, no longer appeared to be a fabled story, so great was the prosperity and well-being, the freedom from grief and fear, the joy which pervaded households and people,

μεθ᾽ ἡμέραν τε καὶ νύκτωρ εὐφροσύνας, αἳ μέχρι
μηνῶν ἑπτὰ τῶν πρώτων ἄπαυστοι καὶ συνεχεῖς |
[548] ἐγένοντο.   τῷ δὲ ὀγδόῳ κατασκήπτει
14 βαρεῖα νόσος τῷ Γαΐῳ τὴν πρὸ μικροῦ δίαιταν,
ὅτε ἔζη Τιβέριος, εὐκολωτέραν καὶ διὰ τοῦτο
ὑγιεινοτέραν οὖσαν εἰς πολυτέλειαν μεθαρμοσα-
μένῳ. πολὺς γὰρ ἄκρατος καὶ ὀψοφαγίαι καὶ ἐπὶ
πλήρεσι τοῖς ὄγκοις ἀπλήρωτοι ἐπιθυμίαι θερμο-
λουσίαι τε ἄκαιροι καὶ ἔμετοι καὶ εὐθὺς πάλιν
οἰνοφλυγίαι καὶ ἔφεδροι γαστριμαργίαι, λαγνεῖαι
διὰ παίδων καὶ γυναικῶν, καὶ ὅσα ἄλλα καθαιρε-
τικὰ ψυχῆς καὶ σώματος καὶ τῶν ἐν ἑκατέρῳ
δεσμῶν συνεπέθετο. τὰ δὲ ἐπίχειρα ἐγκρατείας
μὲν ὑγεία καὶ ἰσχύς, ἀκρασίας δὲ ἀσθένεια καὶ
νόσος γειτνιῶσα θανάτῳ.

15 III. Διαγγελείσης οὖν τῆς ὅτι νοσεῖ φήμης, ἔτι
πλοΐμων ὄντων—ἀρχὴ γὰρ ἦν μετοπώρου, τελευ-
ταῖος πλοῦς τοῖς θαλαττεύουσιν, ἀπὸ τῶν πανταχόθεν ἐμπορίων εἰς τοὺς οἰκείους λιμένας καὶ
ὑποδρόμους ἐπανιοῦσι, καὶ μάλιστα οἷς πρόνοια
τοῦ μὴ διαχειμάζειν ἐπὶ ξένης ἐστί—μεθέμενοι τὸν
ἁβροδίαιτον βίον ἐσκυθρώπαζον, συννοίας τε καὶ
κατηφείας πᾶσα οἰκία καὶ πόλις γεγένητο μεστή,
ἰσορρόπῳ λύπῃ τῆς πρὸ μικροῦ χαρᾶς ἀμφικλινοῦς
16 γενομένης. τὰ γὰρ μέρη πάντα τῆς οἰκουμένης
αὐτῷ συνενόσησε, βαρυτέρᾳ νόσῳ χρησάμενα τῆς
κατασχούσης Γάιον· ἐκείνη μὲν γὰρ σώματος ἦν
αὐτὸ μόνον, ἡ δὲ τῶν πανταχοῦ πάντων, ψυχικῆς
εὐσθενείας, εἰρήνης, ἐλπίδων, μετουσίας καὶ ἀπο-
17 λαύσεως ἀγαθῶν. ἀνεπόλουν γὰρ ὅσα καὶ ἡλίκα

10

night and day, and lasted continuously without a
break through the first seven months.

But in the eighth month Gaius was struck down by 14
severe sickness. He had exchanged the recent more
homely and, therefore, healthier way of life which
he had followed while Tiberius was alive, for one
of extravagance. Hard drinking, luxurious feeding
and appetites still unsatisfied when the cavities
were stuffed full, hot baths, ill-timed, and acting as
emetics, followed at once by renewed toping and
gormandizing in its train, lasciviousness venting
itself on boys and women, and everything else that
can destroy soul and body and the bonds in both
which keep them together, joined in the assault.
Self-restraint is rewarded by strength and health,
incontinence by infirmity and sickness bordering on
death.

III. The news of Gaius's illness travelled every- 15
where, since the time still made navigation possible.
For it was the beginning of autumn, the close of the
sailing season when the mariners return from their
trading ports everywhere to their own harbours and
roadsteads, particularly those who take care not to
winter in a foreign country. So people abandoned
their luxurious life and became dismal. Every household and city was filled with anxiety and dejection,
their recent joy being counter-balanced by a grief no
less intense. For every part of the habitable world 16
shared his sickness, and theirs was a sickness more
grievous than that which overcame him. His was of
the body only, theirs was felt by all and everywhere,
affecting the well-being of the soul, their peace, their
hopes and participation and enjoyment of every good
thing. Thoughts of the many great evils which 17

11

PHILO

κακὰ ἐξ ἀναρχίας φύεται· λιμόν, πόλεμον, δεν-
δροτομίας, δηώσεις χωρίων, στερήσεις χρημάτων,
ἀπαγωγάς, τοὺς περὶ δουλείας καὶ θανάτου φόβους
ἀνηκέστους, ὧν ἰατρὸς ἦν οὐδείς, μίαν ἐχόντων
18 θεραπείαν τὸ ῥωσθῆναι Γάιον.   ὅτε γοῦν
ἤρξατο λωφᾶν ἡ νόσος, ἐν βραχεῖ καὶ οἱ μέχρι
περάτων συνῄσθοντο—φήμης γὰρ οὐδὲν ὠκύτερον—, καὶ μετέωρος πᾶσα πόλις ἦν ἀκοῆς ἀεὶ
διψῶσα βελτίονος, ἕως διὰ τῶν ἐπιφοιτώντων παντελὴς ῥῶσις εὐηγγελίσθη, δι' ἣν πάλιν ἐξ ὑπαρχῆς
ἐπὶ τὰς αὐτὰς ἐτρέποντο θυμηδίας, ἰδίαν ἑαυτῶν
νομίζουσαι σωτηρίαν πᾶσαι μὲν ἤπειροι πᾶσαι δὲ
19 νῆσοι. μέμνηται γὰρ οὐδεὶς τοσαύτην μιᾶς χώρας
ἢ ἑνὸς ἔθνους γενέσθαι χαρὰν ἐπὶ σωτηρίᾳ καὶ
καταστάσει ἡγεμόνος, ὅσην ἐπὶ Γαΐῳ συμπάσης
τῆς οἰκουμένης καὶ παραλαβόντι τὴν ἀρχὴν καὶ
20 ῥωσθέντι ἐκ τῆς ἀσθενείας. ὥσπερ γὰρ ἐκ νομάδος
βίου καὶ θηριώδους νῦν πρῶτον ἀρχόμενοι μετα-
[549] βάλλειν πρὸς τὸ σύννομον καὶ | ὁμοδίαιτον καὶ ἐξ
ἐρημίας καὶ σηκῶν καὶ ὑπωρειῶν εἰσοικίζεσθαι
πόλεσι τειχήρεσι καὶ ἐξ ἀνεπιτροπεύτου ζωῆς ὑπὸ
ἐπιτρόπῳ τάττεσθαι νομεῖ τινι καὶ ἀγελάρχῃ τῆς
ἡμερωτέρας ἀγέλης ἐγεγήθεσαν ἀγνοίᾳ τῆς ἀλη-
21 θείας· τυφλώττει γὰρ ὁ ἀνθρώπινος νοῦς πρὸς τὴν
τοῦ συμφέροντος ὄντως αἴσθησιν εἰκασίᾳ καὶ
στοχασμῷ μᾶλλον ἢ ἐπιστήμῃ χρῆσθαι δυνάμενος.
22   IV. Εὐθὺς γοῦν οὐκ εἰς μακρὰν ὁ σωτὴρ καὶ
εὐεργέτης εἶναι νομισθεὶς καί τινας ἀγαθῶν πηγὰς
νέας ἐπομβρήσειν Ἀσίᾳ τε καὶ Εὐρώπῃ πρὸς
εὐδαιμονίαν ἀκαθαίρετον, ἰδίᾳ τε ἑκάστῳ καὶ πᾶσι

12

spring from anarchy occupied their mind : famine, war, ravaging, devastation of estates, loss of property, abductions, fears of enslavement and death, so deadly that no physician could cure them and the only remedy lay in the recovery of Gaius.   So when the 18 sickness began to abate, in quite a short time it was known even to the inhabitants of the ends of the world, for nothing is more speedy than rumour, and every city was on edge, ever craving for a better report until the good news of his complete recovery was announced by the travellers who arrived. At this every continent, every island, returned once more to its former happiness, for they felt that they personally shared in his preservation. For no one 19 remembers any single country or single nation feeling as much delight at the accession or preservation of a ruler, as was felt by the whole world in the case of Gaius, both when he succeeded to the sovereignty and when he recovered from his malady. They felt 20 as if they were beginning for the first time to change a nomadic and brutish for a social and gregarious life, or were passing from desolate life in pens and huts on a mountain side to be settled in a walled city, or from an existence unprotected by a guardian, to take their place under a guardian, a shepherd of the civilized flock. Such was their joy but they did not know the truth. The human mind in its blindness 21 does not perceive its real interest and all it can do is to take conjecture and guesswork for its guide instead of knowledge.

IV. So it was with Gaius. He who had been 22 recently regarded as a saviour and benefactor, who would pour new streams of blessings on Asia and Europe, giving happiness indestructible to each singly

PHILO

κοινῇ, τὸ λεγόμενον δὴ τοῦτο " ἀφ᾽ ἱερᾶς ἤρξατο "[1]
μεταβαλὼν πρὸς τὸ ἀτίθασον, μᾶλλον δὲ ἦν συν-
εσκίαζεν ἀγριότητα τῷ πλάσματι τῆς ὑποκρίσεως
23 ἀναφήνας. τὸν γὰρ ἀνεψιὸν καὶ κοινωνὸν ἀπο-
λειφθέντα τῆς ἀρχῆς καὶ οἰκειότερον αὐτοῦ διάδοχον
—ὁ μὲν γὰρ θέσει υἱωνὸς ἦν, ὁ δὲ φύσει Τιβερίου—
κτείνει προφασισάμενος ἐπιβουλήν, μηδὲ τῆς ἡλικίας χωρούσης ἔγκλημα τοιοῦτον· ἄρτι γὰρ ἐκ
24 παίδων εἰς μειράκιον ὁ δύστηνος μετῄει. καὶ ὥς
γέ φασί τινες, εἰ βραχὺν ἐπεβίω χρόνον Τιβέριος,
ὁ μὲν ἂν ἐκποδὼν ἐγεγένητο Γάιος, δι᾽ ὑποψιῶν
κεχωρηκὼς ἀνηκέστων, ὁ δὲ γνήσιος υἱωνὸς μόνος
ἀπεδέδεικτο ἡγεμὼν καὶ κληρονόμος τῆς παππῴας
25 ἀρχῆς. ἀλλ᾽ ὁ μὲν ὑπὸ τῆς εἱμαρμένης ἔφθη συν-
αρπασθείς, πρὶν ἐπὶ τέλος ἀγαγεῖν τὰ βουλεύματα·
Γάιος δὲ τὴν ἐκ τοῦ παραβαίνειν τὰ πρὸς τὸν
κοινωνὸν δίκαια διαβολὴν ἐνόμιζεν ἀποδράσεσθαι
26 καταστρατηγῶν. τὸ δὲ σόφισμα τοιοῦτον ἦν· συναγαγὼν τοὺς ἐν τέλει, " βούλομαι μέν,"
ἔφη, " τὸν γένει μὲν ἀνεψιὸν εὐνοίᾳ δὲ ἀδελφόν,
ἑπόμενος καὶ τῇ τοῦ τετελευτηκότος Τιβερίου
γνώμῃ, κοινοπραγεῖν τῆς αὐτοκρατοῦς ἐξουσίας·
ὁρᾶτε δὲ καὶ αὐτοὶ νήπιον ἔτι ὄντα κομιδῇ καὶ
χρῄζοντα ἐπιτρόπων καὶ διδασκάλων καὶ παιδα-
27 γωγῶν. ἐπεὶ τί ἂν ἦν μεῖζον ἀγαθὸν ἢ τὰ τοσαῦτα
βάρη τῆς ἡγεμονίας μὴ μίαν ψυχὴν ἢ σῶμα ἓν
ἐπηχθίσθαι, ἀλλ᾽ ἔχειν τὸν δυνησόμενον ἐπελαφρί-
ζειν καὶ συνεπικουφίζειν; ἐγὼ δέ," ἔφη, " παιδα-
γωγοὺς καὶ διδασκάλους καὶ ἐπιτρόπους ὑπερ-

[1] Reiter " ἀφ᾽ ἱερᾶς " ἤρξατο. But ἤρξατο appears to be part of the proverbial phrase.

---

[a] Lit. " began from the sacred line." This line ir the last

14

and all in common, at once " ran amuck " as they say,[a] changing to savagery, or rather revealing the brutality which he used to disguise under the mask of hypocrisy. His cousin, who had been left to share the 23 sovereignty and was more entitled by kinship to the succession, since Gaius was the grandson of Tiberius by adoption while the other was by blood, he put to death on the pretext of conspiracy, though his age in itself precluded such an accusation. For the poor youth was just emerging from boyhood into adolescence. And according to some, if Tiberius had 24 survived a little longer, Gaius would have been put out of the way, lying as he did under fatally damaging suspicions, and his real grandson would have been appointed sole ruler and heir to his grandfather's sovereignty. But Tiberius was snatched away by 25 fate before he had consummated his plans, while Gaius thought that by strategy he would escape the odium which dereliction in his duty to his partner would excite.   He employed the following 26 artifice. Having summoned the chief officials he said, " In accordance with the will of the deceased Tiberius I wish the imperial authority to be shared by him who is my cousin by birth but my brother by affection, though you see yourselves that he is still a mere child and needs guardians and teachers and tutors. For what greater boon could there be than 27 that a single soul or body should cease to be laden with the heavy burden of sovereignty and should have one who would be able to relieve and lighten them ? And I," he continued, " will be more than a guardian, a tutor and a teacher. I will appoint

line of a chessboard, and the actions of anyone who went beyond it would naturally be all " at sea."

PHILO

[550]
28

βαλὼν ἐμαυτὸν μὲν ἤδη γράφω πατέρα, υἱὸν δὲ ἐκεῖνον.'' V. | τούτοις καὶ τοὺς παρόν-
τας ἀπατήσας καὶ τὸ μειράκιον—δέλεαρ γὰρ ἦν ἡ
θέσις οὐκ ἐλπιζομένης ἡγεμονίας, ἀλλ' ἀφαιρέσεως
ἧς εἶχεν ἤδη—τῷ συγκληρονόμῳ καὶ κοινωνῷ[1]
δικαίῳ μετὰ πολλῆς ἀδείας οὐδενὸς ἔτι πεφρον-
τικῶς ἐπεβούλευεν. ἡ γὰρ υἱοῦ παντελὴς ἐξουσία
κατὰ τοὺς τῶν Ῥωμαίων νόμους ἀνάκειται πατρί,
δίχα τοῦ καὶ ἀνυπεύθυνον ἀρχὴν εἶναι τὴν αὐτοκράτορα, μηδενὸς ἐπὶ τοῖς ὁπωσοῦν πεπραγμένοις
29 λόγον ἀπαιτεῖν τολμῶντος ἢ δυναμένου. τοῦτον
μὲν δὴ καθάπερ ἐν τοῖς ἀγῶσιν ἔφεδρον ὑπολαβὼν
εἶναι καταπαλαίει, μήτε συντροφίας μήτε οἰκειότη-
τος μήτε ἡλικίας οἶκτον λαβών, δύστηνον, ὠκύ-
μορον, συνάρχοντα, συγκληρονόμον, τὸν ἐλπισθέντα
ποτὲ καὶ μόνον αὐτοκράτορα διὰ τὴν πρὸς Τιβέριον
ἐγγυτάτω συγγένειαν· υἱωνοὶ γὰρ πατέρων ἀποθανόντων ἐν υἱῶν τάξει παρὰ πάπποις καταριθ-
30 μοῦνται.   λέγεται δὲ ὅτι καὶ κελευσθεὶς
αὐτοχειρίᾳ κτείνειν ἑαυτόν, ἐφεστώτων ἑκατοντάρ-
χου καὶ χιλιάρχου, οἷς εἴρητο μὴ συνεφάψασθαι τοῦ
ἄγους, ὡς οὐκ ἐξὸν αὐτοκρατόρων ἀπογόνους πρὸς
ἑτέρων ἀναιρεῖσθαι—νόμων γὰρ ἐν ἀνομίαις καὶ
ὁσιότητος ἐν ἀνοσιουργίαις ἐμέμνητο κατειρωνευό-
μενος τὴν φύσιν τῆς ἀληθείας—, ἀπείρως ἔχων—
οὐδὲ γὰρ ἕτερόν τινα κτεινόμενον εἶδεν οὐδὲ ἤσκητό
πω ταῖς ὁπλομαχίαις, αἳ μελέται καὶ προγυμνά-
σματα παίδων ἐφ' ἡγεμονίᾳ τρεφομένων εἰσὶ διὰ
τοὺς ἐνισταμένους πολέμους—τὸ μὲν πρῶτον τοὺς
ἥκοντας παρεκάλει τὸν αὐχένα προτείνας ἀνελεῖν.

[1] MSS. κοινωνῶν.

16

myself to be his father and him to be my son."

V. With these words he deceived both 28
the audience and the lad. The adoption was a snare
to assure not the sovereignty which he expected, but
the loss of that which he held already. And Gaius proceeded to plot against his fellow-heir and true partner
with full security and disregard of all opposition, for
the Roman laws assign absolute power over the son
to the father, not to mention his irresponsible authority as emperor, since no one had either the courage
or the power to call him to account for his actions of
any kind. As the victor in the arena throws to the 29
ground the one remaining champion, so dealt he,
without pity for their fellowship in breeding, their
kinship or his youth, with this unhappy lad, and sent
to an early grave his co-regent, his co-heir who had
been expected to be sole emperor as most nearly
related to Tiberius, for grandsons when their fathers
are dead hold the rank of sons in the eyes of their
grandparents. It is said, too, that the 30
boy was ordered to kill himself with his own hands
under the superintendence of a centurion and a
chiliarch, who had been instructed to take no hand
in the sacrilege on the grounds that it was unlawful
that the descendants of emperors should be slain by
others. For amid his lawless and unsanctified deeds
Gaius remembered law and sanctity, a travesty of
their true nature. But the lad lacked skill to do the
deed, for he had never seen anyone else killed and
had not yet been practised in the martial exercises
which in view of the imminent prospect of war are
used to give preliminary training to those who are
being brought up to rule. So at first he stretched
out his neck to the emissaries present and bade them

17

PHILO

31 ὡς δ᾽ οὐχ ὑπέμενον, αὐτὸς λαβὼν τὸ ξίφος ἐπυνθά-
νετο τὸν καιριώτατον τόπον ὑπ᾽ ἀγνοίας καὶ
ἀηθείας, ἵνα εὐσκόπῳ πληγῇ τὴν ἀθλίαν ζωὴν
ἀπορρήξῃ. καὶ οἱ μὲν οἷα διδάσκαλοι κακοδαιμονίας ὑφηγοῦντό τε καὶ ἐδείκνυσαν τὸ μέρος, ᾧ
χρὴ τὸ ξίφος ἐπενεγκεῖν· ὁ δὲ πρώτην καὶ ὑστά-
την μάθησιν ἀναδιδαχθεὶς ἀνδροφόνος αὐτὸς αὑτοῦ
γίνεται βιασθείς, ὁ δύστηνος.

32 VI. Ἐπεὶ δὲ ὁ πρῶτος καὶ μέγιστος ἆθλος οὗτος
Γαΐῳ κατείργαστο, μηδενὸς ἔτι λειπομένου ⟨κοινω-
νοῦ⟩ τῆς ἡγεμονίας πρὸς ὃν ἀποκλινοῦσί τινες τῶν
ἐθελοκακούντων καὶ ἐν ὑποψίαις ὄντων, ἐπὶ δεύτερον εὐθὺς ἐκονίετο τὸν Μάκρωνος, ἀνδρὸς εἰς
[551] πάντα αὐτῷ | συναγωνισαμένου τὰ τῆς ἀρχῆς, οὐ
μόνον ἀποδειχθέντι ἡγεμόνι—κολακείας γὰρ ἴδιον
τὰς εὐπραγίας θεραπεύειν—ἀλλὰ καὶ πρότερον εἰς
33 τὸ τυχεῖν τῆς ἡγεμονίας. ὁ γὰρ Τιβέριος φρονήσει
βαθείᾳ χρώμενος καὶ τῶν κατ᾽ αὐτὸν ἀπάντων
δεινότατος ὢν ἀφανὲς ἀνθρώπου βούλημα συνιδεῖν
καὶ ἐπὶ τοσοῦτον συνέσει διενεγκών, ἐφ᾽ ὅσον καὶ
εὐτυχίᾳ, πολλάκις ὑπεβλέπετο τὸν Γάιον ὡς κακό-
νουν μὲν ἅπαντι τῷ Κλαυδίων οἴκῳ, προσκείμενον
δὲ μόνῳ τῷ μητρῴῳ γένει—καὶ ἐδεδίει περὶ τοῦ
34 υἱωνοῦ, μὴ νέος ἀπολειφθεὶς παραπόληται—, πρὸς
δὲ ἀρχὴν καὶ τοσαύτην ἀνεπιτηδείως ἔχοντα διά
τε τὸ τῆς φύσεως ἄμικτον καὶ ἀκοινώνητον καὶ
τὴν τῶν ἠθῶν ἀνωμαλίαν· ἀλλόκοτα γὰρ αὐτῷ καὶ
ἐπιμανῆ κατεφαίνετο, μηδεμιᾶς σῳζομένης ἀκολου-

---

[a] §§ 32-65. For a very short account of Macro's services
to Gaius and his subsequent fall see *Flaccus* 12-15.
[b] As Gaius could claim through his mother, who was the

dispatch him, and when they could not bring them- 31
selves to do it, he took the sword himself and in his
ignorance and inexperience asked them what was
the most vital spot so that by a well-aimed blow he
might break the thread of his miserable life. And
they playing the part of preceptors in misery gave
their instructions and showed him the part to which
he should apply the sword, and having received this
first and last lesson he was forced to become his
own murderer, poor boy !

VI. ᵃ When Gaius had won this first and principal 32
bout and no partner in his sovereignty was still left
to divert the allegiance of ill-wishers and suspects, he
at once prepared for a second effort, this time against
Macro, who had been throughout his ally in establishing his power, not only after he was appointed
emperor (for flattery never fails to pay court to
success) but also earlier in helping him to get the
sovereignty. For Tiberius, who always acted with 33
profound prudence and was clever above all his con-
temporaries in divining a man's secret wishes, and
as much distinguished for shrewdness as for good
fortune, often looked on Gaius with disfavour as
being ill-disposed to the whole Claudian house and
attached only ᵇ to his mother's family, and he feared
for his grandson that if he was left alone when
young he might be made away with. Moreover he 34
doubted his fitness for an office of such magnitude,
both because of his unsociable and unfriendly nature
and also because of his erratic temperament, for he
showed abnormal and crazy tendencies and main-

daughter of Julia the daughter of Augustus, descent by birth
from Augustus, this might be supposed to weigh with him
more than his descent by adoption through his Claudian
father Germanicus.

35 θίας, μήτε ἐν λόγοις μήτε ἐν ἔργοις. ἃ παντὶ
σθένει κατὰ τὸ παρεῖκον¹ ὁ Μάκρων ἐθεράπευε, τὰς
μὲν ὑπονοίας τοῦ Τιβερίου καὶ ἐν οἷς μάλιστ'
ἐδόκει τὴν διάνοιαν ἑλκοῦσθαι διὰ τὸν ἄληκτον ἐπὶ
36 τῷ υἱωνῷ φόβον ἐξιώμενος. εὔνουν γὰρ καὶ
πειθαρχικὸν ἀπέφαινε τὸν Γάιον καὶ σφόδρα ἡττη-
μένον τοῦ ἀνεψιοῦ, ὡς ἔνεκα φιλοστοργίας καὶ
μόνῳ ἂν ἐθελῆσαι τῆς ἀρχῆς ὑπεκστῆναι· τὴν δὲ
αἰδῶ μὴ λυσιτελῆσαι πολλοῖς, ὑφ' ἧς καὶ Γάιον
37 ἁπλοῦν ὄντα ποικίλον νομίζεσθαι. καὶ ὁπότε μὴ
πείθοι τὰ εἰκότα διεξιών, τὴν ἀπὸ συνθηκῶν ⟨πί-
στιν⟩ ἐπέφερεν, "ἐγγυῶμαι," λέγων, "ἀξιόχρεώς
εἰμι πρὸς πίστιν· ἱκανὰς ἀποδείξεις δέδωκα τοῦ
φιλόκαισαρ ἰδίως καὶ φιλοτιβέριος εἶναι, τὴν ἐπί-
38 θεσιν² καὶ καθαίρεσιν ἐγχειρισθεὶς Σηιανοῦ." καὶ
συνόλως δὲ ἱκανὸς ἦν ἐν τοῖς εἰς Γάιον ἐπαίνοις,
εἰ δεῖ καλεῖν ἀξίως³ ἐπαίνους⁴ τὰς ἀπολογίας, αἳ
πρὸς τὰς ἐξ ὑπονοιῶν αἰτίας καὶ κατηγορίας
ἀδήλους καὶ ἀσαφεῖς⁵ ἐγίνοντο· συνόλως γὰρ ὅσα
περὶ ἀδελφῶν εἴποι τις ἂν ἢ υἱῶν γνησίων ἐγκώμια,
τοσαῦτα καὶ ἔτι πλείω Μάκρων ὑπὲρ Γαΐου διεξῄει
39 πρὸς Τιβέριον. αἴτιον δέ, ὡς ὁ τῶν
πολλῶν λόγος, οὐ μόνον τὸ ἀντιθεραπεύεσθαι πρὸς
αὐτοῦ τὸν Μάκρωνα, πλεῖστον ἢ καὶ σύμπαν ἐν τῇ
ἡγεμονίᾳ δυνάμενον, ἀλλὰ καὶ ἡ Μάκρωνος γυνὴ
διὰ σιωπωμένην αἰτίαν, ἣ καθ' ἑκάστην ἡμέραν
ἤλειφε καὶ συνεκρότει τὸν ἄνδρα μηδὲν ἀνιέναι
σπουδῆς καὶ βοηθείας τῆς ὑπὲρ τοῦ νεανίσκου.

¹ mss. παρῆκον. ² mss. ὑπόθεσιν. ³ mss. ἀξίας.
⁴ mss. ἐπαίνου. ⁵ mss. σαφεῖς.

ᵃ According to Dio lviii. 28 and Tac. *Ann.* vi. 45, Macro
connived at her seduction.

tained no consistency in word or deed. These faults 35 Macro strove with all his might to remedy as opportunity offered and also to eradicate the suspicions of Tiberius on the subject which owing to his ceaseless fear for his grandson seemed to fester most in his mind. Macro represented him as well-disposed and 36 docile and so exceedingly devoted to the service of his cousin that family affection would make him willing to retire and leave him sole emperor. Modesty, he said, in many cases was a disadvantage, and it was his modesty which caused the simpleminded Gaius to be considered cunning. And when 37 the plausibility of his arguments failed to convince Tiberius he would pledge his credit for their truth. " I guarantee it," he said, " I have earned the right to be believed. I have given sufficient proof that I am in a special sense a friend of Caesar, a friend of Tiberius, when the task of attacking and destroying Sejanus was placed in my hand." And in general 38 he was successful with his eulogies of Gaius, if eulogies is a suitable name for the defences directed to meet the vague charges and accusations based on suspicion. For in general the terms in which one might speak in commendation of brothers or sons in the full sense were used in equal or even greater measure of Gaius by Macro, when pleading his cause to Tiberius.

This was due, according to what most 39 people said, not merely to the fact that Gaius in return courted the favour of Macro as possessing a predominant and, indeed, all-powerful influence in the government, but to Macro's wife, though the charge against her was not mentioned. She every day incited and worked upon her husband not to abate his zeal and assistance of the young Gaius.[a]

δεινὸν δὲ γυνὴ γνώμην ἀνδρὸς παραλῦσαι καὶ παρ-
αγαγεῖν, καὶ μάλιστα μαχλάς· ἕνεκα γὰρ τοῦ
40 συνειδότος κολακικωτέρα γίνεται. ὁ δὲ τὴν δια-
φθορὰν μὲν τοῦ γάμου καὶ τῆς οἰκίας ἀγνοῶν,
[552] τὴν | δὲ κολακείαν εὔνοιαν ἀκραιφνεστάτην εἶναι
νομίζων, ἀπατᾶται καὶ λανθάνει τοῖς στρατηγήμασι
τοὺς ἐχθίστους ὡς φιλτάτους προσιέμενος.

41 VII. Εἰδὼς οὖν, ὅτι παρὰ μικρὸν ἐλθόντα μυ-
ριάκις αὐτὸν ἀπολέσθαι διέσωσεν, ἀνυπούλοις καὶ
πεπαρρησιασμέναις ἐχρῆτο ταῖς νουθεσίαις· ἐβούλετο γάρ, ὡς ἀγαθὸς δημιουργός, ἀκαθαίρετον
διαμεῖναι τὸ οἰκεῖον ἔργον, μήτε ὑπ’ αὐτοῦ δια-
42 λυθὲν μήτε ὑφ’ ἑτέρου. ὁπότε οὖν ἢ καταδαρθόντα[1]
ἐν συμποσίῳ θεάσαιτο, περιανίστη στοχαζόμενος
ἅμα μὲν τοῦ πρέποντος ἅμα δὲ καὶ τῆς ἀσφαλείας
—εὐεπιβούλευτον γὰρ ὁ κοιμώμενος—, ἢ τινας
ἐκμανῶς ὀρχηστὰς ὁρῶντα ἢ ἔστιν ὅτε συνορχού-
μενον ἢ ἐπὶ μίμοις αἰσχρῶν καὶ σκωμμάτων μὴ
ὑπομειδιῶντα σεμνότερον ἀλλὰ μειρακιωδέστερον
καγχάζοντα ἢ κιθαρῳδῶν ἢ χορῶν τῆς ἐμμελείας
ἡττώμενον, ἔστιν ὅπου καὶ συνᾴδοντα, ἔνυττε πλησίον καθεζόμενος ἢ κατακεκλιμένος καὶ ἐπέχειν
43 ἐπειρᾶτο. πολλάκις δὲ καὶ ἐπικλίνας πρὸς οὖς,
ἵνα μὴ κατακούοι τις ἕτερος, ἡσυχῇ καὶ πρᾴως
ἐνουθέτει φάσκων· “ οὐδενὶ τῶν παρόντων ἀλλ’
οὐδὲ τῶν ἄλλων ἀνθρώπων ὅμοιον εἶναί σε δεῖ,
οὔτε ἐν θεάμασιν οὔτε ἐν ἀκούσμασιν οὔτε ἐν τοῖς
ἄλλοις ἅπασιν ὅσα κατὰ τὰς αἰσθήσεις, ἀλλὰ προφέρειν ἐπὶ τοσοῦτον ἐν ἑκάστῳ τῶν περὶ τὸν βίον
44 ἐφ’ ὅσον καὶ ταῖς εὐτυχίαις διενήνοχας. ἄτοπον

---

[1] mss. καταδαρθέντα.

22

A wife has great power to paralyse and seduce her husband [a] and particularly if she is a wanton, for her guilty conscience increases her wheedling. The 40 husband, unaware of the corruption of his marriage and household, and thinking that her wheedling is benevolence pure and simple, is deceived and little knows that her artifices are leading him to take his worst enemies to be his dearest friends.

VII. Knowing then that he had saved Gaius over 41 and over again when within an ace of destruction, he gave his admonitions frankly and without disguise, for like a good builder he wished his handiwork to remain proof against destruction or dissolution either by himself or another. So whenever he saw Gaius 42 asleep at a banquet he would wake him up with the double object of preserving propriety and his personal safety, since a sleeping man is an easy target for conspiracy. Or if he saw him frantic with excitement at the sight of dancers and sometimes joining in the dance, or greeting a mime of scandalous scenes and broad jesting with a loud youngster's guffaw, instead of a subdued or sedate smile, or fascinated by the music of harpers or choric singers and occasionally accompanying them, he would sit or lean back at his side and nudge him and try to restrain him. Often, 43 too, bending down to his ear so that no one else should listen, he would admonish him gently and quietly. " As a spectator," he would say, " or listener, or using any other of your senses, you ought not to be like those around you or anyone else at all. In every side of life you ought to be as far above these as you have surpassed them in your good

---

[a] δεῖνον . . . παραλῦσαι read like part of an hexameter.

PHILO

γὰρ τὸν ἡγεμόνα γῆς καὶ θαλάττης νικᾶσθαι πρὸς
ᾠδῆς ἢ ὀρχήσεως ἢ χλευαστικοῦ σκώμματος ἢ
τινος τῶν ὁμοιοτρόπων, ἀλλὰ μὴ ἀεὶ καὶ πανταχοῦ
μεμνῆσθαι τῆς ἡγεμονίας, καθάπερ ποιμένα τινὰ
καὶ ἐπιστάτην ἀγέλης, τὰ πρὸς βελτίωσιν ἀπὸ
παντὸς οὑτινοσοῦν ἐφ' ἑαυτὸν ἕλκοντα καὶ λόγου
45 καὶ πράγματος." εἶτα ἔφασκεν· "ὅταν παρατυγ-
χάνῃς σκηνικοῖς ἀγῶσιν ἢ γυμνικοῖς ἢ τοῖς κατὰ
τὰς ἱπποδρομίας, μὴ σκόπει τὰ ἐπιτηδεύματα,
ἀλλὰ τὴν ἐν τοῖς ἐπιτηδεύμασι κατόρθωσιν, καὶ
46 λάμβανε τὸν τοιοῦτον λογισμόν· εἰ τὰ μηδὲν ὠφε-
λοῦντα τὸν ἀνθρώπινον βίον, τέρψιν δὲ καὶ ἡδονὴν
αὐτὸ μόνον παρέχοντα θεαταῖς, ἐκπονοῦσιν οὕτω
τινές, ὡς ἐπαινεῖσθαί τε καὶ θαυμάζεσθαι καὶ γέρα
καὶ τιμὰς καὶ στεφάνους μετὰ κηρυγμάτων λαμβάνειν, τί χρὴ πράττειν τὸν τῆς ἀνωτάτω καὶ μεγίστης
47 τέχνης ἐπιστήμονα; μεγίστη δὲ καὶ ἀρίστη τέχνη
πασῶν ἐστιν ἡ ἡγεμονία, δι' ἧς πᾶσα μὲν ἡ ἀγαθὴ
καὶ βαθεῖα πεδιάς τε καὶ ὀρεινὴ γεωργεῖται, πᾶσα
δὲ θάλαττα φορτηγοῖς ὁλκάσιν ἀκινδύνως διαπλεῖ-
ται κατὰ τὰς ἀντιδόσεις ὧν ἀλλήλαις ἀγαθῶν
ἀντεκτίνουσιν αἱ χῶραι κοινωνίας ἱμέρῳ, τὰ μὲν
[553] ἐνδέοντα λαμβάνουσαι, ὧν δ' ἄγουσι περιουσίαν |
48 ἀντιπέμπουσαι. φθόνος γὰρ οὐδέποτε πᾶσαν τὴν
οἰκουμένην ἐκράτησεν, ἀλλ' οὐδὲ τὰς μεγάλας
αὐτῆς ἀποτομάς, ὅλην Εὐρώπην ἢ ὅλην Ἀσίαν·
ἀλλ' ἰοβόλου τρόπον ἑρπετοῦ φωλεύει βραχέσιν
εἰσερπύσας χωρίοις ἀνδρὶ ἑνὶ ἢ οἴκῳ ἑνὶ ἤ, εἴ ποτε

---

[a] I understand κατόρθωσις as used in the Stoic sense of the
moral state which produces κατορθώματα, i.e. τὰ κατ' ἀρετὴν

24

fortune. For it is not to be thought of that the 44 sovereign of earth and sea should be overcome by a song or dancing or ribald jesting or anything of the kind, instead of always and everywhere remembering his sovereignty, that he is as a shepherd and master of a flock, and extracting for himself whatever may tend to betterment from everything whatever that is said or done." Then he would continue, " When 45 you are attending theatrical or gymnastic competitions or those of the chariot race, do not pay regard to what the performers actually do, but to the moral achievement[a] shown in their doings, and reason thus with yourself. If there are those who so labour on 46 things which do not profit human life but merely provide pleasure and enjoyment to the spectator, so that they win praise and admiration and rewards and honours and crowns announced by proclamations, what should he do who has learnt the highest and greatest art ? And the best and greatest art is the art of 47 government which causes the good deep soil in lowlands and highlands to be tilled, and all the seas to be safely navigated by merchantships laden with cargoes to effect the exchange of goods which the countries in desire for fellowship render to each other, receiving those which they lack and sending in return those of which they carry a surplus. For envy has 48 never gained the mastery over the habitable world, nor even of the great sections of it, the whole of Europe or the whole of Asia. But like a venomous reptile it creeps into tiny hiding-places, into a single man or a single house or, if the force of its blast be

ἐνεργήματα. The virtue in this case is ἀνδρεία, and it is only in so far as the performers showed this that their performance was worth looking at. *Cf.* Zeller, *Stoics* (Eng. trans.), p. 248.

πολὺς ἄγαν πνέοι, πόλει μιᾷ· πρὸς δὲ μείζονα κύκλον ἔθνους ἢ χώρας οὐ πρόσεισι, καὶ μάλιστα ἀφ’
οὗ τὸ ὑμέτερον γένος τὸ Σεβαστὸν ὄντως ἤρξατο
49 πρυτανεύειν τῶν πανταχοῦ πάντων. ὅσα μὲν γὰρ
εὐημέρει τῶν βλαβερῶν καὶ ἐν μέσοις ἐξητάζετο,
πρὸς ἐσχατιὰς ὑπερόρια καὶ Ταρτάρου μυχοὺς ἤ-
λασε, τὰ δὲ τρόπον τινὰ φυγαδευθέντα τῶν λυσιτε-
λῶν καὶ ὠφελίμων κατήγαγεν ἀπὸ περάτων γῆς
καὶ θαλάττης εἰς τὴν καθ’ ἡμᾶς οἰκουμένην·
ἃ πάντα μιᾷ χειρὶ σῇ κυβερνᾶν ἐπιτέτραπται.
50 παραπεμφθεὶς γοῦν ὑπὸ τῆς φύσεως ἐπὶ πρύμναν
ἀνωτάτω καὶ τοὺς οἴακας ἐγχειρισθεὶς πηδαλιούχει
τὸ κοινὸν ἀνθρώπων σκάφος σωτηρίως, ἐπὶ μηδενὶ
μᾶλλον χαίρων καὶ τερπόμενος ἢ τῷ τοὺς ὑπηκόους
51 εὐεργετεῖν. ἄλλοι μὲν γὰρ ἄλλων ἔρανοι, οὓς
ἀναγκαίως εἰσφέρουσιν ἰδιῶται κατὰ πόλεις· ἄρ-
χοντι δὲ οἰκειότατος ἔρανος, βουλὰς ἀγαθὰς εἰση-
γεῖσθαι περὶ τῶν ὑποτεταγμένων καὶ πράττειν τὰ
βουλευθέντα ὀρθῶς καὶ ἀταμίευτα προφέρειν τὰ
ἀγαθὰ πλουσίᾳ χειρὶ καὶ γνώμῃ, πλὴν ὅσα κατὰ
πρόνοιαν τῆς εἰς τὸ μέλλον ἀδηλότητος ἄξιον
παραφυλάττειν.”
52 VIII. Τοιούτοις κατεπῇδεν ὁ δυστυχής, ὥστε
βελτιῶσαι τὸν Γάιον. ὁ δὲ φίλερις καὶ φιλόνεικος
ὢν ἐπὶ τἀναντία τὴν διάνοιαν ἔτρεπεν, ὥσπερ εἰς
ἐκεῖνα παρακληθείς, καὶ τὸν σωφρονιστὴν ἄντικρυς
ἀπεθάρρει δυσωπεῖν, ἔστι δὲ ὅτε καὶ πόρρωθεν
ἀφικνούμενον ὁρῶν πρὸς τοὺς πλησίον ταυτὶ διε-
53 λάλει· “ πάρεστιν ὁ διδάσκαλος τοῦ μηκέτι μανθάνειν ὀφείλοντος, ὁ παιδαγωγὸς τοῦ μηκέτι παιδὸς

26

overstrong, into a single city. But to the wider circuit of a nation or country it has no entry, particularly since your family, the truly Augustan, began to hold sway over all and everywhere. For 49 all the mischiefs which used to prosper and occupy a central place have been driven by your house into exile and into the utmost corners and recesses of Tartarus, and things beneficial and profitable which lay as though in banishment it has brought back from the ends of the earth and sea into the world of our habitation. The governance of all these has been entrusted to your single hand. Accordingly 50 having under Nature's escort risen to the highest post in the stern, and the tiller placed in your hand, steer in security the common ship of mankind, rejoicing and delighting in nothing so much as in benefiting your subjects. For various are the contributions 51 which private citizens throughout the cities render under compulsion, but the fittest contribution for a ruler is to put forth good proposals for the benefit of his subjects and to execute these proposals in the best way possible and to bring forth good gifts with a bountiful hand and will, reserving nothing save what in provision for the uncertainty of the future may fitly be stored in safe-keeping."

VIII. With such talk the unfortunate man tried to 52 charm Gaius into better ways. But quarrelsome and contentious as he was, he let his inclination turn to the opposite direction as though it was that to which Macro urged him. And he grew bold enough to flout his monitor outright, and sometimes when he saw him coming a little way off he would discourse thus to the bystanders, " Here comes the teacher of 53 one who no longer needs to learn, the tutor of one who

ὄντος, ὁ νουθετητὴς τοῦ φρονιμωτέρου, ὁ τὸν αὐτοκράτορα τῷ ὑπηκόῳ πειθαρχεῖν ἀξιῶν, ἐθάδα
τῆς ἡγεμονικῆς ἐπιστήμης καὶ παιδευτὴν ἑαυτὸν
γράφει, παρὰ τίνι μαθὼν τὰ ἀρχικὰ ἔγωγε οὐκ
54 οἶδα. ἐμοὶ μὲν γὰρ ἐξ ἔτι σπαργάνων μυρίοι
διδάσκαλοι γεγόνασι, πατέρες, ἀδελφοί, θεῖοι, ἀνε-
ψιοί, πάπποι, πρόγονοι μέχρι τῶν ἀρχηγετῶν, οἱ
ἀφ' αἵματος πάντες καθ' ἑκάτερον γένος τό τε
πατρῷον καὶ μητρῷον, αὐτοκρατεῖς ἐξουσίας περι-
ποιησάμενοι, χωρὶς τοῦ κἂν ταῖς πρώταις τῶν
σπερμάτων καταβολαῖς εἶναί τινας δυνάμεις βασι-
55 λικὰς τῶν ἡγεμονικῶν. ὡς γὰρ αἱ τοῦ σώματος
καὶ τῆς ψυχῆς ὁμοιότητες κατά τε τὴν μορφὴν καὶ
σχέσεις καὶ κινήσεις βουλάς τε καὶ πράξεις ἐν τοῖς
σπερματικοῖς σῴζονται λόγοις, οὕτως εἰκὸς ἐν
[554] τοῖς αὐτοῖς ὑπογράφεσθαι τυπωδέστερον | καὶ τὴν
56 πρὸς ἡγεμονίαν ἐμφέρειαν. εἶτα ἐμὲ τὸν καὶ πρὸ
τῆς γενέσεως ἔτι κατὰ γαστρὸς ἐν τῷ τῆς φύσεως
ἐργαστηρίῳ διαπλασθέντα αὐτοκράτορα τολμᾷ τις
διδάσκειν, ἀνεπιστήμων ἐπιστήμονα; ποῦ γὰρ
τοῖς ἰδιώταις πρὸ μικροῦ θέμις εἰς ἡγεμονικῆς
ψυχῆς παρακύψαι βουλεύματα; τολμῶσι δὲ ὑπ'
ἀναισχύντου θράσους ἱεροφαντεῖν καὶ τελεῖν τὰ
57 ἡγεμονικὰ μόλις ἂν ἐν μύσταις ἀναγραφέντες." ἐκ
δὲ τοῦ κατ' ὀλίγον μελετῶν ἀλλοτριοῦσθαι τοῦ
Μάκρωνος ἤρχετο καὶ ψευδεῖς μὲν πιθανὰς δὲ καὶ
εὐπαραγώγους κατ' αὐτοῦ πλάττειν αἰτίας· δειναὶ
γὰρ αἱ εὔθικτοι καὶ μεγάλαι φύσεις εἰκοτολογῆσαι.

---

[a] Or " principles." See note on *De Aet.* 85, and on *De*
28

is no longer in tutelage, the censor of his superior
in wisdom, who holds that an emperor should obey
his subjects, who rates himself as versed in the art
of government and an instructor therein, though in
what school he has learnt its principles I do not
know. For I from the cradle have had a host of 54
teachers, father, brothers, uncles, cousins, grandparents, ancestors, right up to the founders of the
House, all my kinsmen by blood on both the
maternal and paternal sides, who attained to offices
of independent authority, apart from the fact that in
the original seeds of their begetting kinglike potenti-
alities for government were contained. For just as 55
the seminal forces[a] preserve similarities of the body in
form and carriage and gait, and of the soul in projects
and actions, so we may suppose that to the governing
faculty they contain a resemblance in outline. And 56
then does anyone dare to teach me, who even while
in the womb, that workshop of nature,[b] was modelled
as an emperor, ignorance dare to instruct knowledge ?
How can they who were but now common citizens
have a right to peer into the counsels of an imperial
soul ? yet in their shameless effrontery they who
would hardly be admitted to rank as learners dare to
act as masters who initiate others into the mysteries
of government." Step by step he began to practise 57
alienating himself from Macro and also to fabricate
charges against him, which though false were speci-
ous and readily accepted. For quick and highly
gifted natures are clever at producing plausible argu-

Op. 43 (vol. i. p. 475), where reference is given to *S.V.F.*
index p. 93 *a*.

[b] This phrase for the womb has been used several times,
see note on *De Aet.* 66.

PHILO

58 τοιαῦται δὲ ἦσαν αἱ προφάσεις· " ἐμόν ἐστι τοῦ
Μάκρωνος ἔργον Γάιος· μᾶλλον αὐτὸν ἢ οὐχ ἧττον
τῶν γονέων γεγέννηκα· τρίς, οὐχ ἅπαξ, ἀνήρπαστο
ἂν ἐπ' αὐτῷ Τιβερίου φονῶντος, εἰ μὴ δι' ἐμὲ καὶ
τὰς ἐμὰς παρηγορίας· ἀλλὰ καὶ τελευτήσαντος ἔχων
ὑπηκόους τὰς στρατιωτικὰς δυνάμεις εὐθὺς εἰς τὴν
ἐκείνου παρέπεμψα τάξιν, ἀναδιδάσκων ὅτι ἀνδρὸς
ἑνὸς γέγονεν ἔνδεια· μένει δὲ ἄρτιος καὶ πλήρης ἡ
59 ἡγεμονία." τούτοις συνεπείθοντό τινες
ὡς ἀψευδέσιν ἀγνοοῦντες τὸν φένακα τρόπον τοῦ
λέγοντος· οὔπω γὰρ ἦν τὸ πεπλασμένον αὐτοῦ καὶ
ποικίλον τῶν ἠθῶν ἐμφανές. ἀλλὰ γὰρ οὐ πολλαῖς
ὕστερον ἡμέραις ἐκποδὼν ὁ κακοδαίμων γίνεται
σὺν τῇ γυναικί, τῆς περιττῆς εὐνοίας ἀμοιβὰς τὰς
60 ἀνωτάτω τιμωρίας ἀντιλαβών. τοιοῦτόν ἐστιν ἡ
εἰς τοὺς ἀχαρίστους χάρις· ἀντὶ γὰρ ὧν ὠφελή-
θησαν, παρέχουσι τὰς μεγίστας ζημίας τοῖς εὐ-
εργετήσασιν. ὁ γοῦν Μάκρων πάντα ἐπ' ἀληθείας
πραγματευσάμενος μετ' ἐκτενεστάτης σπουδῆς καὶ
φιλοτιμίας, τὸ μὲν πρῶτον ὑπὲρ τοῦ σῶσαι Γάιον,
ἔπειτα δὲ ὑπὲρ τοῦ μόνον τὴν ἡγεμονίαν διαδέξα-
61 σθαι, τοιαῦτα εὕρατο τὰ ἐπίχειρα. λέγεται γάρ,
ὅτι ἠναγκάσθη ὁ δείλαιος αὐτοχειρίᾳ κτεῖναι ἑαυτὸν
καὶ τὴν αὐτὴν ἀνεδέξατο συμφορὰν ἡ γυνή, καίτοι
ποτὲ νομισθεῖσα διὰ συνηθείας αὐτῷ γενέσθαι· βέ-
βαιον δὲ οὐδέν φασι τῶν ἐν ἔρωτι φίλτρων εἶναι διὰ
τὸ τοῦ πάθους ἀψίκορον.
62 IX. Ἐπειδὴ δὲ καὶ ὁ Μάκρων πανοίκιος ἱέρευτο,[1]

[1] mss. ἱερεύετο.

[a] It is strange not to find some words to the effect that
Marco had been heard to say this. For since what follows
30

ments. This was the sort of allegation which he 58 made, " Macro says,[a] ' It is I Macro who made Gaius, I am his begetter more or not less than his parents. Not once only but thrice, when Tiberius wished to kill him he would have been violently removed, had it not been for me and my exhortations. Even when Tiberius was dead, as I had the military forces under my control, I at once brought them over into his camp by teaching them that one man was needed and so his sovereignty remains perfect and complete.' "

Some people accepted these charges as 59 veracious, not knowing the deceptive and cunning character of the speaker, for his artificial and cunning disposition was not yet manifest. However a few days later the unhappy man together with his wife was got rid of and paid the extreme penalty in return for his excessive zeal. This is the gratitude 60 gained by benefits bestowed on the ungrateful. They return the benefits they have received by inflicting the severest penalties on their benefactors. Such were, for example, the rewards which Macro reaped after having busied himself throughout in all sincerity with the most intense zeal and ardour, first to save Gaius's life and secondly to secure his sole accession to the sovereignty. For it is said that the unhappy 61 man was forced to slay himself with his own hand and that his wife submitted to the same fate, though she was supposed to have been at one time Gaius's mistress. But love as they say is a fickle passion, and therefore none of its endearments are stable.

IX. When Macro, too, with his whole house had 62

simply repeats what Philo declares to have been the truth, the falsity could only lie in that he had actually made the boast.

τρίτῳ ἐπαπεδύετο δόλῳ βαρυτέρῳ. πενθερὸς ἐγεγένητο αὐτῷ Μάρκος Σιλανός, μεστὸς φρονήματος
ἀνὴρ καὶ γένει λαμπρός. οὗτος ὠκυμόρου τῆς
θυγατρὸς ἀποθανούσης ἔτι περιεῖπε τὸν Γάιον,
εὔνοιαν προσφερόμενος οὐ πενθεροῦ μᾶλλον ἢ
γνησίου πατρός, ἧς[1] ἐνόμιζεν ἀντιλήψεσθαι κατὰ
νόμον ἰσότητος μεθαρμοσάμενος τὸν γαμβρὸν εἰς
υἱόν. ἐλελήθει δὲ ἄρα ψευδοδοξῶν καὶ ἀπατώ-

[555]   μενος. | ὁ μὲν γὰρ τοὺς τοῦ κηδεμόνος[2] λόγους ἀεὶ
63   διεξῄει μηδὲν ἐπικρυπτόμενος τῶν εἰς βελτίωσιν
καὶ ὠφέλειαν ἠθῶν καὶ βίου καὶ ἡγεμονίας, ἔχων
εἰς παρρησίαν καὶ μεγάλας ἀφορμὰς ὑπερβάλλουσάν
τε εὐγένειαν καὶ τὴν κατ᾽ ἐπιγαμίαν οἰκειότητα·
καὶ γὰρ ἡ θυγάτηρ οὐ πρὸ πολλῶν ἐτεθνήκει χρόνων, ὡς ἀμαυρωθῆναι τὰ δίκαια τῶν κηδεστῶν,
ἀλλὰ μόνον οὐκ ἤσπαιρεν, ἔτι λειψάνων τινῶν
ὑστάτων τοῦ ψυχικοῦ πνεύματος ἐνυπαρχόντων καὶ
64 ἐγκατειλημμένων τῷ σώματι. ὁ δὲ πρὸς ὕβρεως
τὰς νουθεσίας λαμβάνων τῷ πάντων οἴεσθαι φρο-
νιμώτατος καὶ σωφρονέστατος ἔτι δὲ ἀνδρειότατος
εἶναι καὶ δικαιότατος ἤχθαιρε μᾶλλον τῶν ὁμολο-
65 γουμένων πολεμίων τοὺς διδάσκοντας. ὑπολαβὼν
οὖν καὶ τοῦτον εἶναι παρενόχλημα, τὴν πολλὴν
αὐτοῦ ῥύμην τῶν ἐπιθυμιῶν ἐφέξοντα, πολλὰ χαίρειν φράσας τοῖς δαίμοσι τῆς ἀποθανούσης γυναι-
κός, εἰ πατέρα μὲν ἐκείνης ἑαυτοῦ δὲ γενόμενον
πενθερὸν μεταστήσεται, δολοφονεῖ.

66 X. Καὶ τὸ πρᾶγμα ἤδη περιβόητον τοῖς ἐπαλ-

---

[1] mss. ἦν.
[2] mss. τοὺς κηδομένους or τοῦ κηδομένου.

---

[a] Possibly second, i.e before that of Macro, which is

been slaughtered Gaius armed himself to deal a third[a] blow of still more grievous treachery. He had for his father-in-law M. Silanus, a man with plenty of fine spirit and of distinguished family. His daughter died early but he continued to pay the same attentions to Gaius and showed him an affection suited not so much to a father-in-law as to an actual father, thinking that by thus converting his son-in-law into a son he would have it reciprocated by the rule of equality. But he little knew how false and deceptive was his expectation. In all his discourse he talked as a 63 guardian, concealing nothing which might tend to improve and benefit Gaius's character, conduct and government. He had, indeed, strong inducements to speak freely in his pre-eminently noble lineage and his close connexion by marriage. For his daughter had died only a short time before ; the rights of her kinsfolk had grown faint but had all but ceased to struggle for breath although some last remnants of their vitality still existed enclosed in their body. But Gaius took his admonitions as an insult since he 64 thought himself the wisest and most temperate of men and also the bravest and justest and hated his instructors more than his avowed enemies. He con- 65 sidered, too, that Silanus was a nuisance, who would obstruct the torrent of his lusts, and, dismissing all thought of his dead wife's ghostly avengers, should he make away with her father, afterwards his own by marriage, he treacherously murdered him.

X. The matter at once gained notoriety by follow- 66

mentioned by Dio and Suetonius at a later point in their narratives. The death of both Tiberius Gemellus and Silanus is fixed as before 24th May 38, by the records of the Arval Brothers, which note the appointment of their successors at that date. See Balsdon, *Gaius*, pp. 37, 38.

PHILO

λήλοις τῶν πρώτων ἀνδρῶν φόνοις ἐγεγένητο, ὡς
διὰ παντὸς στόματος δυσκάθαρτα ἄγη συνηχεῖσθαι,
φανερῶς μὲν οὐ διὰ δέος, ἠρεμαιοτέρᾳ δὲ τῇ φωνῇ.

67 κἄπειτα ἐκ μεταβολῆς—ὄχλος γὰρ ἀνίδρυτον ἐν
ἅπασι, καὶ βουλαῖς καὶ λόγοις καὶ πράγμασιν—
ἀπιστοῦντες, εἰ οὕτως ἀθρόαν ἐνδέδεκται τροπὴν
ὁ πρὸ μικροῦ χρηστὸς καὶ φιλάνθρωπος ἴσος τε
καὶ κοινωνικὸς εἶναι νομισθεὶς Γάιος, ἀπολογίας
ἐσκόπουν καὶ διερευνῶντες εὕρισκον, ἐπὶ μὲν τῷ
ἀνεψιῷ καὶ συγκληρονόμῳ τοιαῦτα φάσκοντες·

68 " ἀκοινώνητον ἀρχή, θεσμὸς φύσεως ἀκίνητος. οὗτος ἃ παθεῖν ἐμέλλησεν ἂν ὑπ' ἀδυνατωτέρου
προδιέθηκεν ἰσχυρότερος ὤν· ἄμυνα τοῦτ' ἔστιν,
οὐκ ἀνδροφονία. τάχα δὲ καὶ προνοητικῶς ἐπ'
ὠφελείᾳ τοῦ σύμπαντος ἀνθρώπων γένους τὸ μειράκιον ἐκποδὼν γεγένηται, τῶν μὲν τούτῳ τῶν δὲ
ἐκείνῳ προσκληρουμένων, ἐξ ὧν ταραχαὶ ἐμφύλιοί
τε καὶ ξενικοὶ πόλεμοι συνίστανται. τί δὲ ἄμεινον
εἰρήνης; εἰρήνη δὲ ἐξ ἡγεμονίας ὀρθῆς φύεται·
ἡγεμονία δὲ ἀφιλόνεικος καὶ ἀνερίθευτος ὀρθὴ
μόνη, δι' ἧς καὶ τἆλλα πάντα κατορθοῦται."

69 ἐπὶ δὲ Μάκρωνι· " πλέον ἐφυσήθη τοῦ
μετρίου· τὸ Δελφικὸν γράμμα οὐ διανέγνω, τὸ
'γνῶθι σαυτόν'· φασὶ δὲ τὴν μὲν ἐπιστήμην εὐδαιμονίας τὴν δὲ ἄγνοιαν κακοδαιμονίας αἰτίαν εἶναι.
τί παθὼν ὑπηλλάττετο καὶ μετετίθει τὸν μὲν ὑπή-
κοον αὐτὸν εἰς τάξιν ἄρχοντος, τὸν δὲ αὐτοκράτορα
[556] Γάιον | εἰς ὑπηκόου χώραν; οἰκειότατον ἡγεμόνι
μὲν τὸ προστάττειν, ὅπερ ἐποίει Μάκρων, ὑπηκόῳ
34

ing on the successive murders of the foremost men.
And so in every mouth there was common talk about
these inexpiable abominations, though quietly and
in undertones, since fear prevented open discussion.
Then there was a reaction, for a multitude is unstable 67
in everything, intentions, words and deeds. They
could not believe that Gaius, who but now had been
thought kind and humane, showing fairness and
fellowship to all, had undergone at once so complete
a change. They began to look for arguments of
defence and by close search found them. Of his own
cousin and fellow-heir they would talk thus.
" Sovereignty cannot be shared, that is an immutable 68
law of nature. He being the stronger promptly did
to the weaker what the weaker would have done to
him. This is defence, not murder. Perhaps, too, it
was providential and for the benefit of all mankind,
that the lad was put out of the way, since some
would have been partisans of him and others of
Gaius, and it is such things that create disturbances
and wars both civil and foreign. And what is better
than peace ? But peace springs from right government. The only right government is that which is
free from disputes and factions which also causes
everything else to be carried on aright."
Of Macro they said, " His pride extended beyond 69
reasonable limits, he did not read well the Delphic
motto ' Know thyself.' It is a common saying that
knowledge is the source of happiness and ignorance
of unhappiness. What reason had he for reversing
his part and transferring the subject to the rank
of ruler, and Gaius, the emperor, to the place of
a subject ? To command, which is what he did,
befits best the sovereign, and to obey, which is what

δὲ τὸ πειθαρχεῖν, ὅπερ ὑπομένειν ἠξίου Γάιον.''
70 ἐκάλουν γὰρ οἱ ἀνεξέταστοι τὴν παραίνεσιν πρόσ-
ταξιν καὶ τὸν σύμβουλον ἄρχοντα, ἤτοι μὴ συνιέντες ὑπ' ἀναισθησίας ἢ διὰ κολακείαν τὰς φύσεις
τῶν ὀνομάτων ὁμοῦ καὶ πραγμάτων μεταχαράτ-
71 τοντες.   ἐπὶ δὲ Σιλανῷ· '' χλεύης ἄξιον
ὁ Σιλανὸς ἔπαθεν, οἰηθεὶς πενθερὸν τοσοῦτον παρὰ
γαμβρῷ δύνασθαι, ὅσον πατέρα γνήσιον παρ' υἱῷ.
καίτοι πατέρες ἰδιῶται γενομένων ἐν ἀρχαῖς μεγάλαις καὶ ἐξουσίαις υἱῶν ὑποστέλλουσιν, ἀγα-
πητῶς φερόμενοι δευτερεῖα. ὁ δὲ ἠλίθιος, οὐδὲ
πενθερὸς ὢν ἔτι, τὰ μὴ καθ' ἑαυτὸν προσπερι-
ειργάζετο μὴ συνιείς, ὅτι θανάτῳ τῆς θυγατρὸς
συνετεθνήκει καὶ ἡ κατ' ἐπιγαμίαν οἰκειότης·
72 δεσμὸς γὰρ οἴκων ὀθνείων αἱ ἐπιγαμίαι τὴν ἀλλοτριότητα εἰς οἰκειότητα συνάγων, οὗ λυθέντος
λέλυται καὶ τὰ τῆς κοινωνίας, καὶ μάλιστα ὅταν
ἀνεπανορθώτῳ πράγματι λυθῇ, τελευτῇ τῆς εἰς
73 ἀλλότριον οἶκον δεδομένης ἐπὶ γάμῳ.'' τοιαῦτα
ἐν ἅπασι τοῖς συλλόγοις ἐθρύλουν πλεῖστον διδόντες
μέρος τῷ μὴ βούλεσθαι δοκεῖν ὠμὸν εἶναι τὸν
αὐτοκράτορα· χρηστότητα γὰρ καὶ φιλανθρωπίαν
ἐλπίσαντες ὅσην παρ' οὐδενὶ τῶν προτέρων ἐνιδρῦ-
σθαι τῇ Γαΐου ψυχῇ σφόδρα ἄπιστον ἐνόμιζον, εἰ
τοσαύτην καὶ οὕτως ἀθρόαν ἐνδέδεκται μεταβολὴν
πρὸς τἀναντία.
74   XI. Κατεργασάμενος οὖν τρεῖς τοὺς εἰρημένους
ἄθλους ἐκ τριῶν τῶν ἀναγκαιοτάτων μερῶν, δυοῖν
μὲν ἐκ τῆς πατρίδος τοῦ τε βουλευτικοῦ καὶ τοῦ

he deemed Gaius should submit to, befits the subject." For in their thoughtlessness they gave the 70
name of commanding to exhortation and of the ruler
to the counsellor, whether they misunderstood the
matter through stupidity, or in flattery recast the
words and the things signified by them away from
their natural use. Of Silanus, " He was 71
under a ridiculous delusion in thinking that a father-
in-law had the same influence over a son-in-law as a
real father has over his son, though, indeed, in private
life fathers whose sons have obtained high offices and
posts of authority waive their claims and are content
to take the second place. But this silly man even
though he had ceased to be a father-in-law extended
his activities beyond his sphere and did not understand that the death of his daughter carried with it
the death of the matrimonial affinity. For inter- 72
marriage is a lien between unconnected households
bringing the status of stranger into one of affinity,
and if this be broken the community of interests is
broken also, particularly if the break is caused by an
irretrievable event, the death of her whose admission
to a house not her own rested on her marriage."
Such were the ideas on which they dwelt in all their 73
talks, and what principally weighed with them was
their wish to think that the emperor was not cruel.
For as they had hoped that kindness and humanity
were established in his soul in a greater degree than
in any of his predecessors they thought it very in-
credible that he had undergone all at once so complete
a change to the reverse.

XI. Gaius had thus won the three contests de- 74
scribed above in three vitally important departments.
Two of these, the Senate and the Equestrian Order,

τῆς ἱππικῆς τάξεως, τρίτου δὲ τοῦ συγγενικοῦ, καὶ
ὑπολαβὼν τῶν ἰσχυροτάτων καὶ δυνατωτάτων
75 περιγεγενημένος καταπληκτικώτατον δέος ἐνειργά-
σθαι τοῖς ἄλλοις ἅπασι, διὰ μὲν τῆς Σιλανοῦ
σφαγῆς τοῖς βουλευταῖς—ἦν γὰρ οὐδενὸς τῶν ἐν
συγκλήτῳ δεύτερος—, διὰ δὲ τῆς Μάκρωνος τοῖς
ἱππικοῖς—οἷα γὰρ χοροῦ τινος ἡγεμὼν ἐγεγένητο
φερόμενος τὰ πρωτεῖα τιμῆς καὶ εὐδοξίας—, διὰ
δὲ τῆς τοῦ ἀνεψιοῦ καὶ συγκληρονόμου τοῖς ἀφ'
αἵματος ἅπασιν, οὐκέτι ἠξίου μένειν ἐν τοῖς τῆς
ἀνθρωπίνης φύσεως ὅροις, ἀλλ' ὑπερέκυπτε σπου-
76 δάζων θεὸς νομίζεσθαι.   καὶ ἐν ἀρχῇ
ταύτης τῆς παραπληξίας φασὶν αὐτὸν χρήσασθαι
τοιούτῳ λογισμῷ· καθάπερ γὰρ οἱ τῶν ἄλλων
ζῴων ἀγελάρχαι, βουκόλοι καὶ αἰπόλοι καὶ νομεῖς,
[557] οὔτε βόες εἰσὶν οὔτε αἶγες οὔτε ἄρνες, ἀλλ' | ἄν-
θρωποι κρείττονος μοίρας καὶ κατασκευῆς ἐπι-
λαχόντες, τὸν αὐτὸν τρόπον ἀγελαρχοῦντα κἀμὲ
τῆς ἀρίστης ἀνθρώπων γένους ἀγέλης νομιστέον
διαφέρειν καὶ μὴ κατ' ἄνθρωπον εἶναι, μείζονος δὲ
77 καὶ θειοτέρας μοίρας τετυχηκέναι.   ταύτην τὴν ὑπόληψιν ἐνσφραγισάμενος τῇ διανοίᾳ
περιέφερεν ὁ ἠλίθιος ἐν ἑαυτῷ μυθικὸν πλάσμα ὡς
ἀψευδεστάτην ἀλήθειαν. καὶ ἐπειδὴ ἅπαξ ἐθρασύ-
νατο καὶ ἀπετόλμησεν εἰς τοὺς πολλοὺς ἐξενεγκεῖν
τὴν ἀθεωτάτην ἐκθέωσιν αὐτοῦ, τὰ ἀκόλουθα καὶ
συνῳδὰ πράττειν ἐπεχείρει καὶ οἷα δι' ἀναβαθμῶν
ἐκ τοῦ κατ' ὀλίγον εἰς τὸ ἄνω προῄει.
78 ἤρχετο γὰρ ἐξομοιοῦν τὸ πρῶτον τοῖς λεγομένοις
ἡμιθέοις ἑαυτόν, Διονύσῳ καὶ Ἡρακλεῖ καὶ Διοσκούροις, Τροφώνιον καὶ Ἀμφιάραον καὶ Ἀμφί-
λοχον καὶ τοὺς ὁμοίους χρηστηρίοις αὐτοῖς καὶ
38

concerned his relations to his Capital; the third was his family life. So supposing that by his victory over the strongest and most powerful personages he had inspired all the rest with abject fear, the senators by the murder of Silanus who was 75 second to none of the members of that body, the knights by the death of Macro who had become like the leader of a chorus and stood first in honours and reputation among them, and all his blood relations by the death of his cousin and fellow-heir, he no longer considered it worthy of him to abide within the bounds of human nature but overstepped them in his eagerness to be thought a god.   In the 76 first stage of this infatuation he is said to have taken this line of argument. " Those who have charge of the herds of other animals, ox herds, goat herds, shepherds, are not themselves oxen, nor goats nor lambs, but men to whom is given a higher destiny and constitution, and in the same way I who am in charge of the best of herds, mankind, must be considered to be different from them and not of human nature but to have a greater and diviner destiny."

This conception he had firmly sealed 77 in his mind and carried about with him, poor fool, a mythical fiction as if it was an indisputable truth. And when once he had gained courage and was emboldened to publish to the multitude his most godless assumption of godship he tried to make his actions correspond and harmonize with it and gradually as if on stepping-stones advanced to the top.   For he began first of all to 78 liken himself to the so-called demigods, Dionysus and Heracles and the Dioscuri, treating Trophonius and Amphiaraus and Amphilochus and their like and their

ὀργίοις χλεύην τιθέμενος κατὰ σύγκρισιν τῆς ἰδίας
79 δυνάμεως. εἶθ᾽ ὥσπερ ἐν θεάτρῳ σκευὴν ἄλλοτε
ἀλλοίαν ἀνελάμβανε, τοτὲ μὲν λεοντῆν καὶ ῥόπαλον,
ἀμφότερα ἐπίχρυσα, διακοσμούμενος εἰς Ἡρακλέα,
τοτὲ δὲ πίλους ἐπὶ τῆς κεφαλῆς, ὁπότε ἄσκοιτο
εἰς Διοσκούρους· ἔστι δὲ ὅτε κιττῷ καὶ θύρσῳ
80 καὶ νεβρίσιν εἰς Διόνυσον ἠσκεῖτο.   καὶ
ταύτῃ διαφέρειν ἀξιῶν, ὅτι ἐκείνων μὲν ἕκαστος
ἰδίας ἔχων τιμὰς οὐ μετεποιεῖτο ὧν ἐκοινώνουν
ἕτεροι, ὁ δὲ τὰς πάντων ἀθρόων[1] ἐσφετερίζετο
φθόνῳ καὶ πλεονεξίᾳ, μᾶλλον δὲ καὶ αὐτοὺς ἐκεί-
νους, οὐκ εἰς Γηρυόνην τὸν τρισώματον μεταβαλών,
ἵνα τῷ πλήθει παραγάγῃ τοὺς ὁρῶντας, ἀλλ᾽, ὃ δὴ
παραδοξότατον ἦν, ἑνὸς σώματος οὐσίαν μετασχη-
ματίζων καὶ μεταχαράττων εἰς πολυτρόπους μορ-
φάς, Αἰγυπτίου τρόπον Πρωτέως, ὃν εἰσήγαγεν
Ὅμηρος μεταβολὰς παντοίας ἐνδεχόμενον εἴς τε τὰ
στοιχεῖα καὶ τὰ ἐκ τούτων ζῷα καὶ φυτά.
81   Καίτοι τί παρασήμων ἔδει σοι, Γάιε, οἷς ἔθος
ἀσκεῖσθαι[2] τὰ τῶν εἰρημένων ἀφιδρύματα; ἐχρῆν
γὰρ ζηλοῦν τὰς ἐκείνων ἀρετάς. Ἡρακλῆς ἐκά-
θηρε γῆν καὶ θάλατταν ἄθλους ἀναγκαιοτάτους καὶ
ὠφελιμωτάτους ἅπασιν ἀνθρώποις ὑποστὰς ἕνεκα
τοῦ τὰ βλαβερὰ καὶ κακωτικὰ φύσεως ἑκατέρας
82 ἀνελεῖν.   Διόνυσος ἡμερώσας ἄμπελον
καὶ ποτὸν ἐξ αὐτῆς ἀναχέας ἥδιστον ὁμοῦ καὶ
ὠφελιμώτατον ψυχαῖς τε καὶ σώμασι τὰς μὲν ἄγει
πρὸς εὐθυμίαν, κακῶν λήθην καὶ ἀγαθῶν ἐλπίδας

---

[1] mss. ἄθροον.   [2] mss. ἀρκεῖσθαι.

[a] According to Dio lix. 26, he also impersonated goddesses:
Hera, Aphrodite and Artemis.

oracles and celebrations as laughing-stocks compared
with his own power. Then, as in a theatre, he assumed 79
different costumes at different times, sometimes the
lion skin and club, both overlaid with gold, to adorn
himself as Heracles, sometimes caps on his head when
he made himself up as the Dioscuri, or again as Dionysus with ivy, thyrsus and fawn's skin.[a]
And he thought it fit to differ from these in that 80
while each of them held to his own honours and did
not lay claim to those which were shared by others,
he, filled with envy and covetousness, took possession wholesale of the honours of them all, or rather
of the deities themselves. He did not convert
himself into a triple-bodied Geryon to bewilder
the spectators by the multiplication, but performed
a feat which could be least expected by remodelling
and recasting what was nothing but a single body
into manifold forms, like the Egyptian Proteus
whom Homer represented as admitting every kind
of transfiguration both into the elements and into
the animals and plants of which they are the com-
ponents.[b]

And yet what business had you, Gaius, to take the 81
insignia commonly used to adorn the images of the
said deities ? For you should have emulated their
virtues. Heracles purged the earth and the sea,
undergoing trials of endurance most necessary and
profitable for all mankind in order to destroy things
which are mischievous and baneful to either form of
life.   Dionysus cultivated the wild vine and 82
drew pouring from it a drink most delicious and at the
same time profitable to souls and bodies. The soul
he brings into a state of cheerfulness, creating oblivion

---

[b] See *Od.* iv. 454 ff. *Cf. Ebr.* 36.

ἐνεργαζόμενος, τὰ δὲ σώματα ὑγιεινότερα καὶ κρα-
83 ταιότερα καὶ εὐκινητότερα παρασκευάζει· καὶ ἰδίᾳ
τε ἕκαστον ἀνθρώπων[1] βελτίονα ποιεῖ καὶ πολυ-
ανθρώπους οἰκίας καὶ συγγενείας ἐξ αὐχμηροῦ
καὶ ἐπιπόνου βίου μεθαρμόζεται πρὸς ἀνειμένης
σχῆμα καὶ ἱλαρᾶς διαίτης καὶ πάσαις πόλεσιν |
[558] Ἑλληνικαῖς τε καὶ βαρβαρικαῖς εὐωχίας, εὐφροσύνας, θαλίας, ἑορτὰς ἐπαλλήλους παρέχει· πάντων
γὰρ τῶν λεχθέντων αἴτιος ἄκρατος.
84 πάλιν Διοσκούρους λόγος ἔχει κοινώσασθαι τὴν
ἀθανασίαν. ἐπειδὴ γὰρ ὁ μὲν θνητὸς ὁ δὲ ἀθάνατος
ἦν, οὐκ ἐδικαίωσεν ὁ τῆς κρείττονος μοίρας ἀξιω-
θεὶς φιλαυτῆσαι μᾶλλον ἢ πρὸς τὸν ἀδελφὸν εὔνοιαν
85 ἐπιδείξασθαι. φαντασιωθεὶς γὰρ τὸν ἄπειρον αἰῶνα καὶ λογισάμενος, ὅτι αὐτὸς μὲν ἀεὶ βιώσεται,
ὁ δὲ ἀδελφὸς ἀεὶ τεθνήξεται, καὶ μετὰ τῆς ἀθανασίας ἀθάνατον τὸ ἐπ' ἐκείνῳ πένθος ἀναδέξεται,
θαυμαστὴν ἐμεγαλούργησεν ἀντίδοσιν ἀνακερασά-
μενος αὑτῷ μὲν τὸ θνητόν, τῷ δὲ ἀδελφῷ τὸ
ἄφθαρτον, καὶ ἀνισότητα, τὴν ἀδικίας ἀρχήν,
ἐνηφάνισεν[2] ἰσότητι, ἥτις ἐστὶ πηγὴ δικαιοσύνης.
86 XII. Οὗτοι πάντες, ὦ Γάιε, διὰ τὰς ὑπηργμένας
εὐεργεσίας ἐθαυμάσθησαν καὶ ἔτι νῦν θαυμάζονται
καὶ σεβασμοῦ τε καὶ τῶν ἀνωτάτω τιμῶν ἠξιώ-
θησαν. εἰπὲ δὴ καὶ αὐτὸς ἡμῖν, ἐπὶ τίνι γαυριᾷς
87 καὶ πεφύσησαι τῶν παραπλησίων; ἐμιμήσω τοὺς
Διοσκούρους εἰς φιλαδελφίαν; ἵνα ἐντεῦθεν ἄρξω-
μαι. τὸν μὲν ἀδελφὸν καὶ συγκληρονόμον ἐν ἀκμῇ

---

[1] mss. αὐτῶν.   [2] mss. ἐνεκαίνεσεν or ἀνεκοίνωσεν.

[a] Philo has alluded to the story of the Dioscuri, *De Som.* i.

42

of evils and hopes of good, while he renders the body healthier and stronger and more agile. In private life 83 he improves each person and converts large households and families from a squalid and toilsome existence to a free and gay mode of living, and for all cities Greek and barbarian he provides a constant succession of banquets, merrymakings, galas, festivals. For all these owe their existence to Dionysus. Again, 84 the Dioscuri[a] are said to have shared the immortality between them, for since one of them was mortal and the other immortal he who had been judged worthy of the higher destiny did not think it fit to gratify his selfish instinct instead of showing affection to his brother. For having before his eyes the endless ages 85 and reflecting that while he lived for ever his brother would be dead for ever and his mourning for him would be as everlasting as his own existence, he achieved a great and marvellous reciprocation in that he mingled mortality with his own lot and indestructibility with his brother's, and thus made inequality, the source of injustice, vanish in equality, which is the fountain of justice.

XII. All these, Gaius, received and still receive 86 admiration for the benefits for which we are beholden to them[b] and were judged worthy of worship and the highest honours. Tell me yourself what deeds like these have you to make you so boastful and puffed with pride. To begin with the Dioscuri. Did you 87 imitate them in brotherly love ? Your brother and

150 and De Dec. 56. Here he takes the version of the legend in which Castor the mortal was actually killed and then Pollux renounced half his immortality to him.

[b] i.e. benefits in which they took the initiative and not in return for anything which we had done. For this use of ὑπάρχω see Lexicon.

τῆς πρώτης ἡλικίας, ὦ σιδήρειε καὶ ἀνηλεέστατε,
ὠμῶς ἀπέσφαξας, τὰς ⟨δ'⟩ ἀδελφὰς ὕστερον ἐφυ-
γάδευσας· μὴ καὶ αὗται τὸν περὶ ἀφαιρέσεως
88 ἀρχῆς φόβον εἰργάζοντό σοι;   ἐμιμήσω
Διόνυσον; εὑρετὴς καινῶν γέγονας χαρίτων ὡς
ἐκεῖνος; εὐφροσύνης κατέπλησας τὴν οἰκουμένην;
Ἀσία καὶ Εὐρώπη τὰς ἐκ σοῦ γεγενημένας δωρεὰς
89 οὐ χωρεῖ; καινὰς μὲν οὖν τέχνας καὶ ἐπιστήμας
ἀνεῦρες ὡς κοινὸς λυμεὼν καὶ παλαμναῖος, αἷς
μεταβάλλεις τὰ ἡδέα καὶ χαρτὰ πρὸς ἀηδίας καὶ
λύπας καὶ ἀβίωτον βίον τοῖς πανταχοῦ πᾶσι, τὰ
μὲν παρ' ἑτέροις ἀγαθὰ καὶ καλὰ πάντα σφετεριζό-
μενος ἀπλήστοις καὶ ἀκορέστοις ταῖς ἐπιθυμίαις,
τὰ ἀπὸ τῶν ἑῴων, τὰ ἀπὸ τῶν ἑσπερίων, τὰ ἀπὸ
τῶν ἄλλων τοῦ παντὸς κλιμάτων, εἴ τινα ἢ κατὰ
μεσημβρίαν ἦν ἢ πρὸς ἄρκτον, τὰ δὲ ἀπὸ τῆς
σαυτοῦ πικρίας καὶ ὅσα ταῖς ἐπαράτοις καὶ ἰοβόλοις
ψυχαῖς γεννᾶν ἔθος βλαβερὰ καὶ ἐπιζήμια ἀντι-
διδοὺς καὶ ἀντιπέμπων· διὰ ταῦτα ὁ νέος Διόνυσος
90 ἡμῖν ἀνεφάνης;   ἀλλὰ καὶ Ἡρακλέα ἐζή-
λωσας τοῖς ἀκαμάτοις σαυτοῦ πόνοις καὶ ταῖς
ἀτρύτοις ἀνδραγαθίαις, εὐνομίας καὶ εὐδικίας εὐ-
θηνίας[1] τε καὶ εὐετηρίας καὶ τῆς τῶν ἄλλων ἀγαθῶν
ἀφθονίας, ὧν ἡ βαθεῖα εἰρήνη δημιουργός, ἀνα-
πλήσας ἠπείρους τε καὶ νήσους, ὁ ἀγεννέστατος,
ὁ δειλίας μεστός, ὁ τῶν μὲν εἰς εὐστάθειαν καὶ
εὐδαιμονίαν ἁπάντων κενώσας τὰς πόλεις, μεστὰς
[559] δὲ τῶν | εἰς ταραχὰς καὶ θορύβους καὶ τὴν
91 ἀνωτάτω βαρυδαιμονίαν ἀναφήνας· ἐπὶ δὲ ταῖς

---

[1] MSS. εὐσθενείας.

---

[a] For an account of the banishment by Gaius of his sisters

fellow-heir you, iron-hearted and utterly ruthless, cruelly slew in the flower of his prime. Your sisters you afterwards sent into exile.[a] Did they too give you cause to fear that they might rob you of your throne ? Did you imitate Dionysus? 88 Have you become an inventor of new bounties as he was ? Did you fill the inhabited world with joyfulness ? Are the gifts bestowed by you more than Asia and Europe can contain ? Rather the novel 89 arts and sciences, which you as the author of general ruin and destruction discovered, were such that with them you changed what gave pleasure and joy into discomfort and grief and a life which all men everywhere find unworthy of the name. And so insatiable and quenchless were your lusts that you stole all that was good and valuable whether from the east or the west or from all other regions of the world southwards or northwards, and in return you gave and sent them the fruits of your own bitterness and all things mischievous and hurtful that abominable and venomous souls are wont to generate. Was it these which revealed you to us as the new Dionysus ?

Or did you also emulate Heracles in your unwearied 90 labours, your tireless feats of courage ? Did you fill continents and islands with legality and justice, with fertility and prosperity and a lavish supply of the other boons which peace deep-founded creates ?— you the utterly ignoble, brimful of cowardice, who stripped the cities of all that tends to well-being and happiness and turned them into hotbeds of what makes for confusion and tumults and the height of misery. Is it because of the great harvests of your 91

Agrippina and Livilla to the Pontian islands on the charge of adultery and conspiracy see Suet. *Gaius* 24 and Dio lix. 22. 8.

PHILO

τοσαύταις φοραῖς, ἃς ἤνεγκας ἐπ' ὀλέθρῳ, εἰπέ
μοι, Γάιε, ζητεῖς ἀθανασίας μεταλαχεῖν, ἵνα μὴ
ὀλιγοχρονίους καὶ ἐφημέρους ἀλλὰ ἀθανάτους ἀπ-
εργάσῃ συμφοράς; ἐγὼ δὲ νομίζω τοὐναντίον, εἰ
καί τις ἔδοξας γεγενῆσθαι θεός, πάντως ἄν σε
μεταβαλεῖν ἕνεκα τῶν πονηρῶν ἐπιτηδευμάτων εἰς
θνητὴν φύσιν· εἰ γὰρ ἀθανατίζουσιν ἀρεταί, πάντως
92 φθείρουσι κακίαι. μήτε οὖν ἐν Διοσκούροις γράφου
τοῖς φιλαδελφοτάτοις, ὁ σφαγεὺς καὶ λυμεὼν τῶν
ἀδελφῶν γεγονώς, μήτε Ἡρακλέους ἢ Διονύσου
τιμῆς[1] κοινοπράγει τῶν τὸν βίον ὀνησάντων, ὁ κα-
κωτὴς καὶ διαφθορεὺς ὧν ἔδρασαν ἐκεῖνοι.

93 XIII. Τοσαύτη δέ τις περὶ αὐτὸν ἦν λύττα καὶ
παράφορος καὶ παράκοπος μανία, ὥστε καὶ τοὺς
ἡμιθέους ὑπερβὰς ἐπανῄει καὶ ἐπαπεδύετο τοῖς τῶν
μειζόνων καὶ ἀμφιθαλῶν εἶναι δοκούντων σεβα-
94 σμοῖς Ἑρμοῦ καὶ Ἀπόλλωνος καὶ Ἄρεως. Ἑρμοῦ
τὸ πρῶτον, κηρυκείοις καὶ πεδίλοις καὶ χλαμύσιν
ἐνσκευαζόμενος τάξιν τε ἐν ἀταξίᾳ καὶ τὸ ἀκό-
λουθον ἐν συγχύσει καὶ λογισμὸν ἐν φρενοβλαβείᾳ
95 παρεπιδεικνύμενος· εἶτα, ὁπότε δόξειεν
αὐτῷ, τὰ μὲν ἀπετίθετο, εἰς δὲ Ἀπόλλωνα
μετεμορφοῦτο καὶ μετεσκευάζετο, στεφάνοις μὲν
ἀκτινοειδέσι τὴν κεφαλὴν ἀναδούμενος, τόξον δὲ
τῇ εὐωνύμῳ καὶ βέλη κρατῶν χειρί, χάριτας δὲ τῇ

[1] mss. τιμαῖς.

[a] Heracles, Dionysus and the Dioscuri all had mortal
mothers. See note on ἀμφιθαλής Quod Omn. Prob. 20
(vol. ix. p. 510).
[b] Cf. Pausanias ix. 35. 3 Ἀγγελίων τε καὶ Τεκταῖος οἵ γε
Διονύσου τὸν Ἀπόλλωνα ἐργαζόμενοι τοῖς Δηλίοις τρεῖς ἐποίησαν

46

raising, Gaius, whose fruit is destruction, that you
seek to partake of immortality so that you may produce calamities not short-lived nor ephemeral but
everlasting? I think that on the contrary even if it
appeared that you were one of the gods your evil
practices would have caused you to change into the
mortal kind of existence, for if virtues give immortality, vices certainly bring destruction. So then 92
you must not rank with the Dioscuri, those best of
brothers, you who dealt murder and perdition to
your brother, nor share the honour of Heracles or
Dionysus who benefited the life of man, you who
wrought havoc and corruption in what they had
achieved.

XIII. So great a frenzy possessed him, so wild and 93
delirious an insanity that leaving the demigods below
he proceeded to advance upwards and armed himself
to attack the honours paid by their worshippers to the
deities held to be greater and divine on both sides,[a]
Hermes, Apollo and Ares. To take Hermes first, 94
he arrayed himself with herald's staffs, sandals
and mantles, a grotesque exhibition of order in
disorder, consistency in confusion, reason in derange-
ment. Then when it pleased him he 95
would strip them off and change his figure and dress
into Apollo's, his head encircled with garlands of
the sun-rays, wielding a bow and arrows in his left
hand and holding out Graces[b] in his right to signify

ἐπὶ τῇ χειρὶ αὐτοῦ Χάριτας. Pausanias says nothing of the
right hand and Plutarch, De Musica 16, says that the Graces
were carried in the left hand, and the bow in the right. But
coins believed to be copied from the Delian Apollo at Athens,
which itself was a copy of the statue at Delos mentioned by
Pausanias, bear out Philo's statement. See Frazer on Pausanias l.c.

PHILO

δεξιᾷ προτείνων, ὡς δέον τὰ μὲν ἀγαθὰ ὀρέγειν ἐξ
ἑτοίμου καὶ τετάχθαι τὴν βελτίονα τάξιν τὴν ἐπὶ
δεξιά, τὰς δὲ κολάσεις ὑποστέλλειν καὶ τὴν κατα-
δεεστέραν χώραν κεκληρῶσθαι τὴν ἐπ᾽ εὐώνυμα.
96 χοροί τε εὐθὺς εἱστήκεσαν συγκεκροτημένοι, παιᾶ-
νας εἰς αὐτὸν ᾄδοντες, οἱ πρὸ μικροῦ Βάκχον καὶ
Εὔιον καὶ Λυαῖον ὀνομάζοντες καὶ ὕμνοις γεραί-
ροντες, ἡνίκα τὴν Διονυσιακὴν ἀνελάμβανε σκευήν.
97   πολλάκις δὲ καὶ θώρακα ἐνδυόμενος
ξιφήρης προῄει μετὰ κράνους καὶ ἀσπίδος, Ἄρης
ἀνακαλούμενος· καὶ παρ᾽ ἑκάτερα οἱ Ἄρεως τοῦ
καινοῦ [καὶ νέου] θεραπευταὶ συμπροῄεσαν, ἀνδρο-
φόνων καὶ δημοκοίνων θίασος, ὑπηρετήσοντες κα-
κὰς ὑπηρεσίας φονῶντι καὶ διψῶντι ἀνθρωπείου
98 αἵματος.   εἶτα τοῖς ταῦτα ὁρῶσι κατά-
πληξις ἦν ἐπὶ τῷ παραλόγῳ, καὶ ἐθαύμαζον, πῶς
ὁ τἀναντία δρῶν οἷς ἰσότιμος εἶναι προαιρεῖται τὰς
μὲν ἀρετὰς αὐτῶν ἐπιτηδεύειν οὐκ ἀξιοῖ, τοῖς δὲ
παρασήμοις εἰς ἕκαστον σκευάζεται. καίτοι τὰ
περίαπτα ταῦτα καὶ προκοσμήματα ξοάνοις καὶ
ἀγάλμασι προσκαθίδρυται, διὰ συμβόλων μηνύοντα
[560] τὰς ὠφελείας, | ἃς παρέχονται τῷ γένει τῶν ἀν-
99 θρώπων οἱ τιμώμενοι.   πέδιλα Ἑρμῆς ὑποδεῖται
πτερῶν ταρσοὺς ἔχοντα· διὰ τί; ἆρα οὐχ ὅτι
προσήκει τὸν ἑρμηνέα καὶ προφήτην τῶν θείων,
ἀφ᾽ οὗ καὶ Ἑρμῆς ὠνόμασται, τὰ ἀγαθὰ διαγγέλ-
λοντα—κακοῦ γὰρ οὐχ ὅτι θεὸς ἀλλ᾽ οὐδὲ σοφὸς
ἀνὴρ γίνεται μηνυτής—ποδωκέστατόν τε εἶναι καὶ
μόνον οὐ πτηνὸν φέρεσθαι διὰ σπουδὴν ἀνυπέρ-
θετον; ἐπειδὴ τὰ λυσιτελῆ φθάνοντας εὐαγγελίζε-
σθαι προσήκει, καθάπερ τὰ παλίμφημα μέλλοντας,

48

that it was fitting for him to extend good things readily and that these should hold the superior position on the right, while punishment should be kept in the background and allotted the inferior place on the left. And at once at his side singing paeans to 96 him stood drilled choirs of those who but now were calling him Bacchus or Evius or Lyaeus and honouring him with hymns when he was assuming the garb of Dionysus. Often too he would don a 97 breastplate and proceed sword in hand, with helmet and shield, hailed as Ares, and on either side went a procession of the worshippers of the new Ares composed of homicides and official cut-throats to render their base service to a master avid for slaughter and thirsting for human blood. Then those 98 who saw these things were struck with amazement at the strange contradiction, marvelling how one, whose actions were the opposite of those whose honours he purposed to share as their equal, did not think fit to practise their virtues and yet at the same time invested himself with their insignia each in turn. Yet surely these trappings and ornaments are set as accessories on images and statues as symbolically indicating the benefits which those thus honoured provide for the human race. Hermes is shod with sandals like out- 99 stretched wings, why ? Is it not because it befits the interpreter (ἑρμηνεύς) and spokesman of things divine, whence also he gets his name of Hermes, that when he is the harbinger of good, since not even a wise man, much less a god, makes himself the announcer of evil, he should be very swift-footed, travelling with well-nigh the speed of wings in the zeal which brooks no delay. The news of things profitable should be carried quickly, bad news slowly if it is not permitted to

PHILO

100 εἰ μὴ ἐπιτρέποι τις αὐτὰ ἡσυχάζεσθαι. πάλιν
κηρύκειον ἀναλαμβάνει δεῖγμα συμβατηρίων σπον-
δῶν· πόλεμοι γὰρ ἀνοχὰς καὶ διαλύσεις λαμβάνουσι
διὰ κηρύκων εἰρήνην καθισταμένων· οἱ δὲ ἀκήρυ-
κτοι συμφορὰς ἀτελευτήτους ἀπεργάζονται καὶ
101 τοῖς ἐπιφέρουσι καὶ τοῖς ἀμυνομένοις. Γάιος δὲ
πρὸς τίνα χρείαν πέδιλα ἀνελάμβανεν; ἢ ἵνα τὰ δύσ-
φημα καὶ δυσώνυμα, δέον ἡσυχάζεσθαι, βοηδρομῆ-
ται τάχει συντόνῳ πάντῃ συνηχοῦντα; καίτοι τί
κινήσεως ἐπεσπευσμένης ἔδει; μένων γὰρ κακὰ
ἐπὶ κακοῖς ἀμύθητα ὥσπερ ἐξ ἀενάων πηγῶν εἰς
102 ἅπαντα τὰ μέρη τῆς οἰκουμένης ὤμβρει. τί δὲ δεῖ
κηρυκείου τῷ μηδὲν εἰρηναῖόν ποτε μήτε εἰπόντι
μήτε δράσαντι, πᾶσαν δὲ οἰκίαν καὶ πόλιν ἐμφυλίων
ἀναπλήσαντι πολέμων κατά τε τὴν Ἑλλάδα καὶ
βάρβαρον; ἀποθέσθω δὴ τὸν Ἑρμῆν ἀφοσιωσά-
μενος τὴν ἀνοίκειον κλῆσιν, ὁ ψευδώνυμος.
103 XIV. τί δὲ τῶν Ἀπολλωνιακῶν ἐμφερές ἐστι παρ'
αὐτῷ; στέφανον ἀκτινωτὸν φορεῖ, εὖ πως ἀπο-
μαξαμένου τὰς ἡλιακὰς ἀκτῖνας τοῦ τεχνίτου.
ἐκείνῳ δὲ ἥλιος ἢ φῶς συνόλως ἀσπαστόν ἐστιν,
ἀλλ' οὐχὶ νὺξ ⟨καὶ σκότος⟩ καὶ εἴ τι σκότους ἀφεγ-
γέστερον εἰς τὴν τῶν ἐκνόμων ἔργων διάθεσιν;
ἐπειδὴ τὰ μὲν καλὰ περιαυγείας μεσημβρινῆς δεῖ-
ται πρὸς ἐπίδειξιν, τὰ δὲ αἰσχρά φασιν ἐσχατιᾶς
Ταρτάρου, εἰς ὃν ἄξιον συνωθεῖσθαι δεόντως ἐπι-
104 κρυφθησόμενα. μεταθέτω καὶ τὰ ἐν ἑκατέρᾳ χειρὶ

---

a He is alluding to the way in which ἀκήρυκτος comes to be
applied to any truceless or exceptionally bitter conflict,
with no thought whether heralds can enter it or not. *Cf.*

50

leave it untold. Again Hermes assumes the herald's 100
staff as an emblem of covenants of reconciliation, for
wars come to be suspended or ended through heralds
establishing peace; wars where no heralds are admitted *a* create endless calamities both for the as-
sailants and the defenders. But for what useful 101
purpose did Gaius assume the sandals? Was it
that everything of ill report and evil name, instead
of being buried in silence, as it should be, might be
noised abroad with impetuous speed and resound on
every side? And yet what need was there for this
activity in locomotion? Standing where he was, he
rained miseries untold one after the other as from
perennial fountains on every part of the inhabited
world. And what need of the herald-staff had he 102
whose every word and deed was not for peace but
filled every house and city throughout Greece and the
outside world with intestine wars! No, let him shed
Hermes, let him purge himself of his lying claim to a
title so ill-fitting, the impostor!   XIV. As 103
for the appurtenances of Apollo, what is there like
them in Gaius? Apollo wears a crown adorned with
rays, for the craftsman has managed to make a good
copy of the rays of the sun, but was the sun or light
in any form welcome to Gaius and not rather night
and darkness or anything more rayless than darkness
for disposing his lawless actions, since things noble
and beautiful need the full brightness of noonday to
show them forth, but the base and ugly need as they
say deepest Tartarus into which they should be
thrown to lie in the concealment which they deserve?
Let him also transpose what he holds in either hand 104

§ 119. The play upon words involved cannot be reproduced
in English.

καὶ μὴ κιβδηλευέτω τὴν τάξιν. τὰ μὲν βέλη καὶ
τόξα τῇ δεξιᾷ προφερέτω· βάλλειν γὰρ καὶ τοξεύειν
εὐσκόπως οἶδεν ἄνδρας, γυναῖκας, συγγενείας ὅλας,
105 εὐανδρούσας πόλεις, ἐπ' ὀλέθρῳ παντελεῖ. τὰς δὲ
χάριτας ἢ ῥιψάτω θᾶττον ἢ τῇ εὐωνύμῳ συσκια-
ζέτω· τὸ γὰρ κάλλος ᾔσχυνεν αὐτῶν, προσοφθαλ-
μιῶν καὶ προσκεχηνὼς ταῖς μεγάλαις οὐσίαις εἰς
ἁρπαγὰς ἀδίκους, αἷς ἐπικατεσφάττοντο οἱ δεσπόται τῆς εὐτυχίας ἕνεκα κακοδαιμονοῦντες.
106 ἀλλὰ καὶ τὴν ἰατρικὴν Ἀπόλλωνος εὖ πως μετε-
χάραξεν. ὁ μὲν γὰρ σωτηρίων φαρμάκων εὑρετὴς
ἐγένετο πρὸς ὑγείαν ἀνθρώπων, ἀξιῶν καὶ τὰς
ὑφ' ἑτέρων ἐγγινομένας νόσους αὐτὸς ἰᾶσθαι διὰ
τὴν ἐκ φύσεως καὶ ἐπιτηδεύσεως ὑπερβάλλουσαν |
[561] ἡμερότητα. ὁ δὲ ἔμπαλιν νόσους μὲν τοῖς ὑγιαί-
107 νουσι, πηρώσεις δὲ τοῖς ὁλοκλήροις, καὶ συνόλως
θανάτους τοῖς ζῶσι χειροποιήτους πρὸ τοῦ μοιριδίου
χαλεποὺς ἐπέφερε, πάντα τὰ φθοροποιὰ χορηγίαις
ἀφθόνοις παρεσκευασμένος, οἷς, εἰ μὴ ἔφθασε
προαναιρεθεὶς ὑπὸ τῆς δίκης [χρήσασθαι], κἂν τὸ
108 ἐν ἑκάστῃ πόλει δοκιμώτατον ἤδη διέφθαρτο.
πρὸς τοὺς γὰρ ἐν τέλει καὶ πλουσίους εὐτρεπεῖς
ἦσαν αἱ παρασκευαί, καὶ μάλιστα τοὺς ἐν Ῥώμῃ
καὶ τῇ ἄλλῃ Ἰταλίᾳ, παρ' οἷς ἄργυρος καὶ χρυσὸς
τεθησαύρισται τοσοῦτος, ὥστε, εἰ σύμπας ὁ ἐξ
ἁπάσης τῆς ἄλλης οἰκουμένης ἀπὸ περάτων αὐτῶν
συνενεχθείη, πολλῷ καταδεέστερος ἂν εὑρεθῆναι.
διὰ τοῦτο ἀπὸ τῆς πατρίδος ὥσπερ ἀφ' ἱερᾶς

ᵃ Lit. " he began from the sacred line." See § 22, pp. 12-15.

52

and not falsify the arrangement; let him carry the bow and arrows in his right hand, for he knows how to use them both with a true aim against men and women, against whole families, against populous cities to bring them to utter perdition. But the 105 Graces he should either cast quickly away or carry them shaded in his left hand. For he put their beauty to shame when he fixed his greedy eyes and gaping mouth on great estates to work the unjust robberies which were crowned with the slaughter of their owners, whose prosperity was the cause of their miserable end. He also managed to make 106 a fine recasting of Apollo's art of medicine. For Apollo became the inventor of salutary remedies promoting the health of mankind, deigning also to heal himself the maladies engendered by the actions of others in virtue of the supreme kindliness which nature and practice gave him. Gaius on the other 107 hand brought disease to the healthy, crippling to the sound of limb and in general death to the living, death in cruel forms, the work of men anticipating that of fate. Every instrument of destruction he had provided with unstinted liberality whereby, had not his death at the hands of justice forestalled his use of them, all the most highly reputed part of the community in every city would already have perished. For he had all his arrangements ready to deal with 108 the magnates and the rich, particularly those in Rome and the rest of Italy, in whose possession there lay treasured such a great amount of gold and silver that if all contained in all the rest of the inhabited world from its very boundaries was gathered together it would be found to fall far short of it. And there-fore[a] with utter recklessness, he proceeded to cast

53

ἤρχετο τὰ σπέρματα τῆς εἰρήνης ἀπορρίπτειν,[1] ὁ
μισόπολις, ὁ δημοβόρος, ἡ λύμη, τὸ φθοροποιὸν
109 κακόν.   λέγεται μὴ μόνον ἰατρὸς ἀλλὰ
καὶ μάντις ἀγαθὸς Ἀπόλλων εἶναι, χρησμοῖς προ-
λέγων τὰ μέλλοντα πρὸς ὠφέλειαν ἀνθρώπων, ἵνα
μή τις ἐπισκιασθεὶς αὐτῶν[2] περὶ τὸ ἄδηλον ἀπροοράτως καθάπερ τυφλὸς τοῖς ἀβουλήτοις ὡς λυσι-
τελεστάτοις ἐπιτρέχων ἐπεμπίπτῃ, προμαθὼν δὲ
τὸ μέλλον ὡς ἤδη παρὸν καὶ βλέπων αὐτὸ τῇ
διανοίᾳ οὐχ ἧττον ἢ τὰ ἐν χερσὶν ὀφθαλμοῖς σώματος φυλάττηται, προνοούμενος τοῦ μηδὲν ἀνή-
110 κεστον παθεῖν.   ἆρα ἄξιον τούτοις ἀντιθεῖναι τὰ
παλίμφημα Γαΐου λόγια, δι' ὧν πενίαι καὶ ἀτιμίαι
καὶ φυγαὶ καὶ θάνατοι προεμηνύοντο τοῖς πανταχοῦ
τῶν ἐν τέλει καὶ δυνατῶν; τίς οὖν κοινωνία πρὸς
Ἀπόλλωνα τῷ μηδὲν οἰκεῖον ἢ συγγενὲς ἐπιτε-
τηδευκότι; πεπαύσθω καὶ ὁ ψευδώνυμος Παιὰν
τὸν ἀληθῆ Παιᾶνα μιμούμενος· οὐ γὰρ ὥσπερ
τὸ νόμισμα παράκομμα καὶ θεοῦ μορφὴ γίνεται.
111   XV. πάντα γε μὴν ἐλπίσειεν ἄν τις
⟨μᾶλλον⟩ ἢ τοιοῦτον σῶμα καὶ ψυχήν, ἄμφω
μαλακὰ καὶ κατεαγότα, τῇ περὶ ἑκάτερον Ἄρεως
ἀλκῇ δυνηθῆναί ποτε ἐξομοιωθῆναι· ὁ δὲ ὥσπερ
ἐπὶ σκηνῆς ἐναλλάττων πολυειδῆ προσωπεῖα φαντα-
112 σίαις ψευδέσιν ἠπάτα τοὺς ὁρῶντας. φέρε δ' οὖν,
μηδὲν τῶν περὶ σῶμα καὶ ψυχὴν ἐξεταζέσθω[3] διὰ
τὴν ἐν πάσαις σχέσεσι καὶ κινήσεσιν ἀλλοτριότητα

---

[1] ? ἀπορρίπτων.
[2] mss. τῶν. Perhaps, as Mangey and others, to be ex-
punged.   [3] mss. ἐξετάζεσθαι.

---

[a] ἐπεμπίπτειν may mean to fall upon (and seize). But
that they " come a cropper " is suggested by the conclusion
54

away the seeds of peace from his homeland, city-hater, people-devourer, scourge and baleful pest.

Apollo is said to be not only a physician 109 but a good prophet, foretelling by his oracles the future for the benefit of men, lest any of them too beclouded to discern its uncertainties should, with no more foresight than the blind, expect high profit from what prove to be things he little welcomes when he races to them only to stumble and fall upon them,[a] but with foreknowledge of the future as though it were now present and seeing it with his mind as clearly as he sees what lies before him with the eyes of his body, protect and secure himself against any fatal disaster. Can we rightly 110 place beside these those ominous pronouncements of Gaius by which the coming poverty, disfranchisement, exile, death were announced to the highly-placed and powerful everywhere? What fellowship then with Apollo has he whose conduct never showed any affinity or kinship? Falsely does he call himself Paean, let him cease once for all to mimic the true Paean, for a divine form cannot be counterfeited as a coin can be. XV. And 111 surely the last thing one would expect is that such a body and soul as his, both of them feeble and nerveless, could ever be assimilated to the prowess of Ares in both. Yet like an actor wearing in turn many kinds of masks he beguiled the spectators with the deceptive appearances he assumed. Well, one need 112 not examine his characteristics of body and soul, since his every posture and movement showed the

of the very similar passage *Spec. Leg.* iii. 79 ἀπερισκέπτως καὶ ἀπροοράτως σώμασιν ὁμοῦ καὶ πράγμασιν ἐπεμπίπτοντες τυφλῶν τρόπον . . . οὐκ ἐλάττω ὧν διατιθέασι πάσχουσι.

πρὸς τὸν εἰρημένον δαίμονα· τὴν Ἄρεως οὖν, οὐχὶ
τοῦ μεμυθευμένου, τοῦ δὲ ἐν τῇ φύσει λόγου, ὃν
ἀνδρεία κεκλήρωται, δύναμιν οὐκ ἴσμεν ἀλεξίκακον
οὖσαν καὶ βοηθὸν καὶ παραστάτιν ἀδικουμένων, ὡς
113 καὶ αὐτό που δηλοῖ τοὔνομα; παρὰ γὰρ τὸ ἀρή-
γειν, ὅπερ βοηθεῖν ἐστι, κατὰ γλῶτταν Ἄρης
ὠνομάσθαι μοι δοκεῖ, καθαιρετικὸς πολέμων, δημι-
ουργὸς εἰρήνης, ἧς ἐχθρὸς μὲν ἦν ἕτερος, ἑταῖρος[1]
δὲ πολέμων, τὴν εὐστάθειαν εἰς ταραχὰς καὶ
[562] στάσεις μεταρμοζόμενος.
114   XVI. | Ἆρά γε ἤδη μεμαθήκαμεν ἐκ τούτων,
ὅτι οὐδενὶ θεῶν ἀλλ' οὐδὲ ἡμιθέων ἐξομοιοῦσθαι
δεῖ Γάιον, μήτε φύσεως μήτε οὐσίας ἀλλὰ μηδὲ
προαιρέσεως τετυχηκότα τῆς αὐτῆς; τυφλὸν δέ,
ὡς ἔοικεν, ἡ ἐπιθυμία, καὶ μάλισθ' ὅταν προσλάβῃ
κενοδοξίαν ὁμοῦ καὶ φιλονεικίαν μετὰ τῆς μεγίστης
ἐξουσίας, ὑφ' ἧς ἡμεῖς οἱ πρότερον εὐτυχεῖς[2] ἐπορ-
115 θούμεθα. μόνους γὰρ Ἰουδαίους ὑπεβλέπετο, ὡς
δὴ μόνους τἀναντία προῃρημένους καὶ δεδιδαγ-
μένους ἐξ αὐτῶν τρόπον τινὰ σπαργάνων ὑπὸ
γονέων καὶ παιδαγωγῶν καὶ ὑφηγητῶν καὶ πολὺ
πρότερον τῶν ἱερῶν νόμων καὶ ἔτι τῶν ἀγράφων
ἐθῶν ἕνα νομίζειν τὸν πατέρα καὶ ποιητὴν τοῦ
116 κόσμου θεόν. οἱ μὲν γὰρ ἄλλοι πάντες, ἄνδρες,
γυναῖκες, πόλεις, ἔθνη, χῶραι, κλίματα γῆς, ὀλίγου

---

[1] Some mss. omit ἕτερος, others ἑταῖρος.
[2] mss. ἀτυχεῖς.

---

[a] i.e. the Ares which belongs to the order of things which
is governed not by μῦθος but by λόγος, and is the deity whose
special province among the virtues is ἀνδρεία. How Mangey

difference which divided him from the deity in question. Surely we know the power of Ares, not the Ares of mythology, but the Ares of the realm of reason whom courage has taken for its own.[a] That power is a defence from evil, the helper and champion of the wronged as its very name declares. For under the name of Ares I think is disguised ἀρήγω, that is " help." That Ares is the destroyer of wars, the creator of peace. This other[b] was the foe of peace, the friend of wars, the converter of stability into turmoil and faction. 113

XVI. Need we more than these proofs to teach us that Gaius has no right to be likened to any of the gods or demigods either, for his nature, his substance, his purpose in life, is different from theirs ? But passion we see to be a blind thing, particularly when it is reinforced by vanity and ambition, combined with possession of the supreme dominion which made havoc of our former prosperity. For he looked with disfavour on the Jews alone because they alone opposed him on principle, trained as they were we may say even from the cradle, by parents and tutors and instructors and by the far higher authority[c] of the sacred laws and also the unwritten customs, to acknowledge one God who is the Father and Maker of the world. For all others, men, women, cities, nations, countries, regions of the earth, I might almost say 114 115 116

---

understood the words is not clear from his translation " (Martis) eius per quem naturalem fortitudinem intellegimus."

[b] The imperfect shows that the " other " is Gaius rather than the Ares of mythology, though Philo may perhaps mean to equate the two in their vices.

[c] So rather than " long before." For probable examples of this meaning of the phrase see note on *Flaccus* 10.

δέω φάναι πᾶσα ἡ οἰκουμένη, καίτοι στένοντες
ἐπὶ τοῖς γινομένοις, οὐδὲν ἧττον ἐκολάκευον αὐτὸν
ἀποσεμνύνοντες πλέον τοῦ μετρίου καὶ τὸν τῦφον
συναύξοντες. ἔνιοι δὲ καὶ τὸ βαρβαρικὸν ἔθος εἰς
Ἰταλίαν ἤγαγον, τὴν προσκύνησιν, τὸ εὐγενὲς τῆς

117 Ῥωμαϊκῆς ἐλευθερίας παραχαράττοντες. ἐν δὲ
μόνον ἔθνος ἐξαίρετον τῶν Ἰουδαίων ὕποπτον ἦν
ἀντιπράξειν, εἰωθὸς ἑκουσίους ἀναδέχεσθαι θανάτους ὥσπερ ἀθανασίαν, ὑπὲρ τοῦ μηδὲν τῶν πατρίων περιιδεῖν ἀναιρούμενον, εἰ καὶ βραχύτατον
εἴη, διὰ τὸ καθάπερ ἐπὶ τῶν οἰκοδομημάτων
ὑφαιρέσει ἑνὸς καὶ τὰ ἔτι παγίως ἑστάναι δοκοῦντα
συμπίπτειν πρὸς τὸ κενωθὲν χαλώμενα καὶ καταρ-

118 ρέοντα. μικρὸν δὲ οὐκ ἦν τὸ κινούμενον, ἀλλὰ τὸ
μέγιστον τῶν ὄντων, ἀνθρώπου γενητὴν καὶ φθαρ-
τὴν φύσιν εἰς ἀγένητον καὶ ἄφθαρτον ὅσα τῷ
δοκεῖν θεοπλαστῆσαι, ὅπερ ἀσεβημάτων ἔκρινεν
εἶναι χαλεπώτατον—θᾶττον γὰρ ἂν εἰς ἄνθρωπον
θεὸν ἢ εἰς θεὸν ἄνθρωπον μεταβαλεῖν—, δίχα τοῦ
καὶ τὰς ἄλλας τὰς ἀνωτάτω κακίας ἀναδέξασθαι,
ἀπιστίαν ὁμοῦ καὶ ἀχαριστίαν πρὸς τὸν τοῦ κόσμου
παντὸς εὐεργέτην, ὃς τῇ αὑτοῦ δυνάμει τοῖς μέρεσι
πᾶσι τοῦ παντὸς ἀφθόνους περιουσίας ἀγαθῶν ἐκ-
δίδωσιν.

119 XVII. Μέγιστος οὖν καὶ ἀκήρυκτος πόλεμος ἐπὶ
τῷ ἔθνει συνεκροτεῖτο. τί γὰρ ἂν εἴη δούλῳ
βαρύτερον κακὸν ἢ δεσπότης ἐχθρός; δοῦλοι δὲ
αὐτοκράτορος οἱ ὑπήκοοι, καὶ εἰ μηδενὸς ἑτέρου

ᵃ *Cf.* Ar. *Rhet.* i. 5. 9 τὰ βαρβαρικά, οἷον προσκυνήσεις,
where Jebb translates " salaams." See Sandys's note, which
is to the effect that properly speaking προσκ. signifies kissing
the hand to another rather than prostration or salaam, though

the whole inhabited world, groaning though they were at what was happening, flattered him all the same and magnified him out of all proportion and augmented his vanity. Some too even introduced into Italy the barbarian practice of prostrating themselves,[a] a degradation of the high tradition of Roman freedom. One nation only standing apart, 117 the nation of the Jews, was suspected of intending opposition, since it was accustomed to accept death as willingly as if it were immortality, to save them from submitting to the destruction of any of their ancestral traditions, even the smallest, because as with buildings if a single piece is taken from the base, the parts that up to then seemed firm are loosened and slip away and collapse into the void thus made. But that displacement was of nothing 118 petty, but of the greatest of all that exists, when the created and corruptible nature of man was made to appear uncreated and incorruptible by a deification which our nation judged to be the most grievous impiety, since sooner could God change into a man than a man into God. Apart from that it included the supremely evil vices of infidelity and ingratitude to the Benefactor of the whole world who through His power bestows blessings poured in unstinted abundance on every part of the All.

XVII. So then a vast and truceless war was pre- 119 pared against the nation. For what greater curse can a slave have than a hostile master ? Subjects are slaves of the absolute emperor, and if this is not true

the two probably often went together. They appear to be confused by Eur. *Orestes* 1507 προσκυνῶ σ᾿, ἄναξ, νόμοισι βαρβάροισι προσπίτνων, but distinguished by Plato, *Legg.* x. 887 ε προκυλίσεις ἅμα καὶ προσκυνήσεις.

PHILO

τῶν προτέρων διὰ τὸ σὺν ἐπιεικείᾳ καὶ μετὰ νόμων
ἄρχειν, ἀλλά τοι Γαΐου πᾶσαν ἐκτετμημένου τῆς
ψυχῆς ἡμερότητα καὶ παρανομίαν ἐζηλωκότος—
νόμον γὰρ ἡγούμενος ἑαυτὸν τοὺς τῶν ἑκασταχοῦ
νομοθετῶν ὡς κενὰς ῥήσεις ἔλυεν· ἡμεῖς δὲ οὐ
μόνον ἐν δούλοις ἀλλὰ καὶ δούλων τοῖς ἀτιμοτάτοις
ἐγραφόμεθα τοῦ ἄρχοντος τρέποντος¹ εἰς δεσπότην.

[563]
120 XVIII. | ὅπερ συναισθόμενος ὁ Ἀλεξανδρέων μιγὰς
καὶ πεφορημένος ὄχλος ἐπέθετο ἡμῖν, καιρὸν
ἐπιτηδειότατον παραπεπτωκέναι ὑπολαβών, καὶ τὸ
τυφόμενον ἐκ μακρῶν χρόνων μῖσος ἀνέφηνε πάντα
121 κυκῶν καὶ συνταράττων. ὡς γὰρ ἐκδοθέντας εἰς
ὁμολογουμένας καὶ τὰς ἀνωτάτω συμφορὰς ὑπὸ
τοῦ αὐτοκράτορος ἢ πολέμῳ κατακρατηθέντας²
ἐκμανέσι καὶ θηριωδεστάταις ὀργαῖς κατειργάζοντο,
ταῖς οἰκίαις ἐπιτρέχοντες, τοὺς δεσπότας αὐταῖς
γυναιξὶ καὶ τέκνοις ἐλαύνοντες, ὡς κενὰς οἰκητόρων
122 ἀποφῆναι. ἔπιπλα καὶ κειμήλια οὐκέτι ὡς λῃσταὶ
νύκτα καὶ σκότος ἐπιτηροῦντες διὰ φόβον ἁλώσεως
ἔκλεπτον, ἀλλὰ φανερῶς μεθ' ἡμέραν ἐξεφόρουν
ἐπιδεικνύμενοι τοῖς ἀπαντῶσιν, ὥσπερ οἱ κεκληρο-
νομηκότες ἢ πριάμενοι παρὰ τῶν κυρίων. εἰ δὲ
καὶ πλείους συνέθεντο κοινοπραγῆσαι τῶν ἁρπαγῶν,
τὴν λείαν ἐν ἀγορᾷ μέσῃ διενέμοντο, πολλάκις ἐν
ὄψεσι τῶν δεσποτῶν, κατακερτομοῦντες καὶ ἐπι-
123 χλευάζοντες. δεινὰ μὲν οὖν καθ' ἑαυτὰ καὶ ταῦτα·
πῶς γὰρ οὔ; πένητας ἐκ πλουσίων καὶ ἀπόρους
ἐξ εὐπόρων γεγενῆσθαι μηδὲν ἀδικοῦντας ἐξαίφνης
καὶ ἀνοίκους καὶ ἀνεστίους, ἐξεωσμένους καὶ
πεφυγαδευμένους τῶν ἰδίων οἰκιῶν, ἵνα μεθ' ἡμέραν

¹ τρέπω intransitive in the active is otherwise unknown.
τραπέντος has been suggested.
60

of any of his predecessors since they ruled with moderation and observance of the law, it was indeed true of Gaius who had exscinded all kindness from his soul and zealously practised lawlessness. For considering that he himself was a law, he abrogated those laid down by legislators in the several states, treating them as empty talk. And we were ranked not only as slaves but as the most degraded slaves when the ruler changed into a despotic master. XVIII. The promiscuous and unstable rabble of the 120 Alexandrians perceived this, and thinking that a very suitable opportunity had occurred, attacked us and brought to light the hatred which had long been smouldering, reducing everything to chaos and confusion. For treating us as persons given over by the 121 emperor to suffer the extremity of calamity undisguised or as overpowered in war, they worked our ruin with insane and most brutal rage. They overran our houses, expelling the owners with their wives and children, and left them uninhabited. Then they stole 122 the furniture and cherished valuables and, not needing now like robbers through fear of capture to watch for night and darkness, they carried them out openly in daylight and exhibited them to those whom they met as if they had inherited them or bought them from the owners. And if several agreed together to share the pillaging they divided the spoil in midmarket, often before the eyes of the owners, jeering and reviling them the while. These things are horrible 123 in themselves, how could it be otherwise?—when the rich became poor, the well-to-do destitute, suddenly through no fault of their own rendered hearthless and homeless, outcasts and exiles from their own

---

² MSS. κατακριθέντας or κρατηθέντας.

καὶ νύκτωρ ὕπαιθροι διατελοῦντες ἢ ταῖς ἀφ᾽ ἡλίου
φλογώσεσιν ἢ νυκτεριναῖς περιψύξεσι διαφθαρῶσι.
124 κουφότερα δὲ τῶν μελλόντων λέγεσθαι ταῦτα·
συνελάσαντες γὰρ τοσαύτας μυριάδας ἀνδρῶν ὁμοῦ
καὶ γυναικῶν καὶ τέκνων καθάπερ βοσκήματα καὶ
θρέμματα ἐξ ἁπάσης τῆς πόλεως εἰς μοῖραν ἐλα-
χίστην οἷά τινα σηκόν, ᾠήθησαν ὀλίγαις ἡμέραις
σωροὺς ἀθρόων νεκρῶν ἐφευρήσειν ἢ λιμῷ διαφθα-
ρέντων διὰ σπάνιν τῶν ἀναγκαίων, οὐ προευτρεπισ-
μένων τὰ ἐπιτήδεια κατὰ μαντείαν τῶν ἐξαπιναίων
125 κακοπραγιῶν, ἢ δι᾽ ὠθισμὸν καὶ πνῖγος, μηδεμιᾶς
εὐρυχωρίας προσφερομένης, ἀλλὰ καὶ τοῦ πέριξ
ἀέρος κακωθέντος καὶ ὅσον ἦν ἐν αὐτῷ ζωτικὸν
ταῖς ἀναπνοαῖς, εἰ δὲ δεῖ τὸ ἀληθὲς εἰπεῖν, τοῖς
ἐκπνεόντων ἄσθμασιν ἀποβαλόντος,[1] ὑφ᾽ ὧν φλεγό-
μενος καὶ τρόπον τινὰ καταβολῇ πυρετοῦ πιεσθεὶς
θερμὸν καὶ ἄτοπον πνεῦμα διὰ μυκτήρων καὶ
στόματος εἰσέπεμπε, τὸ λεγόμενον κατὰ τὴν παροι-
126 μίαν πῦρ ἐπιφέρων πυρί. τῶν γὰρ ἐντὸς σπλάγχνων ἡ δύναμις ἐκ φύσεως φλογωδεστάτη καθέστη-
κεν, ἣν ὅταν μὲν αἱ θύραθεν αὖραι μετρίως ψυχραὶ
καταπνεύσωσιν, εὐοδεῖ τὰ τῆς ἀναπνοῆς ὄργανα ταῖς
εὐκρασίαις, ὅταν δὲ μεταβάλωσι πρὸς τὸ θερμότε-
ρον, ἀνάγκη δυσοδεῖν πυρὸς ἐπεισρέοντος πυρί.
127   XIX. μηκέτι οὖν ὑπομένειν τὴν δυσ-
[564] χωρίαν | οἷοί τε ὄντες ἐξεχέοντο εἰς ἐρημίας καὶ αἰ-
γιαλοὺς καὶ μνήματα, γλιχόμενοι σπάσαι καθαροῦ
καὶ ἀβλαβοῦς ἀέρος. εἰ δέ τινες ἢ προκατελήφ-
θησαν ἐν τοῖς ἄλλοις μέρεσι τῆς πόλεως ἢ ἀγνοίᾳ

---

[1] So Mangey, but apparently with no ms. authority. Reiter with mss. (one ὑπερβάλλοντος) prints ὑποβαλόντος. But I
cannot see what meaning it can have here.

houses, to dwell night and day under the open sky, and sent to their death by the burning heat of the sun or the freezing cold of the night. But all this is 124 light compared with what is still to be told. After driving all these many myriads of men, women, and children like herds of cattle out of the whole city into a very small portion as into a pen, they expected in a few days to find heaps of dead massed together, perished either by famine through lack of necessaries, since having had no prophetic inkling of the sudden disasters they had not provided what was needed, or else through overcrowding and stifling heat. For no 125 sufficiency of room was obtainable, and the air was vitiated and lost all its life-giving properties through the respirations or, to give them their true name, the gasps of expiring men. Inflamed by these and heavily labouring under something like an attack of fever it injected hot and noisome breath through the mouth and nostrils, adding fire to fire, to use the proverbial phrase. For our internal parts as 126 constituted by nature work[a] at a very great heat, and when the outside airs which ventilate them are fairly cool, the favourable combination keeps the organs of respiration in good order, but when the atmosphere changes to a higher temperature and one stream of fire is added to another these organs are bound to get out of order. XIX. So 127 the Jews, unable to endure any longer the painful want of space, poured out into deserted spots and beaches and tombs, eager to get a breath of pure and innocuous air. And if any were caught in the other parts of the city before they could escape or

[a] δύναμις in this usage seems to imply function as well as nature.

PHILO

τῶν κατασκηψάντων κακῶν ἀγρόθεν παρεγένοντο,
πολυτρόπων ἀπέλαυον συμφορῶν, ἢ καταλευόμε-
νοι ἢ κεράμῳ τιτρωσκόμενοι ἢ πρίνου κλάδοις
καὶ δρυὸς τὰ καιριώτατα[1] μέρη τοῦ σώματος καὶ
μάλιστα κεφαλὴν ἄχρι θανάτου καταγνύμενοι.

128 περικαθήμενοι δὲ ἐν κύκλῳ τινὲς τῶν
ἀργεῖν καὶ σχολάζειν εἰωθότων τοὺς συνεληλα-
μένους καὶ συνεωσμένους εἰς ἐσχατιᾶς βραχύ τι
μέρος, ὡς ἔφην, καθάπερ τοὺς τειχήρεις γεγονότας
ἐπετήρουν, μή τις ὑπεξέλθῃ λαθών. ἔμελλον δὲ
ἄρα οὐκ ὀλίγοι διὰ σπάνιν τῶν ἀναγκαίων ἀλο-
γήσαντες τῆς ἰδίας ἀσφαλείας ἐξιέναι, δέει τοῦ μὴ
λιμῷ πανοίκιοι παραπολέσθαι. τούτων τὰς διαδύ-
σεις[2] καραδοκοῦντες ἐπετήρουν καὶ τοὺς συλληφ-
θέντας εὐθὺς διέφθειρον αἰκιζόμενοι πάσαις αἰκίαις.

129 ἕτερος δὲ λόχος ἦν ἐφεδρεύων τοῖς τοῦ ποταμοῦ
λιμέσι πρὸς ἁρπαγὴν τῶν καταγομένων Ἰουδαίων
καὶ ὧν κατ᾽ ἐμπορίαν ἐκόμιζον· ἐπεισβαίνοντες γὰρ
ταῖς ναυσὶ τὸν φόρτον ἐν ὄψεσι τῶν κυρίων ἐξεφόρουν καὶ αὐτοὺς ἐξαγκωνίζοντες ἐνεπίμπρασαν,
ὕλῃ χρώμενοι πηδαλίοις, οἴαξι, κοντοῖς καὶ ταῖς
130 ἐπὶ τῶν καταστρωμάτων σανίσι. τοῖς
δὲ ἐν μέσῃ τῇ πόλει κατακαιομένοις οἰκτρότατος
ἦν ὄλεθρος· σπάνει γὰρ ἔστιν ὅτε ξύλων φρύγανα
συνεφόρουν καὶ ταῦτα ἀνάψαντες ἐπερρίπτουν τοῖς
ἀθλίοις· οἱ δὲ ἡμίφλεκτοι καπνῷ τὸ πλέον ἢ πυρὶ
διεφθείροντο, τῆς φρυγανώδους ὕλης πῦρ μὲν
ἀμενηνὸν καὶ καπνῶδες ἐξαπτούσης καὶ αὐτίκα
σβεννυμένης, ἀνθρακοῦσθαι δὲ διὰ κουφότητα μὴ

---

[1] mss. κυριώτατα.
[2] So Mangey.—Reiter with mss. διαλύσεις (one ms. δι-
ελεύσεις).

if they came up from the country in ignorance of the disasters which had fallen upon us they experienced manifold misfortunes, being stoned or wounded by tiles or branches of ilex or oak in the most vital parts of the body and particularly in the head, the fracture of which proved fatal.

Some of the habitual idlers and loungers would 128 make a circle round the Jews who, as I have said, had been driven and thrust together into a small part of the extremity of the city, and sit there watching them as though they were in a besieged fortress lest anyone should escape unseen. It was of course certain that several in lack of necessities would, regardless of their own safety, sally out through fear of their whole household being starved to death. A close watch was kept for these attempts to slip through and when any were caught they were at once dispatched by their enemies with every possible maltreatment. There was another 129 company who lay in waiting at the harbours of the river to rob the Jews who put in there and seize the goods which they were bringing for trade. They boarded the vessels and carried out the cargo before the eyes of the owners, whom they pinioned and burnt, using for fuel rudders, tillers, poles and the planks on the decks. Most pitiable was 130 the fate of those who were burnt to death in the middle of the city. For sometimes through lack of proper wood they collected brushwood and after setting it on fire threw it upon the unhappy victims, who perished half burnt more through the smoke than by the fire. For brushwood produces a feeble and smoky flame which is at once extinguished since its slightness prevents it from burning steadily like

131 δυναμένης. πολλοὺς δὲ ἔτι ζῶντας ἱμάσι καὶ βρόχοις περιβαλόντες καὶ ἐπισφίγξαντες τὰ σφυρὰ διὰ μέσης κατέσυρον ἀγορᾶς ἐναλλόμενοι καὶ μηδὲ νεκρῶν ἀπεχόμενοι τῶν σωμάτων· διαρτῶντες γὰρ αὐτὰ κατὰ μέλη καὶ μέρη καὶ πατοῦντες οἱ καὶ τῶν ἀτιθάσων θηρίων ὠμότεροι καὶ ἀγριώτεροι πᾶσαν ἰδέαν ἐξανήλισκον, ὡς μηδὲ λείψανον γοῦν ὃ δυνήσεται ταφῆς ἐπιλαχεῖν ὑπολιπέσθαι.

132 XX. Τοῦ δὲ ἐπιτρόπου τῆς χώρας, ὃς μόνος ἐδύνατο βουληθεὶς ὥρᾳ μιᾷ τὴν ὀχλοκρατίαν καθελεῖν, προσποιουμένου ἅ τε ἑώρα μὴ ὁρᾶν καὶ ὧν ἤκουε μὴ ἐπακούειν, ἀλλ' ἀνέδην ἐφιέντος πολεμοποιεῖν καὶ τὴν εἰρήνην συγχέοντος, ἔτι μᾶλλον ἐξοτρυνόμενοι πρὸς ἀναισχύντους καὶ θρα-
[565] συτέρας ὥρμησαν | ἐπιβουλὰς καὶ συνταξάμενοι στίφη πολυανθρωπότατα τὰς προσευχάς[1]—πολλαὶ δέ εἰσι καθ' ἕκαστον τμῆμα τῆς πόλεως—τὰς μὲν ἐδενδροτόμησαν τὰς δὲ αὐτοῖς θεμελίοις κατέσκαψαν, εἰς ἃς δὲ καὶ πῦρ ἐμβαλόντες ἐνέπρησαν, ὑπὸ λύττης καὶ μανίας ἔκφρονος ἀλογήσαντες καὶ τῶν πλησίον οἰκιῶν· πυρὸς γάρ, ὁπότε λάβοιτο

133 ὕλης, οὐδὲν ὠκύτερον. καὶ σιωπῶ τὰς συγκαθαιρεθείσας καὶ συμπρησθείσας τῶν αὐτοκρατόρων τιμὰς ἀσπίδων καὶ στεφάνων ἐπιχρύσων καὶ στηλῶν καὶ ἐπιγραφῶν, δι' ἃ καὶ τῶν ἄλλων ὤφειλον ἀνέχειν· ἀλλ' ἐθάρρουν ἅτε τὴν ἐκ Γαΐου τίσιν οὐ δεδιότες, ὃν εὖ ἠπίσταντο μῖσος ἄλεκτον ἔχοντα πρὸς Ἰουδαίους, ὡς ὑπονοεῖν, ὅτι οὐδεὶς οὐδὲν αὐτῷ χαρίζοιτο μεῖζον ἢ πάσας κακῶν ἰδέας

134 ἐπιφέρων τῷ ἔθνει. βουλόμενοι δὲ καινοτέραις

---

[1] MSS. ταῖς προσευχαῖς.

coal. Many too, while still alive, they tied with 131
thongs and nooses and, binding fast their ankles,
dragged them through the middle of the market,
leaping on them and not even sparing their dead
bodies. For, more brutal and savage than fierce wild
beasts, they severed them limb from limb and piece
from piece and trampling on them destroyed every
lineament, so that not even the least remnant was left
which could receive burial.

XX. When the governor of the country, who, if he 132
wished, could have by himself suppressed in a single
hour the tyranny of the mob, pretended not to see
what he saw and not to hear what he heard but
allowed them to wage war unrestrainedly and so
wrecked the peace, they became still more excited
and pressed forward to carry out shameless designs
of a bolder kind. They collected great bodies of
men to attack the meeting-houses, of which there are
many in each section of the city. Some they ravaged,
others they demolished with the foundations as well,
others they set fire to and burnt regardless in their
frenzy and insane fury of the fate of the neighbouring
houses, for nothing runs faster than fire when it gets
hold of something to feed it. I say nothing of the 133
tributes to the emperors which were pulled down or
burnt at the same time, the shields and gilded crowns
and the slabs and inscriptions, consideration for which
should have made them spare the rest. But they
were emboldened by having no fear of the vengeance of Gaius. They knew well that he had an
indescribable hatred of the Jews, and so they sur-
mised that nothing anyone could do would gratify
him more than the infliction on the nation of every
kind of ill-treatment. And as they wished to in- 134

67

PHILO

κολακείαις ὑπελθόντες αὐτὸν ἀνυπευθύνοις χρῆσθαι
κατὰ τὸ παντελὲς ταῖς εἰς ἡμᾶς ἐπηρείαις τί
ποιοῦσι; προσευχὰς ὅσας μὴ ἐδυνήθησαν ἐμπρή-
σεσι καὶ κατασκαφαῖς ἀφανίσαι διὰ τὸ πολλοὺς
καὶ ἀθρόους πλησίον οἰκεῖν Ἰουδαίους ἕτερον τρόπον ἐλυμήναντο μετὰ τῆς τῶν νόμων καὶ ἐθῶν
ἀνατροπῆς· εἰκόνας γὰρ ἐν ἁπάσαις μὲν ἱδρύοντο
Γαΐου, ἐν δὲ τῇ μεγίστῃ καὶ περισημοτάτῃ καὶ
135 ἀνδριάντα χαλκοῦν ἐποχούμενον τεθρίππῳ. καὶ
τοσοῦτον ἦν τὸ τάχος καὶ τὸ σύντονον τῆς σπουδῆς,
ὥστε οὐκ ἔχοντες ἐν ἑτοίμῳ καινὸν τέθριππον
ἐκ τοῦ γυμνασίου παλαιότατον ⟨ἐκόμιζον⟩ ἰοῦ
γέμον, ἠκρωτηριασμένον ὦτα καὶ οὐρὰς καὶ βάσεις
καὶ ἕτερα οὐκ ὀλίγα, ὡς δέ φασί τινες καὶ ὑπὲρ
γυναικὸς ἀνατεθὲν τῆς ἀρχαίας Κλεοπάτρας, ἥτις
136 ἦν προμάμμη τῆς τελευταίας. ἡλίκην μὲν οὖν καθ᾽
αὑτὸ τοῦτο τοῖς ἀναθεῖσιν ἐπέφερε κατηγορίαν,
παντὶ τῳ δῆλον. τί γάρ, εἰ [καὶ] καινὸν γυναι-
κός; τί δέ, εἰ παλαιὸν ἀνδρός; τί δέ, εἰ συνόλως
ἐπιφημισθὲν ἑτέρῳ; τοὺς τοιοῦτον ἀνατιθέντας
ὑπὲρ αὐτοκράτορος οὐκ εἰκὸς ἦν εὐλαβηθῆναι,
μή τις γένηται μήνυσις τῷ πάντα σεμνοποιοῦντι
137 τὰ καθ᾽ αὑτὸν διαφερόντως· οἱ δέ γε ἐκ πολλοῦ
τοῦ περιόντος ἤλπιζον ἐπαινεθήσεσθαι καὶ μειζόνων
καὶ λαμπροτέρων ἀπολαύσειν ἀγαθῶν ἕνεκα τοῦ
καινὰ τεμένη προσαναθεῖναι Γαΐῳ τὰς προσευχάς,

---

a The meaning as I understand it is that while the fact that
the statue was an old one, or that that the figure represented
by it was a female, would each of them separately have dis-
qualified the statue, it is unnecessary to press them as the
mere fact that it had been dedicated to someone else was
enough to show its impropriety.

68

gratiate themselves with him by further novelties in flattering and so secure complete immunity for their maltreatment of us, what do you suppose they did ? The meeting-houses which they could not raze or burn out of existence, because so many Jews live massed together in the neighbourhood, they outraged in another way, thereby overthrowing our laws and customs. For they set up images of Gaius in them all and in the largest and most notable a bronze statue of a man mounted on a chariot and four. And 135 so speedy and impetuous were they in their eagerness, that not having a new chariot of the kind at hand they fetched a very old one out of the gymnasium, a mass of rust with the ears, tails, feet and many other parts mutilated, and as some say dedicated to the honour of a woman, the original Cleopatra, great-grand-mother of the last queen of that name. What a serious charge this in itself 136 entailed upon the dedicators is obvious to everyone. What does it matter if it was the new chariot of a woman ? What if it was an old chariot of a man ?[a] As long as the general fact remains that it had been dedicated to someone else ? Might not the authors of an offering of this kind in honour of the emperor reasonably feel alarm lest some information should be laid before one who always particularly insisted on his personal glorification ? No doubt they had 137 extravagant[b] hopes of getting praise and reaping greater and more splendid benefits for turning our meeting-houses into new and additional precincts consecrated to him, though their motive was not

[b] For the common phrase ἐκ πολλοῦ τοῦ περιόντος see note on De Vit. Cont. 63, where among its uses intensification of an action or creation of a superlative are given. So here.

οὐχ ἕνεκα τιμῆς τῆς εἰς ἐκεῖνον, ἀλλ' ὑπὲρ τοῦ
πάντα τρόπον ἐμφορεῖσθαι τῶν ἐπὶ τῷ ἔθνει κακο-
138 πραγιῶν.   ἐναργεῖς δὲ πίστεις | λαβεῖν
[566] ἔστι· πρῶτον μὲν ἀπὸ τῶν βασιλέων· δέκα που
σχεδὸν ἢ καὶ πλειόνων ἐν τριακοσίοις ἔτεσιν ἑξῆς
γενομένων, ἀνάθεσιν εἰκόνων ἢ ἀνδριάντων ἐν
προσευχαῖς οὐδεμίαν ἐποιήσαντο, καίτοι γε οἰκείων
ὄντων καὶ συγγενῶν, οὓς θεοὺς καὶ ἐνόμιζον καὶ
139 ἔγραφον καὶ ἐκάλουν. τί δὲ οὐκ ἔμελλον ἀνθρώπους
γε ὄντας οἱ κύνας καὶ λύκους καὶ λέοντας καὶ
κροκοδείλους καὶ ἄλλα πλείονα θηρία καὶ ἔνυδρα
καὶ χερσαῖα καὶ πτηνὰ θεοπλαστοῦντες, ὑπὲρ ὧν
βωμοὶ καὶ ἱερὰ καὶ ναοὶ καὶ τεμένη κατὰ πᾶσαν
140 Αἴγυπτον ἵδρυνται;   XXI. τάχα που νῦν
φήσουσι τότε οὐκ ἂν εἰπόντες—τὰς γὰρ τῶν ἀρχόντων εὐπραγίας μᾶλλον ἢ τοὺς ἄρχοντας αὐτοὺς
εἰώθασι θεραπεύειν—, ὅτι μείζους μὲν οἱ αὐτοκρά-
τορες τὰ ἀξιώματα καὶ τὰς τύχας τῶν Πτολεμαίων
εἰσί, μειζόνων δὲ καὶ τιμῶν τυγχάνειν ὀφείλουσιν.
141 εἶτα, ὦ πάντων ἀνθρώπων, ἵνα μηδὲν ἀναγκασθῶ
βλάσφημον εἰπεῖν, εὐηθέστατοι, διὰ τί τὸν πρὸ
Γαΐου Τιβέριον, ὃς κἀκείνῳ τῆς ἡγεμονίας αἴτιος
γέγονε, τρία πρὸς τοῖς εἴκοσιν ἔτη γῆς καὶ θαλάσσης ἀναψάμενον τὸ κράτος καὶ μηδὲ σπέρμα
πολέμου μήτε κατὰ τὴν Ἑλλάδα μήτε κατὰ τὴν
βάρβαρον ὑποτυφόμενον ἐάσαντα, τὴν δὲ εἰρήνην
καὶ τὰ τῆς εἰρήνης ἀγαθὰ παρασχόμενον ἄχρι τῆς
τοῦ βίου τελευτῆς ἀφθόνῳ καὶ πλουσίᾳ χειρὶ καὶ
142 γνώμῃ, τῆς ὁμοίας τιμῆς οὐκ ἠξιώσατε; τὸ γένος
ἦν ἐλάττων; ἀλλ' εὐγενέστατος κατ' ἀμφοτέρους
τοὺς γονεῖς. ἀλλὰ τὴν παιδείαν; καὶ τίς ἦν
φρονιμώτερος ἢ λογιώτερος ἐκείνου τῶν κατ' αὐτὸν
70

to honour him but to take their fill in every way of the miseries of our nation. We can 138 find clear proofs of this. Take first the kings of Egypt. In three hundred years there was a succession of some ten or more of these, and none of them had any images or statues set up for them in our meeting-houses by the Alexandrians, although they were of the same race and kin as the people and were acknowledged, written and spoken of by them as gods. It was only natural that they who at any rate 139 were men should be so regarded by those who deified dogs and wolves and lions and crocodiles and many other wild animals on the land, in the water and the air, for whom altars and temples and shrines and sacred precincts have been established through the whole of Egypt. XXI. Perhaps they will 140 now say what they would not have said then, since it is their way to pay more court to the good fortunes of rulers than to the rulers themselves, that the emperors are superior to the Ptolemies in prestige and fortune and deserve to receive superior honours. Tell me, you of all men most foolish, for I do not wish 141 to be forced into abusive language, what of Gaius's predecessor Tiberius from whom he derived his sovereignty, who for twenty-three years was invested with dominion over sea and land and did not let the smallest spark of war smoulder in Greece or the world outside Greece, and to the very end of his life provided peace and the blessings of peace with a rich and unstinting hand and heart? Did you not deem him worthy of like honour? Was he inferior 142 in birth? No, his birth was of the highest on both sides of his parentage. In culture? who was a greater master of thought or of language among

ἀκμασάντων; ἀλλὰ τὴν ἡλικίαν; καὶ ποῖος μᾶλλον ἢ βασιλέων ἢ αὐτοκρατόρων εὐγήρως; οὐ μὴν ἀλλὰ καὶ ἔτι νέος ὢν ὁ πρεσβύτης ἐλέγετο δι' αἰδῶ τὴν περὶ τὴν ἀγχίνοιαν. οὗτος οὖν ὁ τοιοῦτος καὶ τοσοῦτος ὑμῖν παρώφθη καὶ παρεσύρη.

143 Τί δέ; ὁ τὴν ἀνθρωπίνην φύσιν ὑπερβαλὼν ἐν ἁπάσαις ταῖς ἀρεταῖς, ὁ διὰ μέγεθος ἡγεμονίας αὐτοκρατοῦς ὁμοῦ καὶ καλοκαγαθίας πρῶτος ὀνομασθεὶς Σεβαστός, οὐ διαδοχῇ γένους ὥσπερ τι κλήρου μέρος τὴν ἐπωνυμίαν λαβών, ἀλλ' αὐτὸς γενόμενος ἀρχὴ σεβασμοῦ καὶ τοῖς ἔπειτα; ὁ τοῖς μὲν πράγμασι τεταραγμένοις καὶ συγκεχυμένοις ἐπιστάς, ὅτε εὐθὺς παρῆλθεν ἐπὶ τὴν τῶν κοινῶν 144 ἐπιμέλειαν; νῆσοι γὰρ πρὸς ἠπείρους καὶ ἤπειροι πρὸς νήσους περὶ πρωτείων ἀντεφιλονείκουν ἡγεμόνας ἔχουσαι καὶ προαγωνιστὰς Ῥωμαίων τοὺς ἐν τέλει δοκιμωτάτους· καὶ αὖθις τὰ μεγάλα τμήματα τῆς οἰκουμένης, Ἀσία πρὸς Εὐρώπην καὶ Εὐρώπη πρὸς Ἀσίαν, ἡμιλλῶντο περὶ κράτους ἀρχῆς, τῶν Εὐρωπαίων καὶ Ἀσιανῶν ἐθνῶν ἀπὸ ἐσχάτων γῆς ἀναστάντων καὶ βαρεῖς πολέμους |

[567] ἀντεπιφερόντων διὰ πάσης γῆς καὶ θαλάττης πεζομαχίαις ⟨καὶ ναυμαχίαις⟩, ὡς μικροῦ σύμπαν τὸ ἀνθρώπων γένος ἀναλωθὲν ταῖς ἀλληλοκτονίαις εἰς τὸ παντελὲς ἀφανισθῆναι, εἰ μὴ δι' ἕνα ἄνδρα καὶ ἡγεμόνα, τὸν Σεβαστὸν [οἶκον], ὃν ἄξιον καλεῖν 145 ἀλεξίκακον. οὗτός ἐστιν ὁ Καῖσαρ, ὁ τοὺς καταρράξαντας πανταχόθι χειμῶνας εὐδιάσας, ὁ τὰς κοινὰς νόσους Ἑλλήνων καὶ βαρβάρων ἰασάμενος, αἳ κατέβησαν μὲν ἀπὸ τῶν μεσημβρινῶν καὶ

72

those who were in the prime of life in his time ? In
length of days ? and which of the kings or emperors
reached a longer and happier old age, not but what
while still in his youth he was called the old man
out of respect for his shrewdness ? Such and so
great was he who was overlooked and brushed aside
by you.

Again, consider him who in all the virtues trans- 143
cended human nature, who on account of the vastness
of his imperial sovereignty as well as nobility of
character was the first to bear the name of the August
or Venerable, a title received not through lineal
succession as a portion of its heritage but because he
himself became the source of the veneration which
was received also by those who followed him ; who
from the moment that he had charge of the common
weal took in hand the troubled and chaotic condition
of affairs. For islands were engaged with continents 144
in fierce rivalry for primacy, and continents with
islands, all having for their leaders and champions
those of the Romans in great positions who stood
foremost in repute. And again the great regions
which divide the habitable world, Europe and Asia,
were contending with each other for sovereign power
with the nations of both brought up from the uttermost parts of the earth waging grievous war all over
sea and land, battling on either element, so that the
whole human race exhausted by mutual slaughter
was on the verge of utter destruction, had it not
been for one man and leader Augustus whom men
fitly call the averter of evil. This is the Caesar 145
who calmed the torrential storms on every side,
who healed the pestilences common to Greeks and
barbarians, pestilences which descending from the

ἑώων, ἔδραμον δὲ καὶ μέχρι δύσεως καὶ πρὸς
ἄρκτον, τὰ μεθόρια χωρία καὶ πελάγη κατασπεί-
ρασαι τῶν ἀβουλήτων· οὗτός ἐστιν ὁ τὰ δεσμά, οἷς
κατέζευκτο καὶ ἐπεπίεστο ἡ οἰκουμένη, παραλύσας,
146 οὐ μόνον ἀνείς· οὗτος ὁ καὶ τοὺς φανεροὺς καὶ
ἀφανεῖς πολέμους διὰ τὰς ἐκ λῃστῶν ἐπιθέσεις
ἀνελών· οὗτος ὁ τὴν θάλατταν πειρατικῶν μὲν
σκαφῶν κενὴν ἐργασάμενος, φορτίδων δὲ πληρώ-
147 σας. οὗτος ὁ τὰς πόλεις ἁπάσας εἰς ἐλευθερίαν
ἐξελόμενος, ὁ τὴν ἀταξίαν εἰς τάξιν ἀγαγών, ὁ τὰ
ἄμικτα ἔθνη καὶ θηριώδη πάντα ἡμερώσας καὶ
ἁρμοσάμενος, ὁ τὴν μὲν Ἑλλάδα Ἑλλάσι πολλαῖς
παραυξήσας, τὴν δὲ βάρβαρον ἐν τοῖς ἀναγκαιο-
τάτοις τμήμασιν ἀφελληνίσας, ὁ εἰρηνοφύλαξ, ὁ
διανομεὺς τῶν ἐπιβαλλόντων ἑκάστοις, ὁ τὰς
χάριτας ἀταμιεύτους εἰς μέσον προθείς, ὁ μηδὲν
ἀποκρυψάμενος ἀγαθὸν ἢ καλὸν ἐν ἅπαντι τῷ
148 ἑαυτοῦ βίῳ. XXII. τοῦτον οὖν τὸν τοσοῦτον
εὐεργέτην ἐν τρισὶ καὶ τεσσαράκοντα ἐνιαυτοῖς,
οὓς ἐπεκράτησεν Αἰγύπτου, παρεκαλύψαντο, μηδὲν
ἐν προσευχαῖς ὑπὲρ αὐτοῦ, μὴ ἄγαλμα, μὴ ξόανον,
149 μὴ γραφὴν ἱδρυσάμενοι. καὶ μὴν εἴ τινι καινὰς
καὶ ἐξαιρέτους ἔδει ψηφίζεσθαι τιμάς, ἐκείνῳ
προσῆκον ἦν, οὐ μόνον ὅτι τοῦ Σεβαστοῦ γένους
ἀρχή τις ἐγένετο καὶ πηγή, οὐδὲ ὅτι πρῶτος καὶ μέγιστος καὶ κοινὸς εὐεργέτης, ἀντὶ πολυαρχίας ἑνὶ
κυβερνήτῃ παραδοὺς τὸ κοινὸν σκάφος οἰακονομεῖν
ἑαυτῷ, θαυμασίῳ τὴν ἡγεμονικὴν ἐπιστήμην—τὸ

---

^a On the technical law term ἐξελέσθαι εἰς ἐλευθερίαν see
Dict. of Ant. s.v. ἐξαιρέσεως δίκη " If a reputed slave wished

south and the east coursed to the west and north
sowing the seeds of calamity over the places and
waters which lay between. This is he who not only 146
loosed but broke the chains which had shackled and
pressed so hard on the habitable world. This is he
who exterminated wars both of the open kind and
the covert which are brought about by the raids of
brigands. This is he who cleared the sea of pirate
ships and filled it with merchant vessels. This is 147
he who reclaimed every state to liberty,[a] who led
disorder into order and brought gentle manners and
harmony to all unsociable and brutish nations, who
enlarged Hellas by many a new Hellas and hellenized
the outside world in its most important regions, the
guardian of the peace, who dispensed their dues to
each and all, who did not hoard his favours but gave
them to be common property, who kept nothing good
and excellent hidden throughout his life. XXII. This 148
great benefactor they ignored during the forty-three
years in which he was sovereign of Egypt, and set up
nothing in our meeting-houses in his honour, neither
image, nor bust, nor painting. And yet if it was 149
right to decree new and exceptional honours to anyone, he was the proper person to receive them. He
was what we may call the source and fountain-head
of the Augustan stock in general. He was also the
first and the greatest and the common benefactor in
that he displaced the rule of many and committed
the ship of the commonwealth to be steered by a
single pilot, that is himself, a marvellous master of
the science of government. For there is justice in the

to recover his rights as a freeman he could only do so with
the assistance of one who was himself a freeman and was
said ἐξαιρεῖσθαι αὐτὸν εἰς ἐλευθερίαν."

PHILO

γὰρ "οὐκ ἀγαθὸν πολυκοιρανίη"[a] λέλεκται δεόντως, ἐπειδὴ πολυτρόπων αἴτιαι κακῶν αἱ πολυψηφίαι—, ἀλλ' ὅτι καὶ πᾶσα ἡ οἰκουμένη τὰς
150 ἰσολυμπίους αὐτῷ τιμὰς ἐψηφίσαντο. καὶ μαρτυ-
ροῦσι ναοί, προπύλαια, προτεμενίσματα, στοαί, ὡς
ὅσαι τῶν πόλεων, ἢ νέα ἢ παλαιά, ἔργα φέρουσι
μεγαλοπρεπῆ, τῷ κάλλει καὶ μεγέθει τῶν Και-
σαρείων παρευημερεῖσθαι, καὶ μάλιστα κατὰ τὴν
151 ἡμετέραν Ἀλεξάνδρειαν. οὐδὲν γὰρ τοιοῦτόν ἐστι τέμενος, οἷον τὸ λεγόμενον Σεβαστεῖον,
ἐπιβατηρίου Καίσαρος νεώς, ⟨ὃς⟩ ἀντικρὺ τῶν
εὐορμοτάτων λιμένων μετέωρος ἵδρυται μέγιστος
[568] καὶ ἐπιφανέστατος καὶ | οἷος οὐχ ἑτέρωθι κατά-
πλεως ἀναθημάτων, [ἐν] γραφαῖς καὶ ἀνδριάσι
καὶ ἀργύρῳ καὶ χρυσῷ περιβεβλημένος ἐν κύκλῳ,
τέμενος εὐρύτατον στοαῖς, βιβλιοθήκαις, ἀνδρῶ-
σιν, ἄλσεσι, προπυλαίοις, εὐρυχωρίαις, ὑπαίθροις,
ἅπασι τοῖς εἰς πολυτελέστατον κόσμον ἠσκημένον,
ἐλπὶς καὶ ἀναγομένοις καὶ καταπλέουσι σωτήριος.
152 XXIII. ἔχοντες οὖν τοιαύτας ἀφορμὰς
καὶ τοὺς πανταχοῦ πάντας ὁμογνώμονας οὔτε περὶ
τὰς προσευχὰς ἐνεωτέρισαν καὶ καθ' ἕκαστον ⟨τὸ⟩
νόμιμον ἐφύλαξαν· ἢ τινα σεβασμὸν παρέλιπον τῶν
ὀφειλομένων Καίσαρι; καὶ τίς ἂν εὖ φρονῶν

---

[a] Il. ii. 204. The passage is quoted more fully in De Conf.
170.
[b] The other place where this word is known is Thuc. iii.
10. 5, where the Mitylenaeans say that the members of the

76

saying " It is not well that many lords should rule," [a] since multiplicity of suffrages [b] produces multiform evils. But besides all these the whole habitable world voted him no less than celestial honours. These are so well attested by temples, gateways, 150 vestibules, porticoes, that every city which contains magnificent works new and old is surpassed in these by the beauty and magnitude of those appropriated to Caesar and particularly in our own Alexandria.

For there is elsewhere no precinct like 151 that which is called the Sebasteum, a temple to Caesar on shipboard,[c] situated on an eminence facing the harbours famed for their excellent moorage, huge and conspicuous, fitted on a scale not found elsewhere with dedicated offerings, around it a girdle of pictures and statues in silver and gold, forming a precinct of vast breadth, embellished with porticoes, libraries, chambers, groves, gateways and wide open courts and everything which lavish expenditure could produce to beautify it—the whole a hope of safety to the voyager either going into or out of the harbour.   XXIII. Though they had such 152 grounds for action and could command the approval of all men everywhere they brought no violence to bear upon the meeting-houses and observed the law in every respect. Or did they neglect any mark of the reverence that was due to Caesar ? No one in his senses would say that they did.   Why

confederacy of Delos could not unite to resist the encroach-ments of the Athenians διὰ τὴν πολυψηφίαν. It does not seem very appropriate here.

[c] *i.e.* commemorating the voyage of Augustus which led to the surrender of Alexandria on 1st Aug. 30 B.C. Dr. Cook compares coins found in Alexandria bearing the image of a ship with the inscription σεβαστόφορος.

εἴποι; διὰ.τί οὖν ἐστέρησαν;¹ ἐγὼ φράσω μηδὲν
153 ὑποστειλάμενος. ᾔδεσαν αὐτοῦ τὴν ἐπιμέλειαν καὶ
ὅτι τοσαύτην ποιεῖται τῆς βεβαιώσεως τῶν παρ'
ἑκάστοις πατρίων, ὅσην καὶ τῶν 'Ρωμαϊκῶν, καὶ
ὅτι δέχεται τὰς τιμὰς οὐκ ἐπὶ καθαιρέσει τῶν παρ'
ἐνίοις νομίμων τυφοπλαστῶν ἑαυτόν, ἀλλὰ τῷ
μεγέθει τῆς τοσαύτης ἡγεμονίας ἑπόμενος, ᾗ διὰ
154 τῶν τοιούτων πέφυκε σεμνοποιεῖσθαι. τοῦ δὲ μὴ
ταῖς ὑπερόγκοις τιμαῖς δεθῆναι² καὶ φυσηθῆναί ποτε
πίστις ἐναργεστάτη τὸ μηδέποτε θεὸν ἑαυτὸν
ἐθελῆσαι προσειπεῖν, ἀλλὰ κἂν εἰ λέγοι τις δυσ-
χεραίνειν, καὶ τὸ τοὺς 'Ιουδαίους ἀποδέχεσθαι, οὓς
ἀκριβῶς ᾔδει πάντα ἀφοσιουμένους τὰ τοιαῦτα.
155   πῶς οὖν ἀπεδέχετο; τὴν πέραν τοῦ
Τιβέρεως ποταμοῦ μεγάλην τῆς 'Ρώμης ἀποτομὴν
[ἣν] οὐκ ἠγνόει κατεχομένην καὶ οἰκουμένην πρὸς
'Ιουδαίων.³ 'Ρωμαῖοι δὲ ἦσαν οἱ πλείους ἀπελευ-
θερωθέντες· αἰχμάλωτοι γὰρ ἀχθέντες εἰς 'Ιταλίαν
ὑπὸ τῶν κτησαμένων ἠλευθερώθησαν, οὐδὲν τῶν
156 πατρίων παραχαράξαι βιασθέντες. ἠπίστατο οὖν
καὶ προσευχὰς ἔχοντας καὶ συνιόντας εἰς αὐτάς,
καὶ μάλιστα ταῖς ἱεραῖς ἑβδόμαις, ὅτε δημοσίᾳ τὴν
πάτριον παιδεύονται φιλοσοφίαν. ἠπίστατο καὶ
χρήματα συνάγοντας ἀπὸ τῶν ἀπαρχῶν ἱερὰ καὶ
πέμποντας εἰς 'Ιεροσόλυμα διὰ τῶν τὰς θυσίας

¹ Wendland suggested ⟨τιμῆς⟩ ἐστέρησαν. Something is
perhaps needed, but why not ⟨τοῦδ'⟩?
² δεθῆναι is clearly corrupt. Suggestions are οἰδηθῆναι,
ἐπαρθῆναι, διαρθῆναι (or perhaps the simple ἀρθῆναι).
³ So Mangey. I am surprised that Reiter should have
adopted the мss. text by retaining ἣν, which involves putting
the question mark after 'Ιουδαίων. There is little or no point

then did they withhold this from him? I will
answer that question without any reserve. They 153
knew his carefulness and that he showed it in maintaining firmly the native customs of each particular
nation no less than of the Romans, and that he
received his honours not for destroying the institutions of some nations in vain self-exaltation[a]
but in accordance with the magnitude of so mighty a
sovereignty whose prestige was bound to be enhanced
by such tributes. That he was never elated or puffed 154
up by the vast honours given to him is clearly shown
by the fact that he never wished anyone to address
him as a god but was annoyed if anyone used the
word, and also by his approval of the Jews, who he
knew full well regarded all such things with horror.

How then did he show his approval? 155
He was aware that the great section of Rome on the
other side of the Tiber is occupied and inhabited by
Jews, most of whom were Roman citizens emanci-
pated. For having been brought as captives to Italy
they were liberated by their owners and were not
forced to violate any of their native institutions.
He knew therefore that they have houses of prayer 156
and meet together in them, particularly on the sacred
sabbaths when they receive as a body a training in
their ancestral philosophy. He knew too that they
collect money for sacred purposes from their first-
fruits and send them to Jerusalem by persons who

[a] So, I think, rather than as L. & S. revised, citing this
passage, " deceiving himself."

---

in the question " how did he approve of the section beyond
the Tiber?" By the very small change involved in expelling
ἦν after ἀποτομήν, the course of the argument is clearly
shown.

PHILO

157
[569] ἀναξόντων. ἀλλ' ὅμως | οὔτε ἐξῴκισε τῆς Ῥώμης ἐκείνους οὔτε τὴν Ῥωμαϊκὴν αὐτῶν ἀφείλετο πολιτείαν, ὅτι καὶ τῆς Ἰουδαϊκῆς ἐφρόντιζον, οὔτε ἐνεωτέρισεν εἰς τὰς προσευχὰς οὔτε ἐκώλυσε συνάγεσθαι πρὸς τὰς τῶν νόμων ὑφηγήσεις οὔτε ἠναντιώθη τοῖς ἀπαρχομένοις, ἀλλ' οὕτως ὡσίωτο περὶ τὰ ἡμέτερα, ὥστε μόνον οὐ πανοίκιος ἀναθημάτων πολυτελείαις τὸ ἱερὸν ἡμῶν ἐκόσμησε, προστάξας καὶ διαιωνίους ἀνάγεσθαι θυσίας ἐντελεχεῖς ὁλοκαύτους καθ' ἑκάστην ἡμέραν ἐκ τῶν ἰδίων προσόδων ἀπαρχὴν τῷ ὑψίστῳ θεῷ, αἱ καὶ μέχρι νῦν ἐπιτελοῦνται καὶ εἰς ἅπαν ἐπιτελεσθήσονται,

158 μήνυμα τρόπων ὄντως αὐτοκρατορικῶν. οὐ μὴν ἀλλὰ κἂν ταῖς μηνιαίαις τῆς πατρίδος[1] διανομαῖς, ἀργύριον ἢ σῖτον ἐν μέρει παντὸς τοῦ δήμου λαμβάνοντος, οὐδέποτε τοὺς Ἰουδαίους ἠλάττωσε τῆς χάριτος, ἀλλ' εἰ καὶ συνέβη τῆς ἱερᾶς ἑβδόμης ἐνεστώσης γενέσθαι τὴν διανομήν, ὅτε οὔτε λαμβάνειν οὔτε διδόναι ἢ συνόλως τι πράττειν τῶν κατὰ βίον καὶ μάλιστα τὸν ποριστὴν ἐφεῖται, προσετέτακτο τοῖς διανέμουσι ταμιεύειν τοῖς Ἰουδαίοις εἰς τὴν ὑστεραίαν τὴν κοινὴν φιλανθρωπίαν.

159 XXIV. Τοιγαροῦν οἱ πανταχοῦ πάντες, εἰ καὶ φύσει διέκειντο πρὸς Ἰουδαίους οὐκ εὐμενῶς, εὐλαβῶς εἶχον ἐπὶ καθαιρέσει τινὸς τῶν Ἰουδαϊκῶν νομίμων προσάψασθαι· καὶ ἐπὶ Τιβερίου μέντοι τὸν αὐτὸν τρόπον, καίτοι τῶν ἐν Ἰταλίᾳ παρακινηθέντων, ἡνίκα Σηιανὸς ἐσκευώρει τὴν ἐπίθεσιν.

160 ἔγνω γάρ, εὐθέως ἔγνω μετὰ τὴν ἐκείνου τελευτήν,

[1] " πατρίδος suspectum," says Reiter, and a correction to σπυρίδος=sportulae has been suggested. But cf. the application of πατρίς to Jerusalem in § 278. It is an essential part

80

would offer the sacrifices. Yet nevertheless he **157**
neither ejected them from Rome nor deprived them
of their Roman citizenship because they were careful
to preserve their Jewish citizenship also, nor took any
violent measures against the houses of prayer, nor
prevented them from meeting to receive instructions
in the laws, nor opposed their offerings of the first-
fruits. Indeed so religiously did he respect our
interests that supported by wellnigh his whole household he adorned our temple through the costliness of
his dedications, and ordered that for all time continuous sacrifices of whole burnt offerings should be
carried out every day at his own expense as a tribute
to the most high God. And these sacrifices are
maintained to the present day and will be maintained
for ever to tell the story of a character truly imperial.
Yet more, in the monthly doles in his own city when **158**
all the people each in turn receive money or corn, he
never put the Jews at a disadvantage in sharing the
bounty, but even if the distributions happened to
come during the sabbath when no one is permitted
to receive or give anything or to transact any part of
the business of ordinary life, particularly of a lucra-
tive kind, he ordered the dispensers to reserve for
the Jews till the morrow the charity which fell to all.

XXIV. Therefore everyone everywhere, even if he **159**
was not naturally well disposed to the Jews, was
afraid to engage in destroying any of our institutions,
and indeed it was the same under Tiberius though
matters in Italy became troublesome when Sejanus
was organizing his onslaughts. For Tiberius knew the **160**
truth, he knew at once after Sejanus's death that

---

of the argument that Augustus's favour was shown to the
Jews in his own city.

ὅτι τὰ κατηγορηθέντα τῶν ᾠκηκότων τὴν Ῥώμην
Ἰουδαίων ψευδεῖς ἦσαν διαβολαί, πλάσματα Σηιανοῦ τὸ ἔθνος ἀναρπάσαι θέλοντος, ὅπερ ἢ μόνον
ἢ μάλιστα ᾔδει βουλαῖς ἀνοσίοις καὶ πράξεσιν
ἀντιβησόμενον ὑπὲρ τοῦ παρασπονδηθῆναι κινδυ-
161 νεύσαντος αὐτοκράτορος. καὶ τοῖς πανταχόσε
χειροτονουμένοις ὑπάρχοις ἐπέσκηψε παρηγορῆσαι
μὲν τοὺς κατὰ πόλεις τῶν ἀπὸ τοῦ ἔθνους, ὡς οὐκ
εἰς πάντας προβάσης τῆς ἐπεξελεύσεως, ἀλλ' ἐπὶ
μόνους τοὺς αἰτίους—ὀλίγοι δὲ ἦσαν—, κινῆσαι δὲ
μηδὲν τῶν ἐξ ἔθους, ἀλλὰ καὶ παρακαταθήκην
ἔχειν τούς τε ἄνδρας ὡς εἰρηνικοὺς τὰς φύσεις καὶ
τὰ νόμιμα ὡς ἀλείφοντα πρὸς εὐστάθειαν.

162 XXV. Ὁ δὲ Γάιος ἑαυτὸν ἐξετύφωσεν, οὐ
λέγων μόνον ἀλλὰ καὶ οἰόμενος εἶναι θεός. εἶτα
οὐδένας εὗρεν οὔτε Ἑλλήνων οὔτε βαρβάρων ἐπι-
τηδειοτέρους Ἀλεξανδρέων εἰς τὴν τῆς ἀμέτρου
καὶ ὑπὲρ φύσιν ἀνθρωπίνην ἐπιθυμίας βεβαίωσιν·
δεινοὶ γάρ εἰσι τὰς κολακείας καὶ γοητείας καὶ
ὑποκρίσεις, παρεσκευασμένοι μὲν θώπας λόγους,
[570] ἀνειμένοις | δὲ στόμασι καὶ ἀχαλίνοις πάντα φύ-
163 ροντες. θεοῦ κλήσεις οὕτως ἐστὶ σεμνὸν παρ'
αὐτοῖς, ὥστε καὶ ἴβεσι καὶ ἰοβόλοις ἀσπίσι ταῖς
ἐγχωρίοις καὶ πολλοῖς ἑτέροις τῶν ἐξηγριωμέ-
νων θηρίων αὐτῆς[1] μεταδεδώκασιν· ὥστε εἰκότως
ἀταμιεύτοις χρώμενοι ταῖς εἰς θεὸν τεινούσαις
προσηγορίαις ἀπατῶσι μὲν τοὺς ὀλιγόφρονας καὶ
ἀπείρους τῆς Αἰγυπτιακῆς ἀθεότητος, ἁλίσκονται
δὲ ὑπὸ τῶν ἐπισταμένων τὴν πολλὴν αὐτῶν ἠλι-
164 θιότητα, μᾶλλον δὲ ἀσέβειαν. ἧς ἄπειρος ὢν

[1] Reiter's text has αὐτῆς θηρίων, but he notes " transponenda
vidit Mang.," as indeed seems necessary.

82

the accusations made against the Jewish inhabitants of Rome were false slanders, invented by him because he wished to make away with the nation, knowing that it would take the sole or the principal part in opposing his unholy plots and actions, and would defend the emperor when in danger of becoming the victim of treachery. And he charged 161 his procurators in every place to which they were appointed to speak comfortably to the members of our nation in the different cities, assuring them that the penal measures did not extend to all but only to the guilty, who were few, and to disturb none of the established customs but even to regard them as a trust committed to their care, the people as naturally peaceable, and the institutions as an influence promoting orderly conduct.

XXV. But Gaius grew beside himself with vanity, 162 not only saying but thinking that he was God. He then found among the Greeks or the outside world no people fitted better than the Alexandrians to confirm the unmeasured passion which craves for more than is natural to mankind. For the Alexandrians are adepts at flattery and imposture and hypocrisy, ready enough with fawning words but causing universal disaster with their loose and unbridled lips. How much reverence is paid by them to the title of 163 God is shown by their having allowed it to be shared by the indigenous ibises and venomous snakes and many other ferocious wild beasts. It naturally followed that by this unrestricted use of names appertaining to God, while they deceived the little-wits who do not see through Egyptian godlessness, they stand condemned by those who understand their great folly or rather impiety. Failing to 164

PHILO

Γάιος ὑπελάμβανε τῷ ὄντι νομίζεσθαι παρ' Ἀλεξανδρεῦσι θεός, ἐπειδήπερ οὐ πλαγίως ἀλλ' ἄντικρυς ἅπασιν ἐχρῶντο κατακόρως τοῖς ὀνόμασιν,

165 ὅσα τοῖς ἄλλοις ἔθος ἐπιφημίζεσθαι θεοῖς. εἶτα καὶ τὴν περὶ τὰς προσευχὰς νεωτεροποιίαν ἀπὸ καθαροῦ τοῦ συνειδότος καὶ τῆς εἰς αὐτὸν ἀκραιφνοῦς τιμῆς ᾤετο γεγενῆσθαι, τῇ μὲν ταῖς ὑπομνηματικαῖς ἐφημερίσιν, ἃς ἀπὸ τῆς Ἀλεξανδρείας διεπέμποντό τινες, προσέχων—ἥδιστον γὰρ ἦν ἀνάγνωσμα τοῦτο αὐτῷ, ὡς καὶ τὰ τῶν ἄλλων συγγραφέων καὶ ποιητῶν ἀηδέστατα συγκρίσει τῆς ἐν τούτοις χάριτος νομίζεσθαι—, τῇ δὲ καὶ δι' ἐνίους οἰκέτας τοὺς τωθάζοντας ἀεὶ καὶ χλευάζοντας σὺν αὐτῷ.

166 XXVI. Τούτων ἦσαν οἱ πλείους Αἰγύπτιοι, πονηρὰ σπέρματα, κροκοδείλων καὶ ἀσπίδων τῶν ἐγχωρίων ἀναμεμαγμένοι τὸν ἰὸν ὁμοῦ καὶ θυμὸν ἐν ταῖς ψυχαῖς. ἡγεμὼν δὲ οἷά τις ἦν χοροῦ τοῦ Αἰγυπτιακοῦ θιάσου παντὸς Ἑλικών, ἐπάρατον καὶ ἐξάγιστον ἀνδράποδον παρεισφθαρὲν εἰς τὴν αὐτοκρατορικὴν οἰκίαν· ἀπεγεύσατο γὰρ τῶν ἐγκυκλίων κατὰ φιλοτιμίαν τοῦ προτέρου δεσπότου,

167 ὃς αὐτὸν ἐδωρήσατο Τιβερίῳ Καίσαρι. τότε μὲν οὖν οὐδεμιᾶς ἐτύγχανε προνομίας, ὅσα μειρακιώδη χαριεντίσματα Τιβερίου διαμεμισηκότος, ἐπειδὴ πρὸς τὸ σεμνότερόν τε καὶ αὐστηρότερον σχεδὸν

168 ἐκ πρώτης ἡλικίας ἐπικλινῶς εἶχεν. ἐπεὶ δὲ ὁ μὲν ἐτελεύτησε, Γάιος δὲ τὴν ἡγεμονίαν διεδέξατο,

---

a Or " in the regular curriculum of the schools."
b Or simply " zeal " as in § 60. In any case the meaning seems to be that his master wished to give an acceptable

84

understand this Gaius supposed that he was really regarded by the Alexandrians as a god, since they incessantly used plainly and without any indirection terms which other people commonly employ when speaking of God. Then again he thought that the 165 violent proceedings against the meeting-houses had sprung from a clear conscience and from a sincere desire to do him honour. This impression was due partly to the attention he paid to the periodical notifications which were sent at the instance of some persons in Alexandria and made very pleasing reading for him, so much so that in comparison with their charm the works of others either in prose or poetry seemed to him very distasteful. Partly also it was caused by some of his domestics who joined him in perpetual scoffing and mockery.

XXVI. The majority of these were Egyptians, a 166 seed bed of evil in whose souls both the venom and the temper of the native crocodiles and asps were reproduced. The one who played the part of chorus-leader to the whole Egyptian troupe was Helicon, an abominable execrable slave, who had been foisted for ill into the imperial household. For he had received a smattering of a liberal education ^{a} through the ambition ^{b} of his former master, who made a present of him to Tiberius Caesar. In his time indeed he got 167 no high position as Tiberius thoroughly hated all juvenile pleasantries, since from his earliest years he was inclined to solemnity and austerity. But when 168 he died and Gaius succeeded to his sovereignty,

present to Tiberius and therefore had his slave educated for this purpose. Yonge's translation, " in emulation of his master," would, I think, need πρός with acc. rather than the simple genitive.

νέῳ δεσπότῃ παρεπόμενος εἰς ἀνέσεις καὶ τρυφὴν
τὴν διὰ πάσης αἰσθήσεως ἐπιχαλῶντι, " σός,"
εἶπε, " νῦν ὁ καιρός ἐστιν, Ἑλικών, ἐπέγειρε
σαυτόν· ἔχεις πρὸς ἐπίδειξιν ἀκροατὴν καὶ θεατὴν
τὸν πάντων ἄριστον· εὔθικτος[1] εἶ τὴν φύσιν· σκώ-
πτειν καὶ χαριεντίζεσθαι δύνασαι μᾶλλον ἑτέρων·
ἀθύρματα καὶ παιδιὰς ληρώδεις καὶ παρασεσυρ-
μένας οἶδας· τῶν ἐγκυκλίων οὐχ ἧττον πεπαίδευσαι
τὰ ἀχόρευτα· πρόσεστί σοι καὶ τὸ στωμύλον οὐκ
169 ἀτερπές. ἐὰν ἔτι κέντρον ἐγκαταμίξῃς τοῖς τωθα-
σμοῖς ὑποκακόηθες, ὡς μὴ γέλωτα κινεῖν μόνον
ἀλλὰ καὶ πικρίαν ἐκ τοῦ καχυπόνου, τὸν δεσπότην
[571] ὅλον ἥρπακας | εὐφυῶς διακείμενον πρὸς ἀκρόασιν
τῶν μετὰ χλεύης ἐγκλημάτων· ἀναπέπταται γὰρ
αὐτοῦ, ὡς οἶδας, τὰ ὦτα καὶ ἀνωρθίασται πρὸς
τοὺς ἐπιτετηδευκότας συνυφαίνειν τὸ βλασφημεῖν
170 τῷ συκοφαντεῖν. ὕλας δὲ μὴ ζήτει περιττοτέρας·
ἔχεις τὰς κατὰ Ἰουδαίων καὶ τῶν Ἰουδαϊκῶν
ἐθῶν διαβολάς,[2] αἷς ἐνετράφης· ἐξ ἔτι σπαργάνων
ἀνεδιδάχθης αὐτάς, οὐ παρ' ἑνὸς ἀνδρὸς ἀλλὰ τοῦ
γλωσσαργοτάτου μέρους τῆς Ἀλεξανδρέων πόλεως.
171 ἐπίδειξαι τὰ μαθήματα." XXVII. τούτοις τοῖς παραλόγοις καὶ ἐπαράτοις λογισμοῖς
ἐπάρας καὶ συγκροτήσας ἑαυτὸν συνεῖχε καὶ
περιεῖπε τὸν Γάιον, οὐ νύκτωρ, οὐ μεθ' ἡμέραν

[1] mss. εὔθηκτος.
[2] mss. καταβολάς. Perhaps, as Mangey suggested as an alternative, καταβοάς.
86

Helicon, attaching himself to his new master who was relaxing into dissipation and voluptuous enjoyment of every sense, said to himself, " Now is your hour, Helicon! rouse yourself; you have an unrivalled auditor and spectator of your exhibitions ; you are naturally quick of apprehension, you can scoff and jest more than other people, you now how to amuse and to play the fool with drolleries and quips and cranks. Your education has been quite as much in subjects unrecognized in the schools [a] as in those of the regular course ; also your gift of the gab is not without its charm. If you also mix with your jest- 169 ings the sting of a touch of malice so that you stir not only laughter but bitterness born of suspicion, you have your master a complete captive. For he is happily disposed by nature to listen to accusations mixed with derision. His ears as you know are wide open and pricked up to listen to those who have studied to combine abuse with sycophancy. And do 170 not seek for needless abundance of material. You have the obloquy cast upon the Jews and their customs ; in this you were reared ; right from the cradle you were taught it not by one person only but by the noisiest element in the city of the Alexandrians. Display your learning." XXVII. Having 171 stimulated and worked himself up with these perverse and execrable reflections he got a hold of Gaius and paid much court to him. Neither by day nor by night

---

[a] Or perhaps more strongly " base and vicious." Philo may be thinking of Plato, *Laws* 654 A, where ὁ ἀχόρευτος is said to be ἀπαίδευτος, and the πεπαιδευμένος is the ἱκανῶς κεχορευκώς, which is afterwards defined as including not merely dancing and singing well, but showing in them a love for τὰ καλά, and hatred for τὰ αἰσχρά. If this is right, πεπαίδευσαι τὰ ἀχόρευτα is an intentional oxymoron.

ἀφιστάμενος, ἀλλὰ πανταχοῦ συμπαρών, ἵνα ταῖς
ἐρημίαις· καὶ ἀναπαύλαις αὐτοῦ καταχρῆται πρὸς
τὰς κατὰ τοῦ ἔθνους αἰτίας, ἡδονὰς κινῶν τὰς διὰ
σκωμμάτων ὁ πανουργότατος, ἵνα τιτρώσκωσιν
αἱ διαβολαί· τὸν γὰρ ἐπ᾽ εὐθείας κατήγορον οὔτε
ὡμολόγει οὔτε ὁμολογεῖν ἐδύνατο, πλαγιάζων δὲ
καὶ τεχνιτεύων χαλεπώτερος καὶ βαρύτερος ἦν
ἐχθρὸς τῶν ἐπιγεγραμμένων[1] ἄντικρυς τὴν δυσ-
172 μένειαν. φασὶ δὲ ὅτι καὶ τῶν Ἀλεξανδρέων οἱ
πρέσβεις εὖ τοῦτο εἰδότες ἀφανῶς ἐμεμίσθωντο
αὐτὸν μεγάλοις μισθοῖς, οὐ διὰ χρημάτων μόνον
ἀλλὰ καὶ τῶν ἐπὶ τιμαῖς ἐλπίδων, ἃς ὑπέσπειραν
αὐτῷ παρέξειν οὐκ εἰς μακράν, ἐπειδὰν ἀφίκηται
173 Γάιος εἰς Ἀλεξάνδρειαν. ὁ δὲ τὸν καιρὸν ἐκεῖνον
ὀνειροπολῶν, ἐν ᾧ παρόντος τοῦ δεσπότου καὶ
σὺν αὐτῷ σχεδόν τι τῆς οἰκουμένης—οὐ γὰρ ἦν
ἄδηλον, ὅτι κατὰ θεραπείαν Γαΐῳ συνεισβαλεῖ τὸ
δοκιμώτατον καὶ ὅσον τῶν πόλεων ὄψις ἐστὶν
ἀναστὰν ἀπὸ περάτων αὐτῶν—ὑπὸ τῆς μεγίστης
καὶ ἐνδοξοτάτης πόλεως τιμηθήσεται, πάντα ὑπ-
174 ισχνεῖτο.   μέχρι μὲν οὖν τινος τὸν ἐμφω-
λεύοντα ἔνδον πολέμιον ἀγνοοῦντες ἐφυλαττόμεθα
τοὺς ἔξω μόνους· ἐπεὶ δὲ ᾐσθόμεθα, διηρευνῶμεν
περιβλεπόμενοι πάσας ὁδούς, εἴ πως δυνησόμεθα
μαλθάξαι καὶ τιθασεῦσαι τὸν ἄνθρωπον ἐξ ἅπαντος
τρόπου καὶ τόπου βάλλοντα καὶ τοξεύοντα ἡμᾶς

---

[1] Mss. ἀπογεγραμμένων (" registered themselves "), a word
which seems not inappropriate here, where stress is laid on
the open profession. I doubt whether change is necessary,
though ἐπιγ. is very common in Philo.

88

did he leave him but was everywhere in his company, so that he might make full use of his hours of solitude and leisure to press the charges against our nation. An utter villain, he worked upon the pleasure which malicious jesting gives to add a sting to slanders. For he neither owned that he was bringing a direct accusation nor could he have done so, but by his indirect and crafty methods he was a more difficult and formidable enemy than those who straightforwardly ranged themselves among their enemies. It is said also that the envoys of the 172 Alexandrians knew this well and had secretly bribed him with big fees not only in money but also with hopes of honours which they covertly suggested they would procure for him soon when Gaius should come to Alexandria. Elated with visions of that occasion 173 when in the presence of his master and of almost the whole habitable world, since undoubtedly all the men of light and leading[a] in the cities would journey from the furthermost parts to join in homage to Gaius, he would be honoured by the greatest and most illustrious city of them all, he promised everything.

For some time, knowing nothing of the 174 foe who was lurking within, we took precautions against foes outside only, but when we perceived the truth we began to search about and scan every path in the hope that we might be able to appease and soften the heart of a man who in every way and from every place was aiming his javelins and arrows at us so effectively. For he played ball with 175

---

[a] The " eye of the city " is those through whom it sees what it needs, cf. the phrase ὀφθαλμὸς βασιλέως. Or perhaps simply " the choicest part " (so also ὀφθαλμός); cf. ὡς ὄψιν ἐν σώματι Spec. Leg. iv. 157.

175 εὐσκόπως. καὶ συνεσφαίριζε γὰρ καὶ συνεγυμνά-
ζετο καὶ συνελούετο καὶ συνηρίστα καὶ μέλλοντι
κοιμᾶσθαι παρῆν Γαΐῳ, τὴν τοῦ κατακοιμιστοῦ
καὶ κατ᾽ οἰκίαν ἀρχισωματοφύλακος τεταγμένος
τάξιν, ὅση μηδενὶ προσῆν ἄλλῳ, ὡς μόνος ἔχειν
εὐκαιρούσας καὶ σχολαζούσας ἀκοὰς αὐτοκράτορος
τῶν ἔξω διαφειμένας θορύβων εἰς ἀκρόασιν ὧν
176 μάλιστα ἐπόθει. διασυρμοὶ δὲ ἦσαν ἀνακεκραμένοι
κατηγορίαις, ἵνα τοῖς μὲν ἡδονὰς κινῇ, ἡμᾶς δὲ
τὰ μέγιστα βλάπτῃ· τὸ μὲν γὰρ προηγούμενον
ἔργον εἶναι δοκοῦν, ὁ διασυρμός, πάρεργον ἦν
αὐτῷ, τὸ δὲ φαινόμενον πάρεργον, αἱ κατηγορίαι,
177 μόνον καὶ πρῶτον ἔργον. πάντα δὴ κάλων ἀνα-
σείων, ὡς οἱ πνεῦμα δεξιὸν κατ᾽ οἰάκων ἔχοντες,
[572] ἐφέρετο πλησίστιος οὐριοδρομῶν, ἄλλας | ἐπ᾽ ἄλ-
λαις συντιθεὶς καὶ συνείρων αἰτίας. τοῦ δὲ ἐνετυ-
ποῦτο ἡ διάνοια παγιώτερον, ὡς ἄληστον εἶναι τὴν
τῶν ἐγκλημάτων μνήμην.

178 XXVIII. Ἐν ἀπόροις δὲ καὶ ἐν ἀμηχάνοις
ὄντες, ἐπειδὴ πάντα λίθον κινοῦντες ὑπὲρ τοῦ τὸν
Ἑλικῶνα ἐξευμενίσασθαι πάροδον οὐδεμίαν ἀνευ-
ρίσκομεν, μηδενὸς μήτε εἰπεῖν μήτε προσελθεῖν
τολμῶντος ἕνεκα τῆς ἀλαζονείας καὶ βαρύτητος,
ᾗ πρὸς πάντας ἐκέχρητο, καὶ ἅμα διὰ τὸ ἀγνοεῖν,
εἴ τίς ἐστιν αὐτῷ πρὸς τὸ Ἰουδαίων γένος ἀλλοτρί-
ωσις ἀλείφοντι τὸν δεσπότην ἀεὶ καὶ συγκροτοῦντι
κατὰ τοῦ ἔθνους, τὸ μὲν ἔτι πονεῖσθαι περὶ τοῦτο
τὸ μέρος εἰάσαμεν, τοῦ δὲ ἀναγκαιοτέρου περιειχό-
μεθα· γραμματεῖον γὰρ ἔδοξεν ἀναδοῦναι Γαΐῳ
κεφαλαιώδη τύπον περιέχον ὧν τε ἐπάθομεν καὶ
179 ὧν τυχεῖν ἠξιοῦμεν. ἦν δὲ σχεδὸν τοῦτο ἐπιτομή
τις ἱκετείας μακροτέρας, ἣν ἐπεπόμφειμεν πρὸ

90

Gaius, practised gymnastics with him, bathed with him, dined with him and was with him when he was going to bed, as he held the post of chamberlain and Captain of the Guard in the house, a post greater than any that was given to anyone else, so that he alone had convenient and leisurely audiences of the emperor, where he could listen released from outside disturbances to what was most to his heart. Satire 176 was blended with accusations so that while he gave rise to pleasure he did us a maximum of harm, for what seemed the leading feature, the satire, was with him secondary and what appeared secondary, the accusations, were his sole and primary task. So 177 letting out every reef like sailors with a fair wind at the stern, he was carried along at full sail racing before the breeze, while he assembled a string of indictments one after the other. And the impression made on Gaius's mind grew firmer so that his memory of the charges was ineffaceable.

XXVIII. In these straits and difficulties, since 178 while leaving no stone unturned to propitiate Helicon we found no way open, as no one dared to address or approach him because of the arrogance and harshness he showed to all, and also we did not know whether in always inciting and working up his master against the nation he was influenced by a personal dislike of the Jewish race, we ceased to exert ourselves in this direction and confined our efforts to the more pressing side. We determined to give Gaius a document presenting in a summarized form the story of our sufferings and our claims. This document was practically 179 an epitome of a longer supplication which we had sent to him a short time before through the hands

91

PHILO

ὀλίγου δι' Ἀγρίππα τοῦ βασιλέως· ἐκ τύχης γὰρ
ἐπεδήμησε τῇ πόλει μέλλων εἰς Συρίαν κατὰ τὴν
180 δοθεῖσαν αὐτῷ βασιλείαν ἀπαίρειν.[1] * * * ἐλελή-
θειμεν δὲ ἄρα ἔτι ἀπατῶντες ἑαυτούς· καὶ γὰρ
πρότερον, ὅτε εὐθὺς ἠρξάμεθα πλεῖν οἰόμενοι πρὸς
κριτὴν ἀφίξεσθαι τευξόμενοι τῶν δικαίων.
    ὁ δὲ ἦν ἐχθρὸς ἄσπονδος, δελεάζων ὅσα τῷ δοκεῖν
φαιδρῷ τῷ βλέμματι καὶ ἱλαρωτέραις ταῖς προσ-
181 ρήσεσι.   δεξιωσάμενος γὰρ ἡμᾶς ἐν τῷ πρὸς
Τιβέρει πεδίῳ τὸ πρῶτον—ἔτυχε δὲ ἐκ τῶν μη-
τρώων ἐξιὼν κήπων—ἀντιπροσηγόρευσε καὶ τὴν
δεξιὰν χεῖρα κατέσεισεν αἰνιττόμενος εὐμένειαν καὶ
τὸν ἐπὶ τῶν πρεσβειῶν, Ὅμιλον ὄνομα, προσ-
πέμψας, " αὐτός," ἔφη, " τῆς ὑμετέρας ὑποθέσεως
ἀκούσομαι προσευκαιρήσας," ὥστε τοὺς ἐν κύκλῳ
πάντας συνήδεσθαι καθάπερ ἤδη νενικηκόσι καὶ
τῶν ἡμετέρων ὅσοι ταῖς ἐπιπολαίοις παράγονται

---

[1] Reiter here places what he calls (*Prolegomena*, p. 60) a
" lacuna maior." On this see note *b*.

---

a This document of course was quite different from the
complimentary address mentioned in *Flaccus* 103 as sent in
duplicate through Agrippa. The statement made here
seems to me to raise considerable difficulty. The natural
meaning is that it was handed to Agrippa at his visit to
Alexandria in the spring of 38. That the Jews might have
given him a petition setting forth their rights, *i.e.* their claims
to citizenship, is possible enough, and as circumstances had
not changed this, this petition might have been adequate
later. But it also is said to have set forth their sufferings,
i.e. the persecutions and the desecration of the synagogues,
and these could not have been described in a document
handed to Agrippa during this visit, for it is impossible to
suppose that he remained at Alexandria through the pogrom
which culminated at the end of August. The only intelligible

of King Agrippa.[a] For he had chanced to pay a
visit to the city when he was about to sail to Syria
to take up the kingdom which had been given to
him. . . .[b] But we proved to have been unwittingly 180
deceiving ourselves, not for the first time. For it
was the same earlier, when we first started on our
voyage thinking that we should meet a judge and
get our rights.   Actually he was our
mortal foe, beguiling us with the seeming geniality
with which he eyed us and the increased cheeri-
ness of his address. After first greeting us in the 181
plain by the Tiber, as he issued from the gardens
left him by his mother, he repeated his salutation
and waved his right hand signifying goodwill and
sent the official who managed the admission of
ambassadors named Homilus with the message : " I
will hear your statement of the case myself when I
get a good opportunity." Consequently everyone
around us rejoiced with us as though we had already
won the case, and those of our party who were mis-

meaning I can give to the statement is that the visit of
Agrippa had created an intimacy which made him a natural
channel in the subsequent matters for approaching Gaius.
Unless indeed some words are lost. See next note.

  For Agrippa's life and personality see vol. ix. p. 532.

  [b] Reiter gives no reason for supplying a lacuna here
beyond the words " lacunam statuit Cohn." But Cohn's
article in *Philologus* says nothing bearing on it, though he
observes that as the ambassadors are suddenly introduced
in ch. xxvii., some account of the reasons for the embassy
may have been originally given there. I expect that his idea
of a lacuna at this point in ch. xxviii. is a later modification.
I see no reasons for supposing lacunas on any such grounds.
See Introd. pp. xxii. But it is true that a few words to the
effect that Agrippa's visit had led to intimacy with him
might have cleared up the difficulty mentioned in the preceding note.

182 φαντασίαις. ἐγὼ δὲ φρονεῖν τι δοκῶν περιττότερον
καὶ δι' ἡλικίαν καὶ τὴν ἄλλην παιδείαν εὐλαβέ-
στερος ἤμην ἐφ' οἷς ἔχαιρον οἱ ἄλλοι. " διὰ τί
γάρ," ἔφασκον ἀνακινῶν τὸν ἐμαυτοῦ λογισμόν,
" τοσούτων ὄντων πρεσβευτῶν σχεδὸν ἀπὸ πάσης
γῆς ἀφιγμένων, ἡμῶν εἶπε τότε μόνων ἀκούσεσθαι;
τί βουλόμενος; οὐ γὰρ ἠγνόει γε ὄντας Ἰουδαίους,
183 οἷς ἀγαπητὸν τὸ μὴ ἐλαττοῦσθαι. τὸ δὲ δὴ καὶ
προνομίας οἴεσθαι τυγχάνειν παρ' ἀλλοεθνεῖ καὶ
νέῳ καὶ αὐτεξουσίῳ δεσπότῃ μὴ καὶ μανίας ἐγγύς
ἐστιν; ἀλλ' ἔοικε τῇ τῶν ἄλλων Ἀλεξανδρέων |
[573] μερίδι προσκεῖσθαι, ᾗ διδοὺς προνομίαν θᾶττον
ὑπέσχετο δικάσειν, ἐὰν ἄρα μὴ τὸν ἴσον καὶ κοινὸν
ἀκροατὴν ὑπερβὰς ἀντὶ δικαστοῦ γένηται τῶν μὲν
συναγωνιστής, ἡμῶν δὲ ἀντίπαλος."

184 XXIX. Ταῦτα λογιζόμενος ἐσφάδαζον καὶ οὔτε
μεθ' ἡμέραν οὔτε νύκτωρ ἠρέμουν. ἀθυμοῦντος
δέ μου καὶ τὴν ἀνίαν στέγοντος[1]—οὐδὲ γὰρ ἀνενεγ-
κεῖν ἀσφαλὲς ἦν—, ἕτερον κατασκήπτει βαρύτατον
ἐξαπιναίως ἀπροσδόκητον κακόν, οὐχ ἑνὶ μέρει τοῦ
Ἰουδαϊκοῦ τὸν κίνδυνον ἐπάγον, ἀλλὰ συλλήβδην
185 ἅπαντι τῷ ἔθνει. ἀφίγμεθα μὲν γὰρ ἀπὸ Ῥώμης
κόλπον, ἀμείβων τὰς ἰδίας ἐπαύλεις πολλὰς καὶ
εἰς Δικαιάρχειαν ἐπακολουθοῦντες Γαΐῳ· κατ-
εληλύθει δὲ ἐπὶ θάλατταν καὶ διέτριβε περὶ τὸν
186 πολυτελῶς ἠσκημένας. φροντίζουσι δὲ ἡμῖν τῆς
ὑποθέσεως—ἀεὶ γὰρ κληθήσεσθαι προσεδοκῶμεν—
προσέρχεταί τις ὕφαιμόν τι καὶ ταραχῶδες ὑπο-

---

[1] mss. ἄνοιαν (or ἀγνοίαν) στένοντος.

led by short-sighted fancies felt the same. But as 182
I believe myself in virtue of my age and my good
education otherwise to possess a greater amount of
good sense, what gave joy to the others rather
alarmed me. Bestirring my thinking powers I said,
" Why when so many envoys were present from
almost the whole earth did he say that he would
hear us only ? What was his object ? For he must
have known that we were Jews who would be con-
tented if they were not treated worse than others.
To suppose that we shall take precedence with a 183
despot of an alien race, a young man possessing
absolute power, surely borders on madness ; it looks
as if he is attaching himself to the party of the
other Alexandrians and it was to them that he gave
precedence and promised to give judgement quickly,
if indeed he has not discarded the idea of giving a
fair and impartial hearing and instead of a judge
become their advocate and our opponent."

XXIX. Thus thinking I was deeply disturbed and 184
had no rest by day or night. But while in my
despondency I kept my affliction concealed since it
was not safe to let it appear, another very heavy
calamity was suddenly and unexpectedly launched
upon us, which endangered not one part only of the
Jewish race but the whole body of the nation. We 185
had travelled from Rome to Puteoli following Gaius,
who had come down to the sea side and was
spending some time round the bay passing from one to another
of the numerous and expensively furnished country
houses which he owned. While we were anxiously 186
considering the statement of our case, since we were
always expecting to be summoned, there came to
us one with a troubled look in his bloodshot eyes and

95

PHILO

βλεπόμενος, ἄσθματος μεστός, καὶ μικρὸν ἀπὸ
τῶν ἄλλων ἀπαγαγών—πλησίον γὰρ ἦσάν τινες—
" ἠκούσατε," ἔφη, " τὰ καινά; " καὶ μέλλων
ἀπαγγέλλειν ἐπεσχέθη, δακρύων ἀθρόας φορᾶς
187 ἐνεχθείσης. καὶ πάλιν ἀρξάμενος δεύτερον ἐπεσχέθη καὶ τρίτον. ἅπερ ὁρῶντες ἡμεῖς ἐπτοήμεθα
καὶ παρεκαλοῦμεν μηνῦσαι τὸ πρᾶγμα, οὗ χάριν
ἐλθεῖν ἔφασκεν· " οὐ γὰρ ἕνεκα τοῦ διὰ μαρτύρων
κλαίειν· εἰ δὲ ἄξια δακρύων ἐστί, μὴ μόνος ἀπόλαυε
τῆς λύπης· ἐθάδες γεγόναμεν ἤδη κακοπραγιῶν."
188 ὁ δὲ μόλις μὲν ἀναλύζων δὲ ὅμως κεκομμένῳ τῷ
πνεύματί φησιν· " οἴχεται ἡμῶν τὸ ἱερόν· ἀνδριάντα
κολοσσιαῖον ἐσωτάτω τῶν ἀδύτων ἀνατεθῆναι
189 Γάιος προσέταξε Διὸς ἐπίκλησιν αὐτοῦ." θαυ-
μασάντων δὲ τὸ λεχθὲν καὶ πεπηγότων ὑπ᾽ ἐκ-
πλήξεως καὶ μηδὲ προελθεῖν[1] ἔτι δυναμένων—
ἀχανεῖς γὰρ εἱστήκειμεν ὀλιγοδρανοῦντες καὶ
καταρρέοντες περὶ αὑτοῖς, τῶν σωματικῶν τόνων
ἐκνενευρισμένων—, ἕτεροι παρῆσαν τὰς αὐτὰς
190 φέροντες ὠδῖνας. ἔπειτα συγκλεισάμενοι πάντες
ἀθρόοι ἰδίας ὁμοῦ καὶ κοινὰς τύχας ἐθρηνοῦμεν καὶ
οἷα ὑπέβαλλεν ὁ νοῦς διεξῇμεν—λαλίστατον γὰρ
ἄνθρωπος ἀτυχῶν· ἀγωνιάσωμεν[2] ὑπὲρ τοῦ μὴ
εἰς ἅπαν ταῖς ἀνιάτοις[3] παρανομίαις ἀφεθῆναι.

---

[1] mss. προσελθεῖν.
[2] For another punctuation see note *a*.
[3] mss. ἐν αὐτοῖς: see note *a*. If the punctuation there
suggested is accepted, Mangey's conjecture of ἐν ἀστοῖς is
possible. I would also ask for consideration for ἐνιαυσίοις,
i.e. outrages which have now lasted a year.

---

a If this punctuation is right the meaning is " don't let us
be led into making illegal resistance, or perhaps into action

gasping convulsively. He drew us a little way apart
since there were some people standing near and said,
" Have you heard the new tidings ? " and when he
was going to report it he was brought up short, as a
flood of tears streamed from his eyes. He began 187
again and the second time stopped short and so too
a third time. When we saw this we were all in a
flutter and bade him tell us the matter which he said
had brought him there. " For," we said, " you have
not come just to have your weeping witnessed. If
the facts are worth tears do not be the only one to
feel sorrow. We have become inured to misfortunes
by now." He managed with difficulty while sobbing 188
and breathing spasmodically to say, " Our temple is
lost, Gaius has ordered a colossal statue to be set
up within the inner sanctuary dedicated to himself
under the name of Zeus." As we marvelled at his 189
words and, petrified by consternation, could not get
any further, since we stood there speechless and
powerless in a state of collapse with our hearts
turned to water, others appeared bringing the same
woeful tale. Then gathered altogether in seclusion 190
we bewailed the disaster personal to each and common
to all and such thoughts as the mind suggested we
discussed at length. For nothing is more ready of
tongue than a man in misfortune. " Let us struggle," we said, " to save us from delivering ourselves
altogether to fatal acts of lawlessness.[a] We sailed in

which will bring upon us lawless outrages." But I should prefer to put the stop after ἀγωνιάσωμεν instead of after ἀφεθῆναι.
The sense will be " let us face the crisis. It was to save
ourselves from being the victims of outrages that we sailed,"
etc. In this case the παρανομίαι are the outrages we expected
to happen in Alexandria. So substantially Mangey, though
he reads ἀγωνιζόμενοι.

χειμῶνος μέσου διεπλεύσαμεν ἀγνοοῦντες, ὅσος
χειμὼν ἔφεδρός ἐστιν ὁ κατὰ γῆν ἀργαλεώτερος
πολλῷ τοῦ κατὰ θάλατταν· τοῦ μὲν γὰρ ἡ φύσις
αἰτία διακρίνουσα τοὺς ἐτησίους καιρούς, φύσις
δὲ σωτήριον· ἐκείνου δὲ ἄνθρωπος οὐδὲν φρονῶν
ἀνθρώπινον, νέος καὶ νεωτεροποιὸς ἀνημμένος τὴν
[574] ἐφ' ἅπασιν | ἀνυπεύθυνον ἀρχήν· νεότης δὲ μετ' ἐξ-
ουσίας αὐτοκρατοῦς ὁρμαῖς ἀκαθέκτοις χρωμένη
191 κακὸν δύσμαχον. ἐξέσται δὲ προσελθεῖν ἢ διᾶραι
τὸ στόμα περὶ προσευχῶν τῷ λυμεῶνι τοῦ πανιέ-
ρου; δῆλον γὰρ ὡς οὐ φροντιεῖ τῶν ἀφανεστέρων
καὶ τιμῆς ἐλάττονος ἠξιωμένων ὁ τὸν περιση-
μότατον καὶ ἐπιφανέστατον νεών, εἰς ὃν ἀνατολαὶ
καὶ δύσεις ἀποβλέπουσιν ἡλίου τρόπον πανταχόσε
192 λάμποντα, καθυβρίζων. εἰ δὲ καὶ γένοιτό τις ἄδεια
προσόδου, τί χρὴ προσδοκᾶν ἢ θάνατον ἀπαραίτητον; ἀλλ' ἔστω, τεθνηξόμεθα· ζωὴ γάρ τίς ἐστιν
ὁ ὑπὲρ φυλακῆς νόμων εὐκλεέστατος θάνατος. εἰ
δὲ ἐκ τῆς ἡμετέρας τελευτῆς γενήσεται μηδὲν
ὄφελος, οὐ μανία παραπολέσθαι, καὶ ταῦτα πρεσ-
βεύειν δοκοῦντας, ὡς τῶν πεμψάντων μᾶλλον ἢ

---

a The six sections which follow become intelligible if we
recognize that ἰδίου in § 193 refers to the particular interests
of the Alexandrian Jews, especially their claims to citizenship, as opposed to the interests of the nation as a whole, and
not to the personal safety of the ambassadors. Philo and his
colleagues had three courses of action before them. First they
might proceed with their suit, perhaps by sending the document mentioned in § 178 if that had not been sent already.
This was impracticable as far as the synagogue question was
concerned and might probably cost them their lives (§ 191).
Such a death was, indeed, honourable but under the circumstances a mere waste (§ 192). As to the other question, the

midst of the stormy winter, not knowing how great a
storm was awaiting us, a land storm far more dangerous than that of the sea. For that is the work of
nature who divides the annual seasons, and nature
is a preserver. But the other is the work of a man
whose thoughts are not those of a man, a youth with
the recklessness of youth, invested with irresponsible
dominion over all. And youth coupled with absolute
authority is subject to unrestrainable impulses, a
formidable power for evil. *a* Shall we be allowed to 191
come near him and open our mouths in defence of
the houses of prayer to the destroyer of the all-holy
place ? for clearly to houses less conspicuous and
held in lower esteem no regard would be paid by
one who insults that most notable and illustrious
shrine whose beams like the sun's reach every
whither, beheld with awe both by east and west.
And even if we were allowed to approach him un- 192
molested, what have we to expect but death against
which there is no appeal ? Well so be it, we will die
and be no more, for the truly glorious death, met in
defence of laws, might be called life. But if our
decease brings no advantage, is it not madness to
let ourselves perish as well, particularly as we are
supposed to act as ambassadors, so that the disaster

citizenship, to press it when the national existence was in danger
would be felt to be a selfish particularism (§§ 193, 194). The
second alternative was to throw up the whole thing and go
home. This is rejected as unworthy (§ 195). The third was
to wait on quietly in Italy trusting in God and hoping that
the crisis would pass (§ 196). This is probably what actually
happened thanks to Agrippa's intercession, after which the
envoys were admitted and even if unsuccessful, at any rate,
left unharmed. I see no reason to agree with Balsdon,
page 136, that this " laboured defence shows that they were
criticised for neglecting to make any gesture at this point."

193 τῶν ὑπομενόντων εἶναι τὴν συμφοράν; οὐ μὴν
ἀλλὰ καὶ ὅσοι τὰς φύσεις μισοπονηρότατοι τῶν
ὁμοφύλων ἀσέβειαν ἡμῶν κατηγορήσουσιν ὡς, ἐν
ἐσχάτῳ κινδύνῳ τῶν ὅλων σαλευόντων, ἐπιμνησ-
θέντων ὑπὸ φιλαυτίας ἰδίου τινός· τοῖς γὰρ μεγάλοις
τὰ βραχέα καὶ τοῖς κοινοῖς τὰ ἴδια ὑποστέλλειν
ἀναγκαῖον, ὧν οἰχομένων ἔρρει καὶ ἡ πολιτεία.
194 ποῦ γὰρ ὅσιον ἢ θεμιτὸν ἄλλως ἀγωνίζεσθαι,
δεικνύντας ὡς ἐσμὲν Ἀλεξανδρεῖς, οἷς ὁ περὶ τῆς
καθολικωτέρας πολιτείας ἐπικρέμαται κίνδυνος τῆς
Ἰουδαίων; ἅμα γὰρ τῇ τοῦ ἱεροῦ καταλύσει δέος,
μὴ καὶ τὸ κοινὸν τοῦ ἔθνους ὄνομα συναφανισθῆναι
κελεύσῃ ὁ νεωτεροποιὸς καὶ μεγαλουργὸς ἄνθρω-
195 πος. ἀμφοτέρων οὖν τῶν ὑποθέσεων δι᾽
ἃς ἐστάλημεν οἰχομένων, ἴσως φήσει τις· τί οὖν,
οὐκ ᾔδεσαν πραγματεύεσθαι τὴν μετὰ ἀσφαλείας
ἐπάνοδον; πρὸς ὃν εἴποιμι ἄν· ἢ οὐκ ἔχεις ἀνδρὸς
εὐγενοῦς πάθος γνήσιον ἢ οὐκ ἐνετράφης οὐδὲ
ἐνησκήθης τοῖς ἱεροῖς γράμμασιν. ἐλπίδων εἰσὶ
πλήρεις οἱ ὄντως εὐγενεῖς, καὶ οἱ νόμοι τοῖς
ἐντυγχάνουσι μὴ χείλεσιν ἄκροις ἐλπίδας ἀγαθὰς
196 δημιουργοῦσιν. ἴσως ἀπόπειρα ταῦτα τῆς καθ-
εστώσης γενεᾶς ἐστι, πῶς ἔχει πρὸς ἀρετὴν καὶ εἰ
πεπαίδευται φέρειν τὰ δεινὰ λογισμοῖς ἰσχυρογνω-
μοσιν οὐ προκαταπίπτουσα. τὰ μὲν οὖν ἐξ ἀνθρώπων ἅπαντα καὶ ἔρρει καὶ ἐρρέτω· μενέτω
δὲ ἐν ταῖς ψυχαῖς ἀκαθαίρετος ἡ ἐπὶ τὸν σωτῆρα
θεὸν ἐλπίς, ὃς πολλάκις ἐξ ἀμηχάνων καὶ ἀπόρων
περιέσωσε τὸ ἔθνος.
197 XXX. Ταῦτα ἅμα μὲν ὀλοφυρόμενοι τὰς ἀπροσ-

---

would fall more on those who sent us than on the
actual sufferers ? Indeed those among our fellow 193
nationals who most detest wickedness will accuse us
of impiety in selfishly pleading for something which
concerns us in particular, when the existence of all
is tottering in extreme danger. For small things
must needs give way to big and particular to general
interests, the loss of which means the perdition of
the body politic. For what religion or righteousness 194
is to be found in vainly striving to show that we are
Alexandrians, when we are menaced by the danger
which threatens a more universal interest, the cor-
porate body of the Jews ? For it is to be feared that
the overthrow of the temple will be accompanied by
an order for the annihilation of our common name
and nation from the man who deals in revolution
on so great a scale. If then both the 195
causes [a] which we were sent to plead are lost, someone
perhaps will say, ' Well what then ? did they not
know how to manage their safe return ? ' To such
a one I would say, ' Either you have not the genuine
feelings of the nobly born or you were not reared
or trained in the sacred writings.' The truly noble
are always hopeful and the laws create good hopes
for those who take more than a mere sip of their
study. Perhaps these things are sent to try the 196
present generation, to test the state of their virtue
and whether they are schooled to bear dire misfortunes with a resolution which is fortified by reason
and does not collapse at once. So then what man
can do is gone, and let it go. But let out souls retain
indestructible the hope in God our Saviour who has
often saved the nation when in helpless straits.''

XXX. Thus we talked on, at once lamenting 197

101

δοκήτους ἀτυχίας ἅμα δὲ καὶ παρηγοροῦντες ἑαυτοὺς ἐλπίδι μεταβολῆς γαληνοτέρας διεξῇμεν. μικρὸν δὲ ἐπισχόντες πρὸς τοὺς ἀπαγγείλαντας, |

[575] " τί καθ᾽ ἡσυχίαν," εἴπομεν, " κάθησθε, σπινθῆρας αὐτὸ μόνον τοῖς ὠσὶν ἡμῶν ἐνιέντες, ὑφ᾽ ὧν καιόμεθα καὶ πυρπολούμεθα, δέον προσεξηγεῖσθαι καὶ

198 τὰ κεκινηκότα τὸν Γάιον; " οἱ δέ· " τὴν μὲν ἀνωτάτω καὶ πρώτην αἰτίαν ἴστε, ἣν καὶ πάντες ἴσασιν ἄνθρωποι· θεὸς βούλεται νομίζεσθαι, ὑπείληφε δὲ μόνους Ἰουδαίους μὴ πείσεσθαι, οἷς μεῖζον οὐδὲν ἂν προστρίψαιτο κακὸν ἢ λυμηνάμενος τὴν τοῦ ἱεροῦ σεμνότητα. κατήχηται δέ, ὅτι καὶ πάντων ἱερῶν τῶν πανταχοῦ κάλλιστόν ἐστιν ἐξ ἀπείρων χρόνων ἀπαύστοις καὶ ἀφειδέσι δαπάναις ἀεὶ προσκοσμούμενον· δύσερις δὲ καὶ φιλόνεικος ὢν σφετερίσασθαι τοῦτο εἰς ἑαυτὸν διανοεῖται.

199 παρατέθηκται δὲ νῦν μᾶλλον ἢ πρότερον ἐξ ἐπιστολῆς, ἣν ἔπεμψε Καπίτων. φόρων ἐκλογεὺς ὁ Καπίτων ἐστὶ τῶν τῆς Ἰουδαίας, ἔχει δέ πως πρὸς τοὺς ἐγχωρίους ἐγκότως· πένης γὰρ ἀφιγμένος καὶ ἐξ ὧν νοσφίζεται καὶ παρεκλέγει ποικίλον τινὰ καὶ πολὺν πλοῦτον ἠθροικώς, εἶτα εὐλαβηθείς, μή τις αὐτοῦ γένηται κατηγορία, τέχνην ἐπενόησεν, ᾗ διαβολαῖς τῶν ἀδικηθέντων

200 διακρούσεται τὰς αἰτίας. ἀφορμὴν δὲ αὐτῷ δίδωσιν εἰς ὅπερ ἐβούλετο συντυχία τις τοιαύτη. τὴν Ἰάμνειαν—πόλις δέ ἐστι τῆς Ἰουδαίας ἐν τοῖς μάλιστα πολυάνθρωπος—[ταύτην] μιγάδες οἰκοῦσιν, οἱ πλείους μὲν Ἰουδαῖοι, ἕτεροι δέ τινες ἀλλόφυλοι παρεισφθαρέντες ἀπὸ τῶν πλησιοχώρων, οἳ τοῖς τρόπον τινὰ αὐθιγενέσιν ὄντες μέτοικοι κακὰ καὶ

our unexpected misfortunes and comforting ourselves
with a hope of a change to serener conditions. Then
pausing for a little we said to those who had brought
the news, " Why do you sit here silently merely
implanting in our ears the sparks to light the fire
by which we are consumed, instead of proceeding to
tell us the causes which have moved Gaius to do
this ? " They replied, " You know the chief and 198
primary cause which all men also know. He wishes
to be thought a god and has supposed that the only
dissentients will be the Jews on whom he could
inflict no greater injury than the ruin of the sanctity
of their temple. He has been instructed that of all
the temples anywhere it is the most beautiful, ever
from endless ages embellished by ceaseless and un-
sparing expenditure. Quarrelsome and contentious
as he is, he proposes to appropriate it for his own
use. But now his eagerness has become 199
keener than ever before owing to a letter sent to
him by Capito. Capito is the tax-collector for
Judaea and cherishes a spite against the population.
When he came there he was a poor man but by his
rapacity and peculation he has amassed much wealth
in various forms. Then fearing that some accusation
might be brought against him he devised a scheme to
elude the charges by slandering those whom he had
wronged. It chanced that an opportunity for obtain- 200
ing his object was given by the following incident.
Jamneia, one of the most populous cities of Judaea,
is inhabited by a mixture of people, the majority
being Jews with some others of alien races, intruders
for mischief from the dwellers in adjacent countries.
These people being new settlers have made themselves a pest and a nuisance to those who are in a

103

PHILO

πράγματα παρέχουσιν, ἀεί τι παραλύοντες τῶν
201 πατρίων Ἰουδαίοις. οὗτοι παρὰ τῶν ἐπιφοιτώντων
ἀκούοντες, ὅση σπουδῇ κέχρηται Γάιος περὶ τὴν
ἰδίαν ἐκθέωσιν καὶ ὡς ἀλλοτριώτατα διάκειται
πρὸς ἅπαν τὸ Ἰουδαϊκὸν γένος, καιρὸν ἐπιτήδειον
εἰς ἐπίθεσιν παραπεπτωκέναι νομίζοντες αὐτοσχέ-
διον ἀνιστᾶσι βωμὸν εἰκαιοτάτης ὕλης, πηλὸν
σχηματίσαντες εἰς πλίνθους, ὑπὲρ τοῦ μόνον ἐπι-
βουλεύειν τοῖς συνοικοῦσιν· ᾔδεσαν γὰρ οὐκ ἀνεξομένους καταλυομένων τῶν ἐθῶν, ὅπερ καὶ ἐγένετο.
202 θεασάμενοι γὰρ καὶ δυσανασχετήσαντες ἐπὶ τῷ τῆς
ἱερᾶς χώρας τὸ ἱεροπρεπὲς ὄντως ἀφανίζεσθαι
καθαιροῦσι συνελθόντες· οἱ δὲ εὐθὺς ἐπὶ τὸν Κα-
πίτωνα ἧκον, ὃς ἦν τοῦ δράματος ὅλου δημιουργός.
ἕρμαιον δὲ εὑρηκέναι νομίσας, ὅπερ ἐκ πολλῶν
χρόνων ἀνεζήτει, γράφει Γαΐῳ διαίρων τὰ πράγ-
203 ματα καὶ μετεωρίζων.   ὁ δὲ διαγνοὺς[1]
πλουσιώτερον καὶ μεγαλοφρονέστερόν τι ἀντὶ τοῦ
πλινθίνου βωμοῦ τοῦ κατ' ἐπήρειαν ἀνασταθέντος
[576] ἐν Ἰαμνείᾳ κελεύει | κολοσσιαῖον ἀνδριάντα ἐπί-
χρυσον ἐν τῷ τῆς μητροπόλεως ἱερῷ καθιδρυθῆναι,
συμβούλοις χρησάμενος τοῖς ἀρίστοις καὶ σοφωτά-
τοις, Ἑλικῶνι τῷ εὐπατρίδῃ δούλῳ, σπερμολόγῳ,
περιτρίμματι, καὶ Ἀπελλῇ τινι τραγῳδῷ, ὃς ἀκμῇ
μὲν τῆς πρώτης ἡλικίας, ὥς φασιν, ἐκαπήλευσε
τὴν ὥραν, ἔξωρος δὲ γενόμενος ἐπὶ τὴν σκηνὴν
204 παρῆλθεν. ὅσοι δὲ σκηνοβατοῦσιν ἐμπορευόμενοι
θεαταῖς καὶ θεάτροις, αἰδοῦς εἰσι καὶ σωφροσύνης
ἀλλ' οὐκ ἀναισχυντίας καὶ ἀκοσμίας ἐρασταὶ τῆς
ἀνωτάτω· διὰ ταῦτα εἰς τὴν τοῦ συμβούλου

[1] mss. διαγνοὺς (which however is sometimes used in the same sense: v. Stephanus); cf. Flaccus 100.

104

sense indigenous by perpetually subverting some part
of the institutions of the Jews. Hearing from travel- 201
lers visiting them how earnestly Gaius was pressing
his deification and the extreme hostility which he
felt towards the whole Jewish race, they thought that
a fit opportunity of attacking them had fallen in their
way. Accordingly they erected an extemporized
altar of the commonest material with the clay
moulded into bricks, merely as a plan to injure their
neighbours, for they knew that they would not allow
their customs to be subverted, as indeed it turned
out. For, when they saw it and felt it intolerable 202
that the sanctity which truly belongs to the Holy
Land should be destroyed, they met together and
pulled it down. The others at once went off to Capito,
who was the author of the whole episode, and he,
thinking that he had found a piece of luck which he
had long been seeking, wrote to Gaius a highly
exaggerated account of the facts.   Gaius 203
after reading it gave orders that in place of the altar of
bricks erected in wanton spite in Jamneia something
richer and more magnificent, namely a colossal statue
coated with gold, should be set up in the temple of
the mother city. In this he followed the advice of
those excellent and sapient advisers, that member
of the aristocracy Helicon, slave, scrap retailer, piece
of riff-raff, and one Apelles [a] a tragic actor, who, they
say, in the flower of his prime had trafficked his youth-
ful charms, but when the bloom was passed went
on to the stage. Of course performers on the stage 204
whose trade is with theatres and theatre-goers are
lovers of modesty and sobriety, not of shamelessness
and extreme indecency. The reason why Apelles

---

[a] Cf. Suet. Gaius 33 and Dio lix. 5.

τάξιν ὁ Ἀπελλῆς παρῆλθεν, ἵνα βουλεύσηται Γάιος
μεθ᾽ οὗ μὲν ὡς σκωπτέον, μεθ᾽ οὗ δὲ ὡς ἀστέον,
ὑπερβὰς τὰς περὶ τῶν ὅλων σκέψεις, ὡς εἰρηνεύ-
205 εσθαι καὶ ἠρεμεῖσθαι τὰ πανταχοῦ πάντα. ὁ μὲν
οὖν Ἑλικών, σκορπιῶδες ἀνδράποδον, τὸν Αἰγυπ-
τιακὸν ἰὸν εἰς Ἰουδαίους ἤφιεν, ὁ δὲ Ἀπελλῆς τὸν
ἀπὸ Ἀσκάλωνος· ἦν γὰρ ἐκεῖθεν· Ἀσκαλωνίταις
δὲ ἀσύμβατός τις καὶ ἀκατάλλακτος δυσμένεια
πρὸς τοὺς τῆς ἱερᾶς χώρας οἰκήτορας Ἰουδαίους
206 ἐστὶν οὖσιν ὁμόροις.'' ταῦτα ἀκούοντες ἐφ᾽ ἑκάστου ῥήματος καὶ ὀνόματος ἐτιτρωσκόμεθα τὰς
ψυχάς. ἀλλ᾽ οἱ μὲν καλῶν πράξεων καλοὶ σύμ-
βουλοι μικρὸν ὕστερον τὰ ἐπίχειρα εὗρον τῆς
ἀσεβείας, ὁ μὲν ὑπὸ Γαΐου σιδήρῳ δεθεὶς ἐφ᾽ ἑτέ-
ραις αἰτίαις καὶ στρεβλούμενος καὶ τροχιζόμενος
ἐκ περιτροπῆς, ὥσπερ ἐν ταῖς περιοδιζούσαις
νόσοις, ὁ δὲ Ἑλικὼν ὑπὸ Κλαυδίου Γερμανικοῦ
Καίσαρος ἀναιρεθείς, ἐφ᾽ οἷς ἄλλοις ὁ φρενοβλαβὴς
ἠδίκησεν. ἀλλὰ ταῦτα μὲν ὕστερον ἐγένετο.
207 XXXI. Ἡ δὲ περὶ τῆς ἀναθέσεως τοῦ ἀνδριάντος
ἐπιστολὴ γράφεται, καὶ οὐχ ἁπλῶς ἀλλ᾽ ὡς οἷόν
τε ἦν περιεσκεμμένως εἰς ἀσφάλειαν. κελεύει γὰρ
Πετρωνίῳ τῷ τῆς Συρίας ἁπάσης ὑπάρχῳ, πρὸς
ὃν καὶ τὴν ἐπιστολὴν ἐγεγράφει, τῆς παρ᾽ Εὐφράτῃ
στρατιᾶς, ἣ τὴν διάβασιν τῶν ἑῴων βασιλέων καὶ
ἐθνῶν παρεφύλαττε, τὴν ἡμίσειαν ἄγειν ἐπὶ τῆς
Ἰουδαίας τὸν ἀνδριάντα παραπέμψουσαν, οὐχ ἵνα
σεμνοποιήσῃ τὴν ἀνάθεσιν, ἀλλ᾽ ἵνα, εἰ διακωλύοι[1]
208 τις, εὐθὺς ἀπόληται. τί λέγεις, ὦ δέσποτα;

---

[1] mss. διακωλύει.

was advanced to the post of councillor was that Gaius might take advice on the right method of jesting from one and of chanting from the other, having set aside all consideration for the general welfare by which peace and tranquillity of every thing in every place might be maintained. So then Helicon, scorpion 205 in form of a slave, vented his Egyptian venom on the Jews and so too Apelles with the venom of Ascalon. For that was the place he came from, and the Ascalonites have a truceless and irreconcilable hostility to the Jewish inhabitants of the Holy Land on whose borders they live." As we heard this every single 206 word was a wound to our souls. But shortly afterwards these admirable advisers of admirable actions received the reward of their impiety. Apelles for other reasons was thrown by Gaius into chains of iron and tortured by the rack and the wheel in turns [a] like people suffering from recurring fevers. Helicon was put to death by Claudius Germanicus Caesar for the other wrongs which the madman had committed. But these events belong to a later time.

XXXI. Gaius's letter enjoining the dedication of 207 the statue was written not in simple terms but with all circumspection possible to ensure safety. He ordered his viceroy for the whole of Syria, Petronius, to whom the letter was addressed, to bring for the conduct of the statue to Judaea half the army quartered on the Euphrates to guard the passage against the kings and nations of the east. This was done not to add dignity to the dedication but to effect the immediate destruction of anyone who tried to prevent it.

---

[a] Or " periodically " (rack and wheel being regarded as a single process), which suits the figure of recurrent fevers better.

PHILO

προειληφὼς οὐκ ἀνεξομένους, ἀλλ' ὑπερασπιοῦντας
τοῦ νόμου καὶ προαποθανουμένους τῶν πατρίων
πολεμοποιεῖς; οὐ γὰρ ἔοικας δι' ἄγνοιαν ὧν εἰκὸς
ἦν ἀποβήσεσθαι τοῦ περὶ τὸ ἱερὸν ἅψασθαι νεω-
τερισμοῦ, προμαθὼν δὲ ἀκριβῶς τὰ μέλλοντα ὡς
ἤδη παρόντα καὶ τὰ γενησόμενα ὡς χειριζόμενα¹ |

[577] τὴν στρατιὰν εἰσάγειν προσέταξας, ἵνα θυσίαις
ἐναγέσι² πρώταις καθιερωθῇ τὸ ἀφίδρυμα, σφαγαῖς
209 ἀθλίων ἀνδρῶν ὁμοῦ καὶ γυναικῶν.   ὁ
μὲν οὖν Πετρώνιος τὰ ἐπισταλέντα διαναγνοὺς ἐν
ἀμηχάνοις ἦν, οὔτε ἐναντιοῦσθαι δυνάμενος διὰ
φόβον—ᾔδει γὰρ ἀφόρητον οὐ μόνον κατὰ τῶν τὰ
κελευσθέντα μὴ πραξάντων, ἀλλὰ καὶ κατὰ τῶν μὴ
εὐθύς—οὔτε ἐγχειρεῖν εὐμαρῶς· ᾔδει γὰρ ἀνθ' ἑνὸς
θανάτου μυρίους ἄν, εἴπερ δυνατὸν ἦν, ἐθελήσοντας
ὑπομεῖναι μᾶλλον ἢ περιιδεῖν τι τῶν ἀπειρημένων
210 δρώμενον. ἅπαντες γὰρ ἄνθρωποι φυλακτικοὶ τῶν
ἰδίων ἐθῶν εἰσι, διαφερόντως δὲ τὸ Ἰουδαίων
ἔθνος· θεόχρηστα γὰρ λόγια τοὺς νόμους εἶναι
ὑπολαμβάνοντες καὶ τοῦτο ἐκ πρώτης ἡλικίας τὸ
μάθημα παιδευθέντες ἐν ταῖς ψυχαῖς ἀγαλματο-
211 φοροῦσι τὰς τῶν διατεταγμένων εἰκόνας· εἶτα
ἐναργεῖς τύπους καὶ μορφὰς αὐτῶν καθορῶντες
ἀεὶ τοῖς λογισμοῖς αὐτῶν τεθήπασι· καὶ τοὺς μὲν
τιμητικῶς ἔχοντας ἀλλοφύλους αὐτῶν οὐχ ἧττον
τῶν ἰδίων ἀποδέχονται πολιτῶν, τοῖς δὲ ἢ καθαι-
ροῦσιν ἢ χλευάζουσιν ὡς πολεμιωτάτοις ἀπέχθονται·
καὶ πεφρίκασι μὲν ἕκαστον τῶν διηγορευμένων

¹ mss. χειριούμενα or ἐν χειρὶ ἐσόμενα.
² mss. εὐαγέσι.

108

What mean you by this, my lord and master? is it 208
an act of war based on the foreknowledge that they
would not submit but would take up arms to defend
the laws and die for their national institutions?
For surely it was not done in ignorance of the
probable results of any attempt to violate the
temple. No, you foresaw what would take place as
clearly as if it were already present and the future
events as though they were already in hand, and
so you ordered the army to be brought in that the
first sacrifice with which the image was consecrated
might be polluted with the massacre of unhappy
men and women alike. Petronius hav- 209
ing read the instructions was in great difficulties.
Fear made it impossible for him to oppose the
order, for he knew that Gaius crushed irresistibly
not only those who did not carry out his command
but also those who did not do so at once. Neither
could he lightly undertake it, for he knew that the
Jews would willingly endure to die not once but
a thousand times, if it were possible, rather than
allow any of the prohibited actions to be committed.
For all men guard their own customs, but this is 210
especially true of the Jewish nation. Holding that
the laws are oracles vouchsafed by God and having
been trained in this doctrine from their earliest years,
they carry the likenesses of the commandments
enshrined in their souls. Then as they contemplate 211
their forms thus clearly represented they always think
of them with awe. And those of other races who
pay homage to them they welcome no less than their
own countrymen, while those who either break them
down or mock at them they hate as their bitterest
foes. And such dread is inspired by each of the pro-

οὕτως, ὡς ἅπασαν τὴν παρ᾽ ἀνθρώποις εἴτε εὐτυ-
χίαν εἴτε εὐδαιμονίαν χρὴ καλεῖν μηδέποτ᾽ ἂν ὑπὲρ
παραβάσεως καὶ τοῦ τυχόντος ἂν ὑπαλλάξασθαι.

212 περιττοτέρα δὲ καὶ ἐξαίρετός ἐστιν αὐτοῖς ἅπασιν
ἡ περὶ τὸ ἱερὸν σπουδή. τεκμήριον δὲ μέγιστον·
θάνατος ἀπαραίτητος ὥρισται κατὰ τῶν εἰς τοὺς
ἐντὸς περιβόλους παρελθόντων—δέχονται γὰρ εἰς
τοὺς ἐξωτέρω τοὺς πανταχόθεν πάντας—τῶν οὐχ
ὁμοεθνῶν.

213 Εἰς δὴ ταῦτα ἀφορῶν ὁ Πετρώνιος βραδὺς ἦν
ἐγχειρητής, ὅσον τόλμημα μεγαλουργεῖται σκεπτό-
μενος, καὶ συγκαλέσας ὡς ἐν συνεδρίῳ τοὺς τῆς
ψυχῆς ἅπαντας λογισμοὺς τὴν ἑκάστου γνώμην
διηρεύνα καὶ πάντας εὕρισκεν ὁμογνωμονοῦντας
περὶ τοῦ μηδὲν κινεῖν τῶν ἐξ ἀρχῆς καθωσιωμένων,
πρῶτον διὰ τὸ φύσει δίκαιον καὶ εὐσεβές, ἔπειτα
διὰ τὸν ἐπικρεμάμενον κίνδυνον, οὐκ ἐκ θεοῦ μόνον
214 ἀλλὰ καὶ τῶν ἐπηρεαζομένων.   ἔννοιά τε
αὐτὸν εἰσῄει τοῦ ἔθνους, ὅσον ἐστὶν ἐν πολυαν-
θρωπίᾳ, ὅπερ οὐχ ἐδέξατο καθάπερ τῶν ἄλλων
ἕκαστον μιᾶς χώρας τῆς ἀποκεκληρωμένης αὐτῷ
μόνῳ περίβολος, ἀλλ᾽ ὀλίγου δέω φάναι πᾶσα ἡ
οἰκουμένη· κέχυται γὰρ ἀνά τε τὰς ἠπείρους καὶ
νήσους ἁπάσας, ὡς τῶν αὐθιγενῶν μὴ πολλῷ τινι
215 δοκεῖν ἐλαττοῦσθαι. τοσαύτας μυριάδας ἐφέλ-
κεσθαι πολεμίων ἆρ᾽ οὐ σφαλερώτατον; ἀλλὰ
μήποτε γένοιτο συμφρονήσαντας τοὺς ἑκασταχοῦ
πρὸς ἄμυναν ἐλθεῖν· ἄμαχόν τι συμβήσεται χρῆμα·
δίχα τοῦ καὶ τοὺς τὴν Ἰουδαίαν κατοικοῦντας |

[578] ἀπείρους τε εἶναι τὸ πλῆθος καὶ τὰ σώματα γεν-

nouncements that they would never purchase what men deem good fortune or happiness, whichever name is right, by transgressing even in the slightest matters. Still more abounding and peculiar is the 212 zeal of them all for the temple, and the strongest proof of this is that death without appeal is the sentence against those of other races who penetrate into its inner confines. For the outer are open to everyone wherever they come from.

Having these things before his eyes Petronius was 213 slow to set to work. He saw the audacity of so vast an enterprise, and having mustered all the reasoning faculties of his soul, as though in a council, he looked to see what verdict they gave, and found it unanimous against destroying anything which was held sacred from the beginning, primarily from a feeling of natural justice and piety, secondly from the danger threatened not only from God but from the victims of the outrage.   He bethought him of the 214 vast number of people comprised in the nation, which needed to contain it not like every other the circumference of a single country allotted to itself alone, but, one might almost say, the whole habitable world. For it is spread abroad over all the continents and islands so that it seems to be not much less than the indigenous inhabitants. To draw all these myriads 215 into war against him was surely very dangerous. Heaven forbid indeed that the Jews in every quarter should come by common agreement to the defence. The result would be something too stupendous to be combated.[a] But without this the inhabitants of Judea are unlimited in number. Their bodies are

---

[a] χρῆμα is used in the idiomatic sense of something big, of which ὑὸς χρῆμα μέγα is the stock example.

ναιοτάτους καὶ τὰς ψυχὰς εὐτολμοτάτους καὶ
προαποθνῄσκειν αἱρουμένους τῶν πατρίων ὑπὸ
φρονήματος, ὡς μὲν ἔνιοι τῶν διαβαλλόντων εἴποιεν
ἄν, βαρβαρικοῦ, ὡς δὲ ἔχει τἀληθές, ἐλευθερίου καὶ
216 εὐγενοῦς. ἐφόβουν δὲ αὐτὸν καὶ αἱ πέραν Εὐ-
φράτου δυνάμεις· ᾔδει γὰρ Βαβυλῶνα καὶ πολλὰς
ἄλλας τῶν σατραπειῶν ὑπὸ Ἰουδαίων κατεχομένας,
οὐκ ἀκοῇ μόνον ἀλλὰ καὶ πείρᾳ· καθ' ἕκαστον γὰρ
ἐνιαυτὸν ἱεροπομποὶ στέλλονται χρυσὸν καὶ ἄργυρον
πλεῖστον κομίζοντες εἰς τὸ ἱερὸν τὸν ἀθροισθέντα
ἐκ τῶν ἀπαρχῶν, δυσβάτους καὶ ἀτριβεῖς καὶ
ἀνηνύτους ὁδοὺς περαιούμενοι, ἃς λεωφόρους εἶναι
νομίζουσιν, ὅτι πρὸς εὐσέβειαν ἄγειν δοκοῦσι.
217 περιδεὴς οὖν ὡς εἰκὸς ἦν, μὴ πυθόμενοι τὴν
καινουργουμένην ἀνάθεσιν ἐπιφοιτήσωσιν ἐξαίφνης
καὶ περίσχωσιν, οἱ μὲν ἔνθεν οἱ δὲ ἔνθεν, κύκλος
γενόμενοι, καὶ συνάψαντες ἀλλήλοις τοὺς ἐναποληφ-
θέντας μέσους δεινὰ ἐργάσωνται. τοιούτοις μὲν
218 λογισμοῖς χρώμενος ἀπώκνει.   πάλιν δὲ
ὑπὸ τῶν ἐναντίων ἀνθείλκετο, " δεσπότου," λέγων,
" ἡ πρόσταξίς ἐστι καὶ νέου καὶ ὅ τι ἂν βουληθῇ
τοῦτο συμφέρον κρίνοντος καὶ τὸ γνωσθὲν ἅπαξ
ἐπιτελεσθῆναι, κἂν ἀλυσιτελέστατον ᾖ καὶ φιλο-
νεικίας καὶ ἀλαζονείας γέμον, ὅς γε καὶ ὑπερπηδή-
σας τὸν ἄνθρωπον ἐν θεοῖς ἤδη γράφει ἑαυτόν.
ἐπικρέμαται δή μοι κίνδυνος ὁ περὶ ψυχῆς καὶ
ἐναντιωθέντι καὶ εἴξαντι, ἀλλ' εἴξαντι μὲν μετὰ
πολέμου καὶ τάχα ἀμφίβολος[1] καὶ οὐ πάντως
ἀποβησόμενος,[1] ἐναντιωθέντι δὲ ἀπαραίτητος καὶ

---

[1] Perhaps read ἀμφιβόλου . . . ἀποβησομένου, which would
be more logical.

of the finest quality and their souls of the highest courage, preferring to die in defence of their national institutions, moved by a high spirit not as some of their slanderers would say barbaric but in very truth worthy of the free and nobly born. He was frightened 216 also by the forces beyond the Euphrates, since that Babylon and many other satrapies were occupied by Jews was known to him not only by report but by experience. For every year envoys were dispatched for the sacred purpose of conveying to the temple a great quantity of gold and silver amassed from the firstfruits, and these envoys travel over the pathless, trackless, endless routes which seem to them good highroads because they feel that they lead them to piety. So he was naturally much alarmed lest hear- 217 ing of this unprecedented dedication the Jews of those parts might suddenly take to raiding, and coming from different quarters might encircle his troops and joining hands attack them now isolated in their midst with terrible effect. While following this line of reasoning he shrank from action.

Then again he was drawn in the opposite direction 218 by counter-arguments. " The order," he said, " is given by a master who is young and judges that whatever he wishes is beneficial and that what he has once decreed is as good as accomplished, be it ever so unprofitable and charged with contentiousness and arrogance. For he has soared above man's estate and already ranks himself as among the gods. My life is in imminent danger whether I oppose or give way, but while if I give way the danger is the prospect of war the result of which is doubtful, and there is no certainty that it will happen at all, if I oppose, its source is Gaius and it admits of no appeal and no

219 ὁμολογούμενος ἐκ Γαΐου.'' συνελάμβανον δὲ τῇ γνώμῃ ταύτῃ πολλοὶ τῶν συνδιεπόντων τὰ κατὰ Συρίαν αὐτῷ Ῥωμαίων, εἰδότες ὅτι καὶ ἐπ' αὐτοὺς πρώτους αἱ ἀπὸ Γαΐου χωρήσουσιν ὀργαὶ καὶ τιμωρίαι ὡς συναιτίους τοῦ τὸ κελευσθὲν μὴ

220 γενέσθαι. παρέσχε δὲ εἰς ἀκριβεστέραν σκέψιν ἀναχώρησιν ἡ κατασκευὴ τοῦ ἀνδριάντος· οὔτε γὰρ ἀπὸ τῆς Ῥώμης διεπέμψατο—θεοῦ μοι προνοίᾳ δοκῶ τὴν χεῖρα τῶν ἀδικουμένων ἀφανῶς ὑπερ-έχοντος—οὔτε τῶν κατὰ Συρίαν ὅστις ἂν ἄριστος εἶναι δοκιμασθῇ μετακομίζειν προσέταξεν, ἐπεὶ κἂν τῷ τάχει τῆς παρανομίας ταχὺς ἐξήφθη ὁ

221 πόλεμος. καιρὸν οὖν σχὼν[1] εἰς τὴν τοῦ συμφέροντος

[579] διάσκεψιν |—τὰ γὰρ αἰφνίδια καὶ μεγάλα, ὅταν ἀθρόα προσπέσῃ, κατακλᾷ τὸν λογισμόν—προσ-τάττει τὴν κατασκευὴν ἔν τινι τῶν ὁμόρων

222 ποιεῖσθαι. μεταπεμψάμενος οὖν ὁ Πετρώνιος δημιουργοὺς τῶν ἐν Φοινίκῃ τοὺς φρονιμωτάτους δίδωσι τὴν ὕλην· οἱ δὲ ἐν Σιδῶνι εἰργάζοντο.

μεταπέμπεται δὲ καὶ τοὺς ἐν τέλει τῶν Ἰουδαίων ἱερεῖς τε καὶ ἄρχοντας, ἅμα μὲν δηλώσων τὰ ἀπὸ Γαΐου, ἅμα δὲ καὶ συμβουλεύσων ἀνέχεσθαι τῶν ὑπὸ τοῦ δεσπότου προσταττομένων καὶ τὰ δεινὰ πρὸ ὀφθαλμῶν λαμβάνειν· εὐτρεπεῖς γὰρ εἶναι τῶν κατὰ Συρίαν στρατιωτικῶν δυνάμεων

---

[1] mss. σχόντος. I feel some doubt about this correction, which is accepted by Mangey and Reiter. The form of the sentence and the appearance of Petronius's name in the next sentence rather suggest that Gaius and not he is the subject of προστάττει. Is there any objection to this on the ground

114

denial." This latter view was supported by many 219
Romans who shared his administration of Syria, since
they knew that the wrath and vengeance of Gaius
would reach them first as accomplices in making his
orders of none effect. An opportunity for a respite 220
to take a closer consideration was afforded by the
constructing of the statue. For Gaius had not had
one sent from Rome, in my opinion through the
providence of God, who unseen by us stretched out
his hand to protect the wronged, nor did he command
Petronius to select from the statues in Syria the one
approved of as best and send it to Jerusalem. For
speed in the execution of his unlawful purpose would
have led to a speedy outburst of war. So Petronius 221
having got an opportunity for consideration of the
best course to adopt, since great and sudden emer-
gencies when they fall with concentrated force crush
the reasoning faculty, ordered the construction to be
carried out in some one of the adjacent countries
and accordingly sent for the most clever craftsmen 222
to be found in Phoenicia and gave them the material
which they worked up in Sidon. He also
sent for the magnates of the Jews, priests and magistrates, partly to explain Gaius's intentions and partly
to advise them to accept the orders of their lord
and master and keep before their eyes the dire con-
sequences of doing otherwise. For, as he told them,
the more efficient part of the armed forces in Syria

---

of sense ? It was natural that Gaius should tell Petronius to
get a statue made and he may be credited with enough sense
to see that it had better not be made in Judaea itself. In this
case the proper correction would be σχόντι, but even this is
not absolutely necessary. Examples of the genitive absolute
where strict grammar demands another case are not unknown. See Goodwin's *Moods and Tenses* 850.

τὰς μαχιμωτέρας, αἳ πᾶσαν τὴν χώραν καταστορέ-
223 σουσι νεκρῶν. ᾤετο γάρ, εἰ προμαλάξειε τούτους,
δυνήσεσθαι δι' αὐτῶν καὶ τὴν ἄλλην πληθὺν ἅπασαν
ἀναδιδάξαι[1] μὴ ἐναντιοῦσθαι· γνώμης δέ, ὡς εἰκός,
διημάρτανε. πληχθέντας γάρ φασιν ὑπὸ τῶν
πρώτων ῥημάτων εὐθὺς αὐτοὺς ἀήθους[2] κακοῦ
διηγήσει καταπαγῆναι[3] καὶ ἀχανεῖς γενομένους
φοράν τινα δακρύων ὥσπερ ἀπὸ πηγῶν ἀθρόαν
ἐκχεῖν, τὰ γένεια καὶ τὰς τρίχας τῆς κεφαλῆς
224 τίλλοντας καὶ τοιαῦτα ἐπιλέγοντας· " πολλὰ εἰσ-
ηνέγκαμεν εἰς εὐγήρω βίον οἱ λίαν εὐτυχεῖς, ἵνα ὃ
μηδεὶς πώποτε εἶδε τῶν προγόνων ἡμεῖς θεασώ-
μεθα· τίσιν ὀφθαλμοῖς; ἐκκοπήσονται πρότερον
μετὰ τῆς ἀθλίας ψυχῆς καὶ τῆς ἐπωδύνου ζωῆς
ἢ τοιοῦτον ὄψονται κακόν, ἀθέατον θέαν, ἣν οὔτε
ἀκοῦσαι θέμις οὔτε νοῆσαι.''

225 XXXII. Καὶ οἱ μὲν τοιαῦτα ὠλοφύροντο. πυθόμενοι δὲ οἱ κατὰ τὴν ἱερόπολιν καὶ τὴν ἄλλην
χώραν τὸ κινούμενον, ὥσπερ ἀφ' ἑνὸς συνθήματος
συνταξάμενοι, τοῦ κοινοῦ πάθους τὸ σύνθημα
δόντος, ἐξεληλύθεσαν ἀθρόοι καὶ κενὰς τὰς πόλεις
καὶ κώμας καὶ οἰκίας ἀπολιπόντες μιᾷ ῥύμῃ
συνέτεινον εἰς Φοινίκην· ἐκεῖ γὰρ ὢν ἐτύγχανεν
226 ὁ Πετρώνιος. ἰδόντες δὲ τῶν Πετρωνίου τινὲς
ὄχλον ἀμύθητον φερόμενον ἐβοηδρόμουν ἀπαγγέλ-

---

[1] mss. ἀναδιδάξειν. [2] mss. ἀληθοῦς.
[3] mss. καταπλαγῆναι.

116

were ready at hand and would strew the land with the dead. For he thought that if he could start by 223 appeasing them he could use them to instruct all the rest of the population to abstain from opposition. But he failed as might be expected to effect his intention. Smitten by his first words, we are told, as soon as they heard the story of the abnormal calamity they stood riveted to the ground, incapable of speech, and then while a flood of tears poured from their eyes as from fountains they plucked the hair from their beards and heads and finally uttered such words as these, " Did we too for- 224 tunate pay so much to purchase a long and happy life,[a] only to behold what none of our forefathers saw in the past ? How can our eyes bear it ? they shall be torn out and with them the miseries of life, the anguish of our existence, before they look on such a calamity—a sight unfit for them to see, unlawful for the ears to hear, or the mind to imagine."

XXXII. While they were thus lamenting, the 225 inhabitants of the holy city and the rest of the country hearing what was afoot marshalled themselves as if at a single signal, the signal which their common situation gave them, and issued forth in a body leaving cities, villages and houses empty and in one onrush sped to Phoenicia where Petronius chanced to be. Some of his people seeing a vast 226 crowd moving along ran to his aid and made their report in order that he might take precautions

---

[a] If the translation is right it seems to mean that their fortunes and actions had been such that they expected to end their days happily. But the phrasing is odd. Mangey translates " en quo minus beati pervenimus," which I cannot fit into the Greek at all.

PHILO

λοντες, ἵνα φυλάττηται, πόλεμον προσδοκήσαντες.
ἔτι δὲ διηγουμένων, ὁ μὲν ἀφρούρητος ἦν, ἡ δὲ τῶν
Ἰουδαίων πληθὺς ἐξαπιναίως ὥσπερ νέφος ἐπι-
στᾶσα πᾶσαν Φοινίκην ἐπέσχε, κατάπληξιν τοῖς
οὐκ εἰδόσι τὴν τοῦ ἔθνους πολυανθρωπίαν ἐργασα-
227 μένη. καὶ βοὴ μὲν τοσαύτη τὸ πρῶτον ἤρθη μετὰ
κλαυθμῶν καὶ στερνοτυπιῶν, ὡς ἂν μηδὲ τὰς
ἀκοὰς τῶν παρόντων χωρεῖν τὸ μέγεθος· οὐδὲ
γὰρ ἐπαύσατο παυσαμένων, ἀλλ' ἡσυχασάντων ἔτι
συνήχει. ἔπειτα πρόσοδοι καὶ δεήσεις, οἵας ὁ
καιρὸς ὑπέβαλλε· διδάσκαλοι γὰρ τοῦ παρόντος[1]
αὐταὶ αἱ συμφοραί. εἰς τάξεις δὲ ἐξ διενεμήθησαν,
πρεσβυτῶν, νέων, παίδων, πάλιν ἐν μέρει πρεσ-
βυτίδων, γυναικῶν τῶν ἐν ἡλικίᾳ, παρθένων.
228 ἐπεὶ δὲ ὁ Πετρώνιος ἐξ ἀπόπτου κατεφάνη, πᾶσαι
[580] αἱ τάξεις καθάπερ | κελευσθεῖσαι προσπίπτουσιν
εἰς ἔδαφος ὀλολυγὴν θρηνώδη τινὰ μεθ' ἱκετηριῶν
ἀφιεῖσαι. παραινέσαντος δὲ ἀνίστασθαι καὶ προσελθεῖν ἐγγυτέρω, μόλις ἀνίσταντο καὶ καταχεά-
μενοι πολλὴν κόνιν καὶ ῥεόμενοι δακρύοις, τὰς
χεῖρας ἀμφοτέρας εἰς τοὐπίσω περιαγαγόντες
229 τρόπον ἐξηγκωνισμένων, προσῄεσαν. εἶτα ἡ
γερουσία καταστᾶσα τοιάδε ἔλεξεν· " ἄοπλοι μέν
⟨ἐσμεν⟩, ὡς ὁρᾷς, παραγενομένους δὲ αἰτιῶνταί
τινες ὡς πολεμίους. ἃ δὲ ἡ φύσις ἑκάστῳ προσ-
ένειμεν ἀμυντήρια μέρη, χεῖρας, ἀπεστρόφαμεν,
ἔνθα μηδὲν ἐργάσασθαι δύνανται, παρέχοντες αὐτῶν
τὰ σώματα πρὸς εὐσκόπους τοῖς θέλουσιν ἀπο-
230 κτεῖναι βολάς. γυναῖκας καὶ τέκνα καὶ γενεὰς[2]

---

[1] Reiter and Mangey, who suggested πρέποντος, both
suspect παρόντος. Note that τοῦ γὰρ παρόντος συμφοραὶ διδάσκαλοι would form an iambic line.

118

against the war which they expected. They had not finished their story and Petronius still remained unguarded, when the multitude of the Jews suddenly descended like a cloud and occupied the whole of Phoenicia to the profound astonishment of those who did not know how populous the nation was. The first thing to be observed was the great shouting 227 which arose mingled with weeping and smiting of breasts, so great that it was more than the ears of those present could contain. For even when they paused there was no pausing in the sound but it still echoed even amid their silence. The next step was to approach Petronius and make such supplications as the occasion suggested, for great misfortunes themselves teach men what their situation is. They were divided into six companies, old men, young men, boys, and again in their turn old women, grown women, maidens. When Petronius 228 first appeared in the distance all the companies as though at a word of command fell before him to the ground uttering a dirge-like wail with cries of supplication. When he encouraged them to rise and come nearer, they rose with some reluctance and with dust poured all over them, their eyes streaming with tears and both hands set behind them as though they were pinioned, they approached him. Then the body 229 of elders stood and spoke as follows, " We are unarmed as you see, though some accuse us of having come as enemies in war, yet the parts which nature has assigned to each of us for defence, our hands, we have put away where they can do nothing and present our bodies as an easy target for the missiles of those who wish to kill us. We have brought our 230

---

[2] Perhaps read γονέας. See note a on p. 120.

PHILO

ἐπηγαγόμεθά σοι καὶ διὰ σοῦ προσεπέσομεν[1] Γαΐῳ
μηδένα οἴκοι καταλιπόντες, ἵνα ἢ περισώσητε
πάντας ἢ πάντας πανωλεθρίᾳ διαφθείρητε. Πετρώνιε, καὶ τὰς φύσεις ἐσμὲν εἰρηνικοὶ καὶ τὴν
προαίρεσιν, καὶ αἱ διὰ παιδοτροφίαν φιλεργίαι
τοῦτο ἡμᾶς ἐξ ἀρχῆς ἐπαίδευσαν τὸ ἐπιτήδευμα.
231 Γαΐῳ παραλαβόντι τὴν ἡγεμονίαν πρῶτοι τῶν
κατὰ Συρίαν ἀπάντων ἡμεῖς συνήσθημεν, Οὐιτελ-
λίου τότε, παρ᾽ οὗ διεδέξω τὴν ἐπιτροπήν, ἐν τῇ
πόλει διατρίβοντος, ᾧ τὰ περὶ τούτων ἐκομίσθη
γράμματα, καὶ ἀπὸ τῆς ἡμετέρας πόλεως εὐαγ-
γελιουμένη πρὸς τὰς ἄλλας ἔδραμεν ἡ φήμη.
232 πρῶτον τὸ ἡμέτερον ἱερὸν ἐδέξατο τὰς ὑπὲρ τῆς
ἀρχῆς Γαΐου θυσίας, ἵνα πρῶτον ἢ καὶ μόνον
ἀφαιρεθῇ τῆς θρησκείας τὸ πάτριον; ἐξιστάμεθα
τῶν πόλεων, παραχωροῦμεν τῶν οἰκιῶν καὶ κτη-
μάτων, ἔπιπλα καὶ χρήματα καὶ κειμήλια καὶ τὴν
ἄλλην ἅπασαν λείαν εἰσοίσομεν ἑκόντες· λαμβάνειν,
οὐ διδόναι, ταῦτα νομιοῦμεν. ἐν ἀντὶ πάντων
αἰτούμεθα, μηδὲν ἐν τῷ ἱερῷ γενέσθαι νεώτερον,
ἀλλὰ φυλαχθῆναι τοιοῦτον, οἷον παρὰ τῶν πάππων
233 καὶ προγόνων παρελάβομεν. εἰ δὲ μὴ πείθομεν,
παραδίδομεν ἑαυτοὺς εἰς ἀπώλειαν, ἵνα μὴ ζῶντες
ἐπίδωμεν θανάτου χεῖρον κακόν. πυνθανόμεθα
πεζὰς καὶ ἱππικὰς δυνάμεις εὐτρεπίσθαι καθ᾽

---

[1] mss. προσπεσούμεθα. I am not sure that the change is
necessary. Their prostration before Petronius could when
reported in the future to Gaius constitute a prostration before
him.

---

[a] Philo sometimes uses γενεά = " family," cf. § 308. But

120

wives, our children and our families [a] to you, leaving none at home, and have prostrated outselves before Gaius in doing so to you, that you and he may either save us all from ruin or send us all to perish in utter destruction. O Petronius, both by our nature and our principles we are peaceable, and the diligence which parents devote to rearing their children has trained us in this practice from the very first. When 231 Gaius succeeded to the sovereignty we were the first of all the inhabitants of Syria to show our joy, for Vitellius your predecessor as governor was staying in the city, and it was to him that the letter telling the news was sent and it was from our city that rumour to carry the good tidings sped to the others. Was our temple the first to accept sacrifices in behalf 232 of Gaius's reign only that it should be the first or even the only one to be robbed of its ancestral tradition of worship ? We are evacuating our cities, withdrawing from our houses and lands ; our furniture and money and cherished possessions and all the other spoil we will willingly make over. We should think ourselves gainers thereby, not givers. One thing only we ask in return for all, that no violent changes should be made in this temple and that it be kept as we received it from our grandparents and ancestors. But if we cannot persuade you, we give up ourselves 233 for destruction that we may not live to see a calamity worse than death. We hear that forces of cavalry and infantry have been prepared against us if we

it is strange to find it="the rest of the family." So in *Spec. Leg.* iii. 159 we have γύναια τούτων καὶ τέκνα καὶ γονεῖς καὶ τὴν ἄλλην γενεάν. In suggesting γονέας I do not forget that elsewhere he seems regularly to use γονεῖς. But γονέας is a known Attic form and he may have thought it appropriate for a highly rhetorical speech put into the mouth of another.

ἡμῶν, εἰ πρὸς τὴν ἀνάθεσιν ἀντιβαίημεν. οὐδεὶς
οὕτως μέμηνεν, ὡς δοῦλος ὢν ἐναντιοῦσθαι δεσ-
πότῃ· παρέχομεν ἐν ἑτοίμῳ τὰς σφαγὰς ἄσμενοι,
κτεινέτωσαν, ἱερευέτωσαν, κρεανομείτωσαν ἀμαχεὶ
καὶ ἀναιμωτί, πάντα ὅσα κεκρατηκότων ἔργα
234 δράτωσαν. τίς δὲ χρεία στρατιᾶς; αὐτοὶ κατάρ-
[581] ξομεν | τῶν θυμάτων οἱ καλοὶ ἱερεῖς, παραστησό-
μενοι τῷ ἱερῷ γυναῖκας οἱ γυναικοκτόνοι, ἀδελφοὺς
καὶ ἀδελφὰς οἱ ἀδελφοκτόνοι, κούρους καὶ κόρας,
τὴν ἄκακον ἡλικίαν, οἱ παιδοφόνται· τραγικῶν
γὰρ ὀνομάτων δεῖ τοῖς τὰς τραγικὰς συμφορὰς
235 ὑπομένουσιν. εἶτ᾽ ἐν μέσοις στάντες καὶ λουσά-
μενοι τῷ συγγενικῷ αἵματι—τοιαῦτα γὰρ τὰ λουτρὰ
τοῖς εἰς ᾅδου φαιδρυνομένοις—ἀνακερασόμεθα τὸ
236 ἴδιον ἐπικατασφάξαντες αὑτούς. ἀποθανόντων τὸ
ἐπίταγμα γενέσθω· μέμψαιτ᾽ ἂν οὐδὲ θεὸς ἡμᾶς
ἀμφοτέρων στοχαζομένους, καὶ τῆς πρὸς τὸν
αὐτοκράτορα εὐλαβείας καὶ τῆς πρὸς τοὺς καθω-
σιωμένους νόμους ἀποδοχῆς· γενήσεται δὲ τοῦτο,
ἐὰν ὑπεκστῶμεν ἀβιώτου βίου καταφρονήσαντες.
237 ἀκοὴν ἐδεξάμεθα παλαιτάτην ὑπὸ τῶν κατὰ τὴν
Ἑλλάδα λογίων παραδοθεῖσαν, οἳ τὴν τῆς Γοργόνος
κεφαλὴν τοσαύτην ἔχειν δύναμιν ὡμολόγουν, ὥστε
τοὺς προσιόντας εὐθὺς λίθους καὶ πέτρους γίνεσθαι. τοῦτο μύθου μὲν πλάσμα ἔοικεν εἶναι, τὸ
δ᾽ ἀληθὲς αἱ μεγάλαι καὶ ἀβούλητοι καὶ ἀνήκεστοι
συντυχίαι ἐπιφέρουσιν. ὀργαὶ δεσπότου θάνατον
238 ἀπεργάζονται ἢ παραπλήσιόν τι θανάτῳ. νομίζεις,
ὃ μήποτε γένοιτο, παραπεμπόμενον εἰ θεάσαιντο

ᵃ Or " fine priests indeed "—a strange travesty of priest-

oppose the installation. No one is so mad as to oppose a master when he is a slave. We gladly put our throats at your disposal. Let them slaughter, butcher, carve our flesh without a blow struck or blood drawn by us and do all the deeds that conquerors commit. But what need of an army ! our 234 selves will conduct the sacrifices, priests of a noble order *a* : wives will be brought to the altar by wife-slayers, brothers and sisters by fratricides, boys and girls in the innocence of their years by child-murderers. For the tragedian's vocabulary is needed for those who endure tragical misfortunes. Then 235 standing in the midst of our kinsfolk after bathing ourselves in their blood, the right bathing for those who would go to Hades clean, we will mingle our blood with theirs by the crowning slaughter of ourselves. When we are dead let the prescript be 236 carried out ; not God himself could blame us who had a twofold motive, respectful fear of the emperor and loyalty to the consecrated laws. And this aim will be accomplished if we take our departure in contempt of the life which is no life. We have 237 heard a very ancient story handed down by the common consent of learned men of Greece, that the Gorgon's head had such great power that those who looked upon it were turned at once into rocks and stones. The story is no doubt a mythical figment but great and disastrous and irreparable circumstances do bring with them the truth which it conveys. A despot's angry passions do work death or something like death. Think you that if, which 238 Heaven forbid, any of our people should see the

hood, καλοί being used ironically, as perhaps always when applied to persons.

τινες τῶν ἡμετέρων εἰς τὸ ἱερὸν τὸν ἀνδριάντα,
οὐκ ἂν εἰς πέτρους[1] μεταβαλεῖν, παγέντων μὲν
αὐτοῖς τῶν ἄρθρων, παγέντων δὲ τῶν ὀφθαλμῶν,
ὡς μηδὲ κινηθῆναι δύνασθαι, ὅλου δὲ τοῦ σώματος
τὰς φυσικὰς κινήσεις μεταβαλόντος καθ᾽ ἕκαστον
239 τῶν ἐν τῇ κοινωνίᾳ μερῶν αὐτοῦ· τελευταίαν
δέησιν, ὦ Πετρώνιε, ποιησόμεθα δικαιοτάτην· οὔ
φαμεν μὴ δεῖν τὰ κελευσθέντα δρᾶν, ἀλλ᾽ ἀναχώρησιν αἰτούμεθα προσικετεύοντες, ἵνα πρεσβείαν
ἑλόμενοι πέμψωμεν τὴν ἐντευξομένην τῷ δεσπότῃ.
240 τάχα που πρεσβευσάμενοι πείσομεν, ἢ περὶ θεοῦ
τιμῆς πως διεξελθόντες ἢ περὶ νομίμων ἀκαθαιρέ-
των φυλακῆς ἢ περὶ τοῦ μὴ πάντων καὶ τῶν ἐν
ἐσχατιαῖς ἐθνῶν, οἷς τετήρηται τὰ πάτρια, ἔλαττον
ἐνέγκασθαι ἢ περὶ ὧν ὁ πάππος αὐτοῦ καὶ πρόπαππος ἔγνωσαν ἐπισφραγιζόμενοι τὰ ἡμέτερα ἔθη
241 μετὰ πάσης ἐπιμελείας. ἴσως ταῦτα ἀκούων ἔσται
μαλακώτερος· οὐκ ἐν ὁμοίῳ μένουσιν αἱ γνῶμαι
τῶν μεγάλων, αἱ δὲ σὺν ὀργῇ καὶ τάχιστα κά-
μνουσι. διαβεβλήμεθα, τὰς διαβολὰς ἐπίτρεψον
242 ἰάσασθαι· ἀκρίτους καταγνωσθῆναι χαλεπόν. ἐὰν
δὲ μὴ πείσωμεν, τί λοιπὸν ἐμποδών ἐστιν [ἢ]
[582] ταῦτα ἃ καὶ | νῦν διανοῇ πράττειν; ἕως οὐ πε-
πρεσβεύμεθα, μὴ ἀποκόψῃς τὰς ἀμείνους ἐλπίδας
μυριάδων τοσούτων, αἷς οὐχ ὑπὲρ κέρδους ἀλλ᾽
ὑπὲρ εὐσεβείας ἐστὶν ἡ σπουδή. καίτοι γε ἡμάρ-
τομεν τοῦτο εἰπόντες· τί γὰρ ἂν εἴη κέρδος λυσι-
τελέστερον ὁσιότητος ἀνθρώποις;᾽᾽
243 XXXIII. Ταῦτα δὲ διεξῄεσαν ὑπ᾽ ἀγωνίας καὶ
περιπαθήσεως ἄσθματι πολλῷ, κεκομμένῳ τῷ

---

[1] mss. πέτρον.

statue being carried in procession to the temple, they would not be transformed to stone, their joints stiffened and their eyes likewise so that they could not even move, and their whole body in each part of its system changed from its natural motions? Our final prayer, the justest of all, Petronius, will 239 be this. We do not say that you are not bound to do as you are bidden but we add to our supplications a request for a respite so that we may choose a body of envoys and send them to seek an interview with our lord. It may be that by this 240 mission we shall persuade him, pleading in full either the honour due to God or the preservation of our laws undestroyed, or our right to be no worse treated than all the nations, even those in the uttermost regions, who have had their ancestral institutions maintained, or the decisions of his grandfather and great-grandfather in which they ratified our customs with all respect for them. Per- 241 haps when he hears this he will be softened. The judgements of the great do not remain unchanged; if they have been made in anger they soonest lose their strength. We have been slandered, permit us to purge the slanders; it is a grievous thing to be condemned untried. But if we fail to persuade him 242 what remains to hinder you from carrying out your present intention? Wait till we have sent our embassy before you cut away their hopes for better things from all these myriads whose zeal is for their religion and not for gain. And yet we err when we say this, for what more profitable gain can men have than holiness?"

XXXIII. This appeal was made in great agitation 243 and intense emotion accompanied with much gasping

PHILO

πνεύματι, ῥεόμενοι κατὰ τῶν μελῶν ἁπάντων
ἱδρῶτι, μετὰ φορᾶς ἀπαύστων δακρύων, ὡς ἤδη
συναλγεῖν τοὺς ἀκούοντας καὶ τὸν Πετρώνιον—ἦν
γὰρ καὶ τὴν φύσιν εὐμενὴς καὶ ἥμερος—ὑπὸ τῶν
λεχθέντων καὶ ὁρωμένων συνηρπάσθαι· ἐδόκει γὰρ
αὐτῷ καὶ τὰ λεγόμενα εἶναι δικαιότατα καὶ οἰκτρά
244 τις ἡ τῶν ὁρωμένων περιπάθησις. ἐπεξαναστὰς
δὲ μετὰ τῶν συνέδρων ἐβουλεύετο τὰ πρακτέα
καὶ ἑώρα τοὺς μὲν πρὸ μικροῦ παντάπασιν ἐναν-
τιουμένους ἐπαμφοτερίζοντας, τοὺς δὲ ἐνδοιαστὰς
ἐπιρρέποντας ἤδη τῷ πλείονι μέρει πρὸς ἔλεον·
ἐφ' οἷς ἥδετο, καίτοι τὴν φύσιν εἰδὼς τοῦ
προεστῶτος καὶ ὡς ἔστιν ἀπαραίτητος ὀργήν.
245 ἀλλ' εἶχέ τινα καὶ αὐτός, ὡς ἔοικεν, ἐναύσματα
τῆς Ἰουδαϊκῆς φιλοσοφίας ἅμα καὶ εὐσεβείας,
εἴτε καὶ πάλαι προμαθὼν ἕνεκα τῆς περὶ παιδείαν
σπουδῆς εἴτε καὶ ἀφ' οὗ τῶν χώρων ἐπετρόπευσεν,
ἐν οἷς Ἰουδαῖοι καθ' ἑκάστην πόλιν εἰσὶ παμπληθεῖς, Ἀσίας τε καὶ Συρίας, εἴτε καὶ τὴν ψυχὴν
οὕτω διατεθεὶς αὐτήκοῳ καὶ αὐτοκελεύστῳ καὶ
αὐτομαθεῖ τινι πρὸς τὰ σπουδῆς ἄξια φύσει. τοῖς
δὲ ἀγαθοῖς ἀγαθὰς ὑπηχεῖν ἔοικε γνώμας ὁ θεός,
δι' ὧν ὠφελοῦντες ὠφεληθήσονται· ὅπερ κἀκείνῳ
246 συνέβη. τίνες οὖν ἦσαν αἱ γνῶμαι; μὴ κατ-
επείγειν τοὺς δημιουργούς, ἀλλ' ἀναπείθειν εὖ
τετεχνιτευμένον ἀπεργάσασθαι τὸν ἀνδριάντα,
στοχαζομένους καθ' ὅσον ἂν οἷόν τε ᾖ μὴ ἀπολειφ-
θῆναι τῶν διωνομασμένων ἀρχετύπων εἰς πλείο-
νος χρόνου μῆκος, ἐπειδὴ τὰ μὲν αὐτοσχέδια φιλεῖ

ª Or " suggests." For Philo's frequent use of ὑπηχεῖν,
generally carrying with it the idea of a voice heard in-
126

and spasmodic breathing, the sweat streaming over every limb amid a flood of ceaseless tears, so that by now their hearers shared their sorrow, and Petronius who was naturally kindly was quite carried away both by what he heard and what he saw. For he felt that what they said was very just and that the emotion displayed in what he saw was worthy of pity. He rose and retiring deliberated with his 244 fellow-councillors on the course to be taken. He saw that those who had just before been entirely opposed to the Jews were wavering, and that the doubters had thrown most of their weight into the scale of mercy. This pleased him though he knew the nature of his chief and how implacable was his anger. Indeed 245 it appears that he himself had some rudiments of Jewish philosophy and religion acquired either in early lessons in the past through his zeal for culture or after his appointment as governor in the countries where the Jews are very numerous in every city, Asia and Syria, or else because his soul was so disposed, being drawn to things worthy of serious effort by a nature which listened to no voice nor dictation nor teaching but its own. But we find that to good men God whispers [a] good decisions by which they will give and receive benefits, and this was true in his case. What then were his decisions ? He would not press 246 the craftsmen but would urge them to perfect the statue with good artistry and aim as far as possible to take a long time to reach the standard of the widely known exemplars, since work, if perfunctory, is gen-

wardly, often as here the divine voice, see note on *De Som.* i. 164 (vol. v. p. 601). The complete omission of this usage in L. & S., which was remarked on in that note, has since been rectified in the revised edition.

πως ἐπιτέμνεσθαι, τὰ δὲ σὺν πόνῳ καὶ ἐπιστήμῃ
247 μῆκος χρόνων ἐπιζητεῖν. ἣν ᾐτήσαντο πρεσβείαν,
οὐκ ἐπιτρέπειν· ἀσφαλὲς γὰρ οὐκ εἶναι. τοῖς βου-
λομένοις ἐπὶ τὸν πάντων ἡγεμόνα καὶ δεσπότην
ἐκκαλεῖσθαι τὰ πράγματα μὴ ἐναντιοῦσθαι. τῷ
πλήθει μήτε ὁμολογεῖν μήτε ἀρνεῖσθαι· ἑκάτερον
248 γὰρ φέρειν κίνδυνον. ἐπιστέλλειν | Γαΐῳ μηδὲν
[583] μὲν τῶν Ἰουδαίων κατηγοροῦντα, μὴ δηλοῦντα δὲ
ἐπ' ἀληθείας τὰς ἱκετείας καὶ ἀντιβολίας αὐτῶν,
καὶ τῆς περὶ τὴν ἀνάθεσιν βραδυτῆτος αἰτιᾶσθαι
τὸ μέν τι τὴν κατασκευὴν χρόνου μεμετρημένου
δεομένην, τὸ δέ τι καὶ τὸν καιρὸν διδόντα μεγάλας
ἀφορμὰς εἰς ἀναβολὴν εὐλόγους, αἷς συναινέσειν
249 οὐκ ἴσως ἀλλ' ἀναγκαίως καὶ αὐτὸν Γάιον. ἐν
ἀκμῇ μὲν γὰρ τὸν τοῦ σίτου καρπὸν εἶναι καὶ τῶν
ἄλλων ὅσα σπαρτά, δεδιέναι δὲ μὴ κατ' ἀπόγνωσιν
τῶν πατρίων ἄνθρωποι καὶ τοῦ ζῆν καταφρονοῦντες
ἢ δῃώσωσι τὰς ἀρούρας ἢ ἐμπρήσωσι τὴν σταχυη-
φόρον ὀρεινὴν καὶ πεδιάδα, φυλακῆς δὲ χρῄζειν
εἰς ἐπιμελεστέραν τῶν καρπῶν συγκομιδήν, οὐ
μόνον τῶν σπειρομένων ἀλλὰ καὶ ὧν ἡ δενδροφόρος
250 παρέχει. διεγνώκει[1] μὲν γάρ, ὡς λόγος, πλεῖν εἰς
Ἀλεξάνδρειαν τὴν πρὸς Αἰγύπτῳ, πελάγει δὲ οὐκ
ἀξιώσει τοσοῦτος ἡγεμὼν διά τε τοὺς κινδύνους
καὶ διὰ τὸ πλῆθος τοῦ παραπέμποντος στόλου καὶ
ἅμα διὰ τὴν ἐπιμέλειαν τοῦ σώματος, ἃ δὴ πάντα
γίνεται ῥᾳδίως τὸν δι' Ἀσίας καὶ Συρίας κύκλον
251 περαιουμένῳ· δυνήσεται γὰρ καθ' ἑκάστην ἡμέραν
καὶ πλεῖν καὶ ἀποβαίνειν, καὶ μάλιστα τὰς πλείστας
ναῦς ἐπαγόμενος μακράς, ἀλλ' οὐχ ὁλκάδας, αἷς
ὁ παρὰ γῆν πλοῦς ἀνυσιμώτερος, ὡς ταῖς φορτίσι

[1] mss. διέγνωκα μέν.

erally short-lived and to have it executed with pains
and knowledge requires a long time. He would 247
not grant their request for an embassy. It was
not safe. He would not oppose those who wished
to lay the matter before the ruler and master
of them all, but to the general multitude he would
express neither assent nor denial, as both were
dangerous. He would send to Gaius a letter in 248
which, without accusing the Jews or giving a candid
account of their prayers and entreaties, he would
charge the delay in the installation partly to the
work requiring a definite allowance of time for
the construction, partly to the season, which gave
strong grounds for delay, the reasonableness of
which Gaius himself not only might but necessarily
must admit. For the wheat crop was just ripe and 249
so were the other cereals, and he feared that the
Jews in despair for their ancestral rites and in
scorn of life might lay waste the arable land or
set fire to the cornlands on the hills and the plain.
He needed a guard to insure more vigilance in gather-
ing the fruits not only of the cornfields but also those
provided by the orchards. For Gaius had deter- 250
mined, they were told, to sail to Alexandria by Egypt,
but so great a potentate would not think it right to
go by the open sea because of the dangers and the
numbers of ships required for a convoy, and also the
need of providing for his bodily comfort, all which
ends are easily obtained by taking the circuitous route
along Asia and Syria. For he would be able every 251
day to combine the voyage with landing, particularly
as most of the vessels which he would take would
be not merchant ships but warships for which coasting
is more feasible, just as an open sea voyage is for

PHILO

252 διὰ πελάγους ἐστίν. ἀναγκαῖον οὖν καὶ χιλὸν κτήνεσι καὶ τροφὰς ἀφθόνους ἐν ἁπάσαις ταῖς Συριακαῖς πόλεσιν εὐτρεπίσθαι, καὶ μάλιστα ταῖς παράλοις. ἀφίξεται γὰρ παμπληθὴς ὄχλος καὶ διὰ γῆς καὶ διὰ θαλάττης, οὐ μόνον ἀπ' αὐτῆς Ῥώμης καὶ Ἰταλίας ἀναστάς, ἀλλὰ καὶ ἀπὸ τῶν ἐξῆς ἄχρι Συρίας ἐπικρατειῶν ἐπηκολουθηκώς, ὁ μὲν τῶν ἐν τέλει, ὁ δὲ στρατιωτικός, ἱππέων, πεζῶν, τῶν ἐν ταῖς ναυσίν, ὁ δὲ οἰκετικὸς οὐκ ἀποδέων τοῦ

253 στρατιωτικοῦ. δεῖ δὲ χορηγιῶν οὐ πρὸς τὰ ἀναγκαῖα συμμεμετρημένων αὐτῷ[1] μόνον, ἀλλὰ καὶ πρὸς περιττὴν δαψίλειαν, ἢν ἐπιζητεῖ Γάιος. τούτοις ἐὰν ἐντύχῃ τοῖς γράμμασιν, ἴσως πρὸς τῷ μὴ δυσχερᾶναι καὶ τῆς προνοίας ἡμᾶς ἀποδέξεται ὡς ποιησαμένους τὴν ὑπέρθεσιν, οὐ χάριτι τῇ τῶν Ἰουδαίων, ἀλλ' ἕνεκα τῆς τῶν καρπῶν συγκομιδῆς.

254 XXXIV. Ἀποδεξαμένων δὲ τὴν ἐπίνοιαν τῶν συνέδρων, κελεύει γράφεσθαι τὰς ἐπιστολὰς καὶ ἐχειροτόνει τοὺς διακομιοῦντας ἄνδρας εὐζώνους, ἐθάδας δὲ καὶ τῶν κατὰ τὰς ὁδοιπορίας ἐπιτομῶν. καὶ οἱ μὲν ἥκοντες ἀνέδοσαν τὰς ἐπιστολάς, ὁ

[584] δ' ἔτι μὲν ἀναγινώσκων διῴδει | καὶ μεστὸς ἦν

255 ὀργῆς ἐφ' ἑκάστῳ σημειούμενος· ὡς δὲ ἐπαύσατο, συνεκρότει τὰς χεῖρας "εὖ, Πετρώνιε," φάσκων, "οὐκ ἔμαθες ἀκούειν αὐτοκράτορος· αἱ ἐπάλληλοί σε ἀρχαὶ πεφυσήκασιν· ἄχρι τοῦ παρόντος οὐδὲ ἀκοῇ γνωρίζειν μοι δοκεῖς Γάιον, οὐκ εἰς μακρὰν

256 αὐτοῦ πεῖραν ἕξεις. μέλει μὲν γάρ σοι τῶν Ἰουδαϊκῶν νομίμων, ἐχθίστου μοι ἔθνους, ἀλογεῖς δὲ τῶν ἄρχοντος ἡγεμονικῶν προστάξεων. ἐφοβήθης τὸ πλῆθος· εἶτα οὐ παρῆσαν αἱ στρα-

---

[1] mss. αὐτῷ.

130

cargo boats. It would be necessary therefore to have 252 fodder for the beasts and a vast stock of food got ready in all the cities of Syria, particularly on the coast. For a huge crowd would come both by sea and by land, drawn not only from Rome itself and Italy, but also from the successive provinces right up to Syria, a crowd composed partly of persons of high rank, partly of soldiers, infantry and cavalry and marines, while the multitude of servants would be not less than the military. Supplies were needed 253 calculated not merely for absolute necessities but for the excessive expenditure which Gaius demanded. If he reads this letter, thought Petronius, he will probably not merely refrain from anger but approve our forethought, recognizing that the postponement which we have made is not due to favouritism to the Jews but in order to insure the carrying of the harvest.

XXXIV. As his fellow-councillors approved of his 254 policy he ordered the letters to be written, and appointed to carry them persons who were active travellers and also knew how to make short cuts in their journey. When they arrived they delivered the letter, but Gaius while he was still reading was fuming and was filled with wrath as he noted each point. When he stopped reading he smote his hands together 255 and said, " Good, Petronius, you have not learnt to hearken to an emperor ; your successive offices have puffed you with pride. Up to this time you seem to have no knowledge of Gaius even by report ; you will soon know him by actual experience. You concern 256 yourself with the institutions of the Jews, the nation which is my worst enemy ; you disregard the imperial commands of your sovereign. You feared their great numbers. Then had you not with you the military

PHILO

τιωτικαὶ δυνάμεις, ἃς δέδιεν ἔθνη τὰ ἑῷα καὶ
257 ἡγεμόνες αὐτῶν Παρθυαῖοι; ἀλλ' ἠλέησας· εἶτα
οὕτω μᾶλλον ἐνέδωκας ἢ Γαΐῳ; προφασίζου
νῦν ἄμητον, τὸν ἀπροφάσιστον οὐκ εἰς μακρὰν
ἐνδεξόμενος αὐτὸς τῇ κεφαλῇ· συγκομιδὴν αἰτιῶ
καρπῶν καὶ τὰς εἰς τὴν ἡμετέραν ἄφιξιν παρα-
σκευάς· εἰ γὰρ ἀφορία παντελὴς ἐπέσχε τὴν Ἰου-
δαίαν, οὐκ ἦσαν αἱ πλησιόχωροι τοσαῦται καὶ
οὕτως εὐδαίμονες ἱκαναὶ χορηγεῖν τὰ ἐπιτήδεια
258 καὶ τὴν μιᾶς ἔνδειαν ἀναπληρῶσαι; ἀλλὰ τί
προανίσταμαι τῶν χειρῶν; τί δέ μου τῆς γνώμης
προαισθάνονταί τινες· ὁ μέλλων τὰ ἐπίχειρα
καρποῦσθαι γινωσκέτω πρῶτος ἐξ ὧν ἂν πάθῃ.
παύομαι λέγων, φρονῶν δὲ οὐ παύσομαι."
259 καὶ μικρὸν ὅσον ἐπισχὼν τινι τῶν πρὸς ταῖς ἐπιστολαῖς ὑπέβαλε τὰς πρὸς Πετρώνιον ἀποκρίσεις,
ἐπαινῶν αὐτὸν ὅσα τῷ δοκεῖν εἰς τὸ προμηθὲς καὶ
τὴν τοῦ μέλλοντος ἀκριβῆ περίσκεψιν· σφόδρα γὰρ
τοὺς ἐν ἡγεμονίαις εὐλαβεῖτο τὰς πρὸς νεωτεροποιίαν ἀφορμὰς ὁρῶν ἔχοντας ἐν ἑτοίμῳ, καὶ
μάλιστα τοὺς ἐν ταῖς μεγάλαις καὶ μεγάλοις ἐπι-
τάττοντας στρατοπέδοις, ἡλίκα τὰ πρὸς Εὐφράτῃ
260 κατὰ Συρίαν ἐστίν. θεραπεύων οὖν τοῖς ὀνόμασι
καὶ γράμμασιν ἄχρι καιροῦ τὸ ἔγκοτον ἐπεσκίαζε
βαρύμηνις ὤν. εἶτα ἐπὶ πᾶσι γράφει κελεύων
μηδενὸς οὕτω φροντίζειν ἢ τοῦ θᾶττον ἀνατεθῆναι
τὸν ἀνδριάντα· καὶ γὰρ ἤδη τὰ θέρη, τὴν εἴτε
πιθανὴν εἴτε ἀληθῆ πρόφασιν, συγκεκομίσθαι δύνασθαι.
261 XXXV. Μετ' οὐ πολὺ μέντοι παρῆν Ἀγρίππας
ὁ βασιλεὺς κατὰ τὸ εἰωθὸς ἀσπασόμενος Γάιον.

forces which are feared by the nations of the east
and their rulers the Parthians ? Oh but you had 257
compassion ! Then did pity weigh more than Gaius
with you ? Go on, plead the harvest as your pretext ;
the harvest for which no pretext will avail will soon
be visited on your own head. Yes, lay the blame on
the ingathering of the fruits and the preparations
needed for our journey. Why, even if complete
barrenness reigned in Judaea were not the neighbouring countries so many and so prosperous capable of
providing the necessaries and compensating the de-
ficiency in one ? But why should I not sit still till 258
my hands get to work ? why should any people know
my intentions beforehand ? he who is to reap the
reward, let him know of it before others through
personal experience. I stop speaking, but I shall not
stop thinking." After waiting a short 259
time he gave one of his secretaries instructions about
answering Petronius. In these he seemingly praised
him for his forethought and his careful exploration
of future requirements. For he greatly feared the
holders of governorships, he saw that they had re-
sources ready for an uprising, particularly those who
had large provinces and commanded large armies of
the size of those in Syria on the Euphrates. So his 260
language and letters were ingratiating, and though
furiously angry he disguised his rancour waiting for
an opportunity. Then he concluded his letter by
bidding him interest himself in nothing so much as
in hastening the installation of the statue, since the
harvest which he alleged as an excuse, whether truly
or plausibly, could already have been carried.

XXXV. Not long afterwards King Agrippa ap- 261
peared to pay his wonted respects to Gaius. Now he

ἤδει δὲ ἁπλῶς οὐδὲν οὔτε ὧν ἐπεστάλκει ὁ Πετρώνιος οὔτε ὧν ὁ Γάιος ἢ πρότερον ἢ ὕστερον·
ἐτεκμαίρετο μέντοι διὰ τῆς οὐκ ἐν τάξει κινήσεως καὶ τῆς τῶν ὀμμάτων ταραχῆς ὑποτυφομένην
ὀργὴν καὶ ἀνεσκόπει καὶ διηρεύνα ἑαυτὸν πάντη
καὶ πρὸς πάντα μικρά τε αὖ καὶ μεγάλα τὸν λογισμὸν ἀποτείνων, μή τι δέδρακεν ἢ εἶπεν ὧν οὐ χρή.
262 ὡς δὲ συνόλως οὐδὲν εὕρισκεν, ἐτόπασεν, ὅπερ ἦν
εἰκός, ἑτέροις τισὶ πικραίνεσθαι. πάλιν δὲ ὅτε
ὑποβλεπόμενον εἶδε καὶ τετακότα τὰς ὄψεις πρὸς
μηδένα τῶν παρόντων ἢ μόνον ἐπ' αὐτόν, ἐδεδίει |
[585] καὶ πολλάκις ἐρέσθαι διανοηθεὶς ἐπέσχε, τοιοῦτον
λαμβάνων λογισμόν· "ἴσως τὴν ἀπειλὴν πρὸς
ἑτέρους οὖσαν αὐτὸς ἕλξω περιεργίας ὁμοῦ καὶ
προπετείας καὶ θράσους ὑπόληψιν ἐξενεγκάμενος."
263 ἐπτοημένον δ' οὖν καὶ ἀποροῦντα θεασάμενος
αὐτὸν Γάιος—ἦν γὰρ δεινὸς ἐκ τῆς φανερᾶς ὄψεως
ἀφανὲς ἀνθρώπου βούλημα καὶ πάθος συνιδεῖν—
"ἀπορεῖς," εἶπεν "Ἀγρίππα; παύσω σε τῆς
264 ἀπορίας. ἐπὶ τοσοῦτόν μοι χρόνον συνδιατρίψας
ἠγνόησας, ὅτι οὐ τῇ φωνῇ μόνον ἀλλὰ καὶ τοῖς
ὄμμασι φθέγγομαι μᾶλλον ἢ οὐχ ἧττον ἕκαστα
265 διασημαίνων; οἱ καλοί σου καὶ ἀγαθοὶ πολῖται,
παρ' οἷς μόνοις ἐξ ἅπαντος ἀνθρώπων γένους θεὸς
οὐ νομίζεται Γάιος, ἤδη μοι δοκοῦσι καὶ θανατᾶν
ἀφηνιάζοντες· ἐμοῦ κελεύσαντος ἐν τῷ ἱερῷ Διὸς
ἀνδριάντα ἀνατεθῆναι, πανδημεὶ συνταξάμενοι τῆς
πόλεως καὶ τῆς χώρας ὑπεξῆλθον, πρόφασιν ἱκε-
τεύσοντες, τὸ δ' ἀληθὲς ἐναντία τοῖς προστεταγ-
266 μένοις ἐργασόμενοι." μέλλοντος δὲ προσεπιφέρειν
ἕτερα, ὑπ' ἀγωνίας παντοδαπὰς χρόας ἐνήλλαττεν

knew absolutely nothing about the contents of the letter sent by Petronius or of those written earlier and later by Gaius. He judged however by his irregular movements and the disturbance shown in his eyes that anger was smouldering beneath, and he examined and searched himself in every way, setting his reason to work in every direction and on every possibility small or great, to see whether he had done or said something which he should not. But when he could 262 find nothing at all he conjectured naturally enough that Gaius was exasperated by some other persons, but again when he saw him frowning and that his eyes had been fixed on no one else in the company but himself alone, he was frightened and though he was often minded to question him he forbore, reasoning thus : " Perhaps I shall draw upon myself the menace directed to others and have officiousness, rashness and effrontery imputed to me." Gaius, who 263 was skilled in discerning a man's secret wishes and feelings from his open countenance, observed his agitation and perplexity and said, " You are perplexed, Agrippa, I will release you from your perplexity. Have you sojourned with me all this time and 264 not learnt that I speak not only with my voice but quite as much with my eyes in every intimation that I make ? Your excellent and worthy fellow-citizens, 265 who alone of every race of men do not acknowledge Gaius as a god, appear to be courting even death by their recalcitrance. When I ordered a statue of Zeus to be set up in the temple they marshalled their whole population and issued forth from the city and country nominally to make a petition but actually to counteract my orders." He was about to add 266 further charges when Agrippa in deep distress turned

135

ἐν ταὐτῷ γινόμενος αἱμωπός, ὠχρός, πελιδνός.
267 ἤδη δὲ καὶ ἀπὸ κεφαλῆς ἄκρας ἄχρι ποδῶν φρίκη
κατέσχητο, τρόμος τε καὶ σεισμὸς πάντα αὐτοῦ
τὰ μέρη καὶ τὰ μέλη συνεκύκα, χαλωμένων τε
καὶ ἀνιεμένων τῶν σωματικῶν τόνων περὶ ἑαυτῷ
κατέρρει καὶ τὰ τελευταῖα παρεθεὶς μικροῦ κατ-
έπεσεν, εἰ μὴ τῶν παρεστώτων τινὲς ὑπέλαβον
αὐτόν· καὶ κελευσθέντες φοράδην οἴκαδε κομίζουσιν
οὐδενὸς συναισθανόμενον ὑπὸ κάρου τῶν ἀθρόων
268 κατασκηψάντων κακῶν.   ὁ μὲν οὖν Γάιος
ἔτι μᾶλλον ἐξετραχύνθη τὸ κατὰ τοῦ ἔθνους μῖσος
ἐπιτείνων· " εἰ γὰρ Ἀγρίππας," ἔφασκεν, " ὁ
συνηθέστατος καὶ φίλτατος καὶ τοσαύταις ἐνδε-
δεμένος εὐεργεσίαις ἥττηται τῶν ἐθῶν, ὡς μηδὲ
ἀκοὴν ἀνέχεσθαι τὴν κατ' αὐτῶν, ἀλλ' ὑπ' ἐκλύ-
σεως μικροῦ καὶ τελευτῆσαι, τί χρὴ περὶ τῶν
ἄλλων προσδοκᾶν, οἷς μηδεμία πρόσεστιν ὁλκὸς
269 δύναμις εἰς τοὐναντίον;" ὁ δὲ Ἀγρίππας τὴν
μὲν πρώτην ἡμέραν καὶ τὸ πλεῖστον μέρος τῆς
ὑστεραίας ὑπὸ κάρου πιεσθεὶς βαθέος οὐδὲν ἐγνώ-
ριζε τῶν ὄντων, περὶ δὲ δείλην ἑσπέραν μικρὸν
ὅσον τὴν κεφαλὴν ἐπάρας καὶ βεβαρημένους τοὺς
ὀφθαλμοὺς ἐπὶ βραχὺ μόλις διοίξας ἀμαυραῖς καὶ
ἀχλυώδεσι ταῖς ὄψεσι τοὺς ἐν κύκλῳ παρεθεᾶτο,
μήπω γνωρίζειν δυνάμενος ἐπ' ἀκριβὲς τὰς ἑκά-
270 στων ἰδέας.   πάλιν δὲ ὑπενεχθεὶς εἰς ὕπνον ἠρέμει
τῆς προτέρας ὑγιεινοτέρᾳ καταστάσει χρώμενος,
ὡς ἐνῆν ἔκ τε τῆς ἀναπνοῆς καὶ ἐκ τῆς περὶ τὸ
[586] σῶμα σχέσεως τεκμήρασθαι. | περιαναστὰς δὲ
271 ὕστερον ἐπυνθάνετο· "ποῦ τὰ νῦν εἰμι; μήτι
παρὰ Γαΐῳ; μὴ καὶ αὐτὸς πάρεστιν ὁ δεσπότης;"
ἀποκριναμένων δέ· " θάρρει, παρὰ σαυτῷ διατρί-
136

to every kind of colour, blood-red, dead pale and livid all in a moment. And by now from the crown of his 267 head to his feet he was mastered by a fit of shuddering, every part and every limb convulsed with trembling and palpitation. With his nervous system relaxed and unbraced he was in a state of utter collapse, and finally thus paralysed was on the point of falling. But some of the bystanders caught him and, when ordered to bring him home, took him thither on a stretcher, quite unconscious in his coma of the mass of troubles which had fallen upon him. Gaius indeed was still more ex- 268 asperated and pushed his hatred of the nation still further. "If Agrippa," he said, "who is my dearest and most familiar friend and bound to me by so many benefactions, is so under the dominion of its customs that he cannot even bear to hear a word against them and is prostrated almost to the point of death, what must we expect of the others who are not under the influence of any counter-acting force?" On the other hand Agrippa for the first 269 day and the greater part of the next lay sunk in profound coma and knew nothing of what went on. But about the late afternoon he lifted his head slightly and just managed to open his eyes a little, weary as they were, and with their dim and misty vision cast a half look on those around him, unable as yet to distinguish clearly their several forms. Then again 270 he dropped off into sleep and rested quietly in a healthier condition than before, as far as could be judged from his revival and the state of his body. Afterwards he woke up and asked, "Where am I 271 now? At Gaius's? is my lord also present?" They replied, "Cheer up, you are staying in your

272 βεις, Γάιος οὐ πάρεστιν· ἱκανῶς ἠρέμησας ⟨ὑπενεχ-
θεὶς⟩ εἰς ὕπνον· ἀλλ' ἐπιστραφεὶς καὶ μετεωρίσας
σαυτὸν τὸν ἀγκῶνα πῆξον, γνώρισον τοὺς παρόν-
τας· ἴδιοι πάντες εἰσί, φίλων καὶ ἀπελευθέρων καὶ
οἰκετῶν οἱ μάλιστα τιμῶντες καὶ ἀντιτιμώμενοι ''

273 —ὁ δὲ—νήφειν γὰρ ἤρχετο—καθεώρα τὸ παρ' ἑκάστῳ συμπαθές· καὶ κελευσάντων τοὺς πολλοὺς
μεταστῆναι τῶν ἰατρῶν, ἵνα δι' ἀλειμμάτων καὶ

274 τροφῆς καιρίου τὸ σωμάτιον ἀνακτήσωνται, '' πάνυ
γάρ,'' εἶπε, '' φροντιστέον ὑμῖν ἐπιμελεστέρας τῆς
εἰς ἐμὲ διαίτης; οὐ γὰρ ἐξαρκεῖ μοι τῷ βαρυδαί-
μονι λιμὸν ἀκέσασθαι διὰ ψιλῆς καὶ εἰς εὐτέλειαν
ἀπηκριβωμένης τῆς τῶν ἀναγκαίων χρήσεως; οὐδ'
αὐτὰ δὴ ταῦτα προσηκάμην ἄν, εἰ μὴ ἕνεκα τελευταίας βοηθείας, ἣν ὀνειροπολεῖ μου ἡ διάνοια

275 τῷ ταλαιπώρῳ ἔθνει παρασχεῖν.'' καὶ ὁ μὲν
δεδακρυμένος καὶ ἀναγκοφαγῶν δίχα προσοψή-
ματος οὐδὲ κράματος προσενεχθέντος ἠνέσχετο,
ἀλλ' ὕδατος ἀπογευσάμενος, '' ἀπέχει[1] μέν,'' εἶπεν,
'' ἡ τάλαινα γαστὴρ ὃ ἀπῄτει δάνειον· ἐμοὶ δὲ
τί προσήκει ποιεῖν ἢ δεῖσθαι Γαΐου περὶ τῶν
ἐνεστώτων; ''

276 XXXVI. Καὶ δέλτον λαβὼν ταῦτα ἐπιστέλλει·
'' τὴν μὲν κατ' ὄψιν ἔντευξιν, ὦ δέσποτα, φόβος
με καὶ αἰδὼς ἀφείλαντο, ὁ μὲν ἀπειλὴν ἐκτρεπό-
μενος, ἡ δὲ τῷ μεγέθει τοῦ περὶ σὲ ἀξιώματος

---

[1] Reiter prints ἐπέχει from A only. I do not understand
why, for ἀπέχω in the sense of '' receive in full '' is well known,
e.g., St. Matth. vi. 2. No such sense is cited for ἐπέχω.

---

[a] For the medical use of σωμάτιον for a sick man's body
under treatment see examples in L. & S. revised.

[b] πάνυ may be regarded as introducing a question, or an

own house ; Gaius is not here ; you got a good rest 272
when you fell asleep ; now turn round, lift yourself
up, lean upon your elbow and recognize the company present. They are all your own people, those
of your friends and freedmen and servants who most
value you and are valued by you." He was begin- 273
ning to come to his sober senses and observed the
sympathy shown by all, and when the physicians told
most of them to leave the room so that they might
restore their patient [a] with unguents and suitable
nourishment he said, " The idea of troubling your- 274
selves to give me a more elaborate diet ! [b] Isn't it
enough for me, ill-fated wretch that I am, to assuage
hunger merely with the use of bare necessities carefully calculated to maintain economy ?—and even
these I would not have accepted save to insure the
last remaining help which it is the dream of my
heart to give to the unhappy nation." Tearfully he 275
forced himself to swallow some food without anything to season it, and even refused the offer of
a mixed drink, and merely took a taste of water
instead. " The belly," he said, " poor creature,
has been paid in full the debt which it claimed.
What should I now do but make my petition to Gaius
about the present situation ? "

XXXVI. He took a tablet and wrote to him as 276
follows : " My opportunity, my master, of interced-
ing with you face to face has been lost through
fear and reverend shame, fear which could not
confront the menace, reverence which struck me
dumb before the greatness of your dignity. But

ironical affirmation. In either case the sentence indicates a
strong repudiation, though no example of any such use is
given in Stephanus or L. & S.

καταπλήττουσα· γραφὴ δὲ μηνύσει μου τὴν δέησιν,
277 ἣν ἀνθ᾿ ἱκετηρίας προτείνω.   πᾶσιν ἀνθρώποις,
αὐτοκράτορ, ἐμπέφυκεν ἔρως μὲν τῆς πατρίδος,
τῶν δὲ οἰκείων νόμων ἀποδοχή· καὶ περὶ τούτων
οὐδεμιᾶς ἐστί σοι χρεία διδασκαλίας, ἐκθύμως μὲν
στέργοντι τὴν πατρίδα, ἐκθύμως δὲ τὰ πάτρια
τιμῶντι.   καλὰ δὲ ἑκάστοις, εἰ καὶ μὴ πρὸς ἀλή-
θειάν ἐστι, διαφαίνεται τὰ οἰκεῖα· κρίνουσι γὰρ
αὐτὰ οὐ λογισμῷ μᾶλλον ἢ τῷ τῆς εὐνοίας πάθει.
278 γεγέννημαι μέν, ὡς οἶδας, Ἰουδαῖος· ἔστι δέ μοι
Ἱεροσόλυμα πατρίς, ἐν ᾗ ὁ τοῦ ὑψίστου θεοῦ νεὼς
ἅγιος ἵδρυται· πάππων δὲ καὶ προγόνων βασιλέων
ἔλαχον, ὧν οἱ πλείους ἐλέγοντο ἀρχιερεῖς, τὴν
βασιλείαν τῆς ἱερωσύνης ἐν δευτέρᾳ τάξει τιθέμενοι
καὶ νομίζοντες, ὅσῳ θεὸς ἀνθρώπων διαφέρει κατὰ
τὸ κρεῖττον, τοσούτῳ καὶ βασιλείας ἀρχιερωσύνην[1]·
τὴν μὲν γὰρ εἶναι θεοῦ θεραπείαν, τὴν δὲ ἐπιμέλειαν
279 ἀνθρώπων.   ἔθνει δὴ τοιούτῳ προσκεκληρωμένος
καὶ πατρίδι καὶ ἱερῷ δέομαι ὑπὲρ ἁπάντων· τοῦ
μὲν ἔθνους, ἵνα μὴ τὴν ἐναντίαν δόξαν ἐνέγκηται
τῆς ἀληθείας, εὐσεβέστατα καὶ ὁσιώτατα διακεί-
[587] μενον | ἐξ ἀρχῆς πρὸς ἅπαντα τὸν ὑμέτερον οἶκον·
280 ἐν οἷς γὰρ ἐφεῖται καὶ ἔξεστι μετὰ νόμων εὐσεβεῖν,
οὐδενὸς οὔτε τῶν Ἀσιανῶν οὔτε τῶν ἐν Εὐρώπῃ
λείπεται τὸ παράπαν, εὐχαῖς, ἀναθημάτων κατα-
σκευαῖς, πλήθει θυσιῶν, οὐ μόνον ἐν ταῖς κατὰ
τὰς δημοτελεῖς ἑορτὰς ἀναγομέναις, ἀλλὰ καὶ ἐν
ταῖς καθ᾿ ἑκάστην ἡμέραν ἐντελεχέσιν· ἐξ ὧν οὐ
στόματι καὶ γλώσσῃ μηνύουσι τὸ εὐσεβὲς μᾶλλον

---

[1] mss. ἀρχιερωσύνη.

140

my handwriting will declare to you the petition which I put forward instead of the suppliant's olive branch. All men, my emperor, have planted in 277 them a passionate love of their native land and a high esteem for their own laws ; and on this there is no need to instruct you, who love your native city as ardently as you honour your own customs. Every people is convinced of the excellence of its own institutions, even if they are not really excellent, for they judge them not so much by their reasoning as by the affection which they feel for them. I as you know am by birth a Jew, and my 278 native city is Jerusalem in which is situated the sacred shrine of the most high God. It fell to me to have for my grandparents and ancestors kings, most of whom had the title of high priest, who considered their kingship inferior to the priesthood, holding that the office of high priest is as superior in excellence to that of king as God surpasses men. For the office of one is to worship God, of the other to have charge of men. As my lot is 279 cast in such a nation, city and temple I beseech you for them all. For the nation, that it may not get a reputation the reverse of the truth, when from the very first it has been so piously and religiously disposed to all your house. For in all 280 matters in which piety is enjoined and permitted under the laws it stood not a whit behind any other either in Asia or in Europe, in its prayers, its erection of votive offerings, its number of sacrifices, not only of those offered at general national feasts but in the perpetual and daily rites through which is declared their piety, not so much with mouth and tongue as in intentions formed in the secrecy of the soul by those

ἢ ψυχῆς ἀφανοῦς βουλεύμασιν οἱ μὴ λέγοντες, ὅτι
φιλοκαίσαρές εἰσιν, ἀλλ' ὄντες ὄντως.

281 περὶ δὲ τῆς ἱεροπόλεως τὰ προσήκοντά μοι λεκ-
τέον· αὕτη, καθάπερ ἔφην, ἐμὴ μέν ἐστι πατρίς,
μητρόπολις δὲ οὐ μιᾶς χώρας Ἰουδαίας ἀλλὰ καὶ
τῶν πλείστων, διὰ τὰς ἀποικίας ἃς ἐξέπεμψεν ἐπὶ
καιρῶν εἰς μὲν τὰς ὁμόρους, Αἴγυπτον, Φοινίκην,
Συρίαν τήν τε ἄλλην καὶ τὴν Κοίλην προσαγορευο-
μένην, εἰς δὲ τὰς πόρρω διῳκισμένας, Παμφυλίαν,
Κιλικίαν, τὰ πολλὰ τῆς Ἀσίας ἄχρι Βιθυνίας καὶ
τῶν τοῦ Πόντου μυχῶν, τὸν αὐτὸν τρόπον καὶ
εἰς Εὐρώπην, Θετταλίαν, Βοιωτίαν, Μακεδονίαν,
Αἰτωλίαν, τὴν Ἀττικήν, Ἄργος, Κόρινθον, τὰ

282 πλεῖστα καὶ ἄριστα Πελοποννήσου. καὶ οὐ μόνον
αἱ ἤπειροι μεσταὶ τῶν Ἰουδαϊκῶν ἀποικιῶν εἰσιν,
ἀλλὰ καὶ νήσων αἱ δοκιμώταται, Εὔβοια, Κύπρος,
Κρήτη. καὶ σιωπῶ τὰς πέραν Εὐφράτου· πᾶσαι
γὰρ ἔξω μέρους βραχέος, Βαβυλὼν καὶ τῶν ἄλλων
σατραπειῶν αἱ ἀρετῶσαν ἔχουσαι τὴν ἐν κύκλῳ

283 γῆν Ἰουδαίους ἔχουσιν οἰκήτορας. ὥστ' ἐὰν μετα-
λάβῃ σου τῆς εὐμενείας ἡ ἐμὴ πατρίς, οὐ μία
πόλις ἀλλὰ καὶ μυρίαι τῶν ἄλλων εὐεργετοῦνται
καθ' ἕκαστον κλίμα τῆς οἰκουμένης ἱδρυθεῖσαι, τὸ
Εὐρωπαῖον, τὸ Ἀσιανόν, τὸ Λιβυκόν, τὸ ἐν ἠπεί-
ροις, τὸ ἐν νήσοις, πάραλόν τε καὶ μεσόγειον.

284 ἁρμόττει δέ σου τῷ μεγέθει τῆς τοσαύτης τύχης
διὰ τῶν εἰς μίαν πόλιν εὐεργεσιῶν μυρίας ἄλλας
συνευεργετεῖν, ὅπως διὰ πάντων τῶν τῆς οἰκουμένης μερῶν ᾄδηταί σου τὸ κλέος καὶ οἱ μετ'

285 εὐχαριστίας ἔπαινοι συνηχῶνται. φίλων ἐνίων
πατρίδας ὅλας[1] τῆς Ῥωμαϊκῆς ἠξίωσας πολιτείας,

---

[1] mss. ὅλης.

who do not tell you that they love their Caesar but love him in very truth.   As for the holy 281 city, I must say what befits me to say. While she, as I have said, is my native city she is also the mother city not of one country Judaea but of most of the others in virtue of the colonies sent out at divers times to the neighbouring lands Egypt, Phoenicia, the part of Syria called the Hollow and the rest as well and the lands lying far apart, Pamphylia, Cilicia, most of Asia up to Bithynia and the corners of Pontus, similarly also into Europe, Thessaly, Boeotia, Macedonia, Aetolia, Attica, Argos, Corinth and most of the best parts of Peloponnese. And not only are 282 the mainlands full of Jewish colonies but also the most highly esteemed of the islands Euboea, Cyprus, Crete. I say nothing of the countries beyond the Euphrates, for except for a small part they all, Babylon and of the other satrapies those where the land within their confines *a* is highly fertile, have Jewish inhabitants. So that if my own home-city 283 is granted a share of your goodwill the benefit extends not to one city but to myriads of the others situated in every region of the inhabited world whether in Europe or in Asia or in Libya, whether in the mainlands or on the islands, whether it be seaboard or inland. It well befits the magnitude of 284 your great good fortune that by benefiting one city you should benefit myriads of others also so that through every part of the world your glory should be celebrated and your praises mingled with thanksgiving resound. Some of your friends have had their 285 homelands as a whole deemed worthy by you of

a Or " the land round them," the satrapy being identified with its capital.

PHILO

καὶ γεγόνασιν οἱ πρὸ μικροῦ δοῦλοι δεσπόται
ἑτέρων· καὶ τῶν ἀπολελαυκότων τῆς χάριτος μᾶλ-
286 λον ἢ οὐχ ἧττον οἱ δι' οὓς γέγονεν ἥδονται. κἀγώ
τίς εἰμι τῶν εἰδότων μὲν ὅτι δεσπότην ἔχω καὶ
κύριον, κεκριμένων δὲ ἐν τῇ τάξει τῶν ἑταίρων,
[388] ἀξιώματος μὲν ἕνεκα οὐ πολλῶν ὕστερος, | εὐνοίας
287 δὲ οὐδενὸς δεύτερος, ἵνα μὴ λέγω πρῶτος. διά τε
οὖν τὸ πεφυκέναι¹ καὶ διὰ τὸ πλῆθος τῶν εὐεργεσιῶν, αἷς με κατεπλούτισας, θαρρήσας ἂν ἴσως
αἰτήσασθαι τῇ πατρίδι καὶ αὐτός, εἰ καὶ μὴ τὴν
Ῥωμαϊκὴν πολιτείαν, ἐλευθερίαν γοῦν ἢ φόρων
ἄφεσιν, οὐδὲν ἀπετόλμησα τοιοῦτον αἰτήσασθαι,
τὸ δὲ φορητότατον, χάριν σοὶ μὲν ἀζήμιον δοῦναι,
τῇ δὲ πατρίδι λαβεῖν ὠφελιμωτάτην· τί γὰρ ἂν
γένοιτο εὐμενείας ἡγεμόνος ὑπηκόοις ἄμεινον
288 ἀγαθόν; ἐν Ἱεροσολύμοις πρῶτον, αὐτοκράτορ,
ἠγγέλη σου ἡ εὐκταία διαδοχή, καὶ ἀπὸ τῆς ἱεροπόλεως ἐπὶ τὰς παρ' ἑκάτερα ἠπείρους ἐχώρησεν
ἡ φήμη· προνομίας καὶ διὰ τοῦτο τυγχάνειν ἐστὶν
289 ἀξία παρὰ σοί. καθάπερ γὰρ ἐν ταῖς συγγενείαις
οἱ πρεσβύτατοι παῖδες τυγχάνουσι πρεσβείων, ὅτι
πρῶτοι τὸ πατρὸς καὶ τὸ μητρὸς ὄνομα τοῖς
γονεῦσιν ἐφήμισαν, τὸν αὐτὸν τρόπον, ἐπειδὴ τῶν
ἀνατολικῶν πρώτη πόλις αὕτη σε προσεῖπεν
αὐτοκράτορα, δικαία τυγχάνειν πλειόνων ἐστὶν
290 ἀγαθῶν, εἰ δὲ μή, τῶν γοῦν ἴσων. τοσαῦτα δικαιο-
λογηθεὶς καὶ δεηθεὶς ἅμα περὶ τῆς πατρίδος εἰμὶ
τὸ τελευταῖον ἐπὶ τὴν ⟨περὶ⟩ τοῦ ἱεροῦ δέησιν.
τοῦτο, Γάιε δέσποτα, τὸ ἱερὸν χειρόκμητον οὐδεμίαν ἐξ ἀρχῆς μορφὴν παρεδέξατο διὰ τὸ ἔθος τοῦ

¹ Α τὸ πεφυκέναι εὖ, Mangey τὸ ⟨τοιοῦτος⟩ πεφυκέναι.

Roman citizenship, and men who but now were slaves have become masters of others. The pleasure which this gracious action gives to those who have enjoyed it is felt quite as much if not more by those for whose sake it was done. I myself, being one of those who 286 while knowing we have a lord and master have been chosen to rank among your companions, am in dignity inferior to few and in loyalty second to none, I might almost say the first. And though, because I am what 287 I am and in view of the multitude of benefits with which you have enriched me I might perhaps have had the courage to beg myself that my homeland should obtain if not Roman citizenship at least freedom and remission of tribute, I have felt it would be overbold to ask for anything of the kind and only prefer the very modest request of a favour which you will lose nothing by giving and my country will best profit by receiving. For what greater boon can subjects have than the goodwill of their ruler? It 288 was in Jerusalem, my emperor, that your much-prayed-for succession was first announced, and from the holy city the rumour travelled to the mainlands on both sides, and for that reason it deserves to hold the premier place in your esteem. For just as in 289 families the oldest children hold the primacy because they have been the first to give the name of father and mother to their parents, so too this city since it was the first of eastern cities to address you as emperor deserves to receive greater boons than they or at least no less. Having said thus much as a 290 claimant for justice and as a suppliant also on behalf of my native place I come finally to my supplication for the temple. This temple, my Lord Gaius, has never from the first admitted any figure wrought by

PHILO

ἀληθοῦς εἶναι θεοῦ· γραφέων μὲν γὰρ καὶ πλαστῶν
ἔργα μιμήματα τῶν αἰσθητῶν θεῶν εἰσιν· τὸν δὲ
ἀόρατον εἰκονογραφεῖν ἢ διαπλάττειν οὐχ ὅσιον
291 ἐνομίσθη τοῖς ἡμετέροις προγόνοις. Ἀγρίππας
ἐτίμησε τὸ ἱερὸν ἐλθών, ὁ πάππος σου, καὶ ὁ
Σεβαστὸς διὰ τοῦ κελεῦσαι τὰς πανταχόθεν ἀπαρχὰς ἐπιστολαῖς[1] πέμπειν ἐκεῖσε καὶ διὰ τῆς ἐντε-
292 λεχοῦς θυσίας· καὶ ἡ προμάμμη σου * * *[2] ὅθεν
οὐδείς, οὐχ Ἕλλην, οὐ βάρβαρος, οὐ σατράπης, οὐ
βασιλεύς, οὐκ ἐχθρὸς ἄσπονδος, οὐ στάσις, οὐ
πόλεμος, οὐχ ἅλωσις, οὐ πόρθησις, οὐκ ἄλλο τι
τῶν ὄντων οὐδὲν ἐνεωτέρισέ ποτε οὕτως εἰς τὸν
νεών, ὡς ἄγαλμα ἢ ξόανον ἤ τι τῶν χειροκμήτων
293 ἱδρύσασθαι. καὶ γὰρ εἰ τοῖς οἰκήτορσι τῆς χώρας
[589] ἀπήχθοντο δυσμενεῖς ὄντες, ἀλλ' αἰδώς γέ | τις
ἢ φόβος εἰσῄει παραλῦσαί τι τῶν ἐξ ἀρχῆς νενο-
μισμένων ἐπὶ τιμῇ τοῦ ποιητοῦ τῶν ὅλων καὶ
πατρός· ᾔδεσαν γὰρ ἐκ τούτων καὶ τῶν ὁμοιοτρόπων τὰς τῶν θεηλάτων κακῶν φυομένας ἀνηκέστους
συμφοράς. ἧς χάριν αἰτίας ἀσεβὲς σπέρμα σπείρειν
εὐλαβοῦντο δεδιότες, μὴ θερίζειν ἀναγκασθῶσι
τοὺς ἐπ' ὀλέθρῳ παντελεῖ καρπούς.

---

[1] The position of ἐπιστολαῖς seems very strange, if not
impossible. Mangey suggests transposition—presumably in
juxtaposition to κελεῦσαι—or correction to ἀποστολαῖς = " by
missions " (of persons chosen for the purpose). But the
evidence he cites for this use does not seem to do away with
its superfluity after πέμπειν.

[2] The supposed lacuna suggested by Mangey is supported
by Cohn and Reiter. It certainly looks as if some words had
fallen out anticipating what is said of Julia Augusta (Livia)
in § 319, as ἐλθών anticipates the account of Agrippa in

men's hands, because it is the sanctuary of the true
God. For the works of painters and modellers are
representations of gods perceived by sense but to
paint or mould a likeness of the invisible was held by
our ancestors to be against their religion. Your 291
grandfather Agrippa visited and paid honour to the
temple, and so did Augustus by the letters in which he
ordered the first fruits to be sent from every quarter
and by instituting the perpetual sacrifice. Your
great-grandmother too . . . Thus no one, Greek or 292
non-Greek, no satrap, no king, no mortal enemy, no
faction, no war, no storming or sacking of the city,
nor any existing thing ever brought about so great
a violation of the temple as the setting up in it of
an image or statue or any hand-wrought object
for worship. For even if they were ill-disposed and 293
hostile to the inhabitants of the land yet an instinct
of reverence or fear warned them against breaking
down any of the customs observed from the first
in honour of the Maker and Father of all, for they
knew that it was from these and like actions that
the irreparable calamities of divine visitations spring.
Therefore they took good care not to sow the seed
of impiety, lest they should be compelled to reap
its fruits which bring utter destruction.

---

§§ 294–297, and the words about Augustus anticipate §§ 311–
318. But I should not expect more than something like δι' ὧν
ἐδωρήσατο, since ἐτίμησε has all three persons for its subject.
Mangey however thought that something more was required
on the grounds that § 292 has no logical connexion with
§ 291. But if we regard that section as parenthetical there is
a sufficient logical connexion between §§ 290 and 292, and it
is quite in Philo's manner to have causal clauses which
connect with something which has not immediately preceded.
See Introd. pp. xxi-xxiii.

294 XXXVII. "'Αλλὰ τί μοι ξένους καλεῖν μάρτυρας
ἔχοντι πολλοὺς τῶν οἰκειοτάτων σοι παραστῆσαι;
Μάρκος Ἀγρίππας εὐθέως, ὁ πρὸς μητρός σου
πάππος, ἐν Ἰουδαίᾳ γενόμενος, ἡνίκα Ἡρώδης
ὁ ἐμὸς πάππος ἐβασίλευε τῆς χώρας, ἀναβῆναι
μὲν ἀπὸ θαλάττης εἰς τὴν μητρόπολιν ἐν μεσογείῳ
295 κειμένην ἠξίωσε· θεασάμενος δὲ τὸ ἱερὸν καὶ τὸν
τῶν ἱερέων κόσμον καὶ τὴν τῶν ἐγχωρίων ἁγι-
στείαν, ἠγάσθη χρῆμα νομίσας ὑπέρσεμνόν τι καὶ
παντὸς λόγου μεῖζον ἑωρακέναι, καὶ διήγημα οὐδὲν
ἦν ἕτερον αὐτῷ πρὸς τοὺς συνόντας τότε τῶν
ἑταίρων ἢ ὁ τοῦ νεὼ καὶ τῶν κατ' αὐτὸν ἁπάντων
296 ἔπαινος. ὅσας γοῦν ἡμέρας διέτριψεν ἐν τῇ πόλει
κατὰ χάριν τὴν πρὸς Ἡρώδην, ἐφοίτησεν εἰς τὸ
τέμενος τερπόμενος τῇ θέᾳ καὶ τῆς κατασκευῆς
καὶ τῶν θυσιῶν καὶ τῆς περὶ τὰ ἱερουργούμενα
λειτουργίας καὶ τάξεως καὶ τῆς περὶ τὸν ἀρχιερέα
σεμνότητος, ὁπότε ἀσκηθείη τῇ ἱερᾷ στολῇ καὶ
297 κατάρχοι τῶν ἱερῶν. ἀναθήμασι δὲ κοσμήσας
ὅσοις ἐξῆν τὸ ἱερὸν καὶ τοὺς οἰκήτορας εὐεργετήσας
ὅσα μὴ βλάψει χαριζόμενος, Ἡρώδην εὐφημήσας
πολλὰ καὶ εὐφημηθεὶς μυρία, παρεπέμφθη μέχρι
λιμένων, οὐχ ὑπὸ μιᾶς πόλεως, ἀλλ' ὑπὸ τῆς
χώρας ἁπάσης, φυλλοβολούμενός τε καὶ θαυμαζό-
298 μενος ἐπ' εὐσεβείᾳ. τί δὲ ὁ ἕτερός σου
πάππος Τιβέριος Καῖσαρ; οὐχὶ ταὐτὰ φαίνεται
προῃρημένος; ἐν γοῦν τρισὶ καὶ εἴκοσιν ἔτεσιν
οἷς αὐτοκράτωρ ἐγένετο τὴν κατὰ τὸ ἱερὸν ἐκ
μηκίστων χρόνων παραδεδομένην θρησκείαν ἐτήρη-

ᵃ Meaning perhaps such as would not be offensive to
Herod or be felt to be encroaching on his authority.

148

XXXVII. " But why should I cite the testimony of 294
strangers when I can set before you that of many of
your closest kinsmen ?   For instance your maternal
grandfather M. Agrippa, being in Judaea when Herod
my grandfather was king of the country, saw fit to
come up from the coast to the capital situated in the
centre of the land.   But when he surveyed the temple 295
and the rich array of the priests and the worship paid
by the native population he was filled with wonder
thinking that he had seen something to be profoundly
reverenced, something greater than words could
describe.   His discourse to those of his friends who
were there with him consisted of nothing else but
praise of the sanctuary and all that pertained to it.
Thus throughout the days which he spent in the 296
city out of courtesy to Herod he resorted to the
precinct, delighting himself with the spectacle both
of the ornate structure and of the sacrifices and the
ritual observed in the services and the majestic aspect
of the high priest when arrayed in the sacred vest-
ments and conducting the holy rites.   After decking 297
the temple with all the dedicatory gifts which the
law made permissible and benefiting the inhabitants
by granting every favour which he could without
causing mischief [a] and paying many compliments to
Herod and receiving a host of the same from him,
he was escorted to the harbours not by one city only
but by the whole population of the country amid
showers of posies which expressed their admiration
of his piety.   What of your other grand- 298
father Tiberius Caesar ?   Did he not evidently adopt
the same policy ?   At any rate in the twenty-three
years during which he was emperor he maintained the
tradition observed in the temple from distant ages and

149

PHILO

σεν, οὐδὲν αὐτῆς παραλύσας ἢ παρακινήσας μέρος.

299 XXXVIII. ἔχω δέ τι καὶ φιλοτίμημα αὐτοῦ προσ-
διηγήσασθαι, καίτοι μυρίων ἀπολελαυκὼς ὅτε ἔζη
κακῶν· ἀλλὰ τἀληθὲς φίλον καὶ σοὶ τίμιον. Πιλᾶ-
τος ἦν τῶν ὑπάρχων ἐπίτροπος ἀποδεδειγμένος τῆς
Ἰουδαίας· οὗτος οὐκ ἐπὶ τιμῇ Τιβερίου μᾶλλον ἢ
ἕνεκα τοῦ λυπῆσαι τὸ πλῆθος ἀνατίθησιν ἐν τοῖς
κατὰ τὴν ἱερόπολιν Ἡρῴδου βασιλείοις ἐπιχρύσους
[590] ἀσπίδας μήτε | μορφὴν ἐχούσας μήτε ἄλλο τι τῶν
ἀπηγορευμένων, ἔξω τινὸς ἐπιγραφῆς ἀναγκαίας,
ἢ δύο ταῦτα ἐμήνυε, τόν τε ἀναθέντα καὶ ὑπὲρ οὗ
300 ἡ ἀνάθεσις. ἐπεὶ δὲ ᾔσθοντο οἱ πολλοί—καὶ
περιβόητον ἦν ἤδη τὸ πρᾶγμα—, προστησάμενοι
τούς τε βασιλέως υἱεῖς τέτταρας οὐκ ἀποδέοντας
τό τε ἀξίωμα καὶ τὰς τύχας βασιλέων καὶ τοὺς
ἄλλους ἀπογόνους καὶ τῶν παρ' αὐτοῖς τοὺς ἐν
τέλει παρεκάλουν τὸ νεωτερισθὲν περὶ τὰς ἀσπίδας
εἰς ἐπανόρθωσιν ἀγαγεῖν καὶ μὴ κινεῖν ἔθη πάτρια
τὸν πρὸ τοῦ πάντα αἰῶνα διαφυλαχθέντα καὶ πρὸς
301 βασιλέων καὶ πρὸς αὐτοκρατόρων ἀκίνητα. στερ-
ρῶς δὲ ἀντιλέγοντος—ἦν γὰρ τὴν φύσιν ἀκαμπὴς
καὶ μετὰ τοῦ αὐθάδους ἀμείλικτος—, ἀνεβόησαν·
' μὴ στασίαζε, μὴ πολεμοποίει, μὴ κατάλυε τὴν
εἰρήνην· οὐκ ἔστιν ἀτιμία νόμων ἀρχαίων αὐτοκράτορος τιμή. μὴ πρόφασις τῆς εἰς τὸ ἔθνος
ἐπηρείας ἔστω σοι Τιβέριος· οὐδὲν ἐθέλει τῶν
ἡμετέρων καταλύεσθαι. εἰ δὲ φής, αὐτὸς ἐπίδει-
ξον ἢ διάταγμα ἢ ἐπιστολὴν ἢ ὁμοιότροπον, ἵνα

---

[a] Or perhaps " showing his public spirit," as φιλοτιμία is
sometimes used of the munificence of rulers (see Lexicon).
L. & S. revised strangely cite this passage in the sense of " an

150

destroyed or disturbed no part of it.   XXXVIII. I 299
can quote in addition one act showing a fine spirit.[a]
For though I experienced many ills when he was alive,
truth is dear, and is held in honour by you.[b]   One
of his lieutenants was Pilate, who was appointed to
govern Judaea.   He, not so much to honour Tiberius
as to annoy the multitude, dedicated in Herod's
palace in the holy city some shields coated with gold.
They had no image work traced on them nor anything else forbidden by the law apart from the barest
inscription stating two facts, the name of the person
who made the dedication and of him in whose honour
it was made.   But when the multitude understood 300
the matter which had by now become a subject of
common talk, having put at their head the king's four
sons,[c] who in dignity and good fortune were not inferior to a king, and his other descendants and the
persons of authority in their own body, they appealed
to Pilate to redress the infringement of their traditions caused by the shields and not to disturb the
customs which throughout all the preceding ages had
been safeguarded without disturbance by kings and
by emperors.   When he, naturally inflexible, a blend 301
of self-will and relentlessness, stubbornly refused they
clamoured, ' Do not arouse sedition, do not make
war, do not destroy the peace ; you do not honour
the emperor by dishonouring ancient laws.   Do not
take Tiberius as your pretext for outraging the
nation ; he does not wish any of our customs to be
overthrown.   If you say that he does, produce yourself an order or a letter or something of the kind so

act of ambition or ostentation," which is surely quite out of
place.   [b] Or perhaps " reflects honour on you."
    [c] For the account in Josephus cf. Bell. Jud. ii. 169 ff.,
vol. ii. p. 389 L.C.L.

παυσάμενοι τοῦ σοὶ διενοχλεῖν πρέσβεις ἑλόμενοι
302 δεώμεθα τοῦ δεσπότου.' τὸ τελευταῖον τοῦτο μάλιστα αὐτὸν ἐξετράχυνε καταδείσαντα, μὴ τῷ ὄντι
πρεσβευσάμενοι καὶ τῆς ἄλλης αὐτὸν ἐπιτροπῆς
ἐξελέγξωσι τὰς δωροδοκίας, τὰς ὕβρεις, τὰς ἁρ-
παγάς, τὰς αἰκίας, τὰς ἐπηρείας, τοὺς ἀκρίτους καὶ
ἐπαλλήλους φόνους, τὴν ἀνήνυτον καὶ ἀργαλεω-
303 τάτην ὠμότητα διεξελθόντες. οἷα οὖν ἐγκότως
ἔχων καὶ βαρύμηνις ⟨ὢν⟩ ἄνθρωπος ἐν ἀμηχάνοις
ἦν, μήτε καθελεῖν τὰ ἅπαξ ἀνατεθέντα θαρρῶν
μήτε βουλόμενός τι τῶν πρὸς ἡδονὴν τοῖς ὑπηκόοις
ἐργάσασθαι, ἅμα δὲ καὶ τὴν ἐν τούτοις σταθερό-
τητα Τιβερίου μὴ ἀγνοῶν· ἅπερ ὁρῶντες οἱ ἐν
τέλει καὶ συνιέντες, ὅτι μετανοεῖ μὲν ἐπὶ τοῖς
πεπραγμένοις, δοκεῖν δὲ οὐ βούλεται, γράφουσι
304 Τιβερίῳ δεητικωτάτας ἐπιστολάς. ὁ δὲ διαναγνοὺς[1]
οἷα μὲν εἶπε Πιλᾶτον, οἷα δὲ ἠπείλησεν· ὡς δὲ
ὠργίσθη, καίτοι οὐκ εὔληπτος ὢν ὀργῇ, περιττόν
ἐστι διηγεῖσθαι, τοῦ πράγματος ἐξ αὐτοῦ φωνὴν
305 ἀφιέντος. εὐθέως γὰρ οὐδὲ εἰς τὴν ὑστεραίαν
ὑπερθέμενος ἐπιστέλλει, μυρία μὲν τοῦ καινουργη-
θέντος τολμήματος ὀνειδίζων καὶ ἐπιπλήττων,
κελεύων δὲ αὐτίκα καθελεῖν τὰς ἀσπίδας καὶ
μετακομισθῆναι ἐκ τῆς μητροπόλεως εἰς τὴν ἐπὶ
θαλάττῃ Καισάρειαν, ἐπώνυμον τοῦ προπάππου
Σεβαστήν, ἵνα ἀνατεθεῖεν ἐν τῷ Σεβαστείῳ· καὶ
ἀνετέθησαν. οὕτως ἀμφότερα ἐφυλάχθη, καὶ ἡ |
[591] τιμὴ τοῦ αὐτοκράτορος, καὶ ἡ περὶ τὴν πόλιν

---

[1] mss. διαγνούς. See on § 203.

---

[a] So in Jos. *Ant.* xvi. 136, though the epithet Σεβαστή does
not appear elsewhere. It is usually distinguished from

that we may cease to pester you and having chosen
our envoys may petition our lord.' It was this final 302
point which particularly exasperated him, for he
feared that if they actually sent an embassy they
would also expose the rest of his conduct as governor
by stating in full the briberies, the insults, the robberies, the outrages and wanton injuries, the execu-
tions without trial constantly repeated, the ceaseless
and supremely grievous cruelty. So with all his vin- 303
dictiveness and furious temper, he was in a difficult
position. He had not the courage to take down what
had been dedicated nor did he wish to do anything
which would please his subjects. At the same time
he knew full well the constant policy of Tiberius in
these matters. The magnates saw this and understanding that he had repented of his action but did
not wish to appear penitent sent letters of very
earnest supplication to Tiberius. When he had read 304
them through what language he used about Pilate,
what threats he made ! The violence of his anger,
though he was not easily roused to anger, it is
needless to describe since the facts speak for themselves. For at once without even postponing it to 305
the morrow he wrote to Pilate with a host of reproaches and rebukes for his audacious violation of
precedent and bade him at once take down the
shields and have them transferred from the capital
to Caesarea on the coast surnamed Augusta[a] after
your great-grandfather, to be set up in the temple
of Augustus, and so they were. So both objects
were safeguarded, the honour paid to the emperor
and the policy observed from of old in dealing

Caesarea Philippi by ἡ ἐπὶ θαλάσσῃ as here ; v. Pauly-
Wissowa, s.v.

PHILO

306 ἀρχαία συνήθεια. XXXIX. τότε μὲν οὖν ἀσπίδες
ἦσαν, αἷς οὐδὲν ἀνεζωγράφητο μίμημα· νυνὶ δὲ
κολοσσιαῖος ἀνδριάς. καὶ τότε μὲν ἡ ἀνάθεσις ἐν
οἰκίᾳ τῶν ἐπιτρόπων ἦν· τὴν δὲ μέλλουσάν φασιν
ἐσωτάτω τοῦ ἱεροῦ κατ' αὐτὰ τὰ ἄδυτα γίνεσθαι,
εἰς ἃ ἅπαξ τοῦ ἐνιαυτοῦ ὁ μέγας ἱερεὺς εἰσέρχεται
τῇ νηστείᾳ λεγομένῃ μόνον ἐπιθυμιάσων καὶ κατὰ
τὰ πάτρια εὐξόμενος φορὰν ἀγαθῶν εὐετηρίαν τε
307 καὶ εἰρήνην ἅπασιν ἀνθρώποις. κἂν ἄρα τίς που,
οὐ λέγω τῶν ἄλλων Ἰουδαίων, ἀλλὰ καὶ τῶν
ἱερέων, οὐχὶ τῶν ὑστάτων, ἀλλὰ τῶν τὴν εὐθὺς
μετὰ τὸν πρῶτον τάξιν εἰληχότων, ἢ καθ' αὑτὸν
ἢ καὶ μετ' ἐκείνου συνεισέλθῃ, μᾶλλον δὲ κἂν
αὐτὸς ὁ ἀρχιερεὺς δυσὶν ἡμέραις τοῦ ἔτους ἢ καὶ
τῇ αὐτῇ τρὶς ἢ καὶ τετράκις εἰσφοιτήσῃ, θάνατον
308 ἀπαραίτητον ὑπομένει. τοσαύτη τίς ἐστιν ἡ περὶ
τὰ ἄδυτα φυλακὴ τοῦ νομοθέτου μόνα ἐκ πάντων
ἄβατα καὶ ἄψαυστα βουληθέντος αὐτὰ διατηρεῖ-
σθαι. πόσους ἂν οὖν οἴει θανάτους ἑκουσίως
ὑπομένειν τοὺς περὶ ταῦτα ὡσιωμένους, εἰ θεάσαιντο τὸν ἀνδριάντα εἰσκομιζόμενον; ἐμοὶ μὲν
δοκοῦσι γενεὰς ὅλας αὐταῖς γυναιξὶ καὶ τέκνοις
ἀποσφάξαντες ἐπὶ τοῖς τῶν οἰκείων πτώμασιν
ἑαυτοὺς τελευταῖον καθιερεύσειν. ταῦτα μὲν
309 Τιβέριος ἔγνω. τί δὲ ὁ σὸς πρόπαππος,
ὁ τῶν πώποτε γενομένων αὐτοκρατόρων ἄριστος,
ὁ πρῶτος ἀρετῆς ἕνεκα καὶ τύχης Σεβαστὸς
ὀνομασθείς, ὁ τὴν εἰρήνην διαχέας πάντῃ διὰ γῆς
310 καὶ θαλάττης ἄχρι τῶν τοῦ κόσμου περάτων; οὐκ
ἀκοῇ πυνθανόμενος τὰ περὶ τὸ ἱερὸν καὶ ὅτι οὐδέν
ἐστιν ἀφίδρυμα ἐν αὐτῷ χειρόκμητον, ὁρατὸν ἀ-
οράτου μίμημα φύσεως, ἐθαύμαζε καὶ προσεκύνει,

154

with the city. XXXIX. Now at that time it was 306 shields on which no likeness had been painted; now it is a colossal statue. Then too the installation was in the house of the governors; now they say it is to be in the inmost part of the temple in the special sanctuary itself, into which the Grand Priest enters once a year only on the Fast as it is called, to offer incense and to pray according to ancestral practice for a full supply of blessings and prosperity and peace for all mankind. And if any priest, to 307 say nothing of the other Jews, and not merely one of the lowest priests but of those who are ranked directly below the chief, goes in either by himself or with the High Priest, and further even if the High Priest enters on two days in the year or thrice or four times on the same day death without appeal is his doom. So greatly careful was the law-giver to guard 308 the inmost sanctuary, the one and only place which he wished to keep preserved untrodden and untouched. How many deaths think you would those who have been trained to holiness in these matters willingly endure if they should see the statue imported thither? I believe that they would slaughter their whole families, women and children alike, and finally immolate themselves upon the corpses of their kin. This Tiberius knew. But what of 309 your greatgrandfather the best of the emperors that ever were to this day, he who first received the title of Augustus for his virtue and good fortune, who disseminated peace everywhere over sea and land to the ends of the world? Did he not, hearing 310 by report the story of the temple and that it had no work of man's hands, a visible effigy of an invisible being, erected in it, marvel and pay it honour?

φιλοσοφίας οὐκ ἄκροις χείλεσι γευσάμενος ἀλλ'
ἐπὶ πλέον ἑστιαθεὶς καὶ σχεδόν τι καθ' ἑκάστην
ἡμέραν ἑστιώμενος, τὰ μὲν μνήμαις ὧν ἡ διάνοια
προμαθοῦσα τὰ φιλοσοφίας ἀνεπόλει, τὰ δὲ καὶ ταῖς
τῶν συνόντων ἀεὶ λογίων συνδιαιτήσεσι; κατὰ
γὰρ τὰς ἐν δείπνῳ συνουσίας ὁ πλεῖστος χρόνος
ἀπενέμετο τοῖς ἀπὸ παιδείας, ἵνα μὴ τὸ σῶμα
μόνον ἀλλὰ καὶ ἡ ψυχὴ τοῖς οἰκείοις ἀνατρέφοιτο.

311 XL. τεκμηρίοις δὲ ἀφθόνοις πιστώσασθαι δυνάμενος τὸ βούλημα τοῦ Σεβαστοῦ προπάππου σου
δυσὶν ἀρκεσθήσομαι. τὸ μὲν γὰρ πρῶτον ἐπέστειλε
τοῖς ἐπιτρόποις τῶν κατὰ τὴν Ἀσίαν ἐπικρατειῶν,
πυθόμενος ὀλιγωρεῖσθαι τὰς ἱερὰς ἀπαρχάς, ἵνα
ἐπιτρέπωσι τοῖς Ἰουδαίοις μόνοις εἰς τὰ συναγώγια
312 συνέρχεσθαι· μὴ γὰρ εἶναι ταῦτα συνόδους ἐκ
μέθης καὶ παροινίας ἐπὶ συστάσει,[1] ὡς λυμαίνεσθαι
[592] τὰ | τῆς εἰρήνης, ἀλλὰ διδασκαλεῖα σωφροσύνης
καὶ δικαιοσύνης ἀνδρῶν ἐπιτηδευόντων μὲν ἀρετήν,
ἀπαρχὰς δὲ ἐτησίους συμφερόντων, ἐξ ὧν ἀνάγουσι
θυσίας στέλλοντες ἱεροπομποὺς εἰς τὸ ἐν Ἱερο-
313 σολύμοις ἱερόν. εἶτα κελεύει μηδένα ἐμποδὼν
ἵστασθαι τοῖς Ἰουδαίοις μήτε συνιοῦσι μήτε
συνεισφέρουσι μήτε διαπεμπομένοις κατὰ τὰ πάτρια
εἰς Ἱεροσόλυμα· ταῦτα γὰρ εἰ καὶ μὴ τοῖς ῥήμασι,
314 τοῖς γοῦν πράγμασιν ἐπέσταλται. μίαν δὲ ἐπιστολὴν ὑποτέταχα πρὸς τὴν σὴν τοῦ δεσπότου
πειθώ, ἣν Γάιος Νορβανὸς Φλάκκος ἐπιστέλλει

---

[1] Reiter has ἐπισυστάσας on Cohn's conjecture. The mss.
readings recorded are ἐπὶ συστάσει (so Mangey), ἐπὶ συστάσεως
and ἐπισυστάντα. I do not see much reason for ἐπισυστάσας,
which, if taken in the sense of conspiring, would naturally
be followed by a dative, nor any difficulty in ἐπὶ συστάσει.
For σύστασις in this sense cf. De Praem. 75.

For he had not taken a mere sip of philosophy but had feasted on it liberally and continued so to feast almost every day, partly by the memories of the lessons which his mind had conned from its earlier instruction in philosophy, partly by intercourse with the learned who from time to time were in his company. For in the gatherings at his table most of the time was assigned to listening to men of culture [a] so that not only the body but also the soul might be nourished by the food proper to each. XL. While I have a great abundance of evidence to show the wishes of your great-grandfather Augustus I will content myself with two examples. The first is a letter which he sent to the governors of the provinces in Asia, as he had learnt that the sacred first-fruits were treated with disrespect. He ordered that the Jews alone should be permitted by them to assemble in synagogues. These gatherings, he said, were not based on drunkenness and carousing to promote conspiracy and so to do grave injury to the cause of peace, but were schools of temperance and justice where men while practising virtue subscribed the annual first-fruits to pay for the sacrifices which they offer and commissioned sacred envoys to take them to the temple in Jerusalem. Then he commanded that no one should hinder the Jews from meeting or subscribing or sending envoys to Jerusalem according to their ancestral practice. For these were certainly the substance if not the actual words of his instructions. But there is one letter which I subjoin here to convince you, my lord and master, sent by Gaius Norbanus Flaccus

---

[a] This might mean "subjects of culture," but cf. in De Mut. 33 and Quod Omn. Prob. 125, where we have οἱ ἀπὸ παιδείας.

δηλῶν τὰ ὑπὸ Καίσαρος αὐτῷ γραφέντα. ἔστι δὲ
315 τῆς ἐπιστολῆς τὸ ἀντίγραφον τόδε· ‘ Γάιος Νορβανὸς Φλάκκος ἀνθύπατος Ἐφεσίων ἄρχουσι χαίρειν.
Καῖσάρ μοι ἔγραψεν, Ἰουδαίους, οὗ ἂν ὦσιν, ἰδίῳ
ἀρχαίῳ ἐθισμῷ νομίζειν συναγομένους χρήματα
φέρειν, ἃ πέμπουσιν εἰς Ἱεροσόλυμα· τούτους οὐκ
ἠθέλησε κωλύεσθαι τοῦτο ποιεῖν. ἔγραψα οὖν
ὑμῖν, ἵν᾽ εἰδῆτε, ὡς ταῦτα οὕτως γίνεσθαι κελεύει.’
316 ἆρ᾽ οὐκ ἐναργὴς πίστις ἐστίν, αὐτοκράτορ, τῆς
Καίσαρος προαιρέσεως, ᾗ περὶ τὴν τοῦ ἡμετέρου
ἱεροῦ τιμὴν ἐκέχρητο, μὴ βουληθεὶς τῷ κοινῷ τύπῳ
τῶν συνόδων ἀναιρεθῆναι τὰς τῶν Ἰουδαίων εἰς
ταὐτὸ συμφοιτήσεις, ἃς ἀπαρχῶν ἕνεκα ποιοῦνται
317 καὶ τῆς ἄλλης εὐσεβείας; ἕτερον δέ ἐστιν οὐκ
ἀποδέον τούτου δεῖγμα σαφέστατον τῆς βουλή-
σεως τοῦ Σεβαστοῦ· διετάξατο γὰρ ἐκ τῶν ἰδίων
προσόδων ἀνάγεσθαι θυσίας ἐντελεχεῖς[1] ὁλοκαύ-
τους τῷ ὑψίστῳ θεῷ καθ᾽ ἑκάστην ἡμέραν, αἳ καὶ
μέχρι νῦν ἐπιτελοῦνται· ἄρνες εἰσὶ δύο καὶ ταῦρος
τὰ ἱερεῖα, οἷς Καῖσαρ ἐφαίδρυνε τὸν βωμὸν ἐπιστά-
μενος σαφῶς, ὅτι οὐδέν ἐστιν ἀφίδρυμα οὔτε
318 φανερὸν οὔτε ἀφανές· ἀλλὰ γὰρ ὁ τοσοῦτος ἡγεμὼν
καὶ φιλόσοφος[2] οὐδενὸς δεύτερος ἐλογίσατο παρ᾽
ἑαυτῷ, ὅτι ἀναγκαῖόν ἐστιν ἐν τοῖς περιγείοις
ἐξαίρετον ἀπονενεμῆσθαι τόπον ἱερὸν τῷ ἀοράτῳ
θεῷ μηδὲν ὁρατὸν ἀπεικόνισμα περιέξοντα πρὸς
μετουσίαν ἐλπίδων χρηστῶν καὶ ἀπόλαυσιν ἀγαθῶν
319 τελείων.   ὑφηγητῇ τοιούτῳ τῆς εὐσεβείας χρησαμένη καὶ ἡ προμάμμη σου Ἰουλία
Σεβαστὴ κατεκόσμησε τὸν νεὼν χρυσαῖς φιάλαις
καὶ σπονδείοις καὶ ἄλλων ἀναθημάτων πολυτελε-

---

[1] MSS. ἐντελεῖς.

declaring what Caesar had written to him. Here is a transcript of this letter. 'Gaius Norbanus Flaccus proconsul to the magistrates of the Ephesians, greeting. Caesar has written to me that the Jews, wherever they may be, regularly according to their old peculiar custom, make a rule of meeting together and subscribing money which they send to Jerusalem. He does not wish them to be hindered from doing this. I therefore write to you to let you know that this is what he orders to be done.' Is not this a clear proof, my emperor, of the principles which he followed as to the honour due to our temple? He did not think that the form generally adopted about meetings should be applied to do away with the assemblages of the Jews to which they resort for collection of the firstfruits and their other religious observances. Another example no less cogent than this shows very clearly the will of Augustus. He gave orders for a continuation of whole burnt offerings every day to the Most High God to be charged to his own purse. These are carried out to this day. Two lambs and a bull are the victims with which he added lustre to the altar, knowing well that there is no image there openly or secretly set up. Indeed this great ruler, this philosopher second to none, reasoned in his mind that within the precincts of earth there must needs be a special place assigned as sacred to the invisible God which would contain no visible image, a place to give us participation in good hopes and enjoyment of perfect blessings.   Under such an instructor in piety your great-grandmother Julia Augusta adorned the temple with golden vials and libation bowls and a multitude of other sumptuous offerings. What made

315

316

317

318

319

---

² mss. φιλοσοφία (=-ᾳ) or φιλοσοφίας.

στάτων πλήθει· τί παθοῦσα καὶ αὕτη, μηδενὸς
ἔνδον ὄντος ἀφιδρύματος; ἀσθενέστεραι γάρ πως
εἰσιν αἱ γνῶμαι τῶν γυναικῶν ἔξω τῶν αἰσθητῶν
320 μηδὲν ἰσχύουσαι νοητὸν καταλαβεῖν. ἡ δέ γε
[593] καθάπερ ἐν τοῖς ἄλλοις ὅλον | τὸ γένος κἂν τούτῳ
διήνεγκεν, ὑπὸ παιδείας ἀκράτου φύσει καὶ μελέτῃ
περιγεγενημένης,[1] ἀρρενωθεῖσα τὸν λογισμόν, ὃς
οὕτως ὀξυδερκὴς ἐγεγένητο, ὡς μᾶλλον τὰ νοητὰ
καταλαμβάνειν τῶν αἰσθητῶν καὶ ταῦτα νομίζειν
ἐκείνων εἶναι σκιάς.

321 XLI. "Ἔχων οὖν, δέσποτα, τῆς ἡμερωτέρας[2]
προαιρέσεως τοιαῦτα παραδείγματα, πάντα οἰκειό-
τατα καὶ συγγενέστατα ἀφ' ὧν ἐσπάρης καὶ ἀνέβλα-
στες καὶ τοσοῦτον ηὐξήθης, διατήρησον ἃ κἀκείνων
322 ἕκαστος. παρακλητεύουσι τοῖς νόμοις αὐτοκρά-
τορες πρὸς αὐτοκράτορα, Σεβαστοὶ πρὸς Σεβαστόν,
πάπποι καὶ πρόγονοι πρὸς ἔκγονον, πλείους πρὸς
ἕνα, μονονουχὶ φάσκοντες· ἐν ταῖς ἡμετέραις βουλή-
σεσιν ἃ μέχρι καὶ τήμερον ἐφυλάχθη νόμιμα μὴ
καθέλῃς· καὶ γὰρ εἰ μηδὲν ἐκ τῆς καταλύσεως

---

[1] So Mangey with some mss. Others περιγεγενημένη (so
Reiter). See note a.
[2] mss. ἡμετέρας.

---

a The exact meaning, as well as the reading, see note 1, is
uncertain. The one thing certain is that we have an allusion
to the Educational Trinity, Nature, Instruction and Practice,
which occurs so frequently in Philo, particularly in its spiritual
application. See particularly Introd. to vol. vi. pp. x f. and
vol. viii. p. 453. Mangey's translation " ex eruditione pura
quam natura et studio comparaverat," is, I think, impossible.

her too do this, as there was no image there? For the judgements of women as a rule are weaker and do not apprehend any mental conception apart from what their senses perceive. But she excelled all her 320 sex in this as in everything else, for the purity of the training she received supplementing nature and practice *a* gave virility to her reasoning power, which gained such clearness of vision that it apprehended the things of mind better than the things of sense and held the latter to be shadows of the former.

XLI. " So then, my lord, having such patterns of 321 the gentler line of treatment, patterns so closely connected by kinship to yourself, the seed-bed from which you sprang *b* and grew up and rose to such greatness, maintain what each of them also maintained. The cause of the laws is pleaded by emperors to 322 emperor, by Augusti to an Augustus, by grandparents and ancestors to their descendant, by several to one, and you may almost hear them say, ' Do not destroy the institutions which under the shelter of our wills were safeguarded to this day, for even if no sinister result were encountered through their

By παιδείας Philo clearly refers to the instruction received from her ὑφηγητής Augustus, and it is inconsistent with this to say that it was gained by nature and practice. The same applies if reading with Reiter we translate " through instruction she surpassed (her sex) in nature and practice." The translation above seems to me to give the required sense. Livia had the advantage of Augustus's instruction but like everybody else she could not use it properly without the other two. But I cannot find examples of περιγίγνομαι in this sense and I should like to read παραγεγενημένης = " supporting " or " supplementing."

b Or perhaps " most closely akin to those from whom you sprang," τούτων being omitted before ἀφ' ὧν. *Cf. Quod Omn. Prob.* 104 and 123.

αὐτῶν ἀπαντηθείη παλίμφημον, ἀλλ' ἥ γε τοῦ
μέλλοντος ἀδηλότης καὶ τοῖς θαρραλεωτάτοις, εἰ
μὴ καταφρονηταὶ τῶν θείων εἰσίν, οὐ παντελῶς
323 ἐστιν ἄφοβος. ἐὰν καταλέγωμαι τὰς εἰς ἐμαυτὸν
ἐκ σοῦ γενομένας εὐεργεσίας, ἐπιλείψει με ἡ
ἡμέρα, πρὸς τῷ μηδὲ ἁρμόττον εἶναι προηγούμενον
ἔργον πάρεργον ἑτέρου ποιεῖσθαι λόγου· κἂν ἡσυ-
χάζω μέντοι, τὰ πράγματα αὐτὰ βοᾷ καὶ φωνὴν
324 ἀφίησιν. ἔλυσάς με σιδήρῳ δεδεμένον· τίς οὐκ
οἶδεν; ἀλλὰ μὴ χαλεπωτέροις δεσμοῖς, αὐτοκράτορ, ἐπισφίγξῃς· οἱ μὲν γὰρ λυθέντες μέρει
περιβέβληντο τοῦ σώματος, οἱ δὲ νῦν προσδοκώ-
μενοι ψυχῆς εἰσιν, ὅλην αὐτὴν δι' ὅλων μέλλοντες
325 πιέζειν. τὸν ἐπικρεμάμενον ἀεὶ τοῦ θανάτου φόβον
ἀπώσω καὶ τεθνεῶτα τῷ δέει ζωπυρήσας καθάπερ
ἐκ παλιγγενεσίας ἀνήγειρας· διατήρησον τὴν χάριν,
αὐτοκράτορ, ἵνα μὴ ὁ σὸς Ἀγρίππας ἀποτάξηται
τῷ βίῳ· δόξω γὰρ οὐ τοῦ σωθῆναι χάριν ἀφεῖσθαι
μᾶλλον ἢ τοῦ βαρυτέρας ἐνδεξάμενος συμφορὰς
326 ἐπισημότερον τελευτῆσαι. τὸν μέγιστον καὶ εὐ-
τυχέστατον ἐν ἀνθρώποις κλῆρον ἐχαρίσω μοι,
βασιλείαν, πάλαι μὲν μιᾶς χώρας, αὖθις δὲ καὶ
ἑτέρας μείζονος, τὴν Τραχωνῖτιν λεγομένην καὶ τὴν
Γαλιλαίαν συνάψας· μὴ τὰ πρὸς περιουσίαν μοι
χαρισάμενος, ὦ δέσποτα, τὰ ἀναγκαῖα ἀφέλῃς
μηδὲ εἰς φῶς ἀναγαγὼν τηλαυγέστατον ἐξ ὑπαρχῆς
327 εἰς βαθύτατον σκότος ῥίψῃς. ἐξίσταμαι | τῶν
[594] λαμπρῶν ἐκείνων, τὴν πρὸ μικροῦ τύχην οὐ
παραιτοῦμαι, πάντα ὑπαλλάττομαι ἑνός, τοῦ μὴ

---

[a] Or "I do not deprecate my recent (ill) fortune." So
Mangey. This is certainly more in accordance with the

overthrow, still the uncertainty of the future cannot entirely fail to strike fear into the most courageous unless he holds things divine in contempt.' If I should 323 recount the benefits conferred on myself by you, the day will be too short, and besides it is not suitable to treat a primary task as an appendage to another subject. And indeed even if I hold my peace the facts themselves break into speech and cry aloud. You released me bound fast in iron fetters, who does 324 not know it? but do not clamp me, my emperor, with still more grievous fetters, for those which were then unbound encompassed but a part of my body, those which I see before me are of the soul and must press hard on every part of its whole being. You thrust 325 away the ever imminent terror of death, you kindled fresh life in me when dead with fear, you awakened me as though I were born anew. Maintain your bounty, my emperor, that your Agrippa may not bid farewell to life, for it will seem as though my release was not given to save me but that a victim to heavier misfortunes I should come to a more notorious end. The greatest gift of fortune that man can possess 326 you granted to me, a kingdom, in the past of one country, later of another and a greater when you added Trachonitis as it is called and Galilee. Do not after granting me favours in super-abundance take from me bare necessities, and after restoring me to light of fullest radiance cast me anew into deepest darkness. I renounce all that brilliance, I do not 327 beg to keep my shortlived good fortune.[a] I exchange all for one thing only, that the ancestral institutions

common use both of παραιτοῦμαι and πρὸ μικροῦ, but the sentence, if so taken, entirely contradicts what is said in § 323.

κινηθῆναι τὰ πάτρια. τίς γὰρ ἄν μου γένοιτο
λόγος ἢ παρὰ τοῖς ὁμοφύλοις ἢ παρὰ τοῖς ἄλλοις
ἅπασιν ἀνθρώποις; ἀνάγκη γὰρ δυοῖν θάτερον ἢ
προδότην τῶν ἰδίων ἢ σοὶ μηκέτι ὁμοίως φίλον
328 νομισθῆναι· ὧν τί ἂν εἴη μεῖζον κακόν; εἰ μὲν γὰρ
ἐν τῇ τάξει τῶν ἑταίρων ἔτι καταριθμοῦμαι, προ-
δοσίας ἐξοίσομαι δόξαν, ἐὰν μήτε ἡ πατρὶς ἀπαθὴς παντὸς κακοῦ διαφυλαχθῇ μήτε τὸ ἱερὸν
ἄψαυστον· τὰ γὰρ τῶν ἑταίρων καὶ προσπεφευγό-
των ταῖς αὐτοκρατορικαῖς ἐπιφανείαις ὑμεῖς οἱ
329 μεγάλοι διασῴζετε. εἰ δὲ ὑποικουρεῖ τί σου τὴν
διάνοιαν ἔχθος, μὴ δήσῃς ὡς Τιβέριος, ἀλλὰ καὶ
τὴν τοῦ δεθῆναί ποτε αὖθις ἐλπίδα συνανελὼν κέ-
λευσον ἐκποδὼν αὐτίκα γενέσθαι· τί γὰρ ἐμοὶ ζῆν
καλόν, ᾧ μία σωτηρίας ἐλπὶς ἦν τὸ σὸν εὐμενές;''
330 XLII. Ταῦτα γράψας καὶ σφραγισάμενος πέμπει
Γαΐῳ καὶ συγκλεισάμενος οἴκοι κατέμενεν, ἀγω-
νιῶν καὶ συγκεχυμένος καὶ πῶς ἐντύχοι[1] μάλιστα
φροντίζων· οὐ γὰρ βραχὺς ἐπέρριπτο κίνδυνος, ἀλλ'
ὁ περὶ ἀναστάσεως καὶ ἀνδραποδισμοῦ καὶ παν-
τελοῦς πορθήσεως, οὐ μόνον τοῖς τὴν ἱερὰν χώραν
κατοικοῦσιν ἀλλὰ καὶ τοῖς πανταχοῦ τῆς οἰκου-
331 μένης Ἰουδαίοις. λαβὼν δὲ καὶ διαναγινώσκων ἐφ'
ἑκάστῳ τῶν νοημάτων ἅμα μὲν ᾤδει, μὴ κατορ-
θουμένου τοῦ βουλήματος, ἅμα δὲ καὶ ἐπεκλᾶτο
ταῖς δικαιολογίαις ὁμοῦ καὶ δεήσεσι, καὶ τὸν
332 Ἀγρίππαν τῇ μὲν ἐπῄνει, τῇ δὲ ἐμέμφετο· ᾐτι-
ᾶτο μὲν τῆς εἰς τοὺς ὁμοφύλους ἄγαν ἀρεσκείας

---

[1] A strange use of ἐντυγχάνω. Perhaps, as Mangey,
ἂν τύχοι.

---

[a] Or " take shelter under the manifestations."

be not disturbed. For what would be my reputation among either my compatriots or all other men ? Either I must seem a traitor to my people or no longer be counted your friend as I have been ; there is no other alternative, and what greater ill could befall me than these ? For if I still keep my place 328 in the list of your companions I shall lie under an imputation of treachery, unless my homeland is guarded unscathed from every kind of mischief and the temple is untouched. For you great potentates safeguard the interests of your companions and those who take refuge with you by manifestations of your absolute power.ᵃ But if your mind harbour any 329 hostility to me, do not imprison me as Tiberius did, rather do away with any idea of future imprisonment and at the same time bid me take myself out of the way forthwith. For of what value would life be to me whose one hope of salvation lay in your goodwill ? "

XLII. Having written and sealed this letter he 330 sent it to Gaius and shut himself up in his house where he remained greatly agitated and distraught, particularly by anxiety about the turn events might take. For the danger which had fallen upon him was no trifle but one which involved the expulsion, enslavement, and wholesale spoliation of the Jews who dwelt not only in the Holy Land but everywhere through the habitable world. Gaius received the 331 letter and, as he read it, its every sentiment filled him with resentment at the ill-success of his project, yet at the same time he began to bend under the claims for justice coupled with supplication. And from one point of view he praised Agrippa and blamed him from another. He charged him with over-complai- 332

μόνους ἀνθρώπων ἀφηνιάζοντας καὶ ἐκτρεπομένους
αὐτοῦ τὴν ἐκθέωσιν, ἐπῄνει δὲ τὸ μηδὲν ἐν ἑαυτῷ
συσκιάζειν καὶ ἐπικρύπτειν, ἅπερ ἔλεγεν εἶναι
δείγματα ἐλευθεριωτάτων καὶ εὐγενεστάτων ἠθῶν.

333 ἡμερωθεὶς οὖν ὅσα τῷ δοκεῖν ἀποκρίσεων χρη-
στοτέρων Ἀγρίππαν ἠξίωσε, τὸ ἀνωτάτω καὶ
μέγιστον δωρούμενος, τὸ μηκέτι γενέσθαι τὴν
ἀνάθεσιν· καὶ Ποπλίῳ Πετρωνίῳ, τῷ τῆς Συρίας
ἐπιτρόπῳ, κελεύει γραφῆναι μηδὲν ἐπὶ τῷ ἱερῷ
τῶν Ἰουδαίων ἔτι νεώτερον κινεῖν.

334 Ὅμως μέντοι καὶ τὴν χάριν διδοὺς ἔδωκεν οὐκ
ἀκέραιον, ἀλλ᾽ ἀναμίξας αὐτῇ δέος ἀργαλεώτατον·
προσγράφει γάρ· '' ἐὰν δέ τινες ἐν ταῖς ὁμόροις
ἔξω μιᾶς τῆς μητροπόλεως ἐθέλοντες βωμοὺς ἢ
ἱερὰ ἤ τινας εἰκόνας ἢ ἀνδριάντας ὑπὲρ ἐμοῦ καὶ
τῶν ἐμῶν ἱδρύεσθαι κωλύωνται, τοὺς εἴργοντας ἢ
335 παραχρῆμα κολάζειν ἢ εἰς αὐτὸν ἀνάγειν.'' τοῦτο
δὲ οὐδὲν ἦν ἕτερον ἢ στάσεως καὶ ἐμφυλίων πολέμων ἀρχὴ καὶ τῆς δωρεᾶς, ἣν ἐπ᾽ εὐθείας ἐδόκει
παρασχεῖν, πλάγιός τις ἀναίρεσις· ἔμελλον γὰρ οἱ
μὲν κατὰ τὴν πρὸς Ἰουδαίους φιλονεικίαν μᾶλλον
ἢ τὸ πρὸς Γάιον εὐσεβὲς καταπλήσειν τὴν χώραν
[595] ἅπασαν | ἀναθημάτων, οἱ δὲ ἐν ὄψεσι ταῖς αὐτῶν
τὴν τῶν πατρίων ὁρῶντες κατάλυσιν, εἰ καὶ πάντων
ἦσαν πρᾳοπαθέστατοι, μὴ ἀνέχεσθαι, Γάιος δὲ τοὺς
παρακινηθέντας τιμωρίᾳ κρίνων μεγίστῃ ἀνατεθῆναι
336 πάλιν κελεύειν τὸν ἀνδριάντα ἐν τῷ ἱερῷ. προνοίᾳ

sance to his compatriots, who stood alone among mankind in their recalcitrance and refusal to accept his deification. He praised him for disguising and concealing nothing of his real self and this he said proved that he had the characteristics of the truly free and noble. Thus to all appearance mollified he 333 thought good to give kindly answers to Agrippa's request, granting him the chief and principal thing, that the installation should not now take place, and he ordered letters to be sent to Publius Petronius, governor of Syria, that he should forbear to take further steps to violate the tradition of the temple of the Jews.

Nevertheless the concession thus granted by him 334 was not unmixed but had blended with it a very grave cause for alarm. For he added an injunction that if any persons in neighbouring regions outside the capital who wished to set up altars or temples or any images and statues in honour of him or his were prevented from so doing, Petronius was to punish the obstructors at once or send them up to him. Now this was nothing else than a starting point 335 for seditions and civil conflicts and an indirect cancelling of what appeared to be a straightforward gift on his part. For it was to be expected that one party, through hostility to the Jews rather than reverence for Gaius, would fill the whole country with such installations, and the others seeing with their own eyes their ancestral institutions overthrown would not hold their hands even if they were the mildest of men. Then Gaius while awarding the severest punishment to those who had been provoked to violence would again order the statue to be set up in the temple. But by a dispensation 336

δέ τινι καὶ ἐπιμελείᾳ τοῦ πάντα ἐφορῶντος καὶ
σὺν δίκῃ πρυτανεύοντος θεοῦ τῶν ὁμόρων παρε-
κίνησεν οὐδὲν οὐδὲ εἷς, ὡς μὴ χρείαν τινὰ γενέσθαι,
ᾗ πρὸ μετριωτέρας μέμψεως ἀπαραίτητος ἔμελλεν
337 ἀπαντᾶσθαι συμφορά. τί δὲ ὄφελος; εἴποι τις ἄν·
οὐδὲ γὰρ ἠρεμούντων ὁ Γάιος ἠρέμει, μετανοῶν
ἐπὶ τῇ χάριτι ἤδη καὶ τὴν πρὸ μικροῦ ζωπυρῶν
ἐπιθυμίαν· προστάττει γὰρ ἕτερον ἀνδριάντα δη-
μιουργεῖσθαι κολοσσιαῖον χαλκοῦν ἐπίχρυσον ἐν
Ῥώμῃ, μηκέτι τὸν ἐν Σιδῶνι κινῶν, ἵνα μὴ τῇ
κινήσει διαταράξῃ τὸ πλῆθος, ἀλλ' ἠρεμοῦντος καὶ
τῆς ὑπονοίας ἀπηλλαγμένου κατὰ πολλὴν ἡσυχίαν
ἀφανῶς ἐν ταῖς ναυσὶ κομισθέντα λαθὼν τοὺς πολ-
338 λοὺς ἐξαίφνης ἱδρύσηται.   XLIII. τοῦτο δὲ πράξειν ἔμελλεν ἐν παράπλῳ κατὰ τὴν
εἰς Αἴγυπτον ἀποδημίαν. ἄλεκτος γάρ τις αὐτὸν
ἔρως κατεῖχε τῆς Ἀλεξανδρείας, εἰς ἣν ἐπόθει
σπουδῇ πάσῃ παραγενέσθαι καὶ ἀφικόμενος πλεῖστον χρόνον ἐνδιαιτηθῆναι, νομίζων τὴν ἐκθέωσιν,
ἣν ὠνειροπόλει, μίαν ταύτην πόλιν καὶ γεγεννη-
κέναι καὶ συναυξήσειν, καὶ ταῖς ἄλλαις παράδειγμα
γεγενῆσθαι τοῦ σεβασμοῦ, μεγίστην τε οὖσαν καὶ ἐν
καλῷ τῆς οἰκουμένης· τὰ γὰρ τῶν μεγάλων εἴτε
ἀνδρῶν εἴτε πόλεων τοὺς καταδεεστέρους ἄνδρας
339 τε καὶ δήμους ζηλοῦν ἐπιχειρεῖν.   ἦν

ᵃ More literally, " admirably situated for commanding or
serving the habitable world." So rather than " in the finest
situation in the world " (as Mangey), which would need
καλλίστῳ. Thus Stephanus quotes from Lucian (Πλοῖον 15)
ἡ οἰκία ἐν καλῷ τῆς πόλεως οἰκοδομηθεῖσα, but more parallel
to the use here is Xen. Hell. ix. 2. 9 κεῖσθαι τὴν Κέρκυραν ἐν
καλῷ μὲν τοῦ Κορινθιακοῦ κόλπου καὶ τῶν πόλεων αἳ ἐπὶ τοῦτον
καθήκουσι, ἐν καλῷ δὲ τοῦ τὴν Λακωνικὴν χώραν βλάπτειν, ἐν

of the providence and watchful care of God, who surveys and presides over all things with justice, not a single person among the neighbours gave any provocation to violence, so that no occasion arose which would entail a calamity passing beyond a moderate censure and against which no prayers would avail. But what was the use of this? one might 337 say, for if they remained quiet, Gaius did not. He was already repenting of his concession and resuscitating his recent desire. He ordered another bronze statue of colossal size coated with gold to be constructed in Rome. The one in Sidon he forbore from moving, for he did not wish to perturb the multitude by moving it, but intended when they were tranquil and freed from suspicion to have the other conveyed very quietly and secretly on shipboard and suddenly erected unobserved by the mass of the population. XLIII. This he intended to 338 do while coasting along on his voyage to Egypt. For he was possessed by an extraordinary and passionate love for Alexandria. His heart was entirely set upon visiting it and on his arrival staying there for a very considerable time. For he thought this city was unique in that it had both given birth to and would foster the idea of godship which occupied his dreams, and that its vast size and the world-wide value of its admirable situation [a] had made it a pattern to other cities of the worship due to him, since it is true both of individual men and of whole populations that the inferior try to emulate the qualities of the great men and cities respectively.

καλλίστῳ δὲ τῆς τε ἀντιπέραν Ἠπείρου καὶ τοῦ εἰς Πελοπόννησον ἀπὸ Σικελίας παράπλου. There the genitives give the places conveniently reached whether for attack or other purposes.

μέντοι καὶ πρὸς τἆλλα πάντα τὴν φύσιν ἄπιστος,
ὡς, εἰ καί τι χρηστὸν ἐργάσαιτο, μετανοεῖν εὐθὺς
καὶ τρόπον τινὰ δι' οὗ καὶ ταυτὶ λυθήσεται ζητεῖν
340 μετὰ μείζονος ἀνίας καὶ βλάβης. οἷον δή τι λέγω·
δεσμώτας ἔλυσεν ἐνίους ἐπ' οὐδεμιᾷ προφάσει,
πάλιν ἔδησε βαρυτέραν τῆς προτέρας ἐπαγαγὼν
341 συμφοράν, τὴν ἐκ δυσελπιστίας. πάλιν κατέγνω
φυγὴν ἑτέρων θάνατον προσδοκησάντων, οὐκ
ἐπειδὴ συνῄδεσαν αὐτοῖς ἄξια θανάτου πεπραχόσιν
ἢ συνόλως βραχυτέρας ἡστινοσοῦν τιμωρίας, ἀλλὰ
διὰ τὴν ὑπερβάλλουσαν ὠμότητα τοῦ δικαστοῦ μὴ
προσδοκῶντες ἀποφεύξεσθαι. τούτοις ἕρμαιον ἦν
ἡ φυγὴ καὶ ἰσότιμος καθόδῳ τὸν περὶ ψυχῆς
342 ἀνωτάτω κίνδυνον ἀποδεδρακέναι νομίζουσιν. ἀλλ'
οὐ μακρὸς διῆλθε χρόνος, καὶ τῶν στρατευομένων
ἐπιπέμψας τινάς, μηδενὸς καινοτέρου προσπεσόν-
τος, τοὺς ἀρίστους καὶ εὐγενεστάτους ἤδη ζῶντας
[596] ὡς ἐν πατρίσι ταῖς νήσοις καὶ τὴν | ἀτυχίαν
εὐτυχέστατα φέροντας ἀθρόους ἀνῄρει, πένθος
οἰκτρότατον καὶ ἀπροσδόκητον οἴκοις τῶν ἐν
343 Ῥώμῃ μεγάλων προσβαλών. εἰ δέ τισι καὶ δωρεὰν
ἔδωκεν ἀργύριον, οὐχ ὡς δάνειον ἀνέπραττε τόκους
προσκλέγων καὶ ἐπιτοκίας, ἀλλ' ὡς φώριον μετὰ
μεγίστης τῶν λαβόντων ζημίας· οὐ γὰρ ἐξήρκει
τὰ δοθέντα τοῖς ἀθλίοις ἀποτιννύειν, ἀλλὰ καὶ τὰς
οὐσίας ὅλας προσεισέφερον, ἃς ἢ παρὰ γονέων ἢ
παρ' οἰκείων ἢ φίλων ἐκληρονόμουν ἢ ποριστὴν

---

[a] Here the description of Gaius's conduct, interrupted by
the parenthetical section on Alexandria, is resumed. The
arrangement by which a new chapter is begun at § 338 is
unfortunate.

^a In fact in all other matters he was 339 naturally untrustworthy, so that if he did commit any kind action he immediately repented of it and sought some means of cancelling it, thus causing increased affliction and injury. Here is an instance of this 340 sort of thing. He released some prisoners for no reason, and then by imprisoning them again imposed on them a suffering heavier than the former through the bitter disappointment. Again he sentenced 341 others to banishment when they expected death, not because their conscience told them that their action deserved death or even any minor penalty at all, but because in view of the supreme cruelty of their judge they did not expect to get off unpunished. To these banishment was a godsend as good as repatriation, since they felt that they had escaped from the extremity of danger which threatened their lives. But no long time had elapsed when, though no fresh 342 occasion had been given, he sent some of his soldiers on duty to deal with them, and when these men of high excellence and nobility were leading their lives on the islands as though they were their native homes and bearing their misfortunes with the spirit of the favourites of fortune, he proceeded to slaughter them in a body, a blow which brought misery as heartrending as it was unexpected into the households of the great in Rome. So too if he gave a present of money 343 to some he did not treat it as a loan and exact interest and compound interest, but as stolen property entailing very heavy loss for those who took it. For it was not enough for the poor wretches to repay the sums given to them, but they had to contribute as well their whole properties which they inherited from their parents or their relations and friends or

171

344 ἑλόμενοι βίον ἐκτήσαντο αὐτοὶ δι' ἑαυτῶν. οἱ
δ' εὐπάρυφοι καὶ σφόδρ' εὐδοκιμεῖν οἰόμενοι τρόπον
ἕτερον τὸν σὺν ἡδονῇ μετὰ προσποιήσεως φιλικῆς
ἐβλάπτοντο, πάμπολλα μὲν εἰς τὰς ἀκρίτους καὶ
ἀτάκτους καὶ ἐξαπιναίους ἀποδημίας ἀναλίσκοντες,
πάμπολλα δὲ εἰς τὰς ἑστιάσεις· ὅλας γὰρ οὐσίας
ἐξανάλουν εἰς ἑνὸς δείπνου παρασκευήν, ὡς καὶ
345 δανείζεσθαι· τοσαύτη τις ἦν ἡ πολυτέλεια. τοιγαροῦν ἀπηύχοντό τινες ἤδη τὰς δεδομένας ὑπ' αὐτοῦ χάριτας, ὑπολαμβάνοντες οὐκ ὠφέλειαν ἀλλὰ
346 δέλεαρ εἶναι καὶ ἐνέδραν ἀφορήτου ζημίας. τοσαύτη μὲν οὖν τις ἡ περὶ τὸ ἦθος ἦν ἀνωμαλία
πρὸς ἅπαντας, διαφερόντως δὲ πρὸς τὸ Ἰουδαίων
γένος, ᾧ χαλεπῶς ἀπεχθανομένας τὰς μὲν ἐν ταῖς
ἄλλαις πόλεσι προσευχὰς ἀπὸ τῶν κατ' Ἀλεξάνδρειαν ἀρξάμενος σφετερίζεται, καταπλήσας εἰκόνων καὶ ἀνδριάντων τῆς ἰδίας μορφῆς—ὁ γὰρ
ἑτέρων ἀνατιθέντων ἐφεὶς αὐτὸς ἱδρύετο δυνάμει—,
τὸν δὲ ἐν τῇ ἱεροπόλει νεών, ὃς λοιπὸς ἦν ἄψαυστος
ἀσυλίας ἠξιωμένος τῆς πάσης, μεθηρμόζετο καὶ
μετεσχημάτιζεν εἰς οἰκεῖον ἱερόν, ἵνα Διὸς Ἐπι-
347 φανοῦς Νέου χρηματίζῃ Γαΐου.   τί φής;
σὺ μὲν ἄνθρωπος ὢν αἰθέρα καὶ οὐρανὸν ζητεῖς
προσλαβεῖν, οὐκ ἀρκεσθεὶς τῷ πλήθει τῶν τοσούτων
ἠπείρων, νήσων, ἐθνῶν, κλιμάτων, ὧν ἀνήψω τὴν
ἀρχήν; τὸν δὲ θεὸν οὐδενὸς τῶν ἐνταῦθα καὶ
παρ' ἡμῖν ἀξιοῖς, οὐ χώρας, οὐ πόλεως, ἀλλὰ καὶ
τὸν βραχὺν οὕτως περίβολον αὐτῷ καθιερωθέντα
καὶ καθοσιωθέντα χρησμοῖς καὶ λογίοις θεσφάτοις

---

[a] *i.e.* now seen in bodily form. So coins of Antiochus
Epiphanes bear the inscription Ἀντιόχου θεοῦ ἐπιφανοῦς.
Mangey's suggestion that ἐπιφανής in these cases carries the

by choosing a business career acquired through their own efforts. Dignitaries who considered themselves 344 particularly distinguished suffered in another way which served his pleasure under the guise of friendship. His visits to them made without discretion, or order, or warning, cost them huge sums as did also the entertainments which they gave him. For they used to spend their whole substance on providing a single dinner and so run into debt. So vast was the lavish expenditure. And so some came to the point 345 of deprecating the favours bestowed by him, thinking that they were no benefit but a snare to trap them into losses more than they could bear. This great 346 inconstancy of conduct affected all, but particularly the Jewish race. Having conceived a violent enmity to them he took possession of the synagogues in the other cities after beginning with those of Alexandria, by filling them with images and statues of himself in bodily form. For by permitting others to instal them he virtually did it himself. The temple in the Holy City, which alone was left untouched being judged to have all rights of sanctuary, he was proceeding to convert and transmogrify into a temple of his own to bear the name of Gaius, " the new Zeus made manifest." [a] What is this that 347 you say ? do you a mere man seek to annex also ether and heaven, not satisfied with the sum of so many mainlands, islands, nations, regions, over which you assumed sovereignty, and do you deem God worthy of nothing in our world here below, no country, no city, but even this tiny area hallowed for Him and sanctified by oracles and divine messages you propose

same sense as the Latin *praesens*, *i.e.* powerful and ready to help, is perhaps unnecessary.

ἀφελέσθαι διανοῇ, ἵν᾽ ἐν τῷ τῆς τοσαύτης γῆς |
[597] περιβόλῳ μηδὲν ἴχνος μηδὲ ὑπόμνημα καταλειφθῇ
τιμῆς καὶ εὐσεβείας τῆς εἰς τὸν ὄντως ὄντα ἀληθῆ
348 θεόν; καλὰς ὑπογράφεις τῷ γένει τῶν ἀνθρώπων
ἐλπίδας· ἀγνοεῖς ὅτι πηγὰς ἀνατέμνεις ἀθρόων
κακῶν, καινουργῶν καὶ μεγαλουργῶν ἃ μήτε δρᾶν
μήτε λογίζεσθαι θέμις;[1]

349 XLIV. Ἄξιον δὲ ἐπιμνησθῆναι καὶ ὧν εἴδομέν
τε καὶ ἠκούσαμεν μεταπεμφθέντες ἀγωνίσασθαι τὸν
περὶ τῆς πολιτείας ἀγῶνα. εἰσελθόντες γὰρ εὐθὺς
ἔγνωμεν ἀπὸ τοῦ βλέμματος καὶ τῆς κινήσεως,
ὅτι οὐ πρὸς δικαστὴν ἀλλὰ κατήγορον ἀφίγμεθα,
350 τῶν ἀντιτεταγμένων μᾶλλον ἐχθρόν. δικαστοῦ μὲν
γὰρ ἔργα ταῦτα ἦν· καθίσαι μετὰ συνέδρων ἀρι-
στίνδην ἐπιλελεγμένων, ἐξεταζομένης ὑποθέσεως
μεγίστης ἐν τετρακοσίοις ἔτεσιν ἡσυχασθείσης καὶ
νῦν πρῶτον εἰσαγομένης ἐπὶ μυριάσι πολλαῖς τῶν
Ἀλεξανδρέων Ἰουδαίων, ἑκατέρωθεν στῆναι τοὺς
ἀντιδίκους μετὰ τῶν συναγορευσόντων, ἐν μέρει
μὲν ἀκοῦσαι τῆς κατηγορίας, ἐν μέρει δὲ τῆς
ἀπολογίας πρὸς μεμετρημένον ὕδωρ, ἀναστάντα
βουλεύσασθαι μετὰ τῶν συνέδρων, τί χρὴ φανερῶς
ἀποφήνασθαι γνώμῃ τῇ δικαιοτάτῃ· τυράννου δὲ
ἀμειλίκτου δεσποτικὴν ὀφρὺν ἐπανατειναμένου τὰ
351 πραχθέντα. χωρὶς γὰρ τοῦ μηδὲν ὧν ἀρτίως εἶπον
ἐργάσασθαι, μεταπεμψάμενος τοὺς δυεῖν κήπων
ἐπιτρόπους τοῦ τε Μαικήνα καὶ Λαμία—πλησίον

---

[1] Reiter here indicated a lacuna. See Introd. pp. xii, xxiii.

[a] For Josephus's account of this interview see *Ant.* xviii. 8. 1.

to take away, so that in the circumference of this great earth no trace or reminder should be left of the reverence and honour due to the truly existing veritable God? Fine hopes are these which you 348 picture for the human race. Know you not that you are opening the springs of a flood of evil, in these strange and monstrous actions which it is unlawful either to do or conceive?

XLIV. It is right that I should record also both what 349 we saw and what we heard when we were summoned to take a part in the contention about our citizenship.[a] The moment we entered we knew from his look and movements that we had come into the presence not of a judge but of an accuser more hostile than those arrayed against us. For this is what a judge would 350 do: he would sit with assessors selected for their high merit, as the case under examination was of the greatest importance, since nothing had been heard of it for four centuries and it was now for the first time brought up against the many myriads of the Alexandrian Jews [b]: the opposing parties would stand on either side of him with the advocates who would speak for them, and he would listen in turn to the accusation and the defence for the space of water-time allowed! then he would rise and consult with his assessors as to the verdict which in full accordance with justice they would publicly declare. The actual proceedings showed a ruthless tyrant with a menacing frown on his despotic brow. Instead 351 of doing anything that I have just mentioned he sent for the stewards of the two gardens belonging to Maecenas and Lamia near to each other and the

[b] See Introd. pp. xxvi ff.

175

PHILO

δέ εἰσιν ἀλλήλων τε καὶ τῆς πόλεως, ἐν οἷς ἐκ
τριῶν ἢ τεττάρων ἡμερῶν διέτριβε· κεῖθι γὰρ ἐπὶ
παροῦσιν ἡμῖν ἡ κατὰ παντὸς τοῦ ἔθνους ἔμελλε
σκηνοβατεῖσθαι δραματοποιία—κελεύει τὰς ἐπαύλεις αὐτῷ πάσας περιανοιχθῆναι· βούλεσθαι γὰρ
352 μετὰ ἀκριβείας ἑκάστην ἰδεῖν. ἡμεῖς δὲ ὡς αὐτὸν
εἰσαχθέντες ἅμα τῷ θεάσασθαι μετ' αἰδοῦς καὶ
εὐλαβείας τῆς ἁπάσης νεύοντες εἰς τοὔδαφος ἐδε-
ξιούμεθα, Σεβαστὸν Αὐτοκράτορα προσειπόντες·
ὁ δὲ οὕτως ἐπιεικῶς καὶ φιλανθρώπως ἀντιπροση-
γόρευσεν, ὡς μὴ μόνον τὴν ὑπόθεσιν ἀλλὰ καὶ τὸ
353 ζῆν ἀπογνῶναι. σαρκάζων γὰρ ἅμα καὶ σεσηρώς,
" ὑμεῖς," εἶπεν, " ἐστὲ οἱ θεομισεῖς, οἱ θεὸν μὴ
νομίζοντες εἶναί με, τὸν ἤδη παρὰ πᾶσι τοῖς ἄλλοις
ἀνομολογημένον, ἀλλὰ τὸν ἀκατονόμαστον ὑμῖν; "
καὶ ἀνατείνας τὰς χεῖρας εἰς τὸν οὐρανὸν ἐπεφήμιζε
πρόσρησιν, ἣν οὐδὲ ἀκούειν θεμιτόν, οὐχ ὅτι
354 διερμηνεύειν αὐτολεξεί. πόσης εὐθὺς ἀνεπλήσθησαν
ἡδονῆς οἱ τῆς ἐναντίας μερίδος πρέσβεις, ἤδη
κατωρθωκέναι διὰ τῆς πρώτης ἀναφθέγξεως Γαΐου
τὴν πρεσβείαν νομίζοντες· ἐπεχειρονόμουν, ἀνωρ-
[598] χοῦντο, | τὰς θεῶν ἁπάντων ἐπωνυμίας ἐπεφήμιζον
355 αὐτῷ. XLV. γανύμενον δὲ ταῖς ὑπὲρ ἀνθρωπίνην
φύσιν προσρήσεσι θεασάμενος ὁ πικρὸς συκοφάντης
Ἰσίδωρος, " ἔτι μᾶλλον," ἔφη, " δέσποτα, μισήσεις
τοὺς παρόντας καὶ τοὺς ὧν εἰσιν ὁμόφυλοι, ἐὰν
γνῷς τὴν εἰς σὲ κακόνοιαν αὐτῶν καὶ ἀσέβειαν·
ἁπάντων γὰρ ἀνθρώπων ὑπὲρ σωτηρίας τῆς σῆς
θυσίας ἀναγόντων εὐχαριστηρίους, οὐχ ὑπέμειναν
οὗτοι μόνοι θύειν· ὅταν δὲ οὗτοι λέγω, καὶ τοὺς
176

city, in which gardens he had been spending three
or four days. For this was the stage where the
tragedy which was aimed against our whole nation
was to be performed with us who were present as
the immediate victims. He ordered them to leave
all the villas completely open as he wished to make
a careful survey of each of them. When we were 352
brought into his presence the moment we saw him
we bowed our heads to the ground with all respect and timidity and saluted him addressing him
as Emperor Augustus. The mildness and kindness
with which he replied to our greeting was such
that we gave up not only our case but our lives for
lost ! In a sneering, snarling way he said, " Are you 353
the god-haters who do not believe me to be a god,
a god acknowledged among all the other nations but
not to be named by you ? " And stretching out his
hands towards heaven he gave utterance to an invo-
catory address which it was a sin even to listen to,
much more to reproduce in the actual words. How 354
vast was the delight which at once filled the envoys
on the other side ! They thought that Gaius's first
utterance had secured the success of their mission.
They gesticulated, they danced about and invoked
blessings on him under the names of all the gods.
XLV. Seeing that he was delighted at being ad- 355
dressed as of more than human nature the virulent
sycophant Isidorus said, " My lord, you will hate still
more these people here present, and those of whose
nation they are, if you understand their malevolence
and impiety towards you. For when all men were
offering sacrifices of thanksgiving for your preservation they alone could not bear the thought of
sacrificing. And when I say ' they ' I include also

PHILO

356 ἄλλους Ἰουδαίους συμπαραλαμβάνω.'' ἀναβοη-
σάντων δὲ ἡμῶν ὁμοθυμαδόν, '' κύριε Γάιε, συ-
κοφαντούμεθα· καὶ γὰρ ἐθύσαμεν καὶ ἑκατόμβας
ἐθύσαμεν, οὐ τὸ μὲν αἷμα τῷ βωμῷ περισπείσαντες
τὰ δὲ κρέα εἰς θοίνην καὶ εὐωχίαν οἴκαδε κομί-
σαντες, ὡς ἔθος ἐνίοις ποιεῖν, ἀλλ' ὁλόκαυτα τὰ
ἱερεῖα παραδόντες τῇ ἱερᾷ φλογί, καὶ τρίς, οὐχ
ἅπαξ, ἤδη· πρῶτον μὲν ὅτε διεδέξω τὴν ἡγεμονίαν,
δεύτερον δὲ ὅτε τὴν βαρεῖαν νόσον ἐκείνην ἣν πᾶσα
ἡ οἰκουμένη συνενόσησεν ἐξέφυγες, τρίτον δὲ κατὰ
357 τὴν ἐλπίδα τῆς Γερμανικῆς νίκης,'' '' ἔστω,'' φησί,
'' ταῦτα ἀληθῆ, τεθύκατε, ἀλλ' ἑτέρῳ, κἂν¹ ὑπὲρ
ἐμοῦ· τί οὖν ὄφελος; οὐ γὰρ ἐμοὶ τεθύκατε.''
φρίκη βύθιος εὐθὺς κατέσχεν ἡμᾶς ἐπὶ τῷ προτέρῳ
καὶ τοῦτο ἀκούσαντας, ᾗ καὶ μέχρι τῆς ἐπιφανείας
358 ἀνεχύθη. καὶ ταῦθ' ἅμα λέγων ἐπῄει τὰς ἐπαύλεις,
ἀνδρῶνας κατανοῶν, γυναικωνίτιδας, τὰ ἐν ἐπι-
πέδῳ, τὰ ὑπερῷα, ἅπαντα, αἰτιώμενος ἐνίας ὡς
ἐλλιπεῖς κατασκευάς, ἑτέρας ἐπινοῶν καὶ προσδια-
359 τάττων πολυτελεστέρας αὐτός. εἶτα ἡμεῖς ἐλαυνό-
μενοι παρηκολουθοῦμεν ἄνω κάτω, χλευαζόμενοι
καὶ κατακερτομούμενοι πρὸς τῶν ἀντιπάλων ὡς
ἐν θεατρικοῖς μίμοις· καὶ γὰρ τὸ πρᾶγμα μιμεία
τις ἦν· ὁ μὲν δικαστὴς ἀνειλήφει σχῆμα κατηγόρου,
οἱ δὲ κατήγοροι φαύλου δικαστοῦ πρὸς ἔχθραν
ἀποβλέποντος, ἀλλ' οὐ τὴν φύσιν τῆς ἀληθείας.
360 ὅταν δὲ αἰτιᾶται κρινόμενον δικαστὴς καὶ τοσοῦτος,

¹ mss. καὶ or καὶ οὐχ.

ᵃ As sacrifices could only be offered in Jerusalem, they
must mean by '' we '' the Jewish nation, or else (less probably)
that the contributions of money which they sent there were
178

the other Jews." We cried out with one accord, 356
" Lord Gaius, we are slandered ; we did sacrifice
and sacrifice hecatombs too, and we did not just pour
the blood upon the altar and then take the flesh home
to feast and regale ourselves with it as some do, but
we gave the victims to the sacred fire to be entirely
consumed, and we have done this not once but thrice
already, the first time at your accession to the
sovereignty, the second when you escaped the severe
sickness which all the habitable world suffered with
you, the third as a prayer of hope for victory in
Germany." [a] " All right," he replied, " that is true, 357
you have sacrificed, but to another, even if it was for
me ; what good is it then ? For you have not sacrificed
to me." When we heard these words following on
his first remark we were seized by a profound terror
which spread till it became visible in the countenance.
While he was saying this he was going on with his 358
survey of the houses, the different chambers, men's
or women's, the ground floors, the upper floors, all of
them, and some he censured as defective in structure,
and for others he made his own plans and gave orders
that they should be more magnificent. Then driven 359
along we followed him up and down mocked and re-
viled by our adversaries, as they do in the mimes at
the theatres. For indeed the business was a sort of
mime ; the judge had taken on the rôle of accuser, the
accusers the rôle of a bad judge who had eyes only
for his enmity and not for the actual truth. But 360
when the person on trial is accused by a judge and

accompanied with instructions that they were to be applied
to pay for sacrifices for these particular purposes, cf. § 232.
For the bearing of the statement about the German victory
the chronology see Introd. p. xxvii.

ἀνάγκη σιωπᾶν· ἔστι γάρ πως καὶ δι᾽ ἡσυχίας
ἀπολογεῖσθαι, καὶ μάλιστα πρὸς οὐδὲν ὧν ἐπεζήτει
καὶ ἐπεπόθει δυναμένους ἀποκρίνασθαι, τῶν ἐθῶν
καὶ νομίμων τὴν γλῶτταν ἐπεχόντων καὶ τὸ στόμα
361 κλειόντων καὶ ἀπορραπτόντων. ἐπεὶ δὲ ἔνια τῶν
περὶ τὰς οἰκοδομὰς διετάξατο, μέγιστον καὶ σεμνὸν
ἐρώτημα ἠρώτα· "διὰ τί χοιρείων κρεῶν ἀπ-
έχεσθε;" πάλιν πρὸς τὴν πεῦσιν γέλως ἐκ τῶν
ἀντιδίκων κατερράγη τοσοῦτος, τῇ μὲν ἡδομένων
τῇ δὲ καὶ ἐπιτηδευόντων ἕνεκα κολακείας ὑπὲρ
τοῦ τὸ λεχθὲν δοκεῖν σὺν εὐτραπελίᾳ καὶ χάριτι
εἰρῆσθαι, ὡς τινα τῶν ἑπομένων αὐτῷ θεραπόντων
[599] | ἀγανακτεῖν ἐπὶ τῷ καταφρονητικῶς ἔχειν αὐτο-
κράτορος, ἐφ᾽ οὗ καὶ τὸ μετρίως μειδιάσαι τοῖς μὴ
362 πάνυ συνήθεσιν οὐκ ἀσφαλές. ἀποκριναμένων δὲ
ἡμῶν, ὅτι "νόμιμα παρ᾽ ἑτέροις ἕτερα καὶ χρῆσις
ἐνίων ὡς ἡμῖν καὶ τοῖς ἀντιδίκοις ἀπείρηται," καὶ
φαμένου τινός, "ὡς πολλοί γε καὶ τὰ προχειρότατα
ἀρνία οὐ προσφέρονται," γελάσας, "εὖ γε," εἶπεν,
363 "ἔστι γὰρ οὐχ ἡδέα." τοιαῦτα φλυαρηθέντες καὶ
κατακερτομηθέντες ἐν ἀμηχάνοις ἦμεν. εἶτα ὀψέ
ποτε παρασεσυρμένως, "βουλόμεθα μαθεῖν," ἔφη,
364 "τίσι χρῆσθε περὶ τῆς πολιτείας δικαίοις." ἀρξαμένων δὲ λέγειν καὶ διδάσκειν, ἀπογευσάμενος τῆς
δικαιολογίας καὶ συνεὶς ὡς οὐκ ἔστιν εὐκαταφρόνη-
τος, πρὶν ἐπενεγκεῖν τὰ ἐχυρώτερα, συγκόψας καὶ
τὰ πρότερα δρομαῖος εἰς τὸν μέγαν οἶκον εἰσ-
επήδησε καὶ περιελθὼν προστάττει τὰς ἐν κύκλῳ
θυρίδας ἀναληφθῆναι τοῖς ὑάλῳ λευκῇ παραπλη-

---

a The imperfects ἐπεζήτει and ἐπεπόθει show that we have
here a sudden transition from the general to the particular.
We have had an exact parallel in *Flaccus* 118.

that one of such eminence, he must needs hold his peace. For silence too may in a way serve as a defence, particularly to us [a] who could not answer any of the points which he was investigating and wished to press, because our customs and laws muzzled the tongue and closed and stitched up the mouth. But 361 after giving some of his orders about the buildings he put to us this grave and momentous question, " Why do you refuse to eat pork ? " The question was greeted by another outburst of laughter from some of our opponents because they were delighted, while with others it was a studied attempt to flatter him, intended to make the remark seem witty and sprightly. The laughter was so great that some of the servants following him were annoyed at it as showing disrespect for the emperor, with whom even a tempered smile is unsafe except for quite intimate friends. We answered, " Different people have different 362 customs and the use of some things is forbidden to us as others are to our opponents." Then someone said, " Yes, just as many don't eat lamb which is so easily obtainable," whereupon Gaius laughed and said, " Quite right too, for it's not nice." Under such befooling and reviling we were helpless. 363 Then tardily going on a different tack [b] he said, " We want to hear what claims you make about your citizenship." We started to speak and give him the 364 information, but when he had had a taste of our pleading and recognized that it was by no means contemptible, he cut short our earlier points before we could bring in the stronger ones, and dashed at high speed into the large room of the house, and walked round it and ordered the windows all round

[b] Or " with a sarcastic air."

σίως διαφανέσι λίθοις, οἳ τὸ μὲν φῶς οὐκ
ἐμποδίζουσιν, ἄνεμον δὲ εἴργουσι καὶ τὸν ἀφ'
365 ἡλίου φλογμόν. εἶτα προελθὼν ἄνευ σπουδῆς
μετριώτερον ἀνηρώτα· " τί λέγετε; " συνείρειν
δὲ ἀρξαμένων τὰ ἀκόλουθα, εἰστρέχει πάλιν εἰς
ἕτερον οἶκον, ἐν ᾧ γραφὰς ἀρχετύπους ἀνατεθῆναι
366 προσέταττεν. οὕτω τῶν ἡμετέρων σπαραττομένων
καὶ διαρτωμένων καὶ μόνον οὐ συγκοπτομένων καὶ
συντριβομένων δικαίων, ἀπειρηκότες καὶ μηδὲν ἔτι
σθένοντες, ἀεὶ δὲ οὐδὲν ἕτερον ἢ θάνατον προσδοκῶντες, οὐκέτι τὰς ψυχὰς ἐν αὑτοῖς εἴχομεν,
ἀλλ' ὑπ' ἀγωνίας ἔξω προεληλύθεσαν ἱκετεύειν τὸν
ἀληθινὸν θεόν, ἵνα τοῦ ψευδωνύμου τὰς ὀργὰς
367 ἐπίσχῃ. ὁ δὲ λαβὼν οἶκτον ἡμῶν τρέπει τὸν
θυμὸν αὐτοῦ πρὸς ἔλεον· καὶ ἀνεθεὶς πρὸς τὸ
μαλακώτερον, τοσοῦτον εἰπών, " οὐ πονηροὶ μᾶλλον
ἢ δυστυχεῖς εἶναί μοι δοκοῦσιν ἄνθρωποι καὶ
ἀνόητοι μὴ πιστεύοντες, ὅτι θεοῦ κεκλήρωμαι
φύσιν," ἀπαλλάττεται προστάξας καὶ ἡμῖν ἀπέρ-
χεσθαι.

368 XLVI. Τοιοῦτον ἀντὶ δικαστηρίου θέατρον ὁμοῦ
καὶ δεσμωτήριον ἐκφυγόντες—ὡς μὲν γὰρ ἐν
θεάτρῳ κλωσμὸς συριττόντων, καταμωκωμένων,
ἄμετρα χλευαζόντων, ὡς δὲ ἐν εἱρκτῇ πληγαὶ κατὰ
τῶν σπλάγχνων φερόμεναι, βάσανοι, κατατάσεις
τῆς ὅλης ψυχῆς διά τε τῶν εἰς τὸ θεῖον βλασ-
φημιῶν καὶ διὰ τῶν ἐπανατάσεων, ἃς τοσοῦτος
[600] αὐτοκράτωρ | ἐπανετείνετο, μνησικακῶν οὐ περὶ
ἑτέρου, ῥᾳδίως γὰρ ἂν μετέβαλεν, ἀλλὰ περὶ ἑαυτοῦ καὶ τῆς εἰς τὴν ἐκθέωσιν ἐπιθυμίας, ᾗ μόνους
ὑπελάμβανε μήτε συναινεῖν Ἰουδαίους μήτε δύνα-
369 σθαι συνυπογράψασθαι—μόλις ἀνεπνεύσαμεν, οὐκ
182

to be restored with transparent stones, which in the same way as white glass do not obstruct the light but keep off the wind and the scorching sun. Then 365 he advanced in a leisurely way and said in a more moderate tone, " What is it that you say ? " and when we began on the points which came next in the thread of our argument he ran again into another room and ordered original pictures to be put up there. So with the statement of our case thus mangled and 366 disjointed, one may almost say cut short and crushed to pieces, we gave up, for there was no strength left in us, and since we all the time expected nothing else but death, in our deep distress our souls had passed from within us and went forth to supplicate the true God that he should restrain the wrath of the pretender to that name. And God taking compassion on 367 us turned his spirit to mercy ; he relaxed into a softer mood and said just this, " They seem to me to be people unfortunate rather than wicked and to be foolish in refusing to believe that I have got the nature of a god," and saying this he went off bidding us be gone also.

XLVI. Such was this combination of a theatre 368 and a prison in place of a tribunal, theatre-like in the cackling of their hisses, their mockery and unbounded jeering, prison-like in the strokes inflicted on our flesh, the torture, the racking of the whole soul through the blasphemies against God and menaces launched upon us by this mighty despot, who resented the affront not to another, since then he might easily have changed his mind, but to himself and his desire of the deification to which he supposed the Jews alone did not assent and could not pledge themselves to subscribe. From this prison we had 369

183

ἐπειδὴ φιλοζωοῦντες θάνατον κατεπτήχειμεν, ὃν
ἄσμενοι καθάπερ ἀθανασίαν εἱλόμεθα ἄν, εἰ δή τι
τῶν νομίμων ἔμελλεν ἐπανόρθωσιν ἕξειν, ἀλλ'
εἰδότες ἐπ' οὐδενὶ λυσιτελεῖ παρανάλωμα γενησό-
μενοι μετὰ πολλῆς δυσκλείας· ἃ γὰρ ἂν πρέσβεις
ὑπομένωσιν, ἐπὶ τοὺς πέμψαντας λαμβάνει τὴν
370 ἀναφοράν. τούτων μὲν δὴ χάριν ἐπὶ ποσὸν ἐδυνή-
θημεν ἀνακύψαι, τὰ δὲ ἄλλα ἡμᾶς ἐφόβει
διεπτοημένους καὶ ἀποροῦντας, τί γνώσεται, τί
ἀποφανεῖται, ποταπὴ γένοιτ' ἂν ἡ κρίσις· ἤκουσε
γὰρ τῆς ὑποθέσεως, ὃς πραγμάτων ἐνίων παρ-
ήκουσεν; ἐν ἡμῖν δὲ πέντε πρεσβευταῖς σαλεύειν
τὰ τῶν πανταχοῦ πάντων Ἰουδαίων οὐ χαλεπόν;
371 εἰ γὰρ χαρίσαιτο τοῖς ἡμετέροις ἐχθροῖς, τίς ἑτέρα
πόλις ἠρεμήσει; τίς οὐκ ἐπιθήσεται τοῖς συνοι-
κοῦσι; τίς ἀπαθὴς καταλειφθήσεται προσευχή;
ποῖον πολιτικὸν οὐκ ἀνατραπήσεται δίκαιον τοῖς
κοσμουμένοις κατὰ τὰ πάτρια τῶν Ἰουδαίων;
ἀνατετράψεται, ναυαγήσει, κατὰ βυθοῦ χωρήσει
καὶ τὰ ἐξαίρετα νόμιμα καὶ τὰ κοινὰ πρὸς ἑκάστας
372 τῶν πόλεων αὐτοῖς δίκαια. τοιούτοις ὑπέραντλοι
γενόμενοι λογισμοῖς ὑπεσυρόμεθα καταποντού-
μενοι· καὶ γὰρ οἱ τέως συμπράττειν ἡμῖν δοκοῦντες
ἀπειρήκεσαν· καλουμένων γοῦν, ἔνδον ὄντες οὐχ
ὑπέμειναν, ἀλλ' ὑπεξῆλθον διὰ φόβον ἀκριβῶς

---

[a] See *Flacc.* 12 and note.
[b] Balsdon, who translates (p. 161) " for he heard our case
though he paid no attention to some of the facts," whence he
infers that Philo is compelled to admit that Gaius gave a
hearing to the Jewish arguments, is, I think, certainly wrong.
The question mark appended both by Mangey and Reiter is
necessitated by ὅς, which cannot bear the sense which Balsdon
gives it.

escaped and were just able to breathe again, not because we clung to life and cringed from death, which we would gladly have chosen as being immortality, if thereby we were going to get restoration of our institutions, but because we knew that we should prove to have thrown ourselves away for no useful purpose [a] and to our great discredit. For whatever ambassadors suffer recoils upon those who sent them. For the above reasons we were able to 370 lift our heads above water to some extent but the other circumstances alarmed us in our trepidation and suspense as to what he would decide, what verdict he would declare, on what grounds the judgement would be given. For had a hearing been given to our case by him who heard some points only to misunderstand? [b] Surely it was a cruel situation that the fate of all the Jews everywhere should rest precariously on us five envoys. For if he should 371 decide in favour of our enemies, what other city will keep tranquil or refrain from attacking its fellow inhabitants, what house of prayer will be left unscathed, what kind of civic rights will not be upset for those whose lot is cast under the ancient institutions of the Jews? First upset, then shipwrecked, then sunk to the very bottom will be both their peculiar laws and the rights which they enjoy in common in every city. Waterlogged by such con- 372 siderations we were dragged down and submerged in the depths, for those who hitherto seemed to be acting with us gave up. At least when we were summoned [c] they did not stay in and hold their ground but slunk away in fear, knowing full well

[c] Or perhaps " when we called upon them," which gives better sense, though with poorer grammar, cf. note on § 221.

ἐπιστάμενοι τὸν ἵμερον, ᾧ κέχρητο πρὸς τὸ νομίζεσθαι θεός.

373 Εἴρηται μὲν οὖν κεφαλαιωδέστερον ἡ αἰτία τῆς πρὸς ἅπαν τὸ Ἰουδαίων ἔθνος ἀπεχθείας Γαΐου· λεκτέον δὲ καὶ τὴν παλινῳδίαν.[1]

---

[1] ? παλινοδίαν. See note a.

---

a " Counter-story " or " reversal." Presumably this gave an account of Gaius's death and probably also the change of policy adopted by Claudius, as shown in the two edicts recorded by Josephus, *Ant.* xix. 5. If, that is, it was ever written, for it is curious that Eusebius in his brief notice of

THE EMBASSY TO GAIUS, 372-373

the longing which he cherished for being acknowledged as a god.

So now I have told in a summary way the cause 373
of the enmity which Gaius had for the whole nation
of the Jews, but I must also describe the palinode.[a]

the *Legatio*, see Introd. pp. xvii, shows no knowledge of it.
But the word is an odd one, for though Philo uses παλιν-
ῳδεῖν=" repeat " in *De Mut.* 53, the noun itself is only cited
in the sense of recantation. *Cf.* in Philo himself *De Post.*
179, *De Som.* ii. 232. The only sense in which the story of
these events would be a recantation would be that it would
force the doubters of providence to recant. I think παλινοδία,
said by Suidas to=ἐναντία ὁδός, would be a more natural
word.

INDICES TO PHILO

SCRIPTURE INDEX

KEY

INCIDENTS

Blessing of Jacob	Gen. xlix
Passover	Exod. xii
Red Sea	Exod. xiv
Song of Moses	Exod. xv. *Cf.* Deut. xxxii
Manna and Quails	Exod. xvi, Num. xi
Water from Rock	Exod. xvii, Num. xx
Jethro's visit	Exod. xviii
Giving of the Law	Exod. xix ff
Seventy elders	Exod. xxiv. *Cf.* Num. xi
Theophany on Sinai	Exod. xxiv. 10
Golden Calf	Exod. xxxii
Slaughter by Levites	Exod. xxxii
Nadab and Abihu	Lev. x
Spies	Num. xiii
Sabbath broken	Num. xv. 32-36
Korah's revolt	Num. xvi
Edom	Num. xx
Balak and Balaam	Num. xxii-xxiv
Phinehas	Num. xxv
Midianite War	Num. xxv, xxxi
Zelophehad's daughters	Num. xxvii, xxxvi
Blessing of Moses	Deut. xxxiii

189

SCRIPTURE INDEX

Offerings

Lev. i-vii, xxiii. 10, Num. xxviii. 2, Deut. xxvi

Feasts

Lev. xxiii, Num. xxviii, xxix, Deut. xvi ; *cf.* xxvi

Laws and Ordinances, etc.

Atonement	Lev. xvi
Blessing & Cursing	Lev. xxvi, Deut. xxvii, xxviii
Cities of refuge	Exod. xxi. 13, 14, Num. xxxv, Deut. xix
Clean and Unclean	Lev. xi, Deut. xiv
Decalogue	Exod. xx, Deut. v
Great Vow	Num. vi
High Priest	Lev. viii, xvi, xxi
Ius talionis	Exod. xxi. 23-25, Lev. xxiv. 19-21, Deut. xix. 21
Jubilee	Lev. xxv
Leprosy	Lev. xiii, xiv
Levites	Exod. xxxii, *cf.* Num. xxv ; Num. xviii, Deut. x. 9, xxxiii. 9, 10
Nazirite	Num. vi
Rebellious son	Deut. xxi. 18-21
Release	Lev. xxv, Deut. xv
Sabbath-breaking	Exod. xx. 8, xxxi. 13-16, xxxv. 2, 3, Num. xv. 32-36

BIBLICAL REFERENCES

---

[a] These general references to the Pentateuch include those
made to " the Law."

Hypoth. Introd. pp. 407 & n-411, 7.
1n, 7. 5n, 7. 6n, 7. 7n, *De Prov.*
Introd. p. 450

Septuagint [a] :   I. *Leg. All.* i. 1n, 2n, 53n, 66n, ii. 9n,
46n, 59n, iii. 16[N], 20n, 24n, 32[N],
165n, 171n, 203n, 228n
II. *Cher.* 1n, 8[N], 35n, 49[N], 72n,
128n, *Sac.* 5n, 6n, 8n, 12[N], 51n,
59n, 62n, 76n, 77n, 108n, 112n,
136[N], *Det.* 1[N], 12n, 158n, *Post.*
55n, 57[N], 62n, *Gig.* 34n
III. *Quod Deus* 1n, 6[N], 13n, 72n,
82n, 88n, 99n, 111-116[N], 123n,
145n, *Agr.* 1n, 21n, 97n, 170n, 175n,
Plant. 61[N], 73[N], *Ebr.* Introd.
p. 316n, 2[N], 14[N], 24n, 27n,
31[N], 39n, 73n, 79n, 84n & [N],
114-118[N], 127n, 143n, 146n, 149n,
150[N], 152n, *Sob.* 12n, 32[N], 50n,
56[N], 58[N], 66n
IV. *Conf.* 1n, 23n, 44[N], 50n, 56n,
70[N], 81n, 96nn, 103[N], 106[N],
131n, *Mig.* 5n, 19n, 94n, 98n, 99n,
130n, 142n, 155n, 159n, 162n, 164n,
174[N], 206[N], 224nn, *Quis Her.*
118n, 170n, 218n & [N], 243n, 249n,
274n, 275n, 290[N], *Congr.* 8n, 25n,
43n, 139n, 164n
V. *Fug.* 11-13[N], 22n, 132n, 155n,
212n, *Mut.* Introd. p. 128nn, 34n &

[a] This is a list of passages where attention has been drawn
by the Translators to the LXX version in the textual notes,
footnotes, or Appendices.

OLD TESTAMENT

GENESIS

a In these passages Philo bases his argument upon the
use of the plural in " Let us make man . . ."

a Where the A.V. has " unto the plain of Moreh " the LXX reads ἐπὶ τὴν δρῦν τὴν ὑψηλήν. R.V. " unto the *oak* of Moreh."

a Wrongly given as xxxvi. 22.

[a] Where the EV have " an officer of Pharaoh's, captain of the guard " the LXX reads ὁ εὐνοῦχος Φαραὼ ὁ ἀρχιμάγειρος, " the eunuch of Pharaoh and chief cook."

EXODUS

219

a Called " The Song " : III. *Agr.* 81, *Plant.* 48, V. *Som.*
ii. 269. *Cf.* II. *Post.* 167n, III. *Sob.* 10n, V. *Mut.* 182n.

[a] In the footnote (a) to *Decal.* 44 the reference is wrongly
given as ch. xx. 14-19.

  [a] Not only does the LXX have a different order from the Hebrew and English, but there are two versions of the order in the LXX itself : Philo at this point follows the same order as that of Deuteronomy v.
  [b] There are three variations of the order. In the Hebrew and English it is murder, adultery, theft. In the LXX of Exodus it is, as shown above, adultery, theft, murder. In the LXX of Deut. v, and in Philo it is, adultery, murder, theft.
  [c] The Translator's note is not in keeping with the order of the text adopted by Swete.

---

a See note *b* on previous page.
b In the footnote (*b*) to *Decal.* 47 the reference is wrongly
given as ch. xix. 18.

a Cf. Lev. xxiv. 19-21, Deut. xix. 21.

[a] The verse occurs again at xxxiv. 26.

[a] At *Leg. All.* iii. 119 the reference is to the EV; at *Mos.* ii. 113 there is no exact reference; at *Mos.* ii. 114[N] and 115n LXX and EV are mixed, but it is indicated; at *Spec. Leg.* ii. 83 the reference is to the EV; at *Spec. Leg.* iv. 69 no reference is given. At *Mig.* 103f the references are to the LXX.

       a See note *a* on previous page.

LEVITICUS

For the title compare *Plant.* 26 and *Fug.* 170 & n

a In both passages the LXX numeration is followed. At
Quis Her. 131 there is a misprint; for xxxvii. 10 read xxxvi.
10.
b At *Som.* i. 202 the numeration is LXX (EV); in *Mos.*
ii. 114[N] it is EV (LXX).
c In the footnote to *Congr.* 8, for Ex. xxxviii. 5f (xxxvii.
17) read xxxviii. 13, 14 (EV xxxvii. 17).
d The LXX differs considerably from the EV.

a At *Spec. Leg.* i. 151 the reference is to the EV (LXX); at *Quis Her.* 195 it is to the LXX only.

b At *Spec. Leg.* i. 224f the numeration is that of the LXX (EV); but at i. 145f of the EV (LXX); while in *Leg. All.* iii. 133-137, 140 only the EV is given.

c In the footnote to *Leg. All.* iii. 140 there is a misprint. For Lev. vii. 3 read vii. 21 (EV 31).

a *Cf.* Exod. xxi. 23-25, Deut. xix. 21.

NUMBERS

a viii. 24-26 rather than iv. 3ff at *Fug.* 37.

a See note on previous page.

---

[a] Philo uses Δευτερονόμιον (*Leg. All.* iii. 174, *Quod Deus* 50), προτρεπτικοί (*sc.* λόγοι, *Spec. Leg.* iv. 131n) (*Agr.* 78, 172, *Fug.* 142, *Mut.* 42, 236, *Virt.* 47 & n, *Fug.* 170 & n), παραινέσεις (*Agr.* 84, *Spec. Leg.* iv. 131), ᾽Επινομίς (*Quis Her.* 162, 250, *Spec. Leg.* iv. 160 & n & [N]).

[a] Called " The Greater Song " (as distinct from " The Song " of Exod. xv), **I.** *Leg. All.* iii. 105 & n, **II.** *Post.* 167 & n, **III.** *Plant.* 59, *Sob.* 10 & n, **V.** *Mut.* 182 & n, *Som.* ii. 191 ; *cf.* **VIII.** *Virt.* 72.

JOSHUA

JUDGES

RUTH

1 SAMUEL

1 KINGS

2 KINGS

1 CHRONICLES

SCRIPTURE INDEX

2 CHRONICLES

EZRA

JOB

PSALMS

a The numeration given by the Translators for these Psalms has been primarily that of the EV. In many cases the LXX is given in brackets. In all the others the LXX has been given, with or without the EV in brackets.

In a few cases there is a difference of one verse or more between the LXX and the EV, so that the references given by the Translators are slightly inaccurate. I have thought it sufficient to indicate these in the list of corrigenda and simply to print the correct numeration above.

PROVERBS

a See note on previous page.

ECCLESIASTES

SONG OF SOLOMON

ISAIAH

JEREMIAH

SCRIPTURE INDEX

SCRIPTURE INDEX

TOBIT

JUBILEES

NEW TESTAMENT

MATTHEW

SCRIPTURE INDEX

MARK

LUKE

JOHN

ACTS

SCRIPTURE INDEX

HEBREWS

JAMES

1 JOHN

REVELATION

INDEX OF NAMES

Aaron : ' mountainous,' the reason whose thoughts
are lofty and sublime (*Ebr.* 128) ; Speech (*Leg.
All.* iii. 103, *Mig.* 79, 169 & n) or Word (*Leg. All.*
iii. 45, 118 (ἱερὸς λ.) *Quis Her.* 201f, *Mut.* 208), the
logos in utterance (προφορικός, *Mig.* 78, *Det.* 39,
126), the perfect interpreter (*Det.* 132, *cf.* 40,
Mig. 78, 81, 84, *Mut.* 208, *Mos.* i. 84). He is also
the man of gradual improvement (ὁ προκό-
πτων, *Leg. All.* iii. 140, 144, *Som.* ii. 234, 237),
training or practising (ἀσκητής, opp. to τέλειος,
Leg. All. iii. 144), but falling short of consummation (*Som.* ii. 234-237), and so inferior to Moses
(*ib.* ; δεύτερος, *Leg. All.* iii. 128, 132), whom he
is predisposed to obey (*Mos.* i. 85)

Aaron, Speech, is the brother of Moses, Mind (*Det.*
39f, 126-135, *Mig.* 78-84, *cf. Mut.* 208), the
logical nature being the one mother of them both
(*Mig.* 78-84, *cf.* 168f). On the other hand, he is
contrasted with Moses because he receives a less
direct revelation (*Leg. All.* iii. 103, *Mig.* 81) and
access (*Gig.* 52), he is instable (*ib., Som.* ii. 234-
237), he is not whole-hearted in rejecting the
passions (*Leg. All.* iii. 128, 132, 134) and pleasure
(140), he is subject to toil and discipline (135,
144), a learner, imperfect (135, *Som.* ii. 234-237),
making only gradual improvement (see above)

INDEX OF NAMES

II. *Cher.* 40, *Sac.* 1-3, 10f, 14, 51f, 88, 136, *Det.* 1, 32, 37, 42, 45-49, 57 & [N], 61, 68f, 78f, 93, 100, 103, *Post.* 10, 38f, 49, 124, 170-173, (III. *Agr.* 21), IV. *Conf.* 124 & [N], *Mig.* 74, *Congr.* 54 [N], VI. *Abr.* 12n & [N], VIII. *Virt.* 199

Abihu : see Nadab

Abimelech : III. *Plant.* 169 (Gen. xxvi), IV. *Quis Her.* 258, V. *Som.* i. 1-2[N] (Gen. xx), VI. *Abr.* 92-106

Abraham : Abram is πατὴρ μετέωρος, the 'father high-soaring' or 'uplifted father,' signifying the mind which surveys the supra-terrestrial, called 'father' because it cares for its tenets (*Abr.* 82), or because it is the father of our compound being (*Gig.* 62, *cf. Leg. All.* iii. 83), or because it is productive of some wisdom (*Mut.* 68). This is the mind of the lover of learning, the meteorologist or astrologer, given to nature-study (*Gig.* 62f, *Mut.* 70f, 76, *cf. Abr.* 82, 84), associated with Abram's residence in Chaldaea and contrasted with his departure from there and his new name (*Leg. All.* iii. 83f,[a] *cf.* 244, *Cher.* 4, *Gig.* 62, *Mut.* 66-71, 76, *Abr.* 81-84)

Abraham is πατὴρ ἐκλεκτὸς ἠχοῦς, the 'elect father of sound,' signifying the good man's reasoning (*Gig.* 64, *cf. Cher.* 7), because reason (*Gig.* 64) or mind (*Cher.* 7, *Mut.* 66, *Abr.* 83, 99) is father of the uttered word (ὁ γεγωνὸς or προφορικὸς λόγος). This is the man of wisdom (*Mut.* 69f, *Abr.* 84) or man of worth, chosen out of all for his merits (*Gig.* 63), who pursues ethical philosophy

---

[a] In *Leg. All.* iii. 83f Philo may be coupling this with a favourable interpretation, 'the mind which contemplates the Deity'; but probably there too he is alluding to the change of name.

(*Mut.* 76), the man of God (*Gig.* 63). See *Cher.* 7, *Gig.* 63f, *Mut.* 66, 69f, 76, *Abr.* 81-84

He is called the wise man or Sage (*passim* ; see p. 278, n), or the man of worth,[a] the good man (ὁ σπουδαῖος, *Leg. All.* iii. 217, *Mig.* 110, 129, *Quis Her.* 129, *Mut.* 31, 201, *Som.* ii. 256), pious (*Leg. All.* iii. 10), faithful (*Post.* 173), just (*Leg. All.* iii. 9, *Decal.* 38, cf. *Abr.* 232), perfect (*Leg. All.* iii. 203, 244, *Quod Deus* 4, *Quis Her.* 275, *Mut.* 270, cf. *Abr.* 244 & n, 270, *Virt.* 217, *Sac.* 7), the lover of God (φιλόθεος,[b] *Cher.* 7, *Post.* 21, *Abr.* 50, cf. 170) and beloved of God (θεοφιλής, *Abr.* 50, 89, cf. 273, *Sob.* 56 & [N], *Som.* i. 193f). He is the elder (πρεσβύτερος, Gen. xxiv. 1 ; by virtue of his right reasoning, *Sob.* 17, 18 & [N], or wisdom, *Abr.* 270, 274), the most ancient (πρεσβύτατος, *Virt.* 212), the first (*Abr.* 272, 276), the founder of the race (*Quis Her.* 279, *Som.* i. 167, *Mut.* 88, *Abr.* 98, 276, cf. 56, *Mos.* i. 7, *Virt.* 206f, cf. *Praem.* 166 & n). He is regarded as a prophet (*Quis Her.* 258f, 263-266, *Virt.* 218). (See further below)

Abraham at first dwelt in Chaldaea, signifying mere opinion (*Gig.* 62, *Mig.* 187) and the study of the supra-terrestrial (*Cher.* 4, *Gig.* 62, *Mut.* 67f) or astrology (*Congr.* 45n, 49, *Mut.* 16, 71, *Som.* i. 53, 161, *Abr.* 69, 77, 82, *Virt.* 212 & n, *Praem.* 58), the study of nature and its causes (*Congr.* 48f,

---

[a] ἀστεῖος, *Mig.* 130, *Quis Her.* 276, *Mut.* 175, 180, 193, 252, *Som.* ii. 244, *Abr.* 83, 85, 90, 118, 214, 225, 242, 274. The English translations vary.

[b] Compare also φιλάρετος (*Abr.* 68, cf. 220, 224), φιλοδίκαιος (225), φιλομαθής (*Congr.* 68, 73, 111, *Mut.* 70, cf. 270), φιλόσοφος (*Mut.* 70, cf. *Cher.* 45, *Mig.* 149, *Abr.* 224, 271) ; cf. also *Abr.* 271 (with φρόνησις), *Mig.* 197 (with ἐπιστήμη).

Mut. 76, *cf. Quis Her.* 289, *Abr.* 69f), a poly-
theistic creed (*Virt.* 214, *cf. Mig.* 184 & n).[a] But
he awoke or was awakened to the falsity of this
(*Abr.* 70, 78-80, *Virt.* 214, *Abr.* 88) and departed
from Chaldaea and dwelt in Haran, the land of
sense-perception (*Mig.* 176f, 184-189, 195, *Som.*
i. 41-44, 47, 52-60, *Abr.* 72 & n). Then in obedience to divine command, or by free impulse (*Abr.*
88 ; contrast 67, *cf. Virt.* 214), he left Haran and
his kindred and his father's house (*Abr.* 67, 85-88,
Virt. 214 ; ' body, sense and speech,' *Det.* 159,
Mig. 1-12, 192, 195).[b] Soon after God appeared
to him (*Det.* 159, *Mig.* 192, 195, *Som.* i. 59f, *Abr.*
70f, 77-80, 84, 88, *Virt.* 214, *Praem.* 58).[b] So this
was a spiritual emigration (*Abr.* 66, 68f), an advance from self-knowledge to the vision and
knowledge of God (*Mig.* 1-12, 192, 195, *Quis Her.*
287-289, *Congr.* 48f, *Abr.* 72 & n, 77-80, 87f, *cf.*
Mut. 16, *Som.* i. 59f, *Abr.* 70f, *Virt.* 214f, *Praem.*
58, *Leg. All.* iii. 244), to wisdom (*Mut.* 70f) and
virtue (*Mut.* 70-76) and truth (*Mig.* 1-12, *Virt.*
214, *Praem.* 58), a true stripping of the soul (*Leg.*
All. ii. 59, *cf. Mig.* 192 & n, *Som.* i. 43). There-
after his name was changed (see above).[c] Mean-

---

[a] In *Cher.* 4, *Mig.* 178-181, *Mut.* 67f (*cf. Gig.* 62) Philo's
view of the sojourn in Chaldaea is favourable or partly favourable. It is unfavourable or partly unfavourable in *Abr.* 69f,
79, 84, 88, *Virt.* 212f, *Praem.* 58, *Mig.* 179, 194, *Congr.*
48f, *Som.* i. 161.

[b] Often Philo directly links the vision of God with Abraham's earlier migration from Chaldaea (*Quis Her.* 287-289,
Congr. 48f, *Mut.* 16, 70-73, *Som.* i. 161, *Abr.* 69-71, 80, *cf.*
84, 88, *Virt.* 214, *Praem.* 58).

[c] The similarity of Gen. xii. 7 and xvii. 1 has made it easy
for Philo to connect the change of name (xvii. 5) with the
emigrations from Chaldaea and Haran (xi. 31, xii. 1).

while, when compelled by famine to enter Egypt (*Quis Her.* 286-289) his marriage [a] was protected as a reward for his departure from Haran (*Abr.* 90-98). His separation from Lot (*Abr.* 211-225) showed his kindness (208ff) and peaceableness (216, 225) ; the quarrel represented a conflict of principles in the soul (220-223 & n, *cf. Mig.* 150 & [N]). On the other hand, his courageous and warlike nature (225) was revealed by his conflict with Chederlaomer and the kings ; this was a victory over the four passions and five sense-faculties (*Ebr.* 105, *Conf.* 26, *Congr.* 92f, *Abr.* 236-244), over evil and wrongdoings (*Ebr.* 24, *Quis Her.* 286-289), a victory of reason or the Word (*Abr.* 243f), of the friendly and perfect number, Ten (*Congr.* 91-93, *Abr.* 244), establishing democracy (*Abr.* 242 & n). In this Abraham revealed his kindness and trust in God (*Abr.* 232, *cf. Virt.* 22n) and might (*Ebr.* 105f). His refusal to accept any spoil from the king of Sodom was the obedience of the man of worth who dissociates himself from evil (*Leg. All.* iii. 24 & n, 197) and acknowledges only God (*Ebr.* 105f)

When God made promise of a son, "Abraham believed God and He counted it to him for righteousness " : that is, his virtue or expectation was rewarded with faith, the one sure good (*Mig.* 44, *Abr.* 268, 273, *Virt.* 216, *Praem.* 27, 49f & [N]). His faith in God is in contrast to trust in reasonings (*Leg. All.* iii. 228), the inconstancy of created things (*Quod Deus* 4, *Praem.* 28-30), lower things (*Quis Her.* 92f), externals (*Abr.* 269),

[a] Sarah is Virtue (*Leg. All.* iii. 218, *Post.* 62, etc.), or Wisdom (*Congr.* 72f).

sense-perception (*Praem.* 28-30). On the other hand, his faith is not absolute, such as that of God (*Mut.* 181f, 186, *cf.* 201, 218 ; *cf. Quis Her.* 94f). His union with Hagar was advised by Sarah because he was still Abram, inquiring into supra-mundane things (for Hagar is School-learning or the Culture of the Schools ; *Leg. All.* iii. 244) and the things of sense (*Congr.* 81, 88). Abram's name was changed to Abraham when his character improved and he became perfect (see Scripture Index, *s.v.* Gen. xvii. 1, *Leg. All.* iii. 244, *Cher.* 4, *Gig.* 63, *Mut.* 65, 70f, 76, *cf.* 83f, 87). His laughter at God's promise of a son is variously justified : it was because he was about to beget Happiness (*Leg. All.* iii. 85-87, 218, *cf. Mut.* 166) ; because of his joy in God as the sole cause of good gifts (*Mut.* 154-156) ; the doubt was one of the mind only, and quite momentary (175-180), but sincere (193 & n, *cf. Abr.* 110f). His entertainment of the three strange visitors showed his kindliness (*Abr.* 107), generosity (110) and piety (114), and God's recognition of his wisdom (118). Allegorically the incident represents Abraham's vision of God and His potencies (*Cher.* 106, *Abr.* 119-132). The birth of Isaac was promised as a thank-offering for their stay (*Sac.* 122, *Abr.* 110). Abraham interceded for Sodom because he believed that God would spare the rest for the sake of the least particle of virtue (*Mig.* 122f, *Mut.* 228) : scanty goodness by God's favour expands ; this is signified by the number Ten (*Sac.* 122, *Congr.* 109), which God accepted, *viz.*, the lower training or education (*Mut.* 228). *Cf. Abr.* 164-166

INDEX OF NAMES

Abraham's greatest action was his readiness to
sacrifice Isaac (*Abr.* 167-207) ; he was steadfast
in his love for God (170), and it was an offering
made in piety (177, 198) and obedience (192), an
allegory of the offering of joy to God (200-207).
Attention is drawn to his moderation in grief
over the loss of Sarah (245f, 255-261). For this
he was hailed as a king (261, *Virt.* 216 & n, 218)
—an example of a ruler appointed for ever by
Nature herself (*Mut.* 151). This kingship in the
mind illustrates the principle that the sage alone
is king (*Mut.* 152f & [N], *Som.* ii. 244, *Abr.* 261,
cf. Mig. 196f) and that this kingship is a gift from
God in reward for virtue (*Abr.* 261, *Virt.* 216).[a]
Abraham's purchase of the cave of Machpelah
(see Scripture Index, *s.v.* Gen. xxiii. 3ff) and his
marriage to Keturah (*Sac.* 43f, *cf. Congr.* 34f,
Virt. 207 ; contrast *Cher.* 40) are both mentioned.
Finally, Gen. xxv. 8 (LXX) is interpreted as not
implying death : Abraham, being a fully purified
soul, inherited incorruption and passed direct to
heaven (*Sac.* 5-7, *Quis Her.* 276-289)

He had been a man of wealth and power (*Det.* 14,
Mig. 94, *Abr.* 209 & n, 252 ; contrast *Mut.* 152) ;
though his life was comparatively short (*Sob.* 17,
Quis Her. 291), he had lived in harmony with
nature (*Mig.* 128) and with the will of God (*Leg.
All.* iii. 197), Whose worthy servant (*Quis Her.* 8f)
and companion (*Gig.* 64) he was, enjoying access
(*Post.* 27, *Mig.* 132) and intimacy (*Cher.* 18, *Gig.*
62f, *Ebr.* 94, *Quis Her.* 289). God was his instructor (*Som.* i. 173, *cf. Sac.* 5-7) and standard in

[a] For Philo's interest in Gen. xxv. 5, 6, see Scripture Index.

all things (*Cher.* 31) ; for, recognizing his meanness before Him (*Quod Deus* 161), his was the soul that hides away wickedness and longs for all beauteous things (*Leg. All.* iii. 27, *cf. Abr.* 48-51), flying from himself and taking refuge in God (*Leg. All.* iii. 39), stretching Godwards (*Ebr.* 105f), the very type of the pilgrim soul (*Quis Her.* 280). He was a man of vision (*Ebr.* 107, *Som.* ii. 226f, *Abr.* 70f, 79f, *Praem.* 30, 58, *cf. Det.* 159) and a man of God (*Gig.* 63), inspired by divine spirit, whereby his whole being and character were refined (*Virt.* 217).

He is numbered in the second (and higher) Patriarchal triad of those who yearn for virtue, signifying that virtue which comes by Teaching (*Congr.* 35f, *Mut.* 12, *Som.* i. 168-172, *Mos.* i. 76, *Praem.* 27, 49 & [N], *cf. Mig.* 125 & [N].[a] See *s.vv.* Isaac, Jacob). Thus he was the grandfather of Jacob's early training and knowledge (*Sac.* 43 & n, *Sob.* 65, *Mut.* 270, *Abr.* 50, *Som.* i. 47 & n & [N], 70 ; contrast 171f, *cf. Quod Deus* 92 & [N]) and the starting-point for that of Moses (*Post.* 174). He was thus himself a learner (*Congr.* 63, 122, *Som.* i. 171) and pupil of God (see above), apt to learn because he despaired of himself (*Som.* i. 60) and was eager for knowledge (*Mut.* 88), and because he combined attention, memory (*cf. Mig.* 125 & [N], *Mut.* 84, 270) and the valuing of deeds before words (*Congr.* 68), and retained what he had learned and so remained constant (*Mut.* 84, *cf. Post* 27). Thus, taught by natural zeal, he was not only one who obeyed the law,

---

[a] Here Abraham is described as one of the threefold divisions of eternity or time (αἰῶνος μέτρα).

but rather himself a law and an unwritten statute (*Abr.* 275f)

Philo often mentions his particular qualities of character : in addition to the epithets already mentioned, he alludes to his virtue,[a] his piety,[b] his holiness (*Abr.* 198, cf. *Praem.* 24), spiritual refinement (*Virt.* 217), justice (*Abr.* 219, 225, 232), sincerity (*Mut.* 193 & n), obedience (*Abr.* 60, 88, 192, 276), faith (see Scripture Index *s.v.* Gen. xv. 6) and faithfulness (*Quis Her.* 129) and constancy (see above), his wisdom,[c] sound sense (φρόνησις, *Mig.* 164, *Abr.* 219, 271), moderation (σωφροσύνη, *Abr.* 219, cf. 256-261), reason (*Abr.* 256, *Praem.* 30, cf. *Leg. All.* iii. 9), knowledge (*Congr.* 153, 156, *Som.* i. 59f, 160, *Praem.* 61, cf. *Quis Her.* 93), confidence blended with caution (*Quis Her.* 22) ; his courage (*Abr.* 225, 219) and war-like quality (225), yet peaceableness (*ib.*), love of tranquillity (216) and solitude (87) ; his kindness of heart (107, 208, 232), hospitality (114,

[a] ἀρετή, *Leg. All.* iii. 24, 244f, *Cher.* 40, *Post.* 62, 75f, *Mig.* 167 & n, *Congr.* 35, *Mut.* 71, 83f, *Som.* ii. 90, 255-258, *Abr.* 51f, cf. 60, 219f, 221, cf. 224, 244, 261, 269, *Mos.* i. 76, *Praem.* 27.

[b] εὐσέβεια, *Leg. All.* iii. 209, *Mut.* 76, 155, *Abr.* 60f, 98-208, esp. 114, cf. 177, 198f, 208, *Virt.* 218.

[c] σοφία, *Cher.* 45, *Post.* 174, *Sob.* 55f, *Conf.* 77-79, *Congr.* 48, 73ff, 153, 156, *Mut.* 32, 69, 71, 270, *Som.* i. 66, *Abr.* 118, 219f, 224, 271, *Mos.* i. 76, *Praem.* 27, 49 & [N]. ' Wise ' is the most frequent epithet of Abraham : *Leg. All.* iii. 210, 217, 244, *Cher.* 7, 10, 18 (πάνσοφος), 31, 106, *Sac.* 122, *Det.* 59, 124, *Post.* 18, 27, *Plant.* 73, *Ebr.* 24, 105, *Sob.* 17, 65, *Conf.* 26, 77-79, *Mig.* 13, 94, 109, 122, 129, 140, *Quis Her.* 1, 88, 91, 258, 280, 313, *Congr.* 48, 92, 109, 119, *Fug.* 200, *Mut.* 69-71, 152, 155, 270, *Som.* i. 214, *Som.* ii. 89f, 226, 244, 255, *Abr.* 68, 77, 80, 83f, 118, 132, 142, 168, 199, 202, 213, 229, 255, 261, 272, 275, *Praem.* 58.

cf. 167), domestic authority (116), fatherly affection (170, 194-199), conjugal faithfulness (*Congr.* 73, 78-80), sexual continence (*Cher.* 40, *Mut.* 31-34, *Abr.* 253 & n) ; his industry (*Plant.* 73-77), law-abidingness and stability (*Quis Her.* 289, *Abr.* 276); he was great and lofty in character (*Abr.* 199), worthy of our affection (88), the very pattern of nobility (*Virt.* 219, *cf. Abr.* 98, 276)

212n, *Praem.* 23[N], 24-30, 49 & [N], 57f & nn, 61, 166 & n, IX. *Flacc.* 74n, *Hyp.* 6. 1n

Ada : wife of Lamech (*Post.* 75, 112), means ' Witness ' (79), bearing witness to the success of worthless things and being borne witness to as helping to accomplish them (83). Represents the Epicurean school (79[N])

Adam : For Philo Adam is generic man rather than an actual individual ; and in fact he treats the story of Eve's creation from Adam as an allegorical myth (*Leg. All.* ii. 19, *cf.* I. Gen. Introd. p. xiii). As such Adam stands for the mind of man, and occasionally for the soul

" There are two races of men, the one made after the (Divine) Image, and the one moulded out of the earth " (*Leg. All.* ii. 4) ; Philo generally distinguishes the two accounts of creation given in Gen. i. 27 and ii. 7 ; the first is the genus man, male and female, the second is the species (*Leg. All.* ii. 13). In *Op.* 134 he says that the first is not an objective being at all, but an idea, type or seal, incorporeal. Generally the contrast is between the spiritual man made after the image of God and the earthly man made out of clay. In *Quis Her.* 56f the point of contrast is not the two creations but the two elements in man, the spiritual (Gen. i. 27 and ii. 7, " God breathed into him the breath of life ") and the earthly (ii. 7, made from clay). In *Plant.* 18-20 the two creations are taken together as complementary rather than contrasted ; so, too, in the fine passage in *Virt.* 203-205 (*cf. Op.* 72-76, where Philo builds upon the use of the plural in ' Let us make,' accounting thus for the evil in man).

When contrasted, the points of contrast are the material and the manner of the constitution of each (*Op.* 134, *Leg. All.* i. 31, 33, 42, 88, *Plant.* 44f, *cf. Quis Her.* 56f), their character (*Leg. All.* i. 53-55, 92-96, *Plant.* 45, *cf. Quis Her.* 56f), their status and function in Eden (*Leg. All.* i. 53-55, 88f, 92-96, *Plant.* 44f).

The direct equation of Adam with Mind is made frequently (*Leg. All.* i. 90, 92, iii. 50, 185, (222), 246, *Cher.* 10, 57 (*Plant.* 42, 46, *Quis Her.* 52, 257, *Virt.* 204)) ; in many more instances Philo assumes this equation and launches into his interpretation (*e.g., Leg. All.* i. 42, 55, ii. 49f, *Quis Her.* 231). It is in respect of the mind within the soul that Adam or man is said to be made after the image of God (*Op.* 69, *Virt.* 204). This mind may be said to partake of spirit, for its reasoning faculty possesses robustness (*Leg. All.* i. 42). It is the less material mind, having no part in perishable matter, endowed with a constitution of a purer and clearer kind : it is the heavenly mind (88, 90), immortal (*Op.* 134, *Plant.* 44), the child of God (*Virt.* 204). This is the mind to whom God affords secure knowledge of virtue and the double advantage of practising and remembering it (*Leg. All.* i. 89). It possesses virtue instinctively, and so needs no command or prohibition from God (*ib.* 92). Usually the emphasis is on the likeness and proximity to God ; but in *Quis Her.* 231 (*cf. Leg. All.* iii. 96) Philo deduces from " *after* the *image* of God " that the likeness was at third hand

It is less easy to define the other type of mind, the one signified by the man moulded from the

earth (*Plant.* 32, 34, 41f, 44, *Congr.* 90, *Abr.* 12 ;
cf. Som. ii. 70, *Abr.* 56, *Virt.* 203), because Philo
is sometimes comparing it unfavourably with the
first creation, and sometimes favourably with
the creation of Sense-Perception (Eve). The
man moulded from the earth is the first objective
creation by the Artificer, but not His offspring
(*Leg. All.* i. 31 ; but see *Virt.* 204). Nevertheless it is, more strictly speaking, this mind which
is called Adam (*Leg. All.* i. 90, *Cher.* 57, *Plant.*
42 ; *cf. Op.* 165. But see *Quis Her.* 261). He is
mind mingling with, but not yet blended with,
body. This earth-like mind is also corruptible,
were not God to breathe into it a power of real
life, making it a soul, endowed with mind and
actually alive (*Leg. All.* i. 32). This was ' of
grace ' on God's part, Who has thus created no
soul barren of virtue (34). Furthermore, it
means that man could not plead that his sin was
due to ignorance (33-35). It is only by this in-
breathing that the soul of man conceives of God
(38). The mind in turn shares this inspiration
with the unreasoning part of the soul (40). On
the other hand, this breathing into the mind
made out of matter is insubstantial air compared
with the spirit of the image-mind (42). It is
placed amid virtue (*Eden*, 47) because it is
rational (*Plant.* 42) ; but in contrast to the image-
mind, it neither remembers nor practises it, but
has facility for apprehending it only (*Leg. All.* i.
55). Such a mind is the more earthly and perishable (88, 90) ; it is incapable of knowing itself
(91) ; it can have no part in wisdom indepen-
dently of command and exhortation (92) ; it is

neutral, being neither bad nor good (93, 95); it cannot be alone, for it is closely linked with the senses, passions, and vices (*Leg. All.* ii. 4). Here Philo begins to treat of it in relation to Eve or Sense-Perception. The mind prior to the creation of sense-perception is the older (*Cher.* 60) and princely part of the soul, as opposed to the irrational portion (*Leg. All.* ii. 6). It is mind without body (*Leg. All.* ii. 22, iii. 49, *Cher.* 58); with many powers and faculties lying dormant (*Leg. All.* ii. 22, 37), but an incomplete soul (24, *cf. Op.* 166, *Cher.* 59f). From one of these faculties, a quiescent state of perception, God made the *activity* of perception (*Leg. All.* ii. 35-37, 40, 45). This was done while the mind was asleep, for that means the waking of sense (25, *Quis Her.* 257; but see *Leg. All.* ii. 31). This sense-perception poured light into the mind (*Cher.* 61). For the sake of sense-perception the mind abandons both God and His wisdom, resolving itself into the inferior order of flesh (*Leg. All.* ii. 49f). Sense-perception has a certain independence of mind (iii. 56-58; contrast ii. 41); when it is subservient to mind, good results (i. 50, iii. 221f): but the reverse is profitless. The nakedness of Adam and Eve typifies the nakedness of the neutral mind, clothed neither with vice nor with virtue (ii. 53, *cf.* iii. 55). It is irrational and amoral (ii. 64f). This infant-like state (53) is prior to that of apprehension (70).[a] It is in *Leg.*

---

[a] Notice that whereas the neutral state of the moulded mind was contrasted with the goodness of the image-mind in *Leg. All.* i. 93, 95 above, and that because it was prior to the creation of sense-perception, here the neutrality is that of

283

All. iii. 246f that Philo seems to develop this
theme of neutrality most fully, in terms of Gen.
iii. 17 : Adam is the neutral mind, for in so far as
he is mind, his nature is neither bad nor good,
but under the influence of virtue and vice it is
his wont to shift towards good and bad. The
doings of the whole soul (does Philo mean mind
and sense-perception ?) are blameworthy when
it allows wickedness to regulate them. In pain
does the bad man all his life long avail himself of
his own vitality ; his only motive for joy is supplied by righteousness and good sense and the
virtues. Thus the neutral mind is given the high
calling of deciding its own destiny (*Plant.* 45).
The Fall ended all neutrality, and Adam becomes
the foolish mind [a] or the bad man (*Leg. All.* iii.
200, 216, 251f, *Cher.* 10). His flight from God
leads only to the error of self-sufficiency (*Leg.
All.* iii. 28-31). He is expelled from Eden or
Virtue for ever (*Leg. All.* i. 55, *Cher.* 10, *Plant.*
46). His vanity of soul is later revealed in his
naming his son as Cain or ' Possession ' (*Cher.* 57,
63 ; *cf. Leg. All.* ii. 68-70)

Adam is often referred to as the ' first founder of
the race ' (*Op.* 79, 136, 142, *Mut.* 64, *cf. Abr.* 56,
Virt. 199) or, simply, ' the first man ' (*Op.* 136,
140, 148, 151, 156, *Leg. All.* ii. 14f, *Plant.* 34, *Abr.*
12, 56, *Virt.* 203). He is the first ' world-citizen '
(*Op.* 3 & [N], 142 & [N]). In contrast with his
later folly and wickedness, he is wise (*Op.* 148,
Mut. 64, *cf. Leg. All.* ii. 15), surpassing all later men

Adam and Eve, prior to the eating of the fruit of the tree of
knowledge.
[a] But see below.

in body and soul, the bloom of the race (*Op.* 140), the noblest of things earthborn and of perishable creatures, a miniature heaven (*Op.* 82, *cf. Virt.* 203), a being naturally adapted for sovereignty (*Op.* 84), and so a king, viceroy of God (148, *cf. Mut.* 63). It was because of this kingship that he was made responsible for the naming of the creatures (*ib.*); but also because of his wisdom (148, *Mut.* 64), and because God was testing him, to make him exert some faculty of his own (149), testing, too, his character, to see how he would welcome, name, and make use of wealth, pleasure, etc. (*Leg. All.* ii. 16-18); also because he was to be regarded as the beginning of the use of speech (*ib.* 14f, 18), God carefully avoiding being responsible for letters and parts of speech (*Mut.* 63f). But in fact these names were signs of moral values (*Mut.* 65). By thus assigning the giving of names to one man incongruity and inconsistency were avoided (*Leg. All.* ii. 15). Adam was placed in Eden that his choice might be tested (*Op.* 155, *Plant.* 32, 41, *Virt.* 205). There woman became for him the beginning of a blameworthy life : bodily pleasure led to his fall (*Op.* 151, 165). His crime was that he honoured the two before the One, the created rather than the Creator (*Som.* ii. 70), the false rather than the true (*Virt.* 205). He was expelled [a] from the garden by God, evil-mindedness expelled from holy boundaries by the Good (*Congr.* 171); thus he forfeited immortality and happiness and en-

---

[a] The departure from Eden is usually an expulsion or an involuntary act (*Post.* 10); but in *Plant.* 34 and *Leg. All.* i. 55 Adam is said to run away or migrate.

INDEX OF NAMES

Omn. Prob. 125, *Vit. Cont.* 21, *Flacc.* Introd. pp.
295-299, 2, 23, 26, 28, 43, 45, 47, 74, 78, 80, 103,
110, 141, 163, **X.** *Leg.* Introd. pp. xi, xii, xvii,
xviii, xxi n, xxiv & n, xxvi & n, xxvii, 120-141,
150, 162-166, 170, 172f, 183, 194, 250, 338, 346, 350

Aloeidae : **IV.** *Conf.* 4

Amalek : ' a people licking out,' so ' Passion,' which
" eats up the whole soul and licks it out, leaving
behind in it no seed or spark of virtue " ; through
it all the war of the soul is fanned into flame
(**I.** *Leg. All.* iii. 186f, *cf.* **IV.** *Mig.* 143f, *Congr.* 54-
56).   It represents the very opposite of the
Practiser, whom it attacks (**III.** *Ebr.* 24, **IV.** *Mig.*
143f), **VI.** *Mos.* i. 214n, 215ff, **VIII.** *Virt.* 22n

Aminadab : **II.** *Post.* 76 (Exod. vi. 23)

Ammonites : descendants of Lot's daughters, by
incest, according to Gen. xix. 38 (**II.** *Post.* 176f,
VII. *Spec. Leg.* i. 333n).   They refused hospitality
to Israel before the entry into Canaan, and so
were to be shut out from the congregation of the
Lord (Deut. xxiii. 3, 4 ; **I.** *Leg. All.* iii. 81) ; but
they are also excluded, in Philo's mind, because
of their impure descent, by which they inherit
the nature of sense-perception (**II.** *Post.* 177,
VII. *Spec. Leg.* i. 333n, 327[N]).   They signify
those who attribute creation to (mind and) sense-
perception (**II.** *Post.* 177).   See also Moabites

Amorites : ' talkers ' (**I.** *Leg. All.* iii. 232, **IV.** *Quis Her.*
302), a figure of the uttered word (ὁ γεγωνὸς
λόγος), especially plausible, sophistical speech
(*Quis Her.* 302, 304) or unanalysed ways of
thought (308).   In **III.** *Quod Deus* 99 they represent the inward feelings which chase (Deut. i.
43f) those who do not achieve righteousness.

INDEX OF NAMES

Arphaxad : son of Shem, begotten when he was a hundred years old (Gen. xi. 10). Means ' he disturbed affliction ' : the soul's offspring harasses and destroys injustice, afflicted and full of evils as it is (V. *Mut.* 189). Philo is discoursing upon the perfect number one hundred

Artemis : VII. *Decal.* 54

Asa : (IV. *Conf.* 149)

Ascalon : IX. *Prov.* 2. 64, X. *Leg.* 205

Asenath : wife of Joseph, daughter of the priest of Heliopolis (Gen. xli. 45). Signifies the Senses, daughters of Mind (V. *Som.* i. 78 & n)

Asher : means ' felicitation ' and symbolizes natural wealth, which has the reputation of conferring felicity (V. *Som.* ii. 35). But he was the son of Leah's handmaid, and so in IV. *Mig.* 95 he is the symbol of counterfeit (bastard) wealth, outward and visible (*cf.* III. *Sob.* 12[N])

Asia, Asians : II. *Cher.* 63, III. *Quod Deus* 175, V. *Som.* ii. 54, VI. *Jos.* 134, *Mos.* i. 263, ii. 19f, IX. *Quod Omn. Prob.* 94, 132, *Aet.* 141, *Flacc.* 46, X. *Leg.* 10, 22, 48, 88, 144, 245, 250, 280f, 283, 311

Assyria, Assyrians : means ' directing ' and stands for pleasure, which thinks that it can direct the course of human weakness (I. *Leg. All.* i. 69, 85-87). Philo is interpreting Gen. ii. 14, where the river Tigris (self-mastery) is said to flow over against Assyria. VI. *Mos.* i. 23 & [N], Assyrian letters

Athena : I. *Leg. All.* i. 15

Athens, Athenians : I. *Op.* 104, VI. *Abr.* 10, *Mos.* ii. 19, VII. *Spec. Leg.* iii. 22, IX. *Quod Omn. Prob.* 47, 127-129, 132, 137n, 140

Athos : V. *Som.* ii. 118

INDEX OF NAMES

Atlantic : **III.** *Ebr.* 133

Atlantis : **IX.** *Aet.* 141

Attica, Attic : **II.** *Post.* 94, **IX.** *Flacc.* 156, 173, **X.** *Leg.* 281

Augusta : see *s.vv.* Caesarea, Julia

Augustan House : **IX.** *Flacc.* 23, 49, 81, 103f, **X.** *Leg.* 48, 149, 322

Augustus : G. Julius Caesar Octavianus, first Emperor, 27 B.C.–A.D. 14, grandfather of Gaius Caesar (Caligula), **IX.** *Flacc.* 50, 74, 105, **X.** *Leg.* 143-158, 291, 305, 309-319, 322

Augustus : Gaius Caesar (Caligula), third Emperor, A.D. 37-41, **X.** *Leg.* 240, 322, 352. See *s.v.* Gaius

Aunan : **IV.** *Mig.* 164, 165 & n. Means ' eyes,' and so stands for the vision-lover, since the eyes of the soul are opened by cheerfulness. Eshcol (good natural ability) and Aunan are rewarded with Mamre (the contemplative life) for inheritance (Gen. xiv. 24)

Autolycus : **IX.** *Vit. Cont.* 57

Avillius : see Flaccus

Baal : **VI.** *Mos.* i. 276n

Baal-Peor : " And Israel joined himself unto Baal-Peor " (Num. xxv. 3), perhaps ' Baal of Peor ' ; in any case the reference is to heathen cult. It occurs in the context of the incident of Phinehas leading to the Midianite war (see **VIII.** *Virt.* 34[N]), described in **VI.** *Mos.* i. 300-304, **VIII.** *Virt.* 34-46. So Philo interprets : Midianites (those ' sifted out ' as unfit), initiated in the unholy rites of Baal-Peor, and widening all the orifices of the body to receive the streams which pour in from outside (for the meaning of Baal-

290

INDEX OF NAMES

Peor is ' mouth of skin (or leather) above '—
ἀνωτέρω στόμα δέρματος), flood the ruling mind
and sink it (V. *Mut.* 106f). So Midian is also described as the nurse of things bodily, and Baal-
Peor as her offspring, the heavy leathern weight
(δερμάτινον ὄγκον, IV. *Conf.* 55 ; here Philo is
interpreting Num. xxxi. 49 with xxv in mind).
In Deut. iv. 3, 4 the Israelites are reminded of
the fate of their fellows who sinned in following
Baal-Peor and perished ; this allusion underlies
Philo's exposition in V. *Fug.* 56, VII. *Spec. Leg.* i.
31 & n, 345 & n

Babel : or ' Confusion ' (Gen. xi. 9, LXX, A.V. mg.),
II. *Post.* 81, IV. *Conf.* 1, 183-195, IV. *Quis Her.*
228n, V. *Som.* ii. 283-290, 283n & [N], VIII. *Praem.*
23 [N], 111[N]

Babylon, Babylonia : II. *Gig.* 66, V. *Som.* ii. 59,
VI. *Abr.* 188, *Mos.* i. 5, 34, VIII. *Virt.* 223, X. *Leg.*
216, 282. Only in *Gig.* 66 does Philo allegorize ; Nimrod (' desertion ') has Babylon (' alteration ') as the beginning of his kingdom (Gen.
x. 10, LXX), for with every deserter change and
alteration of purpose are the first steps

Bacchants, Bacchic, Bacchus : III. *Plant.* 148, IX. *Vit.
Cont.* 85, X. *Leg.* 96

Balaam : ' foolish (or ' vain,' μάταιος) people ' (*Cher.*
32, *Conf.* 159 & n, *Mig.* 113), a sophist, an empty
(μάταιος) conglomeration of incompatible and
discordant notions (*Det.* 71), a dealer in auguries
and prodigies and in the vanity of unfounded
conjecture (*Quod Deus* 181, *Conf.* 159, *Mut.* 202),
dwells in Mid-River Land, for his understanding
is submerged (*Conf.* 66) ; he is no heavenly
growth, but a creature of earth (*Quod Deus* 181).

With his soothsaying mock wisdom he defaces
the stamp of heaven-sent prophecy (*Mut.* 202)

Balak : means ' foolish,' for it is the pitch of folly to
hope that God should be deceived and His purpose upset by the devices of men (IV. *Conf.* 65,
on Num. xxiii. 7f). The whole story of Balak
and Balaam is told at length in VI. *Mos.* i. 263-
300, 305.

Beersheba : the ' well of the oath ' is so named by
Abraham and by Isaac (Gen. xxi. 31, III. *Plant.*
73f, 78 ; xxvi. 33, *Plant.* 78-84, V. *Som.* i. 8, 12,
14, 40). It is from Beersheba that Isaac departs
to go to Haran (xxviii. 10, *Som.* i. 4, 5 & n, 6-13,
42, 61, 68). It represents the inexhaustible
nature of knowledge (*Plant.* 78-84, *Som.* i. 42) ;
also the endless quest of the fourth cosmic region,
heaven (*Som.* i. 14-24)

Benjamin : means ' Son of days ' (*Mut.* 92f, *Som.* ii.
36) and symbolizes vainglory, for the day is
illumined by the sunlight visible to our senses,
to which we liken vainglory (*Mut.* 92). This
name is given him by his father, the head of the
house, the reason ; but the soul (Rachel) calls
him a Son of Sorrow, knowing by experience the
unhappiness that goes with vainglory. Rachel

died on giving birth to him, for the conception and birth of vainglory, the creature of sense, is in reality the death of the soul (*Mut.* 94-96). In *Som.* ii. 36, 41 the interpretation of his name is quite neutral : he is a symbol of time, both that of youth and that of old age, which are alike measured by days and nights. In *Mig.* 203 it is almost favourable : he is the offspring of sense-perception, and he receives from Joseph five changes of raiment because he deems the senses pre-eminent and deserving of adornment and honour. Naturally in the narrative of Joseph's life he is often mentioned (*Jos.* 167-236)

IV. *Mig.* 203, V. *Fug.* 73, *Mut.* 92-96, *Som.* ii. 33, 36, 41, VI. *Jos.* 167-236, 234n

Benoni : ' Son of my sorrow ' (*Mut.* 94-96). See *s.v.* Benjamin

Bered : Hagar's well was between Kadesh (holy) and Bered (in evils) ; he that is in gradual progress (Hagar symbolizes School learning) is on the border-land between the holy and the profane (V. *Fug.* 213)

Bethel : IV. *Conf.* 74, V. *Som.* i. 228 & n

Bethuel : father of Rachel (II. *Post.* 76), means ' Daughter of God ' and signifies Wisdom, an ever-virgin daughter, who by reason alike of her own modesty and the glory of Him that begot her hath obtained a nature free from every defiling touch. And Wisdom is not only masculine but father, begetting aptness to learn, sound sense, etc. (V. *Fug.* 48, 50-52). See also Laban

Bezaleel : the craftsman of the Tabernacle (Exod. xxxi. 2ff), filled with the spirit of God (II. *Gig.* 23). The name means ' In the shadow of God,'

for Bezaleel made the copies only : Moses had
already made the original archetypes (I. *Leg.
All.* iii. 102, III. *Plant.* 26f, V. *Som.* i. 206). In
Som. i. 207 his work typifies the variegated (see
207n) fabric of the world, the product of wisdom.
In *Leg. All.* 95-99 it typifies the soul ; God's
shadow is His Word, by which He made the
world ; but this shadow is the archetype for
further creations (and Philo applies this elabo-
rately to Gen. i. 27)

Bias : **IX.** *Quod Omn. Prob.* 153

Bilhah : handmaid of Rachel (**III.** *Quod Deus* 119-121,
VIII. *Virt.* 223 & n, 224). The name means
' swallowing ' and represents the necessary sub-
sistence of the mortal life (**I.** *Leg. All.* i. 94-96,
iii. 146, **IV.** *Congr.* 29f), which in turn is necessary
to the higher, spiritual life (*Congr.* 33). Also
VIII. *Gen.* Introd. p. xviii n

Bithynia : **X.** *Leg.* 281

Boeotia : **X.** *Leg.* 281

Boethus : **IX.** *Aet.* 76 & nn, 78

Brundisium : **IX.** *Flacc.* 26, 152, 173

Brutus : **IX.** *Quod Omn. Prob.* 118

Bura : **IX.** *Aet.* 140 & n

Buzyges, Buzygia : **IX.** *Hyp.* Introd. p. 407 n, 7, 8 &
n & [N]

Caesar : Julius Caesar : **IX.** *Quod Omn. Prob.* 118.
Caesar Augustus : see *s.v.* Augustus. Tiberius
Caesar : see *s.v.* Tiberius. Gaius Caesar
(Caligula) : **IX.** *Flacc.* 25, 35, 40, 42, **X.** *Leg.*
Introd. pp. xviii, xix, 280, 322, 352, 240 ; and
see *s.v.* Gaius. Claudius Germanicus Caesar :
X. *Leg.* 206

INDEX OF NAMES

Caesarea : **X.** *Leg.* 305 & n

Cain : ' possession '; passively (Adam's possession) in *Cher.* 52, 124-126, but otherwise actively, as claiming that all things are his own possession (*Cher.* 57, 64-66, *Sac.* 2, 72, *cf. Det.* 32), and that even when he is incapable of ruling himself (*Cher.* 65f, *Post.* 42). He symbolizes the self-loving principle (*Sac.* 3, 51f, 71, *Det.* 32, 68, 78, *Post.* 21, *cf. Conf.* 128), ascribing all things to mind rather than God (*Sac.* 2f, *cf.* 71f, *Post.* 35, *cf.* 42),[a] impious and godless (*Cher.* 65, *Sac.* 71, *Det.* 50, 103, 119, *Post.* 12, 34f, 42, *cf.* 52, *Conf.* 125) ; he is occupied with the lower, mortal, earthly level of life (*Det.* 119, *cf.* 156f, *Post.* 38, *cf.* 172), and is dead to the life directed by virtue (*Det.* 47, 69f, 78, *cf.* 156, 165f, *Post.* 45, *Conf.* 122), a deserter in the war against wickedness (*Post.* 172, *cf. Det.* 142, 165f), an example of worthlessness (*Det.* 140, 165), wickedness (*Det.* 68, 165, 167-169, *Post.* 172, *Fug.* 64) and depravity (*Conf.* 122). With him Philo associates false opinion and folly (οἴησις, *Cher.* 57 ; εὐήθεια, 65f ; ἄτοπος δόξα, *Sac.* 5 ; ἀφροσύνη, *Det.* 178, *Conf.* 165 ; ἀπόνοια, *Post.* 35). Often in these passages he is consciously contrasted with Abel

Cain was " a tiller of the ground " (Gen. iv. 2), but an unscientific one, no husbandman (*Agr.* 20-25, 27).[b] His quarrel with Abel is interpreted thus : Cain aimed to draw Abel into a dispute and to

---

[a] In *Det.* 167f (on Gen. iv. 15) Philo makes Cain the mind, the eighth part which is ruler of the seven irrational parts of the soul.

[b] This must underlie Philo's remark in *Mig.* 74f that Cain has the cleverness of the town.

master him with plausible sophistries (*Det.* 1, *cf.*
37, *Post.* 38, *Mig.* 74) ; in murdering Abel he
only did away with himself (*Det.* 47, 50, 52, 69f,
78, *cf. Post.* 21 ; *cf. Post.* 45, *Conf.* 122) and
succeeded in slaying only the impression, the
specimen, not the original, the pattern, the class
(*Det.* 75-78) ; Gen. iv. 11 : he stood agape for all
outward things, praying in his greed to take
them in for the destruction of Abel (*Det.* 100-
103) ; he was accursed (*Fug.* 60, *Virt.* 199f,
Praem. 68-73)—indeed he must have been
accursed from the very start (*Det.* 96),—and was
doomed to fear and misery (*Det.* 119, 140, *Conf.*
165, *Virt.* 199f, *Praem.* 71, 72 & n) ; he " went
out from the presence of the Lord " voluntarily
(Adam was driven out) : his was the moral failure
which is of free choice, and therefore worse (*Post.*
10). Cain's wife is the opinion held by an impious man's reasoning faculty (*Post.* 33-39). He
built a city, *i.e.,* he resolved to set up his own
creed (*Post.* 49-51, 52f, 65, *Conf.* 122). Nothing is
said of his death ; so Philo uses this to declare that
folly is a deathless evil (*Det.* 177f, *Post.* 39, *Conf.*
122, *Fug.* 60 & n, 61, 64, *Virt.* 200, *Praem.* 68-73)

II. *Cher.* 12, 52, 53 & [N]-55, 64-66, 124-126, *Sac.*
1-3, 5, 11, 14, 51f, 71f, 88 & n, *Det.* 1, 32, 37, 47f,
50, 57, 61f, 68-70, 74, 75n, 78f, 96, 100, 103f, 119,
140-142, 163-169, 177f, *Post.* 1, 5f, 10, 12, 21, 33-
35, 38f, 40, 42, 45, 48, 49-51, 52, 65, 124, 172,
III. *Agr.* 20-25, 27, 127, *Sob.* 50 & n, IV. *Conf.*
122 & n, 124, 165, *Mig.* 74. *Congr.* 54[N], 171[N]
V. *Fug.* 60 & n, 64 & n. *Mut.* 195f, VI. *Abr.* 12n &
[N], VIII. Gen. Introd. xxi, *Virt.* 199f, *Praem.*
68-72, 68n, 72n

INDEX OF NAMES

Calanus : **IX.** *Quod Omn. Prob.* 93-96 & n & [N]

Caleb : **VI.** *Mos.* i. 232-236. In **V.** *Mut.* 123f, Num.
xiv. 24 is taken as showing there was a total
change of the man himself, because his name
means ' all heart '

Callias : **IX.** *Vit. Cont.* 57

Canaan, Canaanites : Canaan's father Ham saw
Noah's nakedness and told his brothers, and
Noah pronounced a curse on Ham (Gen. ix. 18-
27). That Canaan, not Ham, is cursed leads
Philo to say that it was Canaan reported abroad
the incident (*Leg. All.* ii. 62).[a] This publishing
represents the accomplishment of evil which
until then was only purposed (*ib.*) ; this hints at
what Philo develops in another treatise, namely
that Ham is vice in the quiescent state, but
Canaan, which means ' tossing,' is vice when it
passes into active movement (*Sob.* 30-34, 44-48,
Congr. 81-88). Thus the Exodus is from passion
(Egypt) to vice (*Congr.* 84), Canaan also symbolizing the stage of adolescence (82, 85). In *Sac.*
90 he applies ' tossing ' differently : the land of
the Canaanites is where reason is tossed to and
fro. In *Post.* 122 the reference suggests that the
Canaanites (' the people of the land ') stand for
opposing doctrines.

I. *Leg. All.* ii. 62, **II.** *Sac.* 90, *Post.* 122, **III.** *Sob.* 30-
34, 44-48, 51, 69, **IV.** *Congr.* 71, 81-88, 87n, 121,
V. *Fug.* 87, **VI.** Gen. Introd. p. xiv n, *Abr.* 77n,
85n, 133, *Mos.* i. 163, 214n, 220, (250) & n,

---

[a] God's curse makes Canaan slave to Ham's brothers ;
the fool is slave of the virtuous, either for improvement or
for chastisement (*Sob.* 69).

INDEX OF NAMES

VII. *Spec. Leg.* iii. 29n, VIII. *Spec. Leg.* iv. 219n,
Virt. 202, 221 [N], IX. *Quod Omn. Prob.* Introd.
p. 4, *Hyp.* 6, 1n

Capito : **X.** *Leg.* 199-202

Carabas : **IX.** *Flacc.* 34n, 36-40

Carthage : **III.** *Quod Deus* 174

Castor and Pollux : **VII.** *Decal.* 56 & [N], **X.** *Leg.*
78-92

Castus : **IX.** *Flacc.* 86f

Cenchreae : **IX.** *Flacc.* 155

Chaereas : **IX.** *Quod Omn. Prob.* 125

Chaldaea, Chaldaeans : Chaldaea was famed for astrology (*Mig.* 178, *Som.* i. 53, *Abr.* 69), and so
Abraham's connexion with Chaldaea is taken to
imply he too was an astrologer (*Ebr.* 94, *Mig.*
177-181, *Quis Her.* 96f, *Abr.* 69-72, 82, *Virt.* 212
& n, *Praem.* 58), though at other times Philo
makes the identification only allegorically. It
is called, rather contemptuously, the ' Chaldaean
δόξα—creed, opinion,' (*e.g. Gig.* 62, *Mig.* 187),
and is contrasted unfavourably even with Haran
(sense-perception). It represents the attempt to
regard the physical universe as the only reality
and to attribute causation to the heavenly bodies,
thus honouring the created world before the
Creator (*Mig.* 179, *Quis Her.* 97, 280, *Congr.* 49,
Mut. 16, *Abr.* 69, *Virt.* 212f). Only once does
Philo translate the name : in *Quis Her.* 97 he
says it corresponds to ' even tenour or levelness ' ;
it was the even tenour of the heavenly bodies
that suggested this creed

In the later treatises ' Chaldaean ' is used for
' Hebrew ' tongue (*Abr.* 8 & n, 12, 99, 201, *Mos.*
ii. 26, 31, 38, 40, 224, *Praem.* 14, 23, 31, 44).

Moses and Jacob are called Chaldaeans (*Mos.* i. 5, *Hyp.* 6. 1 & n), and Moses is said to have been trained in Chaldaean astronomy (*Mos.* i. 23 & n)

II. *Gig.* 62, III. *Ebr.* 94, IV. *Mig.* 177-181, 184 & n, 187, *Quis Her.* 96-99, 277, 280, 289, *Congr.* 49f, V. *Mut.* 16, *Som.* i. 52-54, 161, VI. *Abr.* 8 & n, 12, 62n, 67-72, 77, 82, 99, 188, 201, *Mos.* i. 5, 23, ii. 26, 31, 38, 40, 224, VIII. *Virt.* 212n, 212-214, *Praem.* 14, 23, 31, 44, 58, IX. *Hyp.* 6. 1 & n

Chananes : VI. *Mos.* i. 250 & n

Charybdis : V. *Som.* ii. 70 & n

Chedorlaomer : III. *Ebr.* 24

Chemosh : I. *Leg. All.* iii. 225, 231 : Moab's people maimed and blinded ; for Chemosh means ' as a groping,' and groping is characteristic of one who cannot see

Cherubim : The Cherubim with flaming sword guarding Eden are an allegorical figure of the revolution of the whole heaven. One symbolizes the outer sphere of fixed stars, the other the inner contained sphere of the seven planetary zones (*Cher.* 21-24). The Cherubim over the mercy-seat of the ark suggest an alternative interpretation : they are the two hemispheres, circling round the earth ; the flaming sword on this interpretation is the sun (25f, *Mos.* ii. 98). But there is a third and higher interpretation : the Cherubim represent God's two chief potencies cr powers, sovereignty and goodness, the sword is the symbol of reason, which unites them (27-30 ; so too, on the ark, *Quis Her.* 166 & n, *Fug.* 100, *Mos.* ii. 99). Philo translates the Cherubim as recognition or full knowledge (*Mos.* ii. 97 & n)

299

INDEX OF NAMES

Dan : I. *Leg. All.* ii. 94-108, III. *Agr.* 94-123 & 95[N], *Sob.* 58[N], V. *Som.* ii. 35, 39. In *Som.* ii. 35 Dan is the symbol of distinguishing and analysing matters. In *Leg. All.* ii. 94ff and *Agr.* 94ff Philo allegorizes the reference to Dan in the Blessing of Jacob (Gen. xlix. 16-18). Dan, offspring of Bilhah, typifies the soul's second and perishable offspring. His name means ' sifting ' : for this race distinguishes and separates things immortal from those that are mortal. So his father prays that he may prove a lover of self-mastery. (This is worked out in detail according to the text. *Leg. All.* ii. 94-108 ; *cf. Agr.* 95[N] and 94ff)

Dardania : IX. *Quod Omn. Prob.* 115 & n

Darius : (IX. *Quod Omn. Prob.* 132, *cf.* 136)

David : IV. *Conf.* 149, VIII. *Virt.* 221[N], IX. *Quod Omn. Prob.* p. 5 (-6)n

Delos : IX. *Aet.* 120, 121 & n

Delphi : II. *Post.* 113 & [N], IX. *Quod Omn. Prob.* 19, *Prov.* 2. 33, X. *Leg.* 69

Demeter : I. *Op.* 133, VII. *Decal.* 54, *Spec. Leg.* iii. 40 & [N], IX. *Vit. Cont.* 3

Democritus : IX. *Vit. Cont.* 14 & n, 15, *Aet.* 8

Deucalion : VIII. *Praem.* 23 & [N]

Dibon : I. *Leg. All.* iii. 225, 233 ; a name given to going to law, for probabilities and plausible arguments involve trial and disputation and everything of that sort

Dicaearchia (Puteoli) : IX. *Flacc.* 27 & n, X. *Leg.* 185

Dinah : Gen. xxxiv. Means ' judgement ' and signifies the soul's court of justice ; the virgin soul is not to be ravished by the shameless fool (IV. *Mig.* 223, 224 & n, V. *Mut.* 194f)

Diogenes the Babylonian : IX. *Aet.* 77 & n

INDEX OF NAMES

INDEX OF NAMES

φή,[a] *Leg. All.* i. 45, *Post.* 32, *cf. Plant.* 38; 'delight,' *Som.* ii. 242); symbolically it means right and divine reason (*Post.* 32, *cf. Plant.* 37f), wisdom of God (*Som.* ii. 242). It is situated " toward the sun-rising " (Gen. ii. 8) because right reason, wisdom or the heavenly virtues are radiant and without setting (*Leg. All.* i. 46, *Plant.* 40, *Conf.* 61)

In *Op.* 153, *Leg. All.* i. 43, *Plant.* 32, *Conf.* 61 Philo insists upon the impropriety of thinking of a literal garden

I. *Op.* 153-155, *Leg. All.* i. 41, 43-47, 53-56, 63f, 88-90, 96f, 100f, iii. 1, 28-31, II. *Cher.* 1n, 12f, *Post.* 1, 32, 128, III. *Plant.* 32-46, IV. *Mig.* 37, *Congr.* 171 & [N], V. *Som.* ii. 241f

Edom : signifies the earthly one [b] (*Quod Deus* 144), all that is good in outward appearance (for all things whose goodness lies in mere seeming are of earth (148 ; so 166, 180, *Mig.* 146))

II. *Post.* 101, III. *Quod Deus* 144f, 148, 166, 180, IV. *Mig.* 146

Egypt, Egyptians : These nearly always symbolize the body [c] or passions [d] or both [e] ; or the adjec-

[a] So the later LXX ; but Ἐδέμ in Genesis. Eden is from a different Hebrew root than that for ' luxury.'

[b] From I. אדם, man, אדמה, ground, instead of II. אדם, red.

[c] Body, *Leg. All.* ii. 59, 77, iii. 37, 212, 242, *Sac.* 130, *Det.* 38, *Post.* 60-62, *cf.* 158, *cf. Ebr.* 95 & [N], *Ebr.* 208, *cf. Sob.* 13, *Conf.* 70, 92, *Mig.* 23, 154, *Quis Her.* 256, 315, *Congr.* 20f, *Fug.* 180, *cf.* 147f, *Mut.* 173f, 209, *Som.* ii. 258, 277f, *cf. Abr.* 103, *Jos.* 151f.

[d] Passions, *Leg. All.* ii. 84 & [N], 103, iii. 13, 37f, 81, 87, 94, 175, *Sac.* 51, 62, 134, *Det.* 46, 95, *Ebr.* 111, 209, *Conf.* 70, *Mig.* 202, *Quis Her.* 255 & n, *Congr.* 83 (tr. ' sense '), 84f, 87 & n, 163f, *Fug.*, *Mut.* 172, *Som.* ii. 269, 278, 281.

[e] *Sac.* 48, *Post.* 96, 155, *Quod Deus* 111, *Agr.* 64, 88,

303

tives body-loving, passion-loving, pleasure-loving [a] are used. The wickedness and vices of Egypt are also mentioned (*Leg. All.* iii. 38, *Som.* ii. 255, *cf.* 266), and Israel's sojourn there signifies the dissolute and licentious life (*Post.* 156, *cf. Det.* 95) ; or it is a childhood stage to be left behind (*Congr.* 85), its fleshpots contrasted with the wilderness manna (*Quis Her.* 79f). It is earthly (*Congr.* 20)

Other interpretations are also given. Egypt represents sense (αἴσθησις, *Mig.* 77, *Quis Her.* 315, *Congr.* 83, *cf.* 21, *Mut.* 117-119), the mortal element or values (*Det.* 95f, *cf. Quis Her.* 316), the lower education (*Congr.* 20, *cf. Som.* i. 240), unholy doctrines (*Conf.* 36). The King of Egypt is thus the body-loving mind (*Abr.* 103, *Jos.* 151f), the boastful mind (*Ebr.* 111), rebellious against God (*Conf.* 88, *Congr.* 118), the power that flings away all ideas of what is noble (*Det.* 95) ; he is the sovereign of all that is animal and composite (*Sac.* 48), the king of terror (*Mut.* 173).[b] And the Nile, or river Egyptus (*Quis Her.* 315, 316 & n, *Som.* ii. 255-259), represents speech (*Som.* ii. 255-259, 300 & [N]) or the tide of passions (*Conf.* 29f, *Som.* ii. 277f). The arrogance of the Egyptians is mentioned (*Agr.* 62) and their jealousy (*Flacc.* 129) and folly (*Sac.* 51, *Mut.* 170, *cf. Leg.* 163),

---

Conf. 81f, 88-90, *Mig.* 14-16, 18, 20f, 77, 151, 160-162, *Fug.* 18, *Som.* ii. 109, 255f.

[a] φιλοσώματος, *Conf.* 70, *Mig.* 16, *Abr.* 103, *Jos.* 151f; φιλοπαθής, *Sac.* 51, *Mig.* 77, 202 ; φιλήδονος, *Leg. All.* iii. 37f, 212, 242, *Agr.* 88, *cf. Det.* 95, *Mig.* 18, 29, *Quis Her.* 203, 272, *Congr.* 84, *Fug.* 147f, *cf. Mut.* 174, *Som.* ii. 278.

[b] See further *s.v.* Pharaoh.

but especially their godlessness (ἄθεος, *Quis Her.* 203, etc.; *cf. Leg.* 163) in worshipping the animals or the Nile (*Leg. All.* iii. 212, *Fug.* 180 & n, *Jos.* 254, *Mos.* ii. 194-196, *Decal.* 76ff & n & [N], *Vit. Cont.* 8 & n, 9, *Leg.* 163); and the worship of the Golden Calf is usually regarded as a revival of this (*Sac.* 130, *Post.* 2 & [N], 158, 165, *Ebr.* 95 & [N], *Mig.* 160 & [N], *Fug.* 90, *Mos.* ii. 161f & n, 169, 270, *Spec. Leg.* i. 79, iii. 125)

An allusion is made in *Quod Deus* 174, *Jos.* 135 to the great Egyptian empire of ancient times

I. Gen. Introd. p. xvi, *Leg. All.* ii. 59, 77, 83-87 & [N], 103, iii. (3), 13, 37f, 81, 94, 175, 212, (243), II. *Sac.* 48, 51, 62 & [N], 118, 130, 134, *Det.* 38f, 46, 91 [N], 93-95, 177, III. *Quod Deus* 111, 174, *Agr.* 62, 64, 84, 88f, *Ebr.* 36, 95 & [N], 111, 208-210, *Sob.* 13, IV. *Conf.* 29f, 36, 70, 72, 81f, 88-90, 92, *Mig.* 14, 15 & n, 16-26 & n, 29, 54, 76f, 83n, 141, 142n, 151, 154, 159-162 & 160 [N], 200-202, 204, 215, *Quis Her.* 79f, 203, 242 [N], 251, 255f & n, 315f, *Congr.* 1, 20f, 71, 83-87 & n, 118, 163f, V. *Fug.* 18f, 90, 147n, 148, 179f & n, *Mut.* 20, 97, 117-119, 125, 126n, 170-174 & nn, 208f, *Som.* i. 114, 220, 240, ii. 5, 43, 88, 106, 109, 123, 189, 216, 255-259, 266, 269, 277-281, 300 & [N]-302, VI. Gen. Introd. pp. xii, xiii, *Abr.* 92f, 103, 107, 251, *Jos.* 3 [N], 15, 27, 37, 117, 121, 135, 151f, 157 & n, 159, 161, 184, 186, 188, 195f, 201, 203, 237f, 242, 248, 250f, 254f, 259, *Mos.* i. 5f, 17, 21, 23f & nn, 34, 36, (47), 71, 81, 85f, 91, 96, 99, 100ff, 107, 109, 112-118, 120-122, 134ff, 143ff, 147, 149, 163f, 167, 171f, 178f, 193, 202, 210, 216, 237, 240, 247, 284, 290, ii. 1, 19, 29, 161f & n, 169, 193-195, 246,

INDEX OF NAMES

Gen. v. 3-24, *Post.* 41), II. *Post.* 33, 35, 40, 66, IV. *Conf.* 122-127

Enoch (Gen. v. 18-24) : means ' thy gift ' (χάρις σου, *cf.* κεχαρισμένος, *Abr.* 17), and signifies those who acknowledge all as from God the Universal Mind (*Post.* 41f). Enoch's translation (LXX, " he was not found, because God translated him ") indicates that such people are seldom found, because they escape from the wickedness of this life, translated by God (*Post.* 40-44, *Mut.* 34-38). In each case Philo seems to understand the ' translated ' as both an ordinary removal, literal and metaphorical, and as a ' translation ' to immortality (*cf. Quaest. in Gen.* 86, *Abr.* 17[N]). In *Abr.* 17-26, 47 this change is one of heart (repentance) or of abode (seclusion), and the immortality seems to be associated with his finding company with those who are immortalized in their works.[a] In *Praem.* 15-21 the change of abode is a removal from the familiar surroundings of the old life of passion to solitude

II. *Post.* 40-44, V. *Mut.* 34 & n & [N]-38, VI. Gen. Introd. p. x, *Abr.* 17 & n & [N]-26, 47f, VIII. Gen. Introd. p. xxi, *Praem.* 15 & n-21, IX. *Quod Omn. Prob.* 63n

Enos : ' Man ' hopes in God (Gen. iv. 26, LXX), and Enos is thus made the founder of the truly reasonable race (Gen. v. 1) (II. *Det.* 138-140, VI. *Abr.* 7-16, 12n). As the representative of hope he figures in the first triad (Enos, Enoch,

[a] In this treatise Philo is contrasting the triad Enos, Enoch, Noah, who yearn for virtue, with Abraham, Isaac and Jacob, who achieve it (47f).

Noah), contrasted with Abraham, Isaac, and Jacob (**VI.** Gen. Introd. p. x, *Abr.* 7-16, 47f), a type of those who yearn for virtue but do not attain to it. Similarly **VIII.** Gen. Introd. p. xxi, *Praem.* 13 & n, 14

Ephraim : Ephraim is the figurative name of Memory, meaning ' fruitbearing ' : for the soul's proper fruit is to retain what it learns (**I.** *Leg. All.* iii. 90-93, **III.** *Sob.* 27f, **IV.** *Mig.* 205f, *Congr.* 40f, **V.** *Mut.* 97f). In *Leg. All.* iii. 94 & n Ephraim typifies those who (? remember to) sacrifice the Passover in the first month (Num. ix. 6ff). In *Mut.* 97f, 101f his association with Reuben (Gen. xlviii. 5) is fitting, because of the kinship of Memory with natural excellence. In all these passages he is favourably contrasted with his elder brother Manasseh (' recollection ')

Ephron : **IV.** *Conf.* 79. Ephron, from whom Abraham bought Machpelah (Gen. xxiii), means ' clay,' and represents the Hittite preference for mortality, clay, and dust rather than the soul

Epicurus : **II.** *Post.* 2 & [N], **IX.** *Aet.* 8

Equestrian Order : **X.** *Leg.* 74

Equinoxes : **I.** *Op.* 116, *Leg. All.* i. 8 & n

Er : Er, slain by God (Gen. xxxviii. 7), means ' leathern ' and typifies the body, especially as something corpse-like, and those who love it. **I.** *Leg. All.* iii. 69-75, **II.** *Post.* 180

Esau : Philo's interpretation of Esau is nearly always suggested by some phrase from the narratives of Gen. xxv or xxvii rather than by his etymology of the name, which is more than usually absurd. So too Esau is most often named in contrast to Jacob

INDEX OF NAMES

Mainly, Esau typifies the bad man or vice, in pursuit of the passions and bodily lusts,[a] the worse part of the soul (*Fug.* 24, 42f), the base and irrational nature (*Leg. All.* iii. 88f) ; or he represents folly.[b] Here Philo sometimes appeals to a fanciful derivation [c] and progress of ideas, which may be summarized as √עשׂה—ποίημα—fiction, to which belongs folly, or √עץ—δρῦς—oak— stubbornness—folly. Only in *Quis Her.* 251-254 does Philo suggest an altogether different interpretation ; here Esau is passion (πάθος), pursued and supplanted by Jacob, by acquired skill a hunter for the good, in a sense, but slow and procastinating (Jacob anticipated him with the venison)

Other details are suggested by texts. For instance, Esau being a man of the fields (ἄγροικος, in contrast to Jacob, who was a ' simple ' man, ἄπλαστος, dwelling in the city, Gen. xxv. 27, LXX), is interpreted as vice unfit to dwell in the city of virtue, following rustic grossness (*Leg. All.* iii. 2, ἀγροικία), the friend of fiction and make-up (*Plant.* 44, *Congr.* 62, playing on the ἄπλαστος (Jacob) of the text and the derivation Esau— ποίημα). In *Praem.* 59 the text has coloured Philo's description of Esau's character as wild (ἄγριος) and fierce. Esau was hairy, Jacob smooth (xxvii. 11) : thus he is contrasted with

---

[a] *Leg. All.* (ii. 59), iii. 2, 191f, *Sac.* 81 & n, 120 (*contr. Quis Her.* 251-254), 135, *Ebr.* 9f, *Det.* 45f, *Mig.* 208 & n, *Congr.* 129, *Fug.* 24, 43, *Virt.* 210, *Praem.* 62.

[b] *Leg. All.* iii. 193, *Sac.* 17 & [N], *Ebr.* 9f, *Sob.* 26, *Congr.* 61, 175, *Virt.* 209, *Quod Omn. Prob.* 57. Ignorance, *Fug.* 39.

[c] *Sac.* 17 & [N], *Congr.* 61, *Fug.* 39, 42.

INDEX OF NAMES

by fire ; black like the pupil of the eye, she represents the soul's power of vision (*Leg. All.* ii. 67 & [N])

Euboea : **X.** *Leg.* 282

Euodus : **IX.** *Flacc.* 76

Euphrates : **I.** *Leg. All.* i. 63, 72, 85-87, **IV.** *Quis Her.* 315f, **V.** *Som.* ii. 255-258, 300, **VI.** *Abr.* 266, **VIII.** *Virt.* 223, **X.** *Leg.* 10, 207, 216, 259

  (a) Gen. ii. 14, means ' fruitfulness ' and is a figurative name for justice (*Leg. All.* i. 72, 85-87), a virtue which brings gladness to the mind (εὐφραίνουσα)

  (b) Gen. xv. 18, represents the wisdom of God, full of joy and gladness (εὐφροσύνη, *Quis Her.* 315f)

  (c) *Ib.*, represents the soul and the soul's virtues (*Som.* ii. 255-258)

Euripides : **I.** *Leg. All.* i. 7 & n, iii. 202 & n, **VI.** *Jos.* 78 & n, **VIII.** *Spec. Leg.* iv. 47 & n, **IX.** *Quod Omn. Prob.* 25, 99 & n & [N], 101 & n, 102f, 116 & n, 141 & n, 146 & n, 152 & n, *Aet.* 5f, 30, 144

Eurystheus : **IX.** *Quod Omn. Prob.* 120

Eve [a] : Eve is consistently [b] made to represent Sense-perception,[c] the details of the narrative in Gen. ii and iii giving colour to this emphasis or that. Thus sometimes Sense-perception is contrasted with Mind (Adam), sometimes with Pleasure (the serpent) [d]

[a] Eve is mentioned by name comparatively seldom (*Leg. All.* ii. 79-81, *Cher.* 54, 57, 60, *Post.* 33, 124, *Agr.* 95-99, 107f, *Congr.* 171 & [N]).

[b] *Agr.* 95-99 is hardly an exception. See below.

[c] *Op.* 165, *Leg. All.* ii. 5f, 9, 14, 24, 38-45, 49f, 53, 68-70, iii. 49f, 56-68, 182, 184f, 200, 216, 220-224, *Cher.* 40, 43, 57-65, *Post.* 124-126, 170 ; *cf. Agr.* 95-99.

[d] Eve is contrasted with the animals, the passions, in *Leg.*

311

INDEX OF NAMES

The creation of man " male and female " (*Op.* 76,
Leg. All. ii. 13, *Quis Her.* 164) calls for no comment ; but the creation of Eve from Adam's side
(Gen. ii. 18ff) is seen to have significance. It
must not be taken literally (*Leg. All.* ii. 19 ; *cf.*
Op. 156f). We learn that man's helper is a
created one, formed subsequent to man (*Leg.
All.* ii. 5, 24 ; *cf.* 73), and represents Sense or
Sense-perception (αἴσθησις), which completes
man's soul (*ib.* 24, *Cher.* 58-60), adding to the
activity of mind the passivity of the senses (*ib.*
38f) ; thus turning a quiescent potentiality into
a reality, an activity (38, 40, 44f), and pouring
light into the mind (*Cher.* 61). This creation out
of Adam reveals that the starting-point of sense
is mind (*Leg. All.* iii. 185). Adam united to his
wife as " one flesh " indicates the degrading of
mind into sense-perception (ii. 49f, *cf.* *Gig.* 65),
and the begetting of bodily pleasure (*Op.* 152f) ;
thus woman is for man the beginning of a blameworthy life (*Op.* 151). Their nakedness (*Leg. All.*
ii. 53, 68-70 ; contrast iii. 56-58) suggests the
imperfection and powerlessness of mind and
sense-perception, each of which can dominate
the other

The Temptation and Fall is also a myth (μύθου
πλάσματα, *Op.* 156). The serpent represents
pleasure, and appropriately " beguiles " the
senses first and through them reaches the mind
(*Op.* 165), which apprehends simultaneously (*Leg.

All. ii. 5f, 9-14 ; with Adam, mind, in *Leg. All.* ii. 38-43,
49f, 56-58, 222-224, *Gig.* 65, *Quis Her.* 52f, with the serpent,
pleasure, in *Leg. All.* iii. 61-64, 66-68, 183-185 ; with wisdom
in *Quis Her.* 52f.

All. iii. 59f) ; for sense-perception " gives " without guile (*ib.* 61-64). She is so beguiled by pleasure because she is morally neutral : whether she is good or bad depends upon whether she is in the wise man or the fool (*ib.* 66-68) ; therefore she is not condemned outright like pleasure, but given an opportunity of defence. The disobedience of Adam and Eve having been discovered, God called mind only, not sense-perception, which being irrational cannot receive instruction and is merely included in the call of mind (*ib.* 49f). Questioned, Adam says, " The woman whom Thou gavest with me, she gave me." This indicates that sense is free (" with," not " to "), independent of mind (contrast ii. 68-70) ; it apprehends simultaneously " with " mind and " gives " to it opportunities of apprehending (iii. 56-58)

In *Op.* 157 their crime seems to be chiefly one of omission : they passed by the tree of life immortal, the consummation of virtue

God's curse upon the serpent includes " enmity between thee and the woman, and between thy seed and her seed." This is because pleasure is really a foe to sense (*Leg. All.* iii. 182), and warfare takes place over what is on the boundary between the two realms. They have opposing " seed," for the starting-point for pleasure is passion, while that of sense is mind (184f). The curse upon Eve tells us that as sense she must be subject to grief and with pangs bring forth perception (*Leg. All.* iii. 200, 216). Her resort shall be to her husband—she has two, the lawful one being mind, the other a seducer, known when

313

the objects of perception dominate irrational
sense (220f). The curse upon Adam shows that
it is profitless for mind to listen to sense-perception, for that means the rule of the inferior (222f;
cf. ii. 49f)

The expulsion from Eden illustrates God's expulsion of evil-mindedness from the holy boundaries
(*Congr.* 171 & [N])

" Adam called his wife's name Eve,[a] because she
was the mother of all living " (Gen. iii. 20). In
Cher. 57 this means sense is the source of life to
all living bodies. In *Agr.* 95-99 woman is life,
depending upon the senses and material substances of our bodies (αἰσθήσεως καὶ σαρκῶν
ἐκκρεμαμένη ζωή). In *Quis Her.* 52f (where
Philo is discussing Masek, Gen. xv. 2) Adam
gave sense the name of what was his own death
to her life, for she is the mother of those who are
in truth dead to the life of the soul ; those who
are really living have wisdom for their mother,
but sense they take for a bond-woman

Eve bore Cain ; so sense bears vanity of thought
(*Cher.* 57, *cf.* 61-65). This, which implies the
union of mind with sense, is reprehensible, and
that is why men like the patriarchs did not know
women (*Cher.* 40, 43). On the other hand, Eve's
giving birth to Seth is more favourably regarded :
the senses are watered from the mind and so
broaden and extend their powers

I. Gen. Introd. p. xiii, *Op.* 76, 151-153, 156f, 165,
167, *Leg. All.* ii. 1, 5, 8f, 13f, 19, 24, 38-45, 49f, 53,
68-70, 73, 79, 81, iii. 1, 49f, 56-68, 182, 184f, 188,
200, 216, 220-224, II. *Cher.* 40, 43, 53f, 57-65,

[a] See note *a* on p. 311.

INDEX OF NAMES

Sac. 1, *Post.* 33, 124-126, 170, *Gig.* 65, III. *Agr.* 95-99, 107f, *Ebr.* 4n, IV. *Quis Her.* 52f, 164, *Congr.* 171 & [N], VI. *Mos.* i. 263 [N], VIII. *Virt.* 199

Evilat : I. *Leg. All.* i. 63, 66f, 74f, 85f, is the kindly and gracious disposition where lies God's greatest treasure, prudence (66f) ; it is folly ' in travail ' for the foolish mind travails for its desires but is powerless to bring to birth (74f, 85f)

Evius : **X.** *Leg.* 96

Flaccus Avillius : **IX.** *Flacc. passim*

Flaccus, G. Norbanus : **X.** *Leg.* 314f

Gad : **V.** *Som.* ii. 35, 40. Symbol of piratical attack and counter-attack

Gaidad : son of Enoch (Gen. iv. 18), ' flock,' symbolic of the irrational faculties (II. *Post.* 66, 69)

Gaius Caesar : **IX.** *Flacc.* 9-15, 22, 25f, 31f, 35, 40, 42, 97-100, 108f, 114, 126, 150, 180ff, **X.** *Leg.* 32-39, 41-119, 133f, 136f, 141, 162-165, 168, 180-209, 218, 230-232, 239-242, 244, 247-251, 253-373

Gaius Flaccus : **X.** *Leg.* 314f

Galilee : **X.** *Leg.* 326

Ganymede : **IX.** *Prov.* 2. 7

Geloans : III. *Ebr.* 174

Genesis : I. *Op.* 12, II. *Post.* 127, VI. *Abr.* 1, **IX.** *Aet.* 19

Geon : one of the four rivers of Gen. ii. 13 ; means ' breast ' or ' butting ' (κερατίζων), figurative of courage (I. *Leg. All.* i. 63, 68, 85f, II. *Post.* 128)

Germanicus : see Caesar

Germany, Germans : **V.** *Som.* ii. 121f & [N], **X.** *Leg.* 10, 356 & n

Geryon : **X.** *Leg.* 80

INDEX OF NAMES

Gideon : ' robbers' hold,' ready to destroy Penuel (Judges viii. 9). **IV.** *Conf.* 129-132, *cf.* **VIII.** *Praem.* 4-6[N]

Gilead : ' migration of witness ' : for God caused the soul (Jacob) to migrate from the passions (Laban), and bore witness to it . . . etc. (**I.** *Leg. All.* iii. 16, 19). ' Heap of witness ' : for the mind is witness of each man's secret purposes (**II.** *Post.* 59 & [N]). Also **IV.** *Congr.* 43

Gog : **VI.** *Mos.* i. 290n

Gomorrah : **III.** *Ebr.* 222, **V.** *Som.* i. 85, ii. 191f (' measure,' figuring those who make man the measure of all), **VI.** *Abr.* 1 & n, *Mos.* ii. 52-65, 263, *cf.* i. 207, **IX.** *Aet.* 147[N]

Gorgon : **X.** *Leg.* 237

Goshen : **VI.** *Jos.* 256n

Graces, The : **VI.** *Abr.* 54, *Mos.* ii. 7, **X.** *Leg.* 95, 105

Great Bear : **I.** *Op.* 114, **VII.** *Spec. Leg.* ii. 57

Greece [a] : **III.** *Quod Deus* 173, **VI.** *Jos.* 134, *Mos.* i. 21, ii. 18, **VII.** *Spec. Leg.* iii. 16, **VIII.** *Praem.* 165, **IX.** *Quod Omn. Prob.* 73, 94, 132, 138, 140, *Vit. Cont.* 14, 57, *Prov.* 2. 15, 66, **X.** *Leg.* 141, 147, 237

Greek, Greeks [a] : **I.** *Op.* 127, *Leg. All.* ii. 15, **II.** *Cher.* 91, **III.** *Plant.* 14, 67, *Ebr.* 193, **IV.** *Conf.* 6, 68, *Quis Her.* 214, **V.** *Mut.* 35, 179, **VI.** *Abr.* 136, 180, 267, *Jos.* 30, 56, 134, *Mos.* i. 2, 21, 23, ii. 12, 18, 20, 23, 27, 40, **VII.** *Decal.* 153, *Spec. Leg.* i. 211, ii. 44, 165, iii. 15, **VIII.** *Spec. Leg.* iv. 61, 120, *Praem.* 8, 23, **IX.** *Quod Omn. Prob.* 88, 94, 96, 98, 140, *Vit. Cont.* 14, 21, 42, 48, 68, *Aet.* 57, **X.** *Leg.* 8, 83, 145, 162, 237, 292

Greek language, The [a] : **I.** *Op.* 127, **IV.** *Conf.* 6, 68,

---

[a] Some overlapping in these three divisions is inevitable.

316

Hades : a mythical place (**IV.** *Congr.* 57), the resort of those who look to created things (**IV.** *Quis Her.* 45), the spiritually blind (*ib.* 78) ; the life of the bad, a life of damnation and bloodguiltiness, the victim of every curse (ὁ ἀλάστωρ καὶ παλαμναῖος καὶ πάσαις ἀραῖς ἔνοχος, *Congr.* 57) ; *cf.* **V.** *Som.* i. 151. Also **VI.** *Mos.* ii. 281, **X.** *Leg.* 235

Hagar : Hagar, Sarah's handmaid, is consistently contrasted with her, Sarah being Virtue or Wisdom,[a] while Hagar is the Lower Education of the Schools.[b] (What this comprised is sometimes told us : *Congr.* 11f, 15ff, 74ff, 142, 144, 146ff.) The School-learning is the step towards the perfection represented by her mistress,[c] and is necessary (*Congr.* 24), but represents a stage of in-

---

[a] Sarah is philosophy in *Congr.* 79, 145 ; knowledge and wisdom, *ib.* 156 ; better judgement (γνώμη), *Fug.* 205 ; good sense (φρόνησις), *ib.* 207.

[b] The lower education, ἡ μέση παιδεία, in *Cher.* 3, 6, *Post.* 130, *Congr.* 12, 14, 20, 22, *Mut.* 255 (μέσαι τέχναι, *Congr.* 140, *cf.* 128 ; παιδεία, *Congr.* 23, 72f, 121, *Som.* i. 240). παιδεύματα (*Leg. All.* iii. 244) and προπαιδεύματα (*Cher.* 8, 10, *Congr.* 152, 180, *Fug.* 2, 213, *Mut.* 263) are also used ; and the adjective ἐγκύκλιος, *Leg. All.* iii. 244, *Cher.* 2, 6 & [N], *Sac.* 43f, *Congr.* 14, 19f, 23, 72f, 79, 121, 155, *Fug.* 213, *Som.* i. 240.

[c] In *Congr.* 79 the handmaid-mistress relationship is used twice over to convey Encyclia-Philosophy, Philosophy-Wisdom.

completeness (ἀτελής, *Fug.* 207) and gradual progress only (ψυχὴ προκόπτουσα, *ib.* 202, 213, *cf.* 211), something temporary (*Congr.* 12) ; this is typified in Hagar being Abraham's concubine, not his wife (*ib.* 23, 154-156)

Hagar's name means ' sojourning ' ; for the aspirant to virtue sojourns with the subjects of the Schools (*Leg. All.* iii. 244 & [N]) ; or it signifies that the student of secular learning only sojourns and is not domiciled with wisdom (*Sac.* 43f, where Philo also identifies the ' alien sojourner ' with the lower knowledge itself ; *cf. Congr.* 20, 22f). She is an Egyptian (Gen. xvi. 1) : so the student of the Schools must necessarily be associated with the body (Egypt) and its senses to apprehend knowledge (*Congr.* 20) ; but this disqualifies her from seeing God Himself (*Som.* i. 240 & n ; see below)

Abraham's union with Hagar, sponsored by Sarah (*Congr.* 72), occurs before he is perfect, while he is still Abram and concerned with supramundane things (*Leg. All.* iii. 244), ten years after his arrival in Canaan, while the soul had passed the stage of the senses and passions and was able to apprehend and choose between virtue and vice (*Congr.* 81f), when it was mature enough to begin the training of the Schools (*ib.* 121f, *cf.* 88). Hagar's conception led to a feud with Sarah (*ib.* 127-129, 158)—not the jealousy of women, but the conflict of two minds of different quality (180). Hagar fled, voluntarily (*Cher.* 3, contrasting the expulsion later), to escape the stern search for virtue (*Cher.* 6 & [N] ; but contrast *Fug.* 213), throwing away achievements for un-

certainties (*Fug.* 205f), a flight prompted by
shame (*Fug.* 5f, 203, 213). But an angel (? conviction, *Fug.* 6) finds her (*Cher.* 3, *Fug.* 5f, 202ff,
211-213; contrast *Som.* i. 240) by a spring (wisdom : Hagar is not said to draw from it, *Fug.*
202), and she returns [a]

Hagar is expelled with her sophist son Ishmael
after the birth of Isaac (*Leg. All.* iii. 245, *Cher.* 3,
8f, *Post.* 130, 132, *Sob.* 8f). Again she is found
by a well (knowledge : and she draws for Ishmael,
Post. 130, 132, 137) and she is preserved by God.
In *Abr.* 247-254 Philo gives a summary of the
story, somewhat idealized

I. Gen. Introd. pp. xviif, *Leg. All.* iii. 244 & [N],
II. *Cher.* 3, 6, 8, *Sac.* 43, *Post.* 130, 132, 137, III.
Sob. 8, IV. *Congr.* p. 449n, 1, 11f, 20, 22-24, 71f,
81, 88, 121f, 127-129, 139, 153-158, 180, V. *Fug.*
1, 5f, 202f, 211 & n, 212, *Mut.* 255, *Som.* i. 240
& n, VI. *Abr.* 247-254

Ham : a name for vice in the quiescent state ; by
interpretation ' heat '—a sign of fever in the
body and of vice in the soul (*Sob.* 44). See also
s.v. Canaan, III. *Sob.* 1, 6, 32, 44f, 47f, VIII. *Virt.*
202

Hamor : irrational being (ἄλογος φύσις), for Hamor
means ' ass ' (IV. *Mig.* 224 & n). Folly or un-
intelligence (ἄνοια, V. *Mut.* 193f)

Hannah : the gift of the wisdom of God, for Hannah
means ' her grace ' (III. *Quod Deus* 5, *Ebr.* 145-
152, V. *Mut.* 143, 144[N], *Som.* i. 254). Hannah's
song (1 Sam. ii. 1-10, esp. *v.* 5) suggests that she
represents the soul sterilized to wickedness and

[a] Further details in the story belong rather to Ishmael, *q.v.*

mortal sowing but holding fast to the ' seventh '
and mother of its peace (V. *Mut.* 143f, III. *Quod
Deus* 10f, VIII. *Praem.* 159 & n, 160)

Haran : the country of sense-perception, understanding's bodily tenement (*Mig.* 187, 197, 207-
214, *Som.* i. 53, 68) ; for Haran is ' hole,' and
holes are figures for eyes, ears, etc. (*Mig.* 188,
Som. i. 59). So Haran stands also for the organs
of sense (*Mig.* 195 & n, *Fug.* 45, *Som.* i. 41, *Abr.*
72)

Abraham's father, Terah (the explorer of sense ;
Socrates ; self-knowledge), lived and died in
Haran (*Som.* i. 47-59).   It is to Haran that he
and Abraham migrate, teaching us to discard
the speculations of astrology in favour of the
Socratic study of ourselves (*Mig.* 176-197, esp.
185-189, *cf.* 137f ; *Fug.* 45f, *Som.* i. 55 & n-58,
Abr. 70-80, 72n) ; and it is a necessary intermediate stage in the soul's progress (*Mig.* 198f).
But Abraham leaves it to go on to immortality
and the knowledge of God (*Mig.* 189-195, *Som.*
i. 47, 60, *Abr.* 72n, 85-88)—for to despair of oneself is the first step (*Som.* i. 60, *cf.* 56 ; *Mig.*
195)

In the Jacob stories also Haran is significant. His
mother wisely counsels him to flee to Haran
(Gen. xxvii. 43-45), for compromise with the
senses may sometimes be the best course (*Mig.*
208 & n-213). In *Fug.* 45f this is the advice to
know ourselves.   In either case it is to be a
temporary measure (*Mig.* 211, *Fug.* 46, *Som.* i.
45f). Jacob goes to Haran (Gen. xxviii. 10, *Som.*
i. 4, 5 & n, 41-45, 61, 68, 70) from Beersheba
(' well of knowledge ') : if a man cannot com-

mune with the understanding by itself, he wins
in sense-perception a second-best refuge (*ib.* 44).
Laban's shepherds tell him they are of Haran
(Gen. xxix. 4) : their flocks are the irrational
faculties, fittingly associated with the senses
(*Mig.* 212f). But Jacob too eventually leaves
Haran to live in the fear of God (*ib.* 214f, *cf.*
5 & n)

IV. *Mig.* 176f, 184 & n-195 & n (esp. 187f), 197f,
207[N], 208-216, 210[N], 212n, V. *Fug.* 23, 45f,
Som. i. 4, 5 & n, 41-45, 55n, 56n, 61, 68, 70,
VI. *Abr.* 62n, 67, 72 & n, 77 & n-80

Havilah : see *s.v.* Evilat

Hebrew, Hebrews : Hebrew means ' migrant ' ; the
wont of the Hebrews is to quit the objects of
sense-perception and go after those of mind
(*Mig.* 20). Thus Joseph was proved to be a
Hebrew and proved himself one (*ib.*). The
Hebrew women needed no midwives (Exod. i.
19) : the self-taught nature arises by no human
will, but by a God-inspired ecstasy (*Fug.* 168, *cf.*
Mig. 141f & n, *Congr.* 3 & n)

IV. *Mig.* 20, 141f, *Quis Her.* 128, *Congr.* 3, V. *Mut.*
117, *Fug.* 168, VI. *Abr.* 251, *Jos.* 42, 50, 104, 203,
Mos. i. 15f (34ff), 105, 143-147, 179f, 216, 218,
240, 243, 252, 263, 276, 278, 284f, 288f, 295, 305,
311, ii. 32, VIII. *Virt.* 34f

Hebrew language, The [a] : III. *Plant.* 169, *Sob.* 45,
IV. *Conf.* 68, 129f, *Mig.* 13, *Congr.* 40, V. *Som.* ii.
250, VI. *Abr.* (8 & n, 12), 17, 27f, 57, (99, 201),
Jos. 28, (*Mos.* ii. 26, 31, 38, 40, 97, 224), VII.

---

[a] In the later treatises Philo tends to use Χαλδαῖοι, Χαλδαϊστί;
these references are included, in brackets.

INDEX OF NAMES

Decal. 159, *Spec. Leg.* ii. 41, 86, 145, (VIII. *Praem.* 14, 23, 31, 44), (**X**. *Leg.* 4)

Hebron : Hebron means 'coupling' or 'union' (συζυγή) and 'comradeship' (συνεταιρίς) and is a figurative title for our body, because it is coupled with a soul and has established a comradeship with it. So Jacob sent Joseph out of the vale of Hebron (Gen. xxxvii 14) to stir him from the hollows of the body and senses (**II**. *Det.* 15-17). In **II**. *Post.* 60-62 Philo gives a similar interpretation of Num. xiii. 22, but says the 'union' may also be that of the soul with virtue (so Gen. xxiii. 9, 19). Hebron is also called a treasure-house, guarding personal monuments of knowledge and wisdom (Num. xiii. 22, *Post.* 60-62 & [N])

Helene : **IX**. *Flacc.* 156

Heliceia : **IX**. *Aet.* 140 & n

Helicon : **X**. *Leg.* 166-178, 203-206

Heliopolis : **II**. *Post.* 54, 57 & [N] ; the mind, sun-like, sending forth its proper light, causes all forms and conditions to be clearly apprehended. So **V**. *Som.* i. 77f

Hellas : see *s.v.* Greece

Hellespont : **V**. *Som.* ii. 118

Hephaestus : **VII**. *Decal.* 54 & [N] ; **IX**. *Vit. Cont.* 3, *Aet.* 68

Hera : **VII**. *Decal.* 54 & N, **IX**. *Vit. Cont.* 3

Heracleitus : **I**. *Leg. All.* i. 108, iii. 7 & [N], **IV**. *Quis Her.* 214, **V**. *Fug.* 61 & n, **IX**. *Aet.* 111 & n, *Prov.* 2. 67

Heracles : **IX**. *Quod Omn. Prob.* 99-104, 101n, 120, 127 & n, 128, **X**. *Leg.* 78f, 81, 90-93 & n

Hermes : **VII**. *Decal.* 54 & n, **IX**. *Quod Omn. Prob.* 101 & n, **X**. *Leg.* 93 & n-102 ; *cf.* **IV**. *Quis Her.* 224

322

INDEX OF NAMES

Herod : Herod the Great, grandfather of Agrippa (*q.v.*), **IX**. *Flacc.* 25, **X**. *Leg.* 294-300

Heroes' City (Goshen) : **VI**. *Jos.* 256 & n

Heshbon : ' reasonings,' so quibbling riddles, full of obscurity, **I**. *Leg. All.* iii. 225-233

Hesiod : **IX**. *Aet.* 17, 18 & n, 19

Heth : **V**. *Fug.* 25 [N], *Som.* ii. 89, 90 & n : Abraham, to avoid giving provocation, did obeisance to the sons of Heth (Gen. xxiii. 7), the enemies of reason who remove instruction (Heth is ' removing '), that he might obtain Machpelah

Hiddekel : see *s.v.* Tigris

Hippocentaurs : **VII**. *Spec. Leg.* iii. 45

Hippocrates : **I**. *Op.* 105, 124, **IX**. *Vit. Cont.* 16 & n

Homer : **I**. Gen. Introd. p. xvi n, **IV**. *Conf.* 4, **VI**. *Abr.* 10, **IX**. *Quod Omn. Prob.* 31, *Vit. Cont.* 17 & n & [N], **X**. *Leg.* 80 [a]

Homilus : **X**. *Leg.* 181

Hor : Hor (LXX "Ωρ, E.V. Hur) supports Moses' hands (Exod. xvii. 12) : that is, the wise man's doings are steadied by truth (Hor is ' light '). Similarly Num. xx. 25 : Aaron goes up into Mt. Hor to die, for the end and goal of the Word (Aaron) is truth (**I**. *Leg. All.* iii. 45 ; *cf.* **VI**. *Mos.* i. 214n)

Hormah : **III**. *Quod Deus* 99

Hoshea : Moses changes the name of Hoshea to Joshua (Num. xiii. 17), thus transforming the individual who embodies a state to the state itself ; for Hoshea is ' he,' *i.e.* a particular individual, ' is saved,' and Joshua is ' salvation ' (**V**. *Mut.* 121 & n)

Hur : see *s.v.* Hor

[a] For many quotations from Homer, without his name, see Index to Translators' Notes.

INDEX OF NAMES

Hydra : **V.** *Som.* ii. 14
Hypotaenia : **IX.** *Flacc.* 45

Iberus : **V.** *Som.* ii. 123 & [N], **IX.** *Flacc.* 2 & n
Iliad : **IX.** *Vit. Cont.* 17. (Without naming the *Iliad*,
    Philo also quotes from it in **III.** *Agr.* 41, **VI.** *Mos.*
    i. 61, **VII.** *Decal.* 69 & n, **IX.** *Quod Omn. Prob.* 31)
India, Indians : **V.** *Som.* ii. 56, 59, **VI.** *Abr.* 182, **VIII.**
    Praem. 89, **IX.** *Quod Omn. Prob.* 74 & [N], 93-96,
    Aet. 128f
Ion : **IX.** *Quod Omn. Prob.* 134 & [N]
Ionia, Ionian, Ionic : **V.** *Som.* ii. 55 (Ionic carvings),
    VIII. *Spec. Leg.* iv. 102 (Ionians and luxury), **IX.**
    Flacc. 154 (Ionian Gulf)
Isaac : Isaac means ' laughter,' [a] the soul's gladness
    (*Leg. All.* iii. 43, 87),[b] or Happiness (*ib.* 217-219)
    in generic form (τὸ εὐδαιμονίας γένος, *Cher.* 8,
    106, *Det.* 60, *Post.* 134), joy, the best of the good
    emotions,[c] given by God to soothe and cheer
    truly peaceful souls (*Mut.* 131). But chiefly he
    represents the virtue [d] or wisdom [e] or knowledge [f]
    which is self-learned or self-taught,[g] that which
    is by nature [h]

---

[a] *Leg. All.* i. 82, ii. 82, iii. 43, 87, 217-219, *Cher* .8, 106,
Det. 60, 124f, *Post.* 134, *Plant.* 168f, *Mut.* 137, 157, 161,
166f, *Abr.* 201-204, *Spec. Leg.* ii. 54, *Praem.* 31.
[b] So *Mut.* 157-161 ; *cf.* γέλως ἐνδιάθετος, 131.
[c] εὐπαθειῶν ἀρίστη χαρά, *Congr.* 36, *Mut.* 1, 130f, 264, *Abr.*
201-204, *Praem.* 31-35, 50 ; *cf.* *Mut.* 261, *Spec. Leg.* ii. 54.
[d] ἀρετή, *Mig.* 125, *Congr.* 34-36, *Som.* i. 167-169, *Abr.* 52,
54, *Praem.* 31, 50.
[e] σοφία, *Post.* 78, *Quod Deus* 4, *Sob.* 9, *Congr.* 37, *cf.* 111.
[f] ἐπιστήμη, *Sob.* 9, *Som.* i. 160.
[g] See notes *a* and *b*, p. 326.
[h] φύσις, *Mut.* 88, *Som.* i. 160, 167, 171, *Abr.* 52, 54,
Praem. 31 ; φυσική, *Abr.* 52.

Thus he belongs to the second and higher triad of those who yearn for virtue,[a] not so much men as values—Abraham (by teaching), Isaac (by nature [b]), Jacob (by practice). All alike are God-lovers and God-beloved (*Abr.* 48-56), all are wise men (*Som.* i. 167) ; but Isaac's is the higher gift (*Sac.* 5-7 & [N], *Som.* i. 169), so he is often favourably contrasted with the other two,[c] though once Philo inconsistently admits that nature cannot be complete without them (*Abr.* 53) ; and once he seems to indicate limitation in Isaac's apprehension of God (*Som.* i. 68 & n). This identification of Isaac with natural ability is not explained (see VI. Gen. Introd. p. xi & n)

Some other contrasts are interesting. Philo subordinates Abraham to Isaac even when following the narrative of Gen. xxii (*Mig.* 166f & n) ; when interpreting " The Lord God of Abraham thy father and the God of Isaac " (*Som.* i. 160f, 166-171) ; and God taught Abraham but begat Isaac (*ib.* 173). Jacob falls short of Isaac in the apprehension of the divine (*Som.* i. 68 & n). Ishmael, though elder in years, is spiritually junior to Isaac (*Sob.* 7-9 ; *cf.* *Mut.* 262f)

The usual epithet (' self-taught ') for Isaac is αὐτο-

[a] This trinity appears in *Sac.* 5-7 & [N], *Sob.* 38n, *Mig.* 125 & [N], *Congr.* 34-38, *Mut.* 12 & [N], *Som.* i. 166-173, *Abr.* 48-56, *Praem.* 24-51, *cf.* *Leg. All.* ii. 59. See Vol. VI, Gen. Introd. pp. x-xii.

[b] But Isaac is ' perfection ' in *Mut.* 12 ; see [N].

[c] *E.g.* *Som.* i. 167-173 ; *Congr.* 34-38, his is legitimate rather than ' concubine ' knowledge ; *Mut.* 88, he keeps the same name throughout ; *Leg. All.* ii. 59, ' nakedness ' from passion.

325

INDEX OF NAMES

μαθής [a]; sometimes αὐτοδίδακτος [b] and αὐτήκοος [c] are linked with it.[d] But φύσις (natural
ability) is also used.[e] He is wise [f] and noble
(ἀστεῖος, *Som.* i. 171, *Abr.* 52, cf. γενναῖος in
Som. ii. 10), a lover of self-discipline (σωφροσύνη,
Congr. 175), a man of faith (*Som.* i. 68), holy
(ὅσιος, *Abr.* 52, cf. 172), excellent (ἄριστος,
Congr. 175 ; σῶμα κάλλιστος, ψυχὴν ἄριστος, *Abr.*
168), perfect in virtues [g] (*Sob.* 8f, cf. *Congr.* 38),
the perfect good,[h] one who is free from passion
(ἀπαθὲς εἶδος) and inviolable (ἀτρώτου γένους
εἶδος, *Det.* 46 & n),[i] who has left behind his own
self (*Quis Her.* 68). He is a prophet (*ib.* 261),
and one of the founders of the race (*Mut.* 88 ; cf.
Som. i. 167)

Isaac was the child promised (see *s.v.* Gen. xv. 4,
xvii. 6f) to Abraham (the good man, etc.) and

---

[a] αὐτομαθής, *Sac.* 6 & [N], 120[N], *Det.* 30, *Quod Deus* 4,
Post. 78, *Plant.* 168, *Ebr.* 60, 94, *Sob.* 38n, 65, *Conf.* 74, 81,
Mig. 29f, 101, 125 & [N], 140, 166, 167 & n, *Congr.* 24n,
34, 36, 38, 111, *Fug.* 166, *Mut.* 1, 12 & [N], 88, 137, 255,
263, *Som.* i. 68, 160, 168f, 194, ii. 10, *Praem.* 27, 59. *Cf.*
μαθητὴς Θεοῦ, *Sac.* 7 ; ἱκανὸς διδάσκειν καὶ μανθάνειν οὐ δεόμενος,
Mig. 140.

[b] αὐτοδίδακτος, *Post.* 78, *Fug.* 166, *Mut.* 88, *Som.* i. 160, ii.
10, *Praem.* 27, 59.

[c] αὐτήκοος, *Plant.* 168, *Sob.* 65, *Som.* i. 160, 168f, *Praem.*
27, 50.

[d] αὐτουργός, *Plant.* 168.

[e] φύσις, *Plant.* 168, *Fug.* 168, *Mut.* 88, *Som.* i. 160, 167-
171, *Abr.* 52, 54, *Praem.* 31.

[f] πάνσοφος, *Cher.* 47, *Sac.* 43 ; σοφός, *Sob.* 9, *Fug.* 200,
Som. i. 167. *Cf.* note e, p. 324.

[g] ἀρετή, *Cher.* 40. *Cf.* note d, p. 324.

[h] τέλειον ἀγαθόν, *Mut.* 188, cf. 88, 166 ; ἀγαθὸς καὶ τέλειος,
Som. i. 162 ; τέλειος, *Sac.* 43 ; cf. τελειότης, *Mut.* 12 & [N].

[i] See further below, on Gen. xxvi. 2.

Sarah (virtue) in their old age. They both greet this with laughter, and the offspring of them both is laughter itself (*Leg. All.* iii. 217f).[a] God's covenant would be with him (Gen. xvii. 19) ; this praise even before his birth is because joy gladdens in anticipation, and therefore God held Isaac worthy of his great name and of a great endowment (*ib.* 85-87). This male child (one free from all womanish feelings—πάθος) is to be named by the feeling he raises in Abraham, namely joy (*Mut.* 261).[b] Isaac is the most perfect thank-offering given to Abraham by the divine potencies after their visit (Gen. xviii. 9f, *Cher.* 106) ; while his answer to their question, " Where is Sarah ? " is fitting : Virtue is in the soul, but Happiness can only come with the exercise of it—that is, when Sarah conceives and bears Isaac, happiness in its totality (*Det.* 60). " It had ceased to be with Sarah after the manner of women " (xviii. 11) : this favourite text [c] applies to Isaac, for happiness is conceived when we are dead to the passions (*Cher.* 8 & [N]), when virtue is free from alloy (*Post.* 134), and the self-taught nature requires us to forsake those human ways of custom and mere reasoning (*Fug.* 167f, cf. *Ebr.* 60). Sarah " conceived and bare " (xxi. 2) not a man,[d] but a most pure thought, beautiful, not by practice but by nature (*Fug.* 167). Abraham was then one hundred years old (xxi. 5), the number irradiated by the self-taught nature,

---

[a] How they could laugh before laughter was born is discussed in *Mut.* 157, 166.

[b] See note c, p. 324. [c] See *s.v.* Sarah.

[d] *Cf. Mig.* 140-142, *Mut.* 130f, *Som.* i. 172, *Abr.* 54f.

INDEX OF NAMES

Isaac, who is joy, the best of the good emotions [a]
(*Mut.* 1, 188). " The Lord has made laughter
for me " (xxi. 6, LXX) : as Isaac and laughter are
the same, this means that God made or begat
Isaac ; for He Himself is the Father of the perfect nature, sowing and begetting happiness in
men's souls (*Leg. All.* iii. 219, *Mut.* 130f, 137,
Som. i. 173).[b] Sarah's rejoicing (" all that hear
me will laugh with me ") calls for fellowship in
joy when one hears that Virtue has given birth
to Happiness (*Leg. All.* ii. 82. *cf.* iii. 218f). The
child gives rather than receives nourishment
(' suck,' xxi. 7), being capable of teaching and
not needing to learn (*Mig.* 140 & [N] and perhaps
29). The same interpretation is given for his
being weaned (*Sob.* 7-9, *Mig.* 29, *Som.* ii. 10)

Abraham's (intended) sacrifice of Isaac is variously
explained. It is, of course, no human being, but
the fruit of a rich and fertile soul which is offered
(*Mig.* 142, *Leg. All.* iii. 209) ; the sum offering of
the mind that has reached the summit (*ib.* 139 &
n, *cf. Abr.* 172) ; a fitting thank-offering, which
illustrates what it is not to beget for oneself (*Quod
Deus* 4) : a perfect, undivided, whole burnt-offer-
ing (*cf. Som.* i. 194), because Isaac had no passion
which breeds corruption (*Sac.* 110) ; the sacrifice
of the good emotion of the understanding, that is,
joy, showing that rejoicing is most clearly associated with God alone (*Abr.* 202, *Leg. All.* iii. 209).

[a] See note *c*, p. 324.
[b] So too *Cher.* 45, *Det.* 124f, where Isaac is also the offspring of wisdom, *i.e.* of Abraham (*cf. Abr.* 194) ; and *Mig.*
139-142, offspring of the soul, *i.e.* Sarah (*cf. Quod Deus* 4,
where the soul is Abraham).

328

INDEX OF NAMES

Such an acknowledgement God fully rewards by
returning the gift ; so Isaac is saved (*ib.* 177, 203f)
One further topic in the story [a] : " so they went
both of them together " (xxii. 8) means with
equal speed of mind rather than body along the
road to holiness (*Abr.* 172) ; that is, the learner's
virtue along with that of the self-taught, the
pair being now capable of winning virtue's prize
in equal measure (*Mig.* 166 & n, 167) [b]
" Isaac went into the plain to meditate at the even-
tide " (Gen. xxiv. 63, LXX). This means that he
quits his own mind to be with God (*Leg. All.* iii.
43, *Det.* 29, *cf. Quis Her.* 68 on Gen. xv. 4, *Leg.
All.* i. 82) ; the plain signifies the conquest of
opposing principles, and Isaac is the champion
unopposed who finds the field empty of all his
adversaries (*Det.* 29-31)
" Abraham gave all that he had [c] unto Isaac. But
unto the sons of the concubines . . . Abraham
gave gifts " (xxv. 5, 6) : The real substances,
the perfect virtues, are the possessions of the
perfect and true-born only (*Sac.* 43) ; so Isaac
alone receives substantial realities, graven on the
heart (in contrast to idols, Gen. xxxi. 35) of the
wise, the self-taught nature (*Congr.* 74). These
' substances ' or ' realities ' are the natural laws
(*Mig.* 94 & n & [N], *cf. Leg. All.* iii. 197)

[a] Philo also treats of Abraham's binding of Isaac (*Quod
Deus* 4) and their dialogue (*Fug.* 132-136, *Abr.* 173).

[b] " When this higher stage is reached the old antithesis
between labour and natural gifts, between art the imitator
and nature the creator, is wiped out." (Translator's note *ad
loc.*)

[c] τὰ ὑπάρχοντα is each time taken as the philosophical term
τὰ ὑπαρκτά, ' realities.' See *Mig.* 94[N].

Isaac was warned not to enter Egypt (xxvi. 2, 3).
This means he was always spiritually ' naked '
of passions and vices (*Leg. All.* ii. 59, *Det.* 46), and
dwells in Wisdom-land (*Mig.* 29f, *Som.* i. 160).
In *Conf.* 81 Philo perversely interprets the text
to teach that the good man is a *sojourner* in the
body but *dwells* in wisdom. His ' sporting ' with
Rebecca (xxvi. 8) was a divine pursuit (*Cher.* 8 &
n & [N]), the sacred sporting of the soul with
the one who waits patiently for all that is beautiful (*Plant.* 168-170)

Philo interprets Gen. xxiv. 67 so that he can qualify
Isaac's *taking* a wife (rather than *receiving* one
from God) ; so Isaac is included with those who,
self-taught, are ready to accept from God Reason
or Knowledge, the partner in the life of the wise
(*Post.* 77f). No concubines of Isaac are mentioned : for the self-taught nature wants neither
the practice (Jacob) nor the teaching (Abraham)
which entails the need of the concubine as well
as the legitimate forms of knowledge ; he is the
husband of no slavish arts, but of the queen and
mistress of virtue, constancy (*Congr.* 34-38, 111).
Philo goes further : Isaac and the other lovers
of wisdom and those of like spirit did not know
women, but rather rejected sense.[a] Their wives
are called women, but are really virtues, Rebecca
being ' steadfastness in excellence ' (*Cher.* 40f,
47, *cf. Post.* 62)

Of Isaac's death (xxxv. 29, " he was added to his
people "—γένος) it is said that self-learnt knowledge is translated into the genus of the im-

---

[a] αἴσθησις is Philo's regular interpretation of Eve or
generic woman.

INDEX OF NAMES

perishable and fully perfect (*Sac.* 6f & [N])

I. *Leg. All.* i. 82, ii. 59, 82, iii. 43, 85-87, 177, 209, 217-219, II. *Cher.* 8 & n & [N], 40f, 47, 106, *Sac.* 5-7 & [N], 43, 64, 110, 120[N], *Det.* 29-31, 46 & n, 60, 124f, *Post.* 62, 77f, 134, III. *Quod Deus* 4, 92 & [N], *Plant.* 78f, 168-170, *Ebr.* 60, 94, 119f, *Sob.* 7-9, 38n, 65, IV. *Conf.* 74, 81, *Mig.* 26n, 29, 94, 101, 125 & n & [N], 126, 139, 140 & [N], 142n, 166, 167 & n, *Quis Her.* 8, 68, 251, 261, *Congr.* 24n, 34-38, 70, 111, 175, V. *Fug.* 48, 132, 166f, 200, *Mut.* 1, 12 & [N], 13, 88, 130f, 137, 157, 161, 166f, 175-177, 188, 190, 218, 230, 252f, 255, 261-264, *Som.* i. 3, 14, 38, 68 & n, 159 & n, 160, 162f, 166-173, 194f, *Som.* ii. 10, VI. Gen. Introd. pp. x, xi & n, xii, xvi f, *Abr.* 485-6, 168-177, 188, 192-207, VII. *Spec. Leg.* ii. 54, VIII. *Virt.* 207 & n, 208, *Praem.* 24, 27, 31-35, 50, IX. *Quod Omn. Prob.* 70[N]

Ishmael: bastard [a] son of Abraham by Hagar. Hagar is the προπαιδεύματα of the Schools, the lower learning ; and so her son [b] represents sophistry.[c] He is contrasted with the true-born son, Isaac : Ishmael, though elder in years, is spiritually junior to Isaac,[d] his sophistry contrasts with

---

[a] νόθος, *Sob.* 8, cf. *Fug.* 208.

[b] Ishmael is closely linked with Hagar in *Cher.* 8, *Post.* 130-132, *Congr.* 127-129, *Fug.* 204, 208-212 & n, *Mut.* 255.

[c] σοφιστεία, *Cher.* 9, *Sob.* 9 ; σοφιστής, *Cher.* 8, 10, *Sob.* 9, *Congr.* 129, *Fug.* 209-211.

[d] Gen. xxi. 14-16 uses παιδίον of Ishmael, and so he is a ' child ' compared with Isaac. In *Post.* 130f Philo makes this ' child ' the soul just beginning to crave after instruction ; when grown to manhood it becomes the sophist (xxi. 20). In *Fug.* 208 Ishmael is inferior to Israel (*seeing* God), who is a true-born son. Philo evidently has in mind the inferiority of Ishmael (νόθος, *Sob.* 8) to Isaac (γνήσιος).

331

Isaac's wisdom (*Sob.* 8f); he is the progeny of
teaching, Isaac is self-taught (*Mut.* 255, *cf.* 218f,
263). So Hagar and the sophist Ishmael, with
his child's play, are cast out when generic happiness (Isaac) is born, whose ' play ' (with Rebecca)
is divine (*Cher.* 8 & [N])

Philo equates Ishmael with sophistry because he
is the child of Hagar ; but Gen. xxi. 20, " and
he became an archer," is used to develop the
theme, for whatever point he sets forth as a
target, at this he discharges proofs like arrows,
with sure aim (*Post.* 131) ; he is the quarrelsome
sophist who shoots or is shot at with the bow
(*Congr.* 129), loving to argue and shoot at men of
every kind of learning, and of course being shot
at in return (*Fug.* 209-211)

Philo treats Gen. xv. 11f, giving the meaning of
Ishmael's name (see below), and explaining
ἄγροικος as his ' country ' wisdom, compared
with the more civilized, gentle virtue (*Fug.* 208f) ;
and xxi. 19 : Hagar ' watered ' Ishmael with the
same incomplete education as her own (*Post.*
130), with gradual progress (προκοπαῖς, 132).
But it is Abraham's prayer in xvii. 18, " Let
Ishmael live before Thee," which obtains the
fullest treatment (*Mut.* 201-263). *Ishmael* means
' hearing God ' (202, *Fug.* 208)—he was so named
because Hagar was chastened by hearing the
words of God (*Fug.* 208)—so Philo discusses right
and wrong hearing (*Mut.* 201-205). It is spiritual
life which is concerned, that what Ishmael hears
from God may abide and inflame him (209f), that
his may be the sum happiness of living *before God*,
that is, the mind knowing that God's eye is

always watching over him (216f). The prayer teaches that the soul may be inadequate to receive God's greatest gifts (*i.e.* Isaac), but it must dedicate what gifts it has and cherish these lesser ones (220-227). God's answer to the prayer is two gifts rather than one : Ishmael will flourish, but with Isaac the greater gift is given (252f, 255, 263)

I. Gen. Introd. p. xvii, II. *Cher.* 8 & [N], *Post.* 130-132, III. *Sob.* 8f, IV. *Congr.* 127-129, V. *Fug.* 1, 204, 208-212 & n, *Mut.* 201-263 (esp. 201f, 204, 209f, 216f, 252f, 255, 263), VI. *Abr.* 253f, VIII. *Virt.* 206n

Ishmaelites : (VI. *Jos.* 15, 27)

Isidorus : IX. *Flacc.* 20 & [N]-24, 125-127, 135-150, X. *Leg.* 355

Israel [a] : The proper preface to Philo's treatment of the nation is his interpretation of the individual, Jacob, renamed Israel. In some cases Philo links the nation onto the man (*e.g. Mig.* 199-201, *Conf.* 145-148) [b] ; in others he does not distinguish between the two (*e.g. Leg. All.* iii. 15, where Lev. xv. 31 is used to develop teaching on Jacob ; and, for the contrary, *Ebr.* 24, where the nation is called ὁ ἀσκητής, Philo's regular term for Jacob ;

---

[a] Only passages containing the actual word(s) are included, with a few exceptions. Of course Philo often alludes to Israel without mentioning the name ; and that applies particularly to the biographical books. On the other hand, he repeatedly uses texts proper to Israel without any reference to context ; this makes a complete analysis almost impossible. See also Hebrews, Jews, Alexandrians.

[b] Sometimes, of course, Philo's text uses Jacob or Israel for the nation (*e.g.* Num. xxiii. 7, see *Conf.* 72).

cf. 111). In one case it is Isaac with whom Israel is almost equated (*Fug.* 208)

For Philo Israel means ' seeing God,' and so he calls Israel ' the seeing one ' or ' the race of vision.' [a] By Israel he usually means the mind or soul. Sometimes it is the good (or better) mind as a whole,[b] often faced with outward opposition [c] ; sometimes it is the better part of it,[d] contrasted with a lower inward element represented by one of Israel's enemies [e] ; sometimes divisions in Israel represent the conflicting elements of the soul.[f] But it would be unwise to press these distinctions

---

[a] (ὁ) ὁρῶν (τὸν Θεόν), *Leg. All.* ii. 34, iii. 15, 172, 186, 212, *Sac.* 134, *Post.* 63, 89-92, *Plant.* 58, *Sob.* 13, *Conf.* 56, 146, 148, 159, *Mig.* 113, 125, *Quis Her.* 78, *Congr.* 51, *Fug.* 208, *Som.* ii. 44, 172f, *Abr.* 57, *Leg.* 4, *cf. Agr.* 81, *Mig.* 200f, 224, *Congr.* 51, *Som.* ii. 279. τὸ ὁρατικὸν γένος, *Quod Deus* 144, *Conf.* 91f, *Mig.* 18, 54, *Mut.* 109, 189, 258, *Som.* ii. 279 ; ὁρατικός with τρόπος, *Plant.* 60 ; ψυχή, *Ebr.* 111, *Fug.* 139 ; διάνοια, *Mig.* 14 ; νοῦς, *Mut.* 209 ; ὁ ὁρατικός, οἱ ὁρατικοί. *Mig.* 163, *Plant.* 46f. Other expressions are used in *Sac.* 118-120, *Plant.* 58, *Conf.* 72, *Quis Her.* 279, *Fug.* 208, *Mut.* 203, 209, *Som.* i. 114, 172f.

[b] E.g. *Plant.* 58 (ψυχῶν σοφῶν θίασος), *Leg.* 5 ; *cf. Abr.* 58f, *Conf.* 148.

[c] E.g. *Mig.* 14, *Mut.* 209, where Israel is the population of the soul led out from Egypt, the body ; *Mut.* 107, the ruling mind, swamped by Midianite sensuality.

[d] E.g. *Sac.* 119 (μεσαίτατον καὶ ἡγεμονικώτατον τῆς ψυχῆς) and *Abr.* 57 (ὅρασις ἡ διὰ τοῦ τῆς ψυχῆς ἡγεμονικοῦ προφέρει τὰς ἄλλας ὅσαι περὶ αὐτὸ δυνάμεις· αὕτη δέ ἐστι φρόνησις, ὄψις διανοίας).

[e] E.g. Pharaoh (*Det.* 91-95), the Egyptians (*Leg. All.* ii. 34, *Sac.* 134, *Conf.* 91f), Amalek (*Leg. All.* iii. 186).

[f] *Leg. All.* ii. 77f (the Israelites killed by serpents, οὐ τὸ ἄρχον ἐστὶν ἐν ἡμῖν, ἀλλὰ τὸ ἀρχόμενον τὸ λαῶδες), *Mig.* 18 (of the Exodus, τὰ θνητὰ τῆς ψυχῆς καὶ τὰ ἄφθαρτα, κτλ.), *Quis Her.* 78f (of Manna, *cf. Mig.* 199-201, *Agr.* 79-81).

This soul-vision is an unaided faculty, transcending any perception through instruction, symbolized by hearing (*Conf.* 72, 148, *Fug.* 208, *cf. Abr.* 57). It represents the highest kind of seeing, the sight of the truly Existing, superior to the contemplation of the heavens and the trivialities of the sophist (*Congr.* 51f, *cf. Abr.* 58, *Leg.* 5f, *Praem.* 43-46).[a] It is the sight of the understanding, namely wisdom (*Abr.* 57, *Plant.* 58), outstripping reason (*Leg.* 4-6, *cf. Praem.* 43-46). It means the acme of happiness (*Abr.* 58). In one passage Philo allows Israel to be eclipsed ; if any cannot attain to being a son of God, the next place is to be a son of God's First Born, variously entitled as the Word, Israel, etc. Those who do are sons of God's invisible image, the Word, or ' sons of Israel ' (*Conf.* 145-148)

On the nation itself Philo makes little direct comment, though much can be inferred from its symbolical precedence. He calls it ' beloved of God ' (*Mig.* 113) and ' the best of races ' (*Congr.* 51), and describes it as a plant whose root was Abraham (*Quis Her.* 279). In *Mos.* i. 67 he says that the Burning Bush was a symbol of the suffering people

---

[a] But it may be of interest to notice *Quis Her.* 279, where Israel is σκεπτικὸν καὶ θεωρητικὸν τῶν τῆς φύσεως πραγμάτων, and *Som.* ii. 17, νοῦς θεωρητικὸς Θεοῦ τε καὶ κόσμου.

336

is usually ὁ ἀσκητής, the Practiser [a]; but, following the derivation in Gen. xxvii. 36, Philo also uses ὁ πτερνιστής, πτερνίζων, the Supplanter [b]; much less often, Israel, and almost always with reference to the change of name.[c] Jacob symbolizes the soul (e.g. Som. i. 128, 179-181, Abr. 52) or mind (e.g. Quis Her. 256) or reason,[d] especially as the type of those who learn by practise, making gradual progress,[e] with toil.[f] In this he is often compared with Abraham and Isaac.[c] Otherwise his particular significance is mostly suggested by the Genesis narratives, so that we find Jacob repeatedly contrasted with Esau or Laban [c]

When Isaac's wife Rebecca eventually conceived she learned she had twins and that the elder would serve the younger (Gen. xxv. 23, Congr. 129); for God foreknew their potential faculties, and that Jacob, the good character endowed

---

[a] ἀσκητής itself is used nearly sixty times; if we include the cognate words ἀσκητικός, ἄσκησις, ἀσκέω, there are nearly a hundred occurrences. Usually it is ὁ ἀσκητής, occasionally with a noun in apposition (νοῦς, ἀρετή) or with a descriptive genitive (σοφίας, καλῶν); or ἀσκητικός (λόγος, τρόπος, ψυχή διάνοια, βίος, ἀρετή, μελέται). The translators have varied their renderings—Practiser, Self-trained, (self-)disciplined, man of earnest effort, devotee of virtue, etc.

[b] Leg. All. i. 61, ii. 89, iii. 15, 93, 180, Sac. 42, 135, Mig. 200, cf. Quis Her. 252, Mut. 81, Som. i. 171.

[c] See below.

[d] τὸ λογισμόν, Som. i. 180; πρεσβύτερος λόγος, Mut. 94; πρεσβύτερος ὀρθὸς λόγος, Som. ii. 135.

[e] προκόπτω, προκοπή, Det. 5, 51, Sac. 120, Post. 78, Conf. 72.

[f] πόνος, Leg. All. iii. 15, Cher. 46, Sac. 120, Mig. 214, Congr. 35, Fug. 14, Mut. 84-86, 88, Som. i. 120, 127, 168, 179, Jos. 223, cf. 230, Praem. 27, 36. Cf. ἀγωνία, Mut. 81, Som. i. 168.

with reason, would dominate the slavish, base
and irrational Esau (*Leg. All.* iii. 88f, *cf. Congr.*
129, *Praem.* 63). Esau was ἄγροικος, Jacob
ἄπλαστος (xxv. 27). Philo exploits the adjectives
to point the contrast : Jacob's nature is simple,
unfabricated, in contrast to Esau, whose very
name suggests fabrication to Philo (*Plant.* 44).
Jacob dwelt in a house, that is, virtue (*Leg. All.*
iii. 2), but Esau is houseless (*Congr.* 61f). Esau
surrenders to Jacob his birthright (xxv. 29-34).
This is the victory [a] of the practiser of excellence
in his unrelenting warfare against the passions
(*Sac.* 17f, 120), the bad man's power " fainting "
at Jacob's " seething " reason (*ib.* 81 & n).
Though Esau is the elder, Jacob is proved
morally senior (*Sac.* 17f, *Sob.* 26). In the story
of Jacob cheating Esau of their father's blessing,
Jacob says Esau is hairy, he himself smooth
(λεῖος, xxviii. 11). This smoothness signifies
Jacob's nakedness of soul (*i.e.* freedom from
passion ; in *Mig.* 153, singleness of aim), which
his marrying Leah (Λεία) confirms (*Leg. All.* ii.
59 & n). Isaac's surprise at the *speed* with which
the venison was brought (xxvii. 20) also interests
Philo : Jacob found quickly because God imparts wisdom to his disciples and the slow stages
of learning are by-passed (*Sac.* 64, *Quod Deus*
92f, *Ebr.* 120, *Fug.* 168f). Philo contrives other
contrasts with Esau from the same text (see
Quis Her. 252-254 & n). Jacob had hardly gone
out when Esau entered (xxvii. 30, *Ebr.* 9), for the
exodus of virtue works the entrance of evil, and
vice versa—but only to find himself supplanted

[a] *Cf.* p. 339, note *a.*

(xxvii. 36, *Sac.* 134f). This is the soul's victory
over passion (*Leg. All.* iii. 190f, *cf. Mig.* 208, *Quis
Her.* 252n).[a] Esau's blessing says he is to serve
Jacob (xxvii. 40) : it is the chance for the ignorant to learn from the wise (*Leg. All.* iii. 193, *cf.
Quod Omn. Prob.* 57), for the rebellious and war-
ring nature to submit to self-control (*Congr.*
175f) [b]

Rebecca then advised Jacob to flee to her brother
Laban (xxvii. 42-45). This was a flight from
evil (Esau), but also from perfect virtue (his
parents), giving him the chance to know himself
(*Fug.* 42-47), a flight from intellect to the senses,
when discretion required it (*Mig.* 208-211) : it
is politic to avoid action too antithetical (*Fug.*
27), and sense-perception is a useful second-
best refuge (*Som.* i. 41-46). In any case it was
only a temporary measure. Jacob " journeyed
to Haran and met a place " (xxviii. 10f). This
place is the Logos, intermediate to the perception of God (*Som.* i. 68-70),[c] for direct illumina-
tion has been withdrawn (*ib.* 115-117). It is also
the Logos that Jacob uses for the pillow of his
mind (127f). The dream of the Ladder and its
allegorical significance are treated at length

---

[a] In *Mig.* 208 Jacob is said to be τέλειος τὴν ψυχήν (contr.
Fug. 40) ; but perfection is usually associated with the
wrestling victory and his change of name. See below, p. 347,
note *e.*

[b] ἐγκράτεια, *Quis Her.* 254, *Congr.* 31, 175, *Som.* ii. 15.

[c] The ' place ' is on the way to Haran, and might have
been intermediate in a local sense. But Philo seems to
assume that Jacob has arrived at Sense-perception (Haran),
and that (the incident in) this place is on the way to his
vision of God (Israel).

(see *Som.* i. 133-188, and the Analytical Summary, V. pp. 289-291)

When Rachel demanded children of him, thinking that sense-perception and mind can procreate all things (*Post.* 179 ; virtue, *Leg. All.* iii. 180), Jacob expostulated, saying that he was not in the place of God (xxx. 1f), that is, that God is antecedent to the mind and the only Cause (*Leg. All.* ii. 46f)

Jacob and Laban divided the flocks. Jacob's share was the variegated beasts, Laban's those without mark (xxx. 42). This division represents that between things approved by their stamp, awarded by God to the lover of instruction, and those having no mark, assigned to the man of ignorance (*Quis Her.* 180, *Fug.* 9f). The soul can refuse impressions, or it can submissively receive indelible stamps (*ib.* 181). In *Fug.* 11 ἐπίσημος [a] passes to Jacob himself as champion of a theistic philosophy against the materialist Laban ; the world is created, and each thing has been shaped and marked by God's Word. Jacob's dream about the flocks (xxxi. 10ff, *Som.* i. 189-256) refers to the couplings and breedings of thoughts (*Som.* i. 197), the mating of well-endowed souls with perfect virtues (200), ' variegated ' like the branches of knowledge (205). Jacob flees from Laban (xxxi. 20f). This was flight inspired by hatred [b] (*Fug.* 4), shared by the faculties and virtues of the Practiser.[c] It is the soul's flight

---

[a] In *Som.* i. 202 ἐπίσημος may have suggested ' genuine ' coinage ; see note.

[b] The earlier flight from Esau was one of fear.

[c] ἀσκητικαὶ δυνάμεις, *i.e.* Rachel and Leah, Gen. xxxi. 14-16 ; *Fug.* 14f, *cf. Congr.* 31.

from materialism (*ib.* 8), from folly (14), from the passions (22, *Leg. All.* iii. 15-19), to the height and greatness of virtue (Gilead)

The wrestling of Gen. xxxii. 24f marks a stage in the soul's progress, as contrasted with Jacob's victory and new name (xxxii. 28, *Mig.* 200). It is the exercise given by the Logos to the pupil-athlete to develop his strength (*Som.* i. 129, *Mut.* 14 & n; contrast *Mig.* 27). In *Mut.* 14, *Som.* i. 131, it represents the quest for virtue. In *Praem.* 48 it is apparently a wrestling against passions within himself. The numbing of the thigh ligament is the paralysing of conceit (*ib.* 47f), a voluntary disabling (*Som.* i. 131), yet the reward for victory (*Praem.* 47, *Som.* i. 130) ; but in *Mut.* 187 we are told that virtue is not sound-footed in our mortal and bodily nature, but limps a little. Elsewhere the reward is the vision of God (*Mut.* 82, *cf.* *Som.* i. 129). Apart from all this, the ' wrestling ' has provided Philo with a metaphor which he uses frequently to describe the Practiser's conflict against the passions (see below)

After the wrestling Jacob was told, " thy name shall no more be called Jacob, but Israel shall thy name be. Because thou hast been strong with God and mighty with men " (xxxii. 28). The second part of the verse indicates the soul's inward and outward purity ; to win honour in its duty towards the uncreated and the created demands a mind truly midway between the world and God (*Mut.* 44f) ; the soul whole-heartedly following virtue will respect both parents, right reason (father), which teaches it to honour the Father of all, and instruction (mother), which introduces custom and convention (*Ebr.* 80-83). The change of name from Jacob to Israel is for Philo the most significant incident in Jacob's career. Generally it is associated with his wrestling victory : the prize is the vision of God, Israel (*Mig.* 199-201, *Mut.* 81f, *Praem.* 27). Hitherto Jacob has been characterized by learning and progress, now he has attained perfection (*Ebr.* 82, *Som.* i. 119f, *Praem.* 36 ; contrast *Mut.* 87) ; toil in the quest for truth has given place to vision (*Leg. All.* iii. 15, *Praem.* 27) ; hearing [a] is replaced by eyesight (*Ebr.* 82, *Conf.* 72, *Mig.* 38, *Som.* i. 129) ; or, what was seen before, but dimly, is now seen clearly (*Mut.* 81f, *Som.* i. 177, *Praem.* 37) ; the irrational element has been conquered, the soul has achieved intellectual apprehension (*Mig.* 199-201). This is a reminting or remodelling of the soul (μεταχαράττω, *Mig.* 39, *Som.* i. 129f, 171). Different emphases are found according to the context. Thus in *Ebr.* 83 the advance which this change of name represents wins the approval of both parents, right reason and convention (see above). In *Mig.* 199-201 it is shown that seventy and five (the senses) were associated with Jacob, but seventy only (intellectual apprehension) with Israel. In *Sac.* 119f Reuben is son of Jacob but Levi son of Israel, because devout contemplation is proper to the service of God. Vision is an appropriate reward for the Practiser, as faith was for Abraham and joy for Isaac (*Praem.* 27),

[a] Learning depends upon hearing, but the vision of God represents that perfection which does so no longer.

or because an active life goes with youth but a contemplative one suits old age (*ib.* 51 & [N]). In *Som.* i. 238-241 it is said that hitherto Jacob has mistaken the Logos for God, now he sees God Himself. In *Mut.* 83, 87 it is an angel rather than God that renames Jacob (contr. Abraham) because Jacob continues often to be called by his old name : he is not consistently perfect. In *Praem.* 44-46, on the other hand, it is stressed that the revelation of God is given by God Himself : seekers for truth see God through God (*cf.* 39f, and *Som.* i. 240). Philo sometimes gives the impression that it is the climax of Jacob's own achievement (*cf. Som.* i. 171, *Mig.* 199-201, *Mut.* 81f), but then emphasizes that it is a revelation (*e.g. Praem.* 27, 36-39, *cf. Som.* i. 240). The vision of God only revealed that God is, not what He is (*Praem.* 39). Once or twice Israel is used for Jacob without reference to the renaming (*e.g. Leg. All.* ii. 46 & [N],[a] *Quod Deus* 121). Otherwise Israel refers to the nation, see *s.v.* Israel. In *Ebr.* 24 the nation is termed ' the Practiser '

Only a few of Philo's further comments on the narrative need be added. " In my rod I crossed this Jordan " (xxxii. 10) is the mind crossing over the lower nature by schooling (*Leg. All.* ii. 89). The hiding of the strange gods (xxxv. 4) is the hiding, guarding, and destroying of passions (*Leg. All.* iii. 23, 27). " The God who feedeth me from my youth up unto this day, the Angel who delivereth me out of all my ills, bless these boys "

---

[a] ὁ βλέπων, although in a context chronologically earlier than the renaming.

(Jacob's words in xlviii. 15): from this Philo deduces that God rather than the Word feeds Jacob, that is, the principal boons (the various forms of knowledge) are from God Himself, the secondary gifts (remedial) from His Word (*Leg. All.* iii. 177, *Fug.* 66); or, that sustenance is from God rather than created things like rain (*Quod Deus* 157f); or, that God gives the good for virtue-loving souls, while angels have the province of evils for punishment (*Conf.* 181, *Fug.* 67). *Mut.* 41 deals with another phrase, " pleasing *before* God " rather than *to* Him

" Jacob departed and was added to his people " (xlix. 33). Like Abraham, he inherited incorruption and joined the angels, advancing to something better (*Sac.* 5)

Mut. 81f tells of Jacob's practice of virtue and warfare (*Som.* i. 174, 255) against the passions,[a] and this passage happens to contain most of the links in the chain of Philo's terms for this. Jacob is the *supplanter* of Esau, hence the supplanter of the passions (*Leg. All.* ii. 89, iii. 93, *Sac.* 42), which he is even said to hunt (*Quis Her.* 252 & n). He is the practised *wrestler* (πάλην ἠσκηκότος, *Leg. All.* iii. 190), so the struggle is a contest or bout (*Congr.* 31, *Mig.* 200, *Som.* i. 129, 255); the *practised* or *trained* wrestler, so we find athletic metaphors (γεγυμνασμένος, ἀθλητής, etc.).[b]

[a] His struggle is also directed against ignorance (*Det.* 3), the irrational element (*Mig.* 200), vainglory (*Som.* i. 255), effeminacy (*ib.* 126).

[b] γυμνάζω, etc., *Sob.* 65, *Mut.* 84f; ἀθλέω, ἀθλητής, etc., *Mig.* 26f, *Congr.* 70, *Fug.* 43, *Som.* i. 126, 131, 168, 179, *cf. Jos.* 230, *Virt.* 210; and both in *Mig.* 199f, *Som.* i. 129, 251, *Abr.* 48, *Jos.* 26, 223.

INDEX OF NAMES

This of course suggests that the vision of God is a *prize* (see above)

Esau provides the most frequent contrast to Jacob, representing passion [a] or wickedness and vice,[b] folly or ignorance,[c] the irrational.[d] Once Esau and Jacob are types of the twin natures in man (*Praem.* 63). Laban, too, is passion against Jacob's virtue (*Leg. All.* iii. 18-22), but chiefly he represents the (objects of the) senses [e] and corporeal ideas,[f] materialist and atheist philosophy (*Fug.* 8f, 11, 46f); he champions particular qualities against Jacob's theism (*Cher.* 67), the laws of time-order (*Ebr.* 48), sophistry (*ib.* 50); he represents ignorance and lack of schooling,[g] folly,[h] vainglory (*Fug.* 47). With him are associated his daughters,[i] but as the wives of Jacob they are faculties or virtues of the Practiser [j]

But it is the relationship of Abraham and Isaac to Jacob which most interests Philo. The three form an educational trinity representing the spiritual knowledge or virtue which is reached

[a] Passion, *Leg. All.* iii. 2, 190-192, *Sac.* 17f, 42, 81, *Quis Her.* 252-254, *Virt.* 208, *Praem.* 59.

[b] Wickedness, *Sac.* 134f, *Det.* 45f, *Mig.* 208, *Congr.* 129.

[c] Folly, *Sac.* 17, *Ebr.* 10, *Sob.* 26, *Congr.* 61, 175, *Quod Omn. Prob.* 57 ; *cf. Virt.* 209, *Praem.* 59. Ignorance, *Fug.* 39-43.

[d] τὸ φαῦλον καὶ ἄλογον, *Leg. All.* iii. 88f, *Praem.* 59 ; φαῦλον also in *Sac.* 18, *Virt.* 209.

[e] *Leg. All.* iii. 15-17, 20-22, *Ebr.* 46f, *Mig.* 28, *Fug.* 22, 45.

[f] *Leg. All.* iii. 15, *Ebr.* 46f, *Mig.* 28.

[g] *Leg. All.* iii. 20, *cf. Quis Her.* 180, *Fug.* 14.

[h] *Agr.* 42, *Fug.* 14, 16, 45.

[i] *E.g., Cher.* 67, *Leg. All.* iii. 20.

[j] *E.g., Cher.* 40 & [N], *Post.* 62, *Congr.* 24 & n-33, *Quis Her.* 43, *Fug.* 15.

345

by teaching (Abraham), nature (Isaac), practice (Jacob).[a] Most of what Philo has to say about Jacob has been governed by his being the Practiser of virtue : and that rôle was chosen for him because of Philo's wish to reproduce an educational trinity in the Patriarchs. They are compared with each other in these particulars : they are all founders of the race (*Mut.* 88, *cf. Jos.* 172), God names Himself by them (*Mut.* 12, *Mos.* i. 76), their descent has spiritual significance [b] (*Som.* i. 166-170), they have certain qualities in them, whether these are potential or active (*Sob.* 38), they are sojourners only (*Conf.* 79-81), their deaths are a progress to something better (*Sac.* 5-7). They represent learning by teaching, by nature, by practice [c] ; *Mig.* 125 offers a variation on the theme : the Patriarchs are the threefold divisions of eternity (see note). Isaac is once or twice distinguished from Abraham and Jacob [d]

[a] *Sac.* 5-7 & [N], *Sob.* 38 & n, *Conf.* 79-81, *Mig.* 125 & [N], *Congr.* 34-36, *Mut.* 12 & [N], 83-88, *Som.* i. 166-170, *cf.* 160, 173, VI. Gen. Introd. pp. x & n, xi & n, *Abr.* 48-55, *Jos.* 1, *Mos.* i. 76, VIII. Gen. Introd. p. xxi, *Praem.* 24-27, 49-51 & [N], 57ff. The threefold education is also mentioned, without reference to the Patriarchs, in *Leg.* 320.

[b] Abraham is called ' father ' of Jacob in Gen. xxviii. 13. But see also the passages where Philo speaks of Abraham being grandfather of Jacob's knowledge : *Sac.* 43, *Som.* i. 47 & [N], 70, *cf. Quod Deus* 92 & [N].

[c] διδασκαλία, φύσις, ἄσκησις are found in *Sob.* 38 (*Conf.* 79-81), *Abr.* 48-55, *Jos.* 1 (μάθησις for διδασκαλία), *Mos.* i. 76, *Praem.* 24-27, 49-51, 57ff. There is a variation in *Mut.* 12, but see [N].

[d] Their names are changed, Isaac's not (*Mut.* 83-88). They married several women, Isaac only one (*Congr.* 34-36)—but in *Cher.* 40f the patriarchs have nothing to do with women, for they reject sense : their wives are virtues. Isaac might

346

Jacob's character never suffers eclipse with Philo. He is the practiser of virtue, the supplanter of passion, at war for the one against the other (see above). His virtue or his being a type of virtue is constantly referred to,[a] his pursuit of things noble,[b] his wisdom.[c] He is the man of worth.[d] He becomes perfect.[e] We are also told he is wealthy (*Det.* 13f), courageous (*Mut.* 214), holy (*Abr.* 52, *Jos.* 167), a prophet (*Quis Her.* 261), God-loving (*Abr.* 50) and God-beloved (*Sob.* 29, cf. *Som.* i. 243, *Jos.* 167, 200), one of the band of friends of God (*Som.* i. 196)

I. Gen. Introd. p. xii, *Leg. All.* i. 61, ii. 46 & [N], 89, 94-97, 103, iii. 15-23, 88f, 90, 93, 146, 177, 179-181, 190-195, II. *Cher.* 40, 41 & [N], 46, 67, *Sac.*

seem to lag behind ! But Philo is not here thinking of the educational triad.

    [a] *Leg. All.* iii. 2, 15, 22, 89, 93, *Cher.* 40, *Sac.* 17f, 46, 134f, *Det.* 45, *Ebr.* 82f, *Sob.* 15, 65, *Conf.* 181, *Mig.* 27, 200, *Quis Her.* 256, *Congr.* 24, 35, 123, *Fug.* 21, 25, *Mut.* 14, 81, 83, 171f & nn, *Som.* i. 45, 121, 131, 174, 179, *Abr.* 50, 52, *Jos.* 1, 172, 230, *Mos.* i. 76, *Virt.* 210, *Praem.* 65.
    [b] *Sac.* 17, *Sob.* 26, *Mig.* 153, *Fug.* 45, *Som.* i. 126, 131, 251, *Jos.* 4.
    [c] *Leg. All.* iii. 2, 25f, 195, *Sac.* 18, 48, 135, *Ebr.* 48, *Sob.* 27, *Mig.* 101, *Som.* i. 70, 169, 175f, 178, 205, 207, *Jos.* 191, *Mos.* i. 76, *Spec. Leg.* ii. 3, *Virt.* 223, *Praem.* 51. Cf. *Quod Deus* 119, *Quis Her.* 180, *Fug.* 45-47.
    [d] ἀστεῖος, *Leg. All.* iii. 23, 89, 191, *Sac.* 5, *Conf.* 73, *Som.* i. 176.
    [e] He becomes τέλειος by his victory over Esau (*Mig.* 208 ; but contrast *Fug.* 39f, ' child ') ; but in *Som.* i. 213 he is said to be not yet perfect, because Philo mostly thinks of Jacob reaching perfection after his wrestling victory, when he became Israel (*Ebr.* 82, *Mig.* 27, 199-201, 214, *Som.* i. 131). His perfection is through practice : *Agr.* 42, *Conf.* 181, *Congr.* 35. In *Mut.* 83-87 he does not remain consistently perfect even after the change of name.

INDEX OF NAMES

5, 17f, 42, 46-48, 64, 81 & n, 119f, 134f, *Det.* 3-5, 13f, 17, 45, 46 & n, 51 & n, 67, *Post.* 59 & [N], 62, 75f, 78, 89, 179, *Gig.* 22 [N], III. *Quod Deus* 92, 119-121, 157f, *Agr.* 42, *Plant.* 44, 90, 110 & [N], *Ebr.* 9f, 24, 48 & [N], 53, 82f, 120, *Sob.* 12, 15, 26-29, 38 & n, 65 & n, 66, IV. *Conf.* 72-74, 80, 181, 182n, *Mig.* 5, 26-30, 38f, 101, 125 & [N], 153f, 159f, 199-201, 207 & [N]-214, *Quis Her.* 38, 43, 180, 242[N], 251-254 & n, 256, 261, *Congr.* 24 & n, 31-35, 61f, 70, 99, 123, 129, 175f, V. *Fug.* 4, 7-52 (esp. 10, 23-25 & [N], 39-48 & 45[N], 52), 67, 143, *Mut.* 12 & [N]-14, 41, 44-46, 81-88, 92, 94, 97, 171 & n, 172 & n, 187, 210, 214f, *Som.* i. 1-2[N], 3f, 5n, 45-47 & [N], 61, 68-72, 112n, 115 & n-120, 125, 126 & n & [N]-133, 144, 150, 159 & n, 163, 166-182 & n, (183-188), 189f, 196-205, 207f & n, 213, 227f, 238, 240 & n, 249-256, *Som.* ii. 15, 19f, 66, 135, 136n, 141, 207 & n, VI. Gen. Introd. pp. x-xii, xv n, xvi f, *Abr.* 48-56, *Jos.* 1, 4f, 8-14, 20, 22-27, 163-270 (esp. 223, 230), *Mos.* i. 76, 239-242, VII. *Spec. Leg.* ii. 3 & n, VIII. Gen. Introd. pp. xviii, xxi, *Virt.* 6n, 208 & n & [N]-210, 223f, *Praem.* 24-27, 36-39, 40n, 44 & n, 51, 57, 59f, 61n, 63, 65f & n & [N], 78[N], 166n, IX. *Quod Omn. Prob.* 57, *(Flacc.* 74n), *Hyp.* 6. 1 & n

Jamneia : X. *Leg.* 200, 203

Japhet : praised for covering over the soul's sad change (I. *Leg. All.* ii. 63) ; Noah's prayer for Japhet (Gen. ix. 27) is that mind and body and external advantages may all contribute to his attaining the good (III. *Sob.* 59-61 & [N]), though his final home is to be the excellence of the soul (67f). See also III. *Sob.* Introd. p. 441

Jason : IX. *Quod Omn. Prob.* 143

INDEX OF NAMES

---

[a] τῦφος, *Gig.* 50, *Agr.* 43, *Ebr.* 36 (πλάσμα τύφου), 40, *Mut.* 103, 114.

[b] Whitaker began with ' worldling ' in *Sac.* 50 ; used ' uneven ' in *Agr.* 43, and withdrew ' worldling ' ; in *Mut.* 103 he chose ' superfluous.' See his notes on *Sac.* 50 and *Agr.* 43. περισσός is also used in *Gig.* 50.

In Exod. ii. 18, Num. 10. 29, Moses' father-in-law is Raguel, which means 'the shepherding of God.' This change of name reflects a change of character in Jethro, who is won over to the herd of God in admiration of Moses' direction of it (*Mut.* 105). His connexion with Midian [a] signifies that he is the judicial justice-dispensing sort, with seven daughters symbolizing the seven faculties of the unreasoning element (*ib.* 110-120)

II. *Sac.* 50 & [N], *Post.* 77, *Gig.* 50, III. *Agr.* 43 & [N], *Ebr.* 36-45, IV. *Quis Her.* 44, V. *Mut.* 103-114, 104nn, VI. *Mos.* i. 52, 58f, VIII. *Spec. Leg.* iv. 173

Jews, Jewish [b] : In *Mos.* i. 67 Philo says that the Burning Bush was a symbol of the suffering Jews. In *Spec. Leg.* iv. 179 he remarks that the race is in the position of an orphan compared with the nations all around. In *Virt.* 65 he says that what others gain from philosophy the Jews gain from their customs and laws, that is, to know the Cause of all

VI. *Mos.* i. 7, 34, ii. 17, 25, 41, 193, 216, VII. *Decal.* 96, *Spec. Leg.* i. 97, ii. 163, 166, iii. 46, VIII. *Spec. Leg.* iv. 173-175 & n, 179, 224, *Virt.* 65, 108, 206, 212, 226, IX. *Quod Omn. Prob.* 29, 43, 57, 68, 75, *Aet.* 19, *Flacc.* 1, 21, 23f, 29, 43, 45, 47, 49, 54-56,

[a] It is as Jethro he is priest of Midian (Exod. iii. 1). Philo associates this good, judiciary character of Midian with Raguel (*Mut.* 110ff); perhaps he intended us to infer that the bad sense of Midian applies to Jethro, but omitted any explicit statement for lack of a convenient text to illustrate Jethro being ' sifted out.' See Midian.

[b] The references only include the passages in which the word occurs in the Greek text. See also Israel, Hebrews, Alexandrians.

Joseph in this unfavourable light, Philo often ignores texts uncongenial to his thesis, or misrepresents those which he does quote.[a] Nevertheless he does sometimes allow Joseph to have had good qualities [b] and to be a type of the good soul.[c] In the *De Josepho*, however, the whole approach is reversed ; no praise can be too high for the Patriarch (φύλαρχος, *Jos.* i.), and only once does Philo hint at a flaw in his character.[d] Again and again we find what amounts to a categorical denial of things which he has said of him in the earlier works. An indication of this is given in Philo's discussion of Joseph's name. It means, he says, ' Addition '—of external advantages (*Mut.* 89f), of spurious qualities (*Som.* ii. 47), of vanity rather than simplicity (*ib.* 63). But in *Jos.* 28 it is ' Addition of a lord,' and refers —favourably—to his political career. For a further discussion of this see VI. Gen. Introd. pp. xii-xiv

Joseph is the politician,[e] attempting to ' keep in ' with two worlds, the real and the sham, prepared to compromise (*Mig.* 158, 162, *Som.* ii. 14f) and

---

[a] Philo omits, *e.g.*, that Jacob loved Joseph and that he gave him the coat (xxxvii. 3a), and that the Lord was with Joseph and gave him favour with the gaoler (xxxix. 2a, 21) ; he misrepresents xxxix. 1 by applying ' eunuch ' to the Joseph-soul (*Quod Deus* 111 & [N]), xxxvii. 33 by assuming the false allegation there to be true (*Som.* ii. 65f & n, *Jos.* 36), and perhaps 1. 7f (*Mig.* 159f). In *Mig.* 21 (see [N]) the misrepresentation is in Joseph's favour.

[b] Philo lists these in *Mig.* 18-24.

[c] *Fug.* 126-131, *Mut.* 214f.　　[d] *Jos.* 34-36.

[e] ὁ πολιτικός, *Leg. All.* iii. 179, *Jos.* 1, ὁ πολιτικὸς τρόπος, *Fug.* 126, *cf. Mig.* 159, *Som.* i. 221, πολιτεία, *Det.* 6, *Som.* i. 78, 219f. See p. 354, note *c*.

to subordinate truth to expediency or falsehood (*Det.* 7, *Som.* i. 220), accommodating himself to both body and soul (*Mig.* 159, *cf. Som.* ii. 11, i. 78) ; and, being a politician, he is often given to worldly and unspiritual ambitions (*Mig.* 163, *cf. Som.* i. 219f, ii. 12, 16 ; contrast *Fug.* 126), he is eager for vainglory,[a] self-opinionated,[b] presumptuous (*Som.* ii. 99), swollen-headed with vanity [c]

Because Egypt is the scene of his activity, his πολιτεία is connected with the body (*Som.* i. 78, *cf. Mig.* 159) ; his responsible position signifies care for the body (*Post.* 96, *Sob.* 13, *Mut.* 90, *Som.* ii. 42, 46). So Joseph is the lover of the body and its passions,[d] the champion of the body and externals,[e] fond of luxury (*Som.* ii. 9, 16). From his mother he inherited the irrational strain of sense-perception (τὸ ἄλογον αἰσθήσεως, *Som.* ii. 16), and it found expression in his marriage (*Som.* i. 78 & n), his fondness for Benjamin (*Mig.* 203), and his corn laws (*ib.*).[f] Yet Joseph is a Hebrew, ' emigrant ' from sense-perception (*Mig.* 20, *cf. Som.* ii. 107), although in Egypt, he is ruler rather than subject (*Mig.* 20, *Quis Her.* 256), he is proof

---

[a] κενὴ δόξα, *Agr.* 56, *Sob.* 15, *Som.* ii. 12, 16, 42, 78, 93-99, 115, 155, *cf. Mig.* 21 ; δοξομανέω, *ib.* 114.

[b] Δοκησίσοφος, *Leg. All.* iii. 179.

[c] ποικίλος τοῦ βίου τῦφος, *Conf.* 72 ; *cf. Mig.* 161 & [N], *Som.* ii. 46f, 63f, 66, 95, 98, 115, 139.

[d] Ὁ φιλοσώματος καὶ φιλοπαθὴς νοῦς, *Quod Deus* 111, *Mig.* 16 ; see also *Quod Deus* 120, *Agr.* 56, *Som.* ii. 16.

[e] Of the three goods, soul, body, and externals (see *Det.* 7[N]), Joseph is concerned with the lower two : so *Sob.* 13, *Mig.* 22 & n, 203. In *Det.* 7 and *Som.* ii. 9, 11, all three classes are mentioned.

[f] αἴσθησις also in *Mig.* 207, *Som.* ii. 65, 107.

against luxury (*Mut.* 215), from his father he inherited self-control [a]

Joseph began by shepherding the sheep with his half-brothers as a young man [b] (Gen. xxxvii. 2). This association with the sons of Jacob's concubines is fitting, for Joseph's concern is with lower things (*Quod Deus* 119-121) and those who honour spurious goods (*Sob.* 12-15); he pastures the realm of the body (*ib.*) and irrational natures (*Agr.* 55f). Philo ignores Jacob's love for Joseph, but the coat of many colours (xxxvii. 3, ποικίλον χιτῶνα) indicates the complex doctrine (λαβυρινθώδης καὶ δυσέκλυτος δόξα) of the three goods (see above, p. 353, note *e*; *Det.* 6-9, 28); it is the robe of statecraft, variegated with falsehood and sophistry (*Som.* i. 219-225; contrast *Jos.* 32). It also underlies Philo's description of Joseph's character in *Conf.* 72 (ποικίλος τοῦ βίου τῦφος), and probably that in *Som.* ii. 10-16 (δόξα πολυμιγὴς καὶ κεκραμένη) and 66 (ὁ πολυπλοκώτατος . . . τυφοπλαστηθεὶς βίος) [c]

[a] ἐγκρατής. ἐγκράτεια, *Leg. All.* iii. 237-241, *Det.* 19, *Som.* ii. 15, 106, *Jos.* 54f.

[b] ὢν νέος; xlix. 22, νεώτατος. He remains young and immature, *Quod Deus* 119f, *Agr.* 55f, *Sob.* 12-15, *Conf.* 72 (where the translation seems to miss this allusion); *cf. Leg. All.* iii. 242, *Mig.* 205.

[c] Philo's chain of ideas is also πολυπλοκώτατος, and can best be shown by a diagram. For δόξα see *Som.* ii. 15, *Det.* 6-8; the arrows indicate the influence of one idea upon another; for Αἴγυπτος—τῦφος see *Mig.* 160 & [N].

The dreams of the sheaves and the stars (xxxvii. 7-11) reveal the vainglory of Joseph's character (*Som.* ii. 5-7, 30-33, 78, 93-99, 110-116 ; contrast *Jos.* 5-11). His father sends him to join his brothers in the plain (xxxvii. 13-17) to learn to discipline his lower nature (*Det.* 5f, 10-17) ; so he seeks and finds the virtuous family (*Fug.* 126-128)

Joseph was taken to Egypt and sold to Pharaoh's chief cook, a eunuch (xxxix. 1, LXX). So the body-loving mind is enslaved to Pleasure (*Quod Deus* 111).[a] But Potiphar's wife fails to entice him (xxxix. 7-11), and here Joseph appears in a good light as the type of self-control (*Leg. All.* iii. 237-242, *Mig.* 19, 21 &[N], *Som.* ii. 106 ; and see p. 354, note *a*). Unjustly imprisoned, Joseph acts as an interpreter of dreams.[b] In *Mig.* 19 Philo gives him credit for saying God is the author of interpretations ; but in *Cher.* 128 he blames him for saying they are *through* God instead of *by* Him (xl. 8). The interpretation of Pharaoh's dreams resulted in Joseph being set over all the land of Egypt (xli. 41f), which Philo treats caustically (*Som.* ii. 44 ; but see *Mig.* 20). Pharaoh put Joseph in his second chariot : but this is Joseph's conceit (*Som.* ii. 16, 46, *Mig.* 160 & [N] ; contrast *Jos.* 148-150). Pharaoh also changed his name to Psonthomphanech, 'mouth

[a] Philo applies 'eunuch' to the Joseph-soul. See p. 352, note *a*.

[b] *Som.* ii. 42, 78. In view of their context, these titles should probably be regarded as uncomplimentary ; in this book Philo constantly depreciates Joseph's dreams (*Som.* ii. 42, 97, 105, 138 ; contrast *Jos.* 95) and ignores his skill at interpretation.

which judges in answer,' which Philo makes to suggest that fools will look for wise pronouncements from any man who happens to have great wealth (*Mut.* 89-91)

When his father learns that Joseph lives,[a] it means Joseph claimed to have real life—to Jacob's surprise, who expected him to have shared in the death of vain opinions and of the body (*Mig.* 21 & n, *cf. Quis Her.* 256), or to have succumbed to the luxury with which he was surrounded (*Mig.* 214f, *cf. Fug.* 126). Joseph's words in l. 19, " I am of God," also win approval (*Mig.* 22, 160, *Som.* ii. 107, *Jos.* 265f). On his death he was buried in a coffin in Egypt, but he had requested that his bones accompany his people (l. 25f); so the lower side of Joseph's personality is said to have been buried in Egypt (body) and forgotten, but the higher qualities are worthy to be remembered, and leave Egypt with Moses (*Mig.* 16-24, *Som.* ii. 105-109)

I. Gen. Introd. pp. xii & n, xiii, xxii n, *Leg. All.* iii. 90-93, 179f, 237-242, II. *Cher.* 128, *Det.* 5-28, *Post.* 80, 96, III. *Quod Deus* 111 & [N]-116, 119-121, *Agr.* 55-59, *Ebr.* 210, *Sob.* 12-15, 27, IV. *Conf.* 71f, *Mig.* 16 & n-24 & 17[N], 21[N], 23[N], 159-163 & n & 160[N], 203f, 207 & [N], *Quis Her.* 242[N], 251, 256, V. *Fug.* 73, 126-131, *Mut.* 89-91, 97, 170, 171 & n, 215, *Som.* i. 78, 219-225, ii. 5-21, 30, 33, 42-44, 46f, 64-66, 78, 93-116, 135-141, VI. Gen. Introd. pp. xii-xiv & nn, *Jos. passim*,

[a] xlv. 26, the brothers report that Joseph is alive; 28, Jacob rejoices that he is alive; xlvi. 30, he says so to Joseph. For other points in Gen. xlv see *Leg. All.* iii. 179f, *Mig.* 21-23, *Quis Her.* 251, 256, *Mut.* 171, 215.

INDEX OF NAMES

VII. *Spec. Leg.* iii. 51[N], **VIII.** Gen. Introd. p. xviii n, *Praem.* 65[N], **IX.** *Flacc.* 72n, *Prov.* 2. 46n

Joshua : in the incident of Exod. xxxii, Joshua represents a man's *feeling* inward tumult, while Moses is the reasoning side of his nature interpreting the true cause (**III.** *Ebr.* 96-98 & [N], 103f). Joshua's name had been Hoshea, ' he is saved '; it was changed to Joshua, ' salvation '; thus it is a change from an individual to a state, the one mortal, the other permanent, and so the coin was reminted in a better form (**V.** *Mut.* 121 & n-123). Add **VI.** *Mos.* i. 216, (232-236), **VIII.** *Virt.* 55f, 60, 66-70 & n, 72

Jubal : **II.** *Post.* 100-111. Brother of Jobal (*q.v.*) and akin in meaning ; for it means ' inclining now this way, now that ' (μετακλίνων), and it is a figure for the uttered word (ὁ κατὰ προφορὰν λόγος), the unsure speech of the wavering mind (100). He is the inventor of musical instruments, which are inferior to song-birds but, like articulate speech, capable of such *varied* utterance that it is natural that they should be invented by one μετακλίνων λόγους (103-111)

Judaea : **VI.** *Mos.* ii. 31, **IX.** *Hyp.* ii. 1, **X.** *Leg.* 199f, 207, 215, 257, 281, 294, 299

Judah : Philo's interest in Judah is in his name and in the Tamar story. His name means ' confession of praise to the Lord.' [a] This is the crowning virtue, and so there is significance in Leah ceasing to bear after giving birth to Judah (Gen. xxix. 35) [b] and in his being the fourth son : for

[a] *Leg. All.* i. 80, 82, ii. 95f, iii. 26, 146, *Plant.* 134-136, *Ebr.* 94, *Congr.* 125, *Mut.* 136, *Som.* i. 37, ii. 34.
[b] *Leg. All.* i. 80, ii. 95, iii. 146, *Plant.* 134f, *Som.* i. 37f.

357

four is the number of praise and thanksgiving ; Issachar is appropriately so called (' reward '), because he was born next after Judah (xxx. 18), and thanksgiving itself is an all-sufficient reward (*Plant.* 134-136). In *Leg. All.* i. 79-84 Philo compares Judah with Issachar. Judah represents good sense (φρόνησις) as a mystical spiritual condition, Issachar good sense in the action of noble deeds. With this Philo links Judah's name ; for ' thanksgiving ' takes a man out of himself, making him independent of the body, while he acknowledges that even praise is the work, not of the soul, but of God. All this is in the discussion of the precious stones of Gen. ii. 12 ; so Judah is engraved on the ruby of the High Priest's robes, because he is permeated by fire in thanksgiving and drunk with sober drunkenness

Philo varies his interpretation of the Tamar incident, but consistently idealizes it. In *Congr.* 125f he is the lover of learning unveiling knowledge to discover its virtue. In *Fug.* 149-156 the story is an instance of seeking and not finding (by Judah's messenger) invincible virtue. Here Judah is the mind wooing piety (θεοσέβεια) and giving pledges of his sincerity. In *Mut.* 134-136 Tamar's veil prevents her seeing her wooer, though she recognizes his pledges : it is God impregnating the soul, the pledges being His working in the universe. Judah is the thankful character, gratified that no profane element has defiled the divine. In *Som.* ii. 44f Judah is king of the race of vision (Israel), and Tamar is the soul. The pledges are again God's working in the universe, but it is Judah who teaches the soul. In *Virt.* 221f Judah is not mentioned; but see [N]. The description of Judah as ' king ' (*Congr.* 125, *Som.* ii. 44 ; *cf. ἀρχικὸς φύσει, Jos.* 189) seems to depend upon the ' staff ' in the story

I. Gen. Introd. p. xii n, *Leg. All.* i. 80 & n &[N]-84, ii. 95f, iii. 26, 74, 146, III. *Plant.* 134-136, *Ebr.* 94, IV. *Quis Her.* 255 & n, *Congr.* 125f, V. *Fug.* 73f, 149-156, 150[N], *Mut.* 134-136 & 135n, *Som.* i. 37f, ii. 34, 44 & n, 45, VI. *Jos.* 15, 189, 222-231, VIII. *Virt.* 221[N]

Julia Augusta : **X.** *Leg.* 291, 319f
Julius Caesar : see *s.v.* Caesar
Jupiter : **IV.** *Quis Her.* 224

Kadesh : **V.** *Fug.* 195f, 213. The spring at which Rebecca fills her water-pot (Gen. xxiv. 16) is the Divine Wisdom, which waters the fields of knowledge and souls that love the best. Philo identifies this with En-Mishpat (' spring of judgement ' or ' sifting ') at Kadesh (' holy ') in Gen. xiv. 7, and says the Wisdom of God is holy and free from earthy ingredient (= Kadesh) and a sifting of all the universe, separating opposites (= κρίσις). In 213 Hagar's well (xvi. 14) between Bered and Kadesh is the well of School knowledge, so situated because he that is in gradual progress is on the borderland between the holy and the profane, fleeing from the bad but not yet ready to share the perfect good

Keturah : wife or concubine of Abraham (Gen. xxv. 1), meaning ' incense-burning ' ; interpreting xxv. 5f, Philo contrasts true wisdom with school-

---

[a] Where, it seems to me, Philo is playing upon the likeness of Κορέ (LXX) to κόρη, ' maiden ' ; this has not been shown in the translation.

[b] αἰσθητά in *Leg. All.* iii. 15-17, 20-22, *Det.* 4, *Agr.* 42, *Ebr.* 46f, *Mig.* 28, 208-214, *Fug.* 22, 45f ; *cf. Som.* i. 41f.

[c] To this ' Syrian ' contributes also in *Fug.* 44.

variety of things that belong to the world of
sense, including bodies or corporeal ideas ; this
leads Philo to the philosophical concept of the
three ' goods ' or values—those of the soul, the
body, and externals (see *s.v.* Joseph). Laban
has no share in the divine values (*i.e.*, of the·soul ;
Fug. 20) : his philosophy is that of the body and
external things (*Leg. All.* iii. 20, *Ebr.* 46-52 &
[51[N], *cf. Det.* 4) ; here we probably link up
with the αἰσθητὰ καὶ φαινόμενα ἀγαθά of *Agr.*
42. Whether he is drawing upon αἰσθητά generally or σώματα in particular, Philo makes Laban
also represent the *passions* (*Leg. All.* iii. 19-22)

In *Fug.* 8-22, esp. 8-13, Philo might be thought to
reverse Laban's philosophy of ποιότης, variety.
But in fact what he says there is partly governed
by antithesis with Jacob and the terms under
discussion (ἄσημος, ἐπίσημος ; see *s.v.* Jacob),
and partly by his argument, which here is
directed against an *evolutionary philosophy* (11-
13[N], *cf. Som.* i. 45f). Laban's sheep typify
the irrational (*Sac.* 46f), as do his shepherds,
apparently (*Mig.* 212f) ; and Laban enslaves the
rational Jacob (*Leg. All.* iii. 17, *cf.* 19). So he
typifies the *irrational* element. This goes with
his interest in the bodily things [a] and his neglect
of the highest good, that of the soul or mind

Because of his opposition to Jacob, one of the educational triad, Laban comes to be ignorant,
foolish, and unwilling to learn. He loses his
daughters to Jacob, a stripping of the virtues
which leaves him worthless indeed (*Fug.* 15-18) ;
but he is really their foe, a hater of virtue (*Quis*

[a] *Leg. All.* iii. 15, 22, *Ebr.* 46f, *Mig.* 28, *Som.* i. 45f.

361

INDEX OF NAMES

Her. 43f). Or, their going is the departure of his good sense, leaving him ignorant and uneducated (*Leg. All.* iii. 20-22), as does the loss of the arts and branches of knowledge (*Cher.* 67-71). In *Ebr.* 46-55 his attempt to marry the elder to Jacob before the younger was a mistaken adherence to time order and a sophistic flouting of the natural sequence of education—first the School culture and then the higher training in philosophy. As brother of Rebecca he is regarded more leniently than as Laban the Syrian (*Fug.* 44-46, *cf. Leg. All.* iii. 18) ; but as Bethuel he becomes divine Wisdom (*Fug.* 49-52)

I. *Leg. All.* iii. 15-22, II. *Cher.* 67-70, *Sac.* 46f, *Det.* 4, *Post.* 59 & [N], 76, III. *Agr.* 42, *Ebr.* 46-52, IV. *Conf.* 74, *Mig.* 28, 208-214, *Quis Her.* 43f, 180, V. *Fug.* 4, 7-22 & 11-13[N] & 16[N], 44-52 & 45[N], 143, *Som.* i. 1-2[N], 45f, 126n, 189, 202n, 225-227, VIII. *Virt.* 223 & n

Lacedaemonia : see Sparta

Laconian : see Sparta

Laius : VII. *Spec. Leg.* iii. 15

Lamech : II. *Det.* 50f, *Post.* 40f, 46-48, 74f, 79-81, 112, 124. Lamech, whose name means ' humiliation ' or ' lowness ' (ταπείνωσις), appears as a descendant both of Cain and of Seth (Gen. iv. 18, v. 25). The name therefore has a twofold application. There is the ' lowness ' to which the soul is reduced by irrational passions owing to weakness : this is the Cain strain (*cf. Det.* 50) ; and there is the self-imposed check to conceit, an exercise of strength : herein lies Lamech's being a descendant of Seth and father of Noah (*Post.* 40f, 46-48). His grandfather and father

362

(Methuselah, iv. 18) had names indicating soul-death, and his own refers to the low state to which the soul is brought by the birth of passion (*ib.* 74). " Lamech took unto himself two wives " (iv. 19). When a worthless man presumes to take anything to himself it is bound to be evil, and Lamech chose two very great evils (75). He arranged the marriage for himself, because he fancied the mind should proceed to its ends unhindered ; and in his case they were wrong ends (79-81). His words to his wives in Gen. iv. 23 illustrate that, because the soul's actions affect the soul itself, the worthless man's wrongdoing is an injury to himself (*Det.* 50f)

Lamia : **X.** *Leg.* 351

Lampo : **IX.** *Flacc.* 20 & n & [N], 125-135

Leah : ' virtue.' [a] With this Philo fits his interpretation of her name : twice he takes the Greek Λεία, associating this with Jacob's ' smooth ' nakedness of soul (Esau was hairy, Jacob λεῖος, *Leg. All.* ii. 59), and with the ' smooth ' movement of Leah's peaceful virtue (Rachel's is combatant, *Congr.* 25-32) ; otherwise he derives it from Hebrew words, *lo,* ' not,' and *lahah,* ' to be weary.' Thus in *Cher.* 41 Leah means ' rejected and weary '—with sustained practice (of virtue), ' rejected,' because every fool says ' no ' to her and turns from her.[b] In *Mut.* 253-255 the same

[a] In almost every passage. Philosophy contrasted with the lower culture in *Ebr.* 46-53. Beauty of soul (tantamount to virtue) contrasted with that of the body in *Sob.* 12

[b] But see the translation and [N] at *Cher.* 41, where Colson takes the relative to refer to the ἀσκήσεως, immediately antecedent ; I have ventured an alternative rendering, taking Leah as the (admittedly remote) antecedent of ' whom '

363

INDEX OF NAMES

interpretation is given for ' rejected,' but ' weary '
is ' causing weariness through the commands she
lays upon us (Virtue).' In *Mig.* 145 κοπιῶσα is
intransitive, ' growing weary ': for it is the life
of wickedness which causes weariness, and she
in fact refuses to have anything to do with it ;
she ' wearies of ' it

Laban justified marrying Leah to Jacob before
Rachel because she was the elder (Gen. xxix.
26f) : this was to claim that the senior culture,
philosophy, may precede the junior, the School
learning, and that it may be deserted in favour
of the latter. Jacob's reply means he will never
leave philosophy (*Ebr.* 46-53)

" When the Lord saw that Leah was hated, he
opened her womb " (xxix. 31). Most of what
Philo says about Leah revolves round this text.
" Leah was hated " : man hates virtue, but God
honours her by making her the first to bear (*Leg.
All.* ii. 47, *Mut.* 132f) ; men hate virtue, because
she despises their association with sense-perception (Rachel) : but she has fellowship with God
(*Post.* 134f) ; Leah and Rachel together representing the ' mixed ' life, men naturally prefer
the pleasant life of the senses to the austere life
of knowledge and virtue (*Quis Her.* 45-48) ; men
dissent from that to which God assents, namely
virtue and the commands which she lays upon
us (*Mut.* 253-255). God " opened her womb " :
this Philo interprets as the impregnation of
virtue by God Himself (*Leg. All.* ii. 47, *Cher.* 43f ;

('which') : Leah is never ἄσκησις, always virtue ; and in
the close parallel in *Mut.* 253-255 it is Leah and virtue from
which men ' turn away.'

INDEX OF NAMES

cf. Congr. 7, and perhaps *Quis Her.* 50f) ; He is
the husband, but as Leah bore " to Jacob,"
Jacob is the father for whose sake God sowed the
seed in virtue (*Leg. All.* iii. 180, *Cher.* 46, *Mut.*
132f ; but *cf. Congr.* 7) ; by this divine impregnation virtue conceives and bears noble deeds (τὰ
καλά, *Leg. All.* iii. 180, *cf.* 146, *Post.* 135, *Quis
Her.* 50, *Mut.* 255, *cf. Congr.* 31)

After bearing Judah (thankfulness) Leah " left
bearing " (" stood off ''), Gen. xxix. 35. This
indicates that Judah is the crowning virtue (*Leg.
All.* i. 80-82 & n), beyond which Leah could not
go (*Som.* i. 37f) ; and God wanted to balance the
good things of the soul (Leah's sons) with pro-
gressive representatives of the body (from
Rachel and the concubines) (*Leg. All.* iii. 146)

These contrasts with Rachel as sense-perception
are not maintained in *Congr.* 24-33. There the
soul (*Jacob*) is twofold, the reasoning part having
Leah to wife, the unreasoning Rachel. Rachel,
acting through the senses, helps the soul to fight
the passions : she represents the way of war :
Leah is the λεία κίνησις of virtue, most healthy
and peaceful, through whom the Practiser reaps
the higher and dominant blessings. See 24n

I. Gen. Introd. p. xii n, *Leg. All.* i. 80 & n, ii. 47,
59 & n, 94, iii. 20, 146, 180f, II. *Cher.* 41 & [N],
44-46, *Det.* 3, *Post.* 62, 134f, III. *Plant.* 134, *Ebr.*
46-53, *Sob.* 12, IV. *Mig.* 95f, 99, 145 & n, *Quis
Her.* 45-48 & 46n, 50, 175, *Congr.* 7, 24 & n-32,
29[N], 123, V. *Fug.* 15-19 & 16[N], 73, *Mut.* 132,
254f, *Som.* i. 37f, VIII. *Virt.* 221n, 223 & n-225
Lepidus : IX. *Flacc.* 151, 181
Levi, Levites : there are few references to Levi as

365

an individual, and most of them merge into Levi the tribe.[a] The many passages about Levi or Levites as the tribe appointed to the temple service depend upon certain texts. First, Deut. x. 9, " Levi hath no part nor portion with his brethren ; the Lord Himself is his portion." With this is usually linked [b] Deut. xxxiii. 9a, " Saying to his father and mother, I have not seen thee, and he acknowledged not his brethren and his sons he disowned " ; which Philo seldom quotes but often alludes to in the word γένεσις.[c] Thus Philo contrasts Levi with the man who leaves father and mother yet ' cleaves to ' sense-perception (*Leg. All.* ii. 51) ; although Reuben is Jacob's oldest son, Levi, being son of ' Israel,' is spiritually senior, and his ' portion ' is that of the eldest—God Himself (*Sac.* 119f) ; like slayers compelled to flee from home to a city of refuge, Levites too are exiles, having left their families to win an immortal portion (*ib.* 129, *Fug.* 102) ; that is one reason why Levitical cities were chosen for refuge (*Fug.* 88) ; with proselytes, orphans, and widows, Levites [d] are suppliants

[a] *Leg. All.* i. 81, *Sac.* 120, *Ebr.* 94, *Mig.* 224, *Fug.* 73f, 200, *Mut.* 199f, *Som.* ii. 34, 37.

[b] Deut. x. 9 alone in *Sac.* 127, *Det.* 62, *Plant.* 69-72, *Fug.* 102. Deut. xxxiii. 9 alone in (*Det.* 67f), *Plant.* 63f, *Ebr.* 72, *Fug.* 88f. Both in *Leg. All.* ii. 51, *Sac.* 119f, 129, *Congr.* 133, *Mut.* 127, *Som.* ii. 272f.

[c] *Sac.* 120, *Plant.* 63f, *Mut.* 127, *Som.* ii. 273. Colson translated it ' creation ' : and certainly it is contrasted with τὸ ἀγένητον in *Plant.* 63f ; but is there not all the time a play upon its sense of ' family ' or ' kin ,' summarizing Deut. xxxiii. 9 ? Perhaps ' creatures ' or ' creature family ' would convey both.

[d] Philo treats these as three classes with phrases corre-

INDEX OF NAMES

and fugitives, orphans to their creature families,
God being their husband and father (*Som.* ii.
272f); the mind, perfectly cleansed, which re-
nounces all creatures, knows only One, the Un-
create (*Plant.* 62-64); the mind that slays all
that claims kinship with the soul—body, passions,
senses—is one with the Levi-mind, who renounced his family, and with the Phinehas mind
(*Ebr.* 70-74); it is from this great transcendent
soul who holds fast to the Uncreated alone that
Moses is descended on both sides, thus having a
double link with truth (*Congr.* 131-135); and this
portion allotted to the wise is not material possessions, of course, but the greatest spiritual
benefits, given by God to those who serve Him,
who are thereby very kings (*Plant.* 62-72) [a]

The third key passage is Exod. xxxii,[b] the incident
of the Golden Calf and its sequel. Moses asked,
Who is on the Lord's side? The Levites alone
responded, and slaughtered three thousand, not
excluding their own kin. Because of this, says
Philo, they too are in a sense slayers, which is
why their cities are chosen for refuge (*Sac.* 130-
134, *cf. Fug.* 88-90, *Spec. Leg.* iii. 123f, 128); it

sponding to each, using μέν and δέ. But the vocabulary of
the phrases, while appropriate to each, is drawn from terms
used of Levites, so I have amalgamated them.

[a] With Deut. x. 9 in *Plant.* 63 is linked a similar verse,
Num. xviii. 20. In *Mut.* 199f, Deut. xxxiii. 8 is used; and
9b, 10 in *Det.* 62-68. See below.

[b] *Sac.* 130, *Ebr.* 66-74, *Fug.* 90-92, *Mos.* ii. 161-172, 272-
274, *Spec. Leg.* i. 79, iii. 124-126; and the description of
Levi in *Som.* ii. 37 (*cf.* 34) is surely an allusion to this (*cf.
Spec. Leg.* iii. 128). The very similar story of Phinehas (Num.
xxv) is laid under contribution deliberately in *Ebr.* 73f, and
accidentally in *Spec. Leg.* iii. 126.

367

was a slaughter of false doctrines : when the
soul fell the holy thoughts (ἱεροὶ λόγοι), armed
with the proofs of knowledge, championed true
religion (*Sac.* 130) ; it was also a cutting away of
all that is near and dear to the mind : " each his
brother, each his nearest " (xxxii. 27) means the
body, ' brother ' of the soul, and the senses,
' nearest ' to the uttered word [a] (*Ebr.* 65-71, *Fug.*
88-92). This was an instance where right reason
was obeyed rather than custom (*Ebr.* 65, 68).
The reward was the priesthood (*Sac.* 134, *Ebr.*
65, *Mos.* ii. 173, 274, *Spec. Leg.* iii. 125-128)

The fourth passage is Num. xxxv. and its parallels :
the six cities of refuge taken from among the
forty-eight Levitical cities. This was done because the good are a ransom for the bad (*Sac.*
128), because the Levites are themselves virtually exiles, but voluntarily (*Sac.* 129, *Fug.* 88),
because they too are fugitives, but in God (*Sac.*
129), because they too are slayers (*Sac.* 130, *Fug.*
90). Yet another reason is suggested by Exod.
xxi. 13, from which Philo deduces that involuntary
homicide is God's way of punishing : Levites and
homicides, therefore, are both serving God, each
in their way (*Fug.* 93, *Sac.* 133). The non-
allegorical explanation, that Levitical cities

---

[a] ὁ κατὰ προφορὰν (προφορικὸς) λόγος. In *Det.* 63-66, ὁ προφορικὸς λόγος is the Levite's brother minister of Num. viii. 26 ;
while the perfect Levite (having reached fifty) guards the
teachings of virtue, his brother will have the subordinate duties
of teaching those who seek education (παιδεία). Aaron is ὁ
προφορικὸς λόγος : " Aaron the Levite shall speak for thee "
(Exod. iv. 14) means that only to the ἱερεῖ καὶ σπουδαίω λόγω
is it fitting to reveal the thoughts of perfect mind (Moses),
Det. 126, 132.

INDEXOF NAMES

would afford the protection of the sacred office
and territory, is given in *Spec. Leg.* i. 158, iii. 129
& n. In *Sac.* 127 Philo tells why the Levitical
cities are " ransomed for ever " (Lev. xxv. 32).
The fugitive to the city of refuge was a ' suppliant '; the Levites themselves, as we have
seen, were exiles from their kin, casting themselves wholly upon God. So the texts from
Deut. and Num. combine to provide ἱκέτης,
often used of the Levites [a]

The Levites are called φύλακες, ' guardians.' In
Fug. 37, *Det.* 62-66, this is based upon Num. viii.
24-26. But in the latter it leads up to one of the
Deuteronomy texts (xxxiii. 9b, 10), which must
be presumed to underlie *Som.* ii. 272f. The discussion of Num. viii also raises the matter of
symbolic numbers. The Levite begins his
ministry at twenty-five, retires to " guard " at
fifty ; the latter is the number of release from
toil, the former the half-way stage of exercise
and practice (*Det.* 63-66). Elsewhere Philo discusses Levi as ransom for the tenth (*Congr.* 98) ;
and the Levites contribute tenths to make a
hundred, the number of perfection (*Mut.* 2, 191 ;
cf. *Spec. Leg.* 157)

Philo's only etymology of Levi is in *Plant.* 64 : it
means αὐτός μοι, ' He (is precious) to me '

The Levites are the consecrated tribe,[b] to whom
belongs the active ministry and service of God
(*Sac.* 120, 127, *Som.* ii. 34, 272f) ; they represent
the mind that has been perfectly cleansed (*Plant.*

[a] *Sac.* 119, 129, *Det.* 62, *Plant.* 63, *Ebr.* 94, *Quis Her.* 124.
[b] ἡ ἱερωμένη φυλή or cognate phrases, *Sac.* 128f, *Det.* 62,
Quis Her. 124, *Mos.* ii. 186, *Spec. Leg.* ii. 120f, iii. 123, 129.

369

64), perfect virtue (*Sac.* 120, *Mos.* ii. 181, *cf.* *Plant.* 70f). They are the wise, contrasted with the worthless fool (*Sac.* 121, 126, *Plant.* 69-72); they are the representatives of reason [a]; with them is truth (*Congr.* 132, *Ebr.* 70; and *cf. Mos.* i. 177). They are guardians of the oracles and covenants of God, the most excellent exponents of his laws (Deut. xxxiii. 9f, *Det.* 68)

I. *Leg. All.* i. 81, ii. 51, II. *Sac.* 118-135 (for 128-133, *cf. Fug.* 88-93), *Det.* 62-68, (126), 132, 135, III. *Plant.* 62-72, *Ebr.* 65-74, 94, IV. *Mig.* 224, *Quis Her.* 124 & n, *Congr.* 98, 131f & n, 133 & n & [N], 134, 135n, V. *Fug.* 37, 73f, 88-93 (*cf. Sac.* 128-133), 102, *Mut.* 2, 127 & n, 191, 199f, *Som.* ii. 34, 37, 272f, VI. *Mos.* i. 316, ii. 159-186, 272-274, VII. *Spec. Leg.* i. 79 & n & [N], 121n, 156-161, ii. 120f, iii. 123-128, 129n, 130, VIII. *Spec. Leg.* iv. 190n, *Praem.* 54n, 74, 75n

Leviticus : III. *Plant.* 26, *cf.* V. *Fug.* 170 & n

Libya : III. *Quod Deus* 174, V. *Som.* ii. 54, IX. *Aet.* 141, *Flacc.* 43, 45, 152, X. *Leg.* 283

Lot : the name means ' inclination ' or ' leaning ' (ἀπόκλισις [b]) ; for the mind ' inclines,' sometimes turning away from what is good, sometimes from what is bad (*Mig.* 148). In his description of Lot's character in *Abr.* 212 Philo no doubt had this derivation in mind ; but he would also be thinking of the story of Abraham's separation from Lot (Gen. xiii. 1-11, esp. *v.* 9), which he proceeds to tell (212-216) and to allegorize (217-

---

[a] λόγος, *Sac.* 119 ; ὀρθὸς λόγος, *Ebr.* 68, *Congr.* 98 ; λογικός, *Fug.* 90-92.

[b] So *Mig.* 148. ἀποκλίνω in *Som.* i. 86, 246, κλίνω in *Post.* 175, *Mig.* 13, 175. *Cf. Abr.* 212.

224), making Lot stand for the philosophy that pursues externals. In *Mig.* 13 Lot is the soul that inclines to sense-perception, which Abraham thrusts away. He had begun by inclining in a good direction, for he set out with the man of wisdom (xii. 4); but he soon proved a hindrance rather than a help when he inclined back to lack of learning (ἀμαθία), and Abraham had to protect himself by separation (*ib.* 148-150 & [N]). Like his wife (*Fug.* 121f), he was capable of growing up straight and unswerving, but he bent aside his soul (*Mig.* 175). But it was an ἀπόκλισις to virtue when he left Sodom (xix. 23f, *Som.* i. 85f & n, 246). His capture by the four kings (Gen. xiv. 12) refers to the soul's enemies (the four passions, *Mig.* 150 & [N]); the incident and its sequel is described in *Abr.* 225-235

Lot's wife is affected with the same ἀπόκλισις: in *Som.* i. 246-248 we have an allusion to Lot's inclination away from virtue (in entering Sodom), aggravated by sense-perception, so that the soul becomes a monument of its own disaster. In a similar passage (*Fug.* 121f), her looking back is the soul's lazy refusal to exercise its power of reason, having no desire to seek and find, so that the soul becomes lifeless. This speaks of the soul's capability for better things; but in *Leg. All.* iii. 213 we are told God did not allow repentance. The right name for Lot's wife is 'custom'; her nature is hostile to truth, and if we take her with us, she lags behind and gazes round at the old familiar objects and remains among them like a lifeless monument (*Ebr.* 164)

This was the mother of Lot's daughters, Delibera-

tion and Assent ; Lot, their father, was incapable
of rearing any male or perfect growth within his
soul. He is the man not only lacking knowledge
but confident that he has got it—which is even
worse than sheer ignorance. With his two
daughters the mind discusses and assents readily
to every pleasurable suggestion. This could
only happen when the mind is intoxicated (*Ebr.*
162-166). This initiates a long discussion by
Philo on the unreliability of the mind : it cannot
by deliberation find out the truth nor give a right
assent or judgement (166-205 ; see III. *Ebr.*
Introd. pp. 314-316). The same passage (xix.
30-38) is allegorized in *Post.* 175-177, where Philo
is treating " God raised up to me . . . " (Gen.
iv. 25). With that attitude is to be contrasted
that of Lot's daughters (with the same names) ;
their desire to have children by mind is the
assertion that mind can replace God (contrast
" God raised up ") and be the author of everything—a truly sottish idea, created by the strong
drink of folly

The offspring from this unpromising union were
Moab and Ammon (*q.v.*). Their people are to
be excluded from the congregation of the Lord
(Deut. xxiii. 2), for they suppose that sense-
perception and mind can procreate all things
(*Post.* 177)

I. *Leg. All.* iii. 213, II. *Post.* 175-177, III. *Ebr.* 162-
205 (esp. 162-170, 203-205), IV. *Mig.* 13, 148-150
& [N], 175, V. *Fug.* 121f, *Som.* i. 85f & n, 246-248,
VI. Gen. Introd. p. xv n, *Abr.* 212-235, *Mos.* ii.
57f, IX. *Prov.* 2. 8[N]

Lucanian : IX. *Aet.* 12

INDEX OF NAMES

Lyaeus : **X.** *Leg.* 96
Lycurgus : **IX.** *Quod Omn. Prob.* 47, 114.   *Cf.* **VI.** *Mos.*
  ii. 19, **VII.** *Spec. Leg.* iii. 22, **VIII.** *ib.* iv. 102
Lydia : **VI.** *Jos.* 133
Lynceus : **IX.** *Prov.* 2. 7
Lysimachus : **IX.** *Quod Omn. Prob.* 127-130

Macedonians, Macedonia : **II.** *Cher.* 63, *Gig.* 7 & [N]
  (-ia), **III.** *Quod Deus* 173f (both), *Plant.* 12 (-ia),
  VI. *Jos.* 135, **IX.** *Quod Omn. Prob.* 94, 115, **X.** *Leg.*
  281 (-ia)
Machir : **IV.** *Congr.* 39-43.   Machir means ' the
  father's,' and his parentage symbolizes the inferiority of reminiscence and being reminded to
  memory and remembering
Machpelah : Abraham's burial place in Hebron,
  called in the LXX ' the double cave ' (Gen. xxiii).
  In it the patriarchs and their wives were buried
  in pairs, so that it is a treasure house of memories
  (μνῆμαι, probably playing on μνημεῖον in xxiii.
  6 ; see *Som.* ii. 26n), memories of knowledge and
  wisdom (**II.** *Post.* 62 & n).   Along with other
  ' doubles,' it illustrates that the man of worth
  both contemplates the created universe and
  thinks upon the Father who brought it into
  being.   The cave is ' the pair of memories '
  (**V.** *Som.* ii. 26 & n)
Macro : **IX.** *Flacc.* 11-16, 22, **X.** *Leg.* 32-64, 69f, 75
Maecenas : **X.** *Leg.* 351
Maenads : **III.** *Plant.* 148
Maenoles : **III.** *Plant.* 148
Magi : **VII.** *Spec. Leg.* iii. 100 & n & [N], **IX.** *Quod
  Omn. Prob.* 74 & n
Magius Maximus : **IX.** *Flacc.* 74

INDEX OF NAMES

Mahujael (Maiel) : the worthlessness of Cain and his creed is continued in his descendants, Enoch, Gaidad, Maiel, Methuselah, Lamech. The flock of irrational faculties which is Gaidad had for son Maiel, ' away from the life of God,' who also leads an irrational life (**II.** *Post.* 69). He also contributes to Lamech's bad character, whose grandfather he was ; for Mahujael (E.V. ; LXX, Maiel) represents that death of soul which is due to passion (*ib.* 74f)

Maiden, The : see Athena

Maltese Dogs : **VIII.** *Praem.* 89 & [N]

Mamre : the portion awarded to Aunan and Eshcol by Abraham (Gen. xiv. 24), symbolizing the award to natural ability and vision, is awarded the contemplative life ; for Mamre means ' from seeing ' (**IV.** *Mig.* 164 & n, 165)

Manasseh : there are many whose natural gifts differ, as their names show. Such were Ephraim and Manasseh. In blessing them their grandfather Jacob gave precedence to the younger (Gen. xlviii. 19) ; that is because memory (Ephraim) is better than recollection (Manasseh), for the latter is always preceded by forgetfulness. It is older than memory, for in the first stages of education we begin with recollection of what we forget, then advance to remembering. Manasseh is the type of recollection (ἀνάμνησις, opposed to μνήμη) because his name means ' out of forgetfulness ' (*Leg. All.* iii. 90-93, *Sob.* 27-29, *cf. Mig.* 205). To Manasseh's tribe belong Zelophehad's five daughters, showing five is the number of the senses (*Mig.* 205). The contrast between memory and recollection is also made in *Congr.*

39-43. A discussion on legitimate wives and concubines leads Philo to mention Manasseh's marriage to a Syrian concubine (Gen. xlvi. 20, LXX) who bore to him Machir. " Jacob said, Ephraim and Manasseh shall be as Reuben and Simeon to me " (xlviii. 5). Reuben is natural excellence, Simeon learning ; with the relation between these two corresponds that between Ephraim and Manasseh (*Mut.* 97-102). This passage has the same remarks about forgetfulness, memory, recollection

Marah : on the journey from Passion the pilgrim soul is continually tempted by pleasures to return, and Marah marks the bitterness that the soul's toil comes to have. But the Saviour sweetened the waters, producing love of labour (II. *Post.* 156f, IV. *Congr.* 164-166). The passage, Exod. xv. 23-25, ends " . . . and the water was sweetened. There he laid down for him ordinances and judgments . . . "—the statutes were given for chastening, and therefore Marah was appropriate—" . . . and there he tried him," —so that the bitterness is also that of trial in the soul's toil (IV. *Congr.* 163f)

Marea : IX. *Flacc.* 45

Mareotic Lake : IX. *Vit. Cont.* 22

Marin : IX. *Flacc.* 39 & n

Mars : IV. *Quis Her.* 224

Masek : IV. *Quis Her.* 2, 39-42, 51-54, 61. ' From a kiss,' and kissing is not the same as loving, but represents the senses ; she (so LXX) is the mistress of the multitude, the servant of the good, who do not love her, only greet her with a kiss. The offspring of this blood-life is Damascus Eliezer

INDEX OF NAMES

Melchizedek : God made him both ' king ' of ' peace '
(Salem) and priest, without previous qualifica-
tion. He was worthy of it, for he was a ' righteous ' king, no despot. Let him offer to the soul
food full of joy and gladness and induce that
divine intoxication which is sobriety itself. For
he is a priest (Gen. xiv. 18), that is reason, having
his portion in God *a* (*Leg. All.* iii. 79-82). " He
gave him a tenth of all " (xiv. 20) is an example
of that principle seen in all tithes, the offering
of first-fruits to God from all the faculties of our
reason ; and it illustrates that ten is the perfect
number (*Congr.* 98f). Here Melchizedek's priesthood is αὐτομαθὴς καὶ αὐτοδίδακτος. The story
is told in *Abr.* 235. Add I. Gen. Introd. p. xx & n

Memphis : **VI.** *Mos.* i. 118

Mercury : **II.** *Cher.* 22, **IV.** *Quis Her.* 224

Mesopotamia : **II.** *Post.* 76, **IV.** *Conf.* 65f, *Congr.*
70, **V.** *Fug.* 48f, **VI.** *Abr.* 188, *Mos.* i. 264, 278,
VIII. *Virt.* 223n. Isaac advised Jacob to flee into
Mesopotamia (Gen. xxviii. 2) ; this means the
Practiser is to enter the midst of the torrent of
life's river, not overwhelmed by it, but beating
back the current of affairs (*Fug.* 48f). For Mesopotamia is ' Mid-river-land ' (*Conf.* 66). It is the
home of Balaam, whose understanding is submerged in the midmost depths of a river (*ib.*)

Methuselah : **II.** *Post.* 40f, 44f, 73f. His name means
' a sending forth of death.' He is a descendant
both of Seth and of Cain, and his name can be
interpreted in two ways to fit both the good and
the bad strain. In close affinity with Seth he is
the good man from whom death is dismissed, he

a Deut. x. 9, of Levi. Levi also represents reason.

has reaped true life. But as a member of Cain's
house he is at the receiving end of ἐξαποστολὴ
θανάτου, which means he is ever dying to the
life of virtue (41, 44f). With this fits his relationship to soul-death and lowness ; for he is son of
Mahujael and father of Lamech (73f)

Midas : IX. *Quod Omn. Prob.* 136

Midian, Midianites : Midian is ' from judgement,'
and Philo associates with it κρίσις, ' judgement '
or ' sifting.' Moses settles in Midian (Exod. ii.
15), that is, in the examination (κρίσις) of the
things of nature (*Leg. All.* iii. 12f). But ἐκ
κρίσεως can be taken in two senses : it can
mean ' out-sifting,' ' elimination ' ; or it can
mean ' from (belonging to) judgement,' ' judiciary ' (*Mut.* 106 & n, 110). The Midianites in
the story of Phinehas (Num. xxv) come under
the first heading ; their religion was that of
Baal-Peor, drowning the ruling mind beneath
bodily passions, and so they had to be eliminated.
Phinehas killed the Midianitish woman ; and
the Israelites defeated the Midianites (Num.
xxxi). But the other, the good sense, applies
to Raguel, " priest of Midian " (*Mut.* 106-109,
Leg. All. iii. 242) (by implication, the bad sense
perhaps applies to him in his character of
Jethro), whose seven daughter-faculties bring
objects to the mind, their judge and king. Philo
is discussing the double name, Jethro-Raguel
(*Mut.* 103-114). In *Conf.* 55 Midian is called
' the nurse of things bodily ' ; if the reading is
right, Midian must have this connotation from
Baal-Peor, as in *Mut.* 106f. But see [N]. In *Jos.*
15ff the Midianite merchants of Gen. xxxvii are

mentioned, but not named. In *Mos.* i. 295ff and *Virt.* 34ff Philo narrates the two incidents from Numbers ; but only in *Virt.* 34 are the Midianites named. See [N]

I. *Leg. All.* iii. 12f, 242, III. *Agr.* 43, IV. *Conf.* 55 & [N], 57n, V. *Mut.* 103-114, VI. *Jos.* 15, 27, 36, VIII. Gen. Introd. p. xiii n, *Virt.* 22n, 34ff & [N]

Milcah : wife of Nahor. Her name means ' queen ' ; Nahor stayed in Chaldaea, the home of astrology, queen of sciences, and this Milcah symbolizes. It is second best to the true vision of Israel, but better than the Sceptic philosophy, represented by Nahor's concubine (IV. *Congr.* 43-53)

Milky Way : IX. *Prov.* 2. 51

Milo : IX. *Prov.* 2. 7

Miltiades : IX. *Quod Omn. Prob.* 132

Minos : VII. *Spec. Leg.* iii. 43

Minotaur : VII. *Spec. Leg.* iii. 43

Miriam : Miriam criticized Moses for marrying an Ethiopian woman, and was punished (I. *Leg. All.* i. 76). This was sense-perception presuming to find fault with the man of vision (ii. 66f & [N], iii. 103). But her leading the song of the women at the Red Sea in company with Moses is good : it is sense-perception made pure and clean leading Virtue's women along with perfect mind and the men of vision (III. *Agr.* 80f). There is a non-allegorical narrative of this in VI. *Mos.* i. 180, ii. 256, IX. *Vit. Cont.* 87

The unnamed sister who witnessed the finding of the infant Moses (Exod. ii) is referred to in VI. *Mos.* i. 12, 16f, and in V. *Som.* ii. 142 she is given the allegorical name of ' Hope ' ; for she

" spied out from a distance " (ii. 4), looking to
the consummation of his life

Mishael : see *s.v.* Nadab

Mnemosyne : III. *Plant.* 129 & [N]

Moab, Moabites : Ammonites and Moabites were
the descendants of the incestuous union of Lot's
daughters with their father, and for this they
were excluded from the Israelite congregation
(Deut. xxiii. 2). They suppose that sense-perception and mind procreate all things (II. *Post.*
177, I. *Leg. All.* iii. 81, VII. *Spec. Leg.* i. 327[N],
333 & n-336). Num. xxi. 30, " And the women
kindled yet further a fire in Moab," indicates a
conflagration of the mind occasioned by the
senses ; for Moab means ' out of a father,' and
our father is the mind (I. *Leg. All.* iii. 225, 231,
IV. *Mig.* 99f). The " whoredom with the
daughters of Moab " of Num. xxv. 1 stands for
the enervating intercourse with mind's daughters,
the senses (V. *Som.* i. 89, VIII. *Virt.* 34[N])

Moon, The : IV. *Quis Her.* 224

Morning Star, The : II. *Cher.* 22

Moses [a] : The narrative of Moses' infancy is given in
Mos. i. 5-17. He was by race a Chaldaean (*ib.*
5 ; ' Hebrew,' 15), the seventh from Abraham,
a Levite (7, *cf. Post.* 173f) by both his parents,
giving him a double link with truth (*Congr.* 132f
& nn & [N]). He was, we read, " a proper

---

[a] In this analysis only a few references are made to *Mos.*
i and ii. In the final index of passages the many quotations
from or allusions to the Pentateuch, given in the form ' Moses
says ' or ' he says,' are not included ; only those passages
are listed which seem to contribute to the character, career,
or significance of Moses himself. It has been hard to be
consistent ; and I have usually ignored Deuteronomy.

child " (9) : this means he was purest mind (*Congr.* 131f), the Stoic character (*Conf.* 106 & n & [N]), a world-citizen (*ib.*).*ᵃ* His royal education included the learning of Greece and Assyria and Egypt (*Mos.* i. 21-24) ; and he became heir to Pharaoh (32)

Moses " smote the Egyptian and hid him in the sand " (Exod. ii. 11-14, *Mos.* 1. 34-44)—the Egyptian being the bad man who sinks down into his own mind (*Leg. All.* iii. 37-39). This and the subsequent incident represent Moses' attempt to overthrow the domination of the body in two attacks directed against Epicureanism and the Peripatetics (*Fug.* 147 & n, 148). Pharaoh sought his life (a seeking that had no finding, *Fug.* 147), and Moses fled to Midian (*Mos.* i. 45-49) ; or rather, he withdrew from the leader of the passions (*cf. Conf.* 82) to the place of sifting in order to inquire of God (*Leg. All.* iii. 11-14). Midian (Arabia, *Mos.* i. 47) here signifies the judicial type (*Mut.* 110f). At the well the virtue-loving mind delivers the unreasoning faculties from mind's enemies (Exod. ii. 15-22, *Mut.* 110-114). Moses was *given* Zipporah to wife (Exod. ii. 21, *Post.* 77f). Really she was not a woman but a virtue ; for Zipporah, ' bird,' signifies one speeding up to heaven and contemplating divine things (*Cher.* 40-42, 47) ; she is the winged and inspired prophetic nature (*Mut.* 120), perhaps Knowledge or Reason (*Post.* 78). Moses became shepherd to his father-in-law (Exod. iii. 1, *Mos.* i. 60, 63) : that is, Moses' right reason rules the thoughts of the Jethro mind (*Sac.* 50, *Agr.* 43).

ᵃ By a pun on ἀστεῖος.

At the Burning Bush (*Mos.* i. 65-70) the prophet was seeking nature's causes; he was spared from a futile search by the divine warning (" Draw not nigh hither," Exod. iii. 5), and instead he inquired into the nature of the Creator (*Fug.* 161-164). He did not see God Himself (*Fug.* 141, *Mut.* 134), but an angel, the symbol of God's providence (*Mos.* i. 66, *cf. Som.* i. 231f). God promised His presence to Moses (*Mos.* i. 70-76), the secret of successful achievement (*Fug.* 140). He was given three signs (*Mos.* i. 76-82) : God asks the wise man what there is in the active life of his soul, and he answers Schooling, giving it the name of a rod ; when cast away it becomes the serpent Pleasure, which must be seized and disciplined (*Leg. All.* ii. 87-93). Moses protested that he was not eloquent (Exod. iv. 10) : he sets no value upon probabilities and plausibilities, but follows after truth in its purity (*Sac.* 12f & [NN], *Det.* 38, *Mig.* 76f) ; he was tongue-tied with joy, and speech was replaced with fluent thoughts (*Quis Her.* 4). He was made " a god to Pharaoh " (Exod. vii. 1) : the mind is god of the unreasoning part (*Leg. All.* i. 40, *cf. Mig.* 84) ; Moses enjoyed a unique supremacy over the body and the mind which rules it (*Sac.* 9f & [N]) ; the wise is god to the foolish (*Mut.* 125, 128f & n, *Det.* 161f)—not in reality, only in men's imagination (*Det.* 161f, *cf. Quod Omn. Prob.* 43 & n, 44). Moses especially earned this title because of his beneficence (*Mut.* 128f). See also *Som.* ii. 189, *Mos.* i. 158

Philo divides the Ten Plagues (*Mos.* i. 90-146) into those due to the agency of Aaron (96-112) and of Moses (113-125), and those of independent causation

After the Exodus and the Passage of the Red Sea, the Song of Moses (Exod. xv. 1) is the hymn of victory over the passions sung by the army of guardian virtues led by mind in its perfection (*Agr.* 80-83 & [N], *cf. Leg. All.* ii. 102, *Ebr.* 111, *Sob.* 13, *Mos.* i. 180). In the battle against Amalek, Moses held up his hands and Israel prevailed ; but his hands were heavy (Exod. xvii. 11) : when the mind lifts itself up away from mortal things the seeing soul is strengthened against passion (*Leg. All.* iii. 186) ; the wise man's doings are weighty, immovable, upheld by the Word and Truth (*ib.* 45, *Quod Omn. Prob.* 29). At Sinai Moses " drew near unto the thick darkness where God was " (Exod. xx. 21) : that is, in his eager search for God he entered into immaterial conceptions, seeking to reach the unattainable, the transcendent God (*Post.* 14f ; *cf. Mut.* 7 & [N]) ; the people said, " Speak thou with us " (xx. 19) : this illustrates the fact that God tempers His communications, for none could endure His perfection (*Post.* 143f, *cf. Som.* i. 143), and that wise men take God for their guide and teacher, but the less perfect take the wise man (*Quis Her.* 19). Moses led his people up the mountain to the vision of the Existent (xxiv. 10, *Conf.* 95-97). His division of the sacrificial blood (xxiv. 6) represents the twofold nature of wisdom, divine and human (*Quis Her.* 182 & [N]-185). During his forty days and nights in the mount he fasted, entranced by the perfect music of the spheres (*Som.* i. 36). The incident of the

Golden Calf reveals Joshua and Moses as the feeling and the reasoning elements in man (*Ebr.* 96-104, 121-124); fired by his vision of the beautiful, Moses burned the pleasures of the body (*Post.* 158-165)

He pitched the tabernacle outside the camp (xxxiii. 7): this is an instance of that nakedness of soul which is escape from the body and its passions to dwell in virtue (*Leg. All.* ii. 54f, *Gig.* 54, *Det.* 159f); the tent is wisdom, in which the wise man tabernacles, establishing it outside the body because the good man escapes from himself and returns to the apprehension of the One (*Leg. All.* iii. 46-48, *cf. Ebr.* 99), a pilgrim travelling from war to peace, from mortality to the divine life of reasonable and happy souls (*Ebr.* 100). The Lord " spake unto Moses face to face, as a man speaketh unto his friend " (xxxiii. 11; see Scripture Index), and Moses asked that he might know Him (xxxiii. 13): the more perfect mind gets direct apprehension of the First Cause (*Leg. All.* iii. 100-103); he was eager to replace uncertainty with assured confidence (*Post.* 13-16). He required that God's presence should go with him (xxxiii. 15), for he knew his quest was unattainable except by revelation (*Mut.* 8, *cf. Spec. Leg.* i. 41f); the Divine presence and guidance are necessary for the way to the Existent (*Mig.* 170-172, *cf. Fug.* 140 on Exod. iii. 11). Not even Moses was allowed to see God: he was permitted to see only what follows behind Him, His attendant powers (xxxiii. 23, *Post.* 169, *cf. Fug.* 164f, *Mut.* 8-10) or their manifestation in the sensible world (*Spec. Leg.* i. 43n,

47-53 [a]). Deut. v. 31 is also a favourite text
with Philo, "Stand thou here with me": it
shows Moses to have been higher than the trio
Abraham, Isaac, Jacob, for he was trained to soar
above species and genus and was stationed beside
God Himself (*Sac.* 8 & n); it shows the steadfastness of the man of worth (contrasted with
Adam and Cain), who shares the very nature of
God, which is repose (*Post.* 28, *cf. Gig.* 49); and
that the perfect man seeks for quietude (*Quod
Deus* 23-26)

Moses is pre-eminently, of course, the law-giver.[b]
Philo regards Genesis as but the exordium to the
laws (*Op.* 2f), and only alludes to the subsequent
history of Israel (*Praem.* 4 & n & [N]). So great
was Israel's veneration for Moses that whatever
he approved was law for them (*Hyp.* 6. 8f). The
Greeks in their Attic law copied Moses in one
particular at least (*Spec. Leg.* iv. 61, *cf. Aet.*
147ff & [N]). The laws reveal the qualities of
the legislator (*e.g.* his humanity, *Virt.* 80f).
Philo regularly quotes the Pentateuch in the
form 'Moses says' or 'he says,' not only from
the narrative (*e.g. Cher.* 45, 49, 124, *Det.* 86, *Post.*
133), but even when repeating the words attributed to God Himself (*Conf.* 192 & n); and
at times we are given the impression that Moses
shaped the details of his narrative to suit the

___

[a] In spite of Colson's note at *Spec. Leg.* i. 41, I think
there is a difference between that passage, in which Philo
interprets 'my glory' as the Powers, and the other three
passages, where it is God Himself. This affects the interpretation of τὰ ὀπίσω μου.

[b] See below, and p. 386, note *a*.

384

INDEX OF NAMES

symbolical lessons he wishes to give (*e.g. Sob.* 26f). Philo defends the repetitions (*Congr.* 73), anthropomorphisms (*Quod Deus* 57-69), and seemingly bold statements of Moses (*Plant.* 62), and does not allow that such a passage as Gen. vi is mythical (*Gig.* 6, 58).[a] For a comparison between the Law and the Prophets see *Cher.* 49 & [N]. Those who follow the great law-giver's teaching are often called his pupils.[b] In the law we find the philosophy of Moses, which is sometimes held to have anticipated that of later Greek philosophers, and sometimes is contrasted with their theories (*e.g. Op.* 8, 12, 131, *Leg. All.* ii. 14ff, *Quis Her.* 213f, 227f & [N], *Mos.* ii. 12, *Aet.* 19). The Mosaic system is called a polity (πολιτεία *Gig.* 59 & [N], *Quis Her.* 169 & [N], *Spec. Leg.* iii. 51, iv. 55, 100, *Praem.* 4, *cf. Hyp.* 6, 10)

Comparisons and contrasts are made between Moses and other figures. Thus, like Abraham, Isaac, and Jacob, he is said to have married no woman but to have been wedded to a virtue (*Cher.* 40-47, *cf. Leg. All.* ii. 67 ; contrast *Post.* 77) ; yet he excels them in being called to stand beside God Himself (*Conf.* 192 & n). A similar sort of comparison is made between Moses and Noah in *Quod Deus* 109f. The consistency of

---

[a] On the other hand, he tells us not to take some things literally, *e.g.* in *Leg. All.* ii. 19, *cf. Op.* 156f.

[b] γνώριμοι, *Det.* 86, *Post.* 12, *Conf.* 39, *Quis Her.* 81, *Spec. Leg.* i. 59, 345, *Vit. Cont.* 63, *Hyp.* 11. 1 ; θιασῶται, *Quod Deus* 120, *Plant.* 39 ; ἑταῖροι, *Conf.* 62 ; φοιτηταί, *Spec. Leg.* i. 345, ii. 256. In *Spec. Leg.* i. 59 Moses is said to stamp truth upon his disciples. In *Som.* ii. 1 Philo says that, as Moses learned when he did not know, he may teach us too.

Moses is contrasted with the character of his father-in-law Jethro in *Gig.* 50f ; Jethro's presumption in offering advice to Moses is criticized in *Ebr.* 36-45, *Mut.* 103f ; but as Raguel he is held to have joined the people of God in admiration for their leader Moses (*Mut.* 105). Miriam also showed presumption towards Moses (*Leg. All.* ii. 66f, *cf.* iii. 103, i. 76). Joshua reacted to the passionate clamour from the camp, but Moses could not be reached with it, for he was in the presence of God (*Ebr.* 96-103 & [NN]) ; however, Joshua a was worthy pupil and successor to Moses (*Virt.* 51ff). With Bezaleel also there is a contrast : he was instructed by Moses, but Moses was instructed by God (*Leg. All.* iii. 102f) ; he made the shadows of the tabernacle, Moses made the archetypes (*ib.*, and *Plant.* 23, 26f). Most of all, Philo compares and contrasts Moses with Aaron, *q.v.*

Philo makes comparatively little use of Moses as a symbolical figure. He is sometimes the type of the wise man (see below, and p. 387, note *f*) ; he stands for the mind (*e.g. Leg. All.* i. 40) at its purest (*Mut.* 208, *cf. Mos.* ii. 40) or some form of excellence

" The chief of the prophets proves to have many names," says Philo in *Mut.* 125. He derives ' Moses ' from Hebrew to mean ' handling ' (*ib.* 126 & n), or from Egyptian to mean ' water ' (*Mos.* i. 17). Philo's most common title for Moses is ' the law-giver,' a with which must be

---

a θεσμοφύλαξ *Sac.* 50; θεσμοθέτης, *Mig.* 23 ; ὁ τοὺς νόμους προφητεύσας *Spec. Leg.* ii. 104. Otherwise νομοθέτης, νομοθεσία, κτλ.: *Leg. All.* ii. 14, iii. 145, *Cher.* 40, 53, *Sac.* 16, 72,

linked other similar expressions.[a] He is also the
' prophet '[b] and ' revealer,'[c] chief priest,[d] king,[e]
the wise man,[f] perfect,[g] most holy of men,[h] be-

83, 136, *Det.* 62, 105, 115, 135, 147, 171, *Post.* 22, 25, 47, 57,
78, 128, 133, 166, *Gig.* 19, 32, 58, 66, *Quod Deus* 21, 23, 52,
60, 67, 125, *Agr.* 2, 41, 84, 86, 144, *Plant.* 66, 141, *Ebr.* 1, 13,
47, 109, *Sob.* 1, 7, *Conf.* 5, 23, 107, 135, 142, 191, *Mig.* 113,
Quis Her. 21, 55, 163, 292, *Congr.* 120, 132, *Fug.* 120, 173,
188, 194, *Som.* i. 39, 93, 112, 121, ii. 4, *Mos.* i. 1, 7-16, 45-51,
66, 187, 190, 292, *Decal.* 2-17, *Spec. Leg.* i. 15, 234, 319, iii.
42, 102, 151, 167, iv. 39, 143, *Virt.* 22n, 80, 133, 201, *Praem.*
53, 55, *Quod Omn. Prob.* 29, 43, 68, *Aet.* 19, *Hyp.* 6. 8, 7. 11,
11. 1. In *Mos.* ii. 48 God is the true lawgiver.

[a] *E.g.* ' keeper and guardian of the mysteries of the
Existent One ' (*Plant.* 26).

[b] προφήτης. προφητεία, κτλ., *Leg. All.* ii. 1, iii. 43, 173, *Sac.*
130, *Gig.* 49, 56, *Mig.* 15, 151, *Quis Her.* 4, 262, *Congr.* 132,
170, *Fug.* 140, 147, *Mut.* 11, 103, 125f, *Som.* ii. 189, 277, *Mos.*
i. 57, 156, ii. 2-7, 69, 187-191, 209, 213, 229, 246, 250, 253,
257f, 265, 269, 275, 280, 284, 291f, *Decal.* 18f, *Spec. Leg.* ii.
104, 256, iii. 125, *Virt.* 51, *Praem.* 1, 53, 55, *Vit. Cont.* 64,
87 ; θεολόγος, *Praem.* 53 ; ὁ ἱερὸς λόγος, *Quis Her.* 207, cf. 259 ;
ἄνθρωπος θεοῦ, *Det.* 162, *Mut.* 25, 125, 128.

[c] ἱεροφάντης, *Leg. All.* iii. 150, 173, *Sac.* 94, *Post.* 16, 164,
173, *Mig.* 14, *Som.* ii. 3, 29, 109, *Decal.* 18, *Spec. Leg.* i. 41,
Virt. 75, 174 ; θεοπρόπος, *Ebr.* 85, *Conf.* 29, *Fug.* 138 ; θεο-
φράδμων, *Quis Her.* 30, *Mut.* 96, *Mos.* ii. 269 ; ἑρμηνεύς, ἑρ-
μηνεία, κτλ., *Praem.* 55, *Quis Her.* 213 & n, *Mut.* 126, *Mos.* i.
1, *Spec. Leg.* iii. 6, *Post.* 1 ; μάρτυς. μαρτυρέω, *Det.* 138, cf.
Post. 57, *Mig.* 3, *Congr.* 160, *Mut.* 258, *Som.* i. 231, ii. 222,
Abr. 262 (+ θεσπίζω) ; ἐπίσκοπος. *Quis Her.* 30.

[d] *Sac.* 130, *Quis Her.* 182, *Mos.* i. 334, ii. 2-7, 66-71, 75,
cf. 153-158, 187n, 275, 292, *Praem.* 53, 56, cf. θεραπευτὴς
θεοῦ, *Sac.* 13, *Det.* 160.

[e] In *Mos.* ii. 3ff (see also *Mos.* i and ii, Introd. p. 274) and
Praem. 53-56 Philo treats of Moses as king, legislator, prophet,
and high-priest. Moses is also called ' guardian ' and
' leader ' of the nation (*Virt.* 42, *Praem.* 77).

[f] Moses is or symbolizes ὁ σοφός (πάνσοφος) κτλ., in *Leg.
All.* ii. 87, 93, iii. 45, 131, 140f, 144, 147, *Cher.* 41, *Sac.* 9, *Det.*
126, 162, *Post.* 18, 28, 169, 173, *Gig.* 27, 47f, 50, 56, *Quod*

INDEX OF NAMES

loved of God *a* and His friend,*b* truly great.*c* He is a lover of God,*d* and of virtue *e* and of humanity,*f* given to piety *g* and continence (*Mos.* i. 25-31), a man of spiritual vision,*h* the healer of the soul's diseases (*Quod Deus* 67), the nursing father of all things good (*Mig.* 23f) ; indeed he is himself worthy and noble,*i* a true world-citi-

Deus 23-26, cf. 110, Agr. 20, 43, Plant. 27, Ebr. 1, 37, 100, Sob. 20, Conf. 1, 30, 192 & n, Mig. 45f, 76, 113, 201, Quis Her. 19, 21, 55, 301, Congr. 132, Fug. i. 57, 165, Mut. 19, 104, 128, Som. ii. 229, 237, 278, Abr. 13, Mos. i. 4, ii. 67, Spec. Leg. ii. 194, iv. 69, 143, 157, 175, Quod Omn. Prob. 29, 68. Other terms are : φιλομαθής, Fug. 161 ; αὐτομαθής, Leg. All. iii. 135, Post. 77f, cf. Mos. i. 21f, ἐπιστήμη, Agr. 2.

g τέλειος, Leg. All. ii. 91, iii. 100, 131, 134f, 140, 144, 147, Sac. 9f, Det. 132, Quod Deus 23, Agr. 80, Plant. 94, Ebr. 103, Mut. 128, Som. ii. 234, Mos. i. 1 ; cf. Gig. 24-26.

h ἱερώτατος, Leg. All. iii. 185, Cher. 45, Det. 135, Gig. 67, Quod Deus 6, 140, Agr. 85, Plant. 86, 168, Mig. 131, Quis Her. 21, Congr. 89, Mut. 30, 187, Som. i. 121, Abr. 181, Spec. Leg. i. 15, 59, iii. 24, iv. 95, Virt. 175.

a θεόφιλος, θεοφιλής, Op. 5, Leg. All. i. 76, ii. 79, 88, 90, iii. 130, Cher. 49, Sac. 77, Det. 13, Plant. 62, Conf. 95, Mig. 67, Mos. ii. 67, 163, Spec. Leg. i. 41, iv. 175, Virt. 77, Quod Omn. Prob. 44.

b φίλος θεοῦ, based on Exod. xxxiii. 11 : Sac. 130, Ebr. 94, Mig. 45, Quis Her. 21, Som. i. 193f, 231f, Mos. i. 156.

c μέγας, Op. 12, Plant. 18, Ebr. 1, Sob. 49, Mut. 128, Mos. i. 1, Spec. Leg. ii. 51.

d φιλόθεος, Post. 15, 21, Mos. ii. 67, Spec. Leg. i. 42.

e φιλάρετος, Op. 128, Leg. All. ii. 90, iii. 130f, 147, Fug. 157, Mut. 113, Som. ii. 29, Virt. 175 (+φιλόκαλος) ; ἀρετή, Cher. 40, Gig. 48, Som. ii. 230, Mos. i. 48, ii. 66.

f φιλάνθρωπος, Mos. ii. 163, cf. Spec. Leg. ii. 79ff, 104, Virt. 51, 66, 76f, 80, 82ff, 175.

g εὐσέβεια, Praem. 52-56.

h ὁ βλέπων, Leg. All. ii. 93 ; φιλοθεάμων, Ebr. 124 ; ὀξυδερκής, Spec. Leg. ii. 194 ; ὀξυωπία, ib. iii. 91.

i σπουδαῖος, Post. 28, 169, Mos. i. 157 ; ἀστεῖος, a favourite word with Philo, esp. applicable to Moses because it is used

388

zen.[a] He was finally translated, because God prizes the wise man as the world (*Sac.* 8-10)

In the following index only those passages are cited in which Moses the man is mentioned, or which seem in some way to be significant ; thus the repeated quotations from the Pentateuch given as ' Moses says ' are not included. Nor are the words of Moses in Deuteronomy usually included

I. Gen. Introd. pp. xiii, xvii n, *Op.* 1-3, 8, 12, 128, 131, *Leg. All.* i. 40, 60[N], 76, ii. 14f, 54, 66f, 78-81, 87-93, 102-104, iii. 11-14, 37f, 43-48, 100-103, 128-147(-159), 173, 186, 197, 204, 228, II. *Cher.* 40-42, 47, 49 & [N], 56 & [N], 114[N], 130, *Sac.* 8-10, 9 & [N], 12 & [N], 13, 50f, 69, 77, 130, *Det.* 16 & [N], 38-40, 86, 126-138, 160 & [N]-162, 177, *Post.* 1, 12-16, 21, 28-31, 67f, 77f, 136f, 143f, 169, 173f, *Gig.* 24-31, 47-59 & nn & [N], III. *Quod Deus* 23-26, 67, 109f, *Agr.* 2, 43-49, 80f & [N], 94-101, *Plant.* 26f, 46-58, 62, *Ebr.* 36-45, 67, 79, 96-103 & [NN], 111-113, 124, *Sob.* 19f, IV. *Conf.* 29-36, 82, 95-97, 106 & n & [N], 141[N], *Mig.* 14f, 23f, 44-46, 76-85, 122 & n, 168, 169 & n-172, *Quis Her.* 3f, 16-21, 44, 59f, 169 & [N], 182 & [N], 205f, 213f, 228 & [N], 255, 262, *Congr.* 57, 110, 131-133 & [N], V. *Fug.* 140f, 147 & n, 148, 157-165, *Mut.* 7 & [N]-11, 19-21, 25f & n, 103-105 & nn, 113-120, 125-129 & nn, 134, 168, 207-209, *Som.* i. 36, 71, 164f, 188[N], 193f, 206, 231f, ii. 109, 142, 170, 189 & n, 227-234, 237, 277f, 300, VI. Gen. Introd. pp. ix, x, xii, xv-xvii & nn, *Mos.*

of him in Exod. ii. 2 : *Conf.* 106, *Quis Her.* 19, *Congr.* 132, *Som.* ii. 227, 230, *Mos.* i. 9.

[a] *Conf.* 106 & n & [N], *Mos.* i. 157.

Nadab and Abihu must be included in several references to Moses' nephews (*Leg. All.* iii. 133, *Mos.* ii. 142ff, *Virt.* 53, 59, *Praem.* 78). Their names are explained in Philo's exposition of Exod. xxiv. 1 : Nadab means 'voluntary' honouring of God ; Abihu, ' my father,' signifies the man sensible enough to have God for his father rather than master, whom he thus approaches fearlessly and affectionately (*Mig.* 168f & n). They are simply ' holy principles ' (*Som.* ii. 67). But the significant passage for Philo is Lev. x. 1ff, which he contrives to interpret wholly in favour of Nadab and Abihu. The " strange fire " which they offered was their zeal, ' alien ' to creation but akin to God (*Som.*

---

a Colson used both ' Nazarite ' and ' Nazirite,' but the latter more often. Both are correct.

VI. *Mos.* i. 6, 99-101, 202, VIII. *Praem.* 90. For
   its allegorical significance see Egypt

Nimrod : means 'desertion,' and typifies the fleshly
   outlook of the earth-born " giants," who are
   held to have 'deserted' the good (II. *Gig.* 65f)

Noah : In Gen. v. 29 Lamech names his son Noah,
   and a punning explanation derives the name
   from a Hebrew root meaning 'rest.' By his
   birth Philo means us to understand the birth of
   righteous reasoning to the soul, whereby all
   painful ambitions, griefs, and wickednesses are
   banished (*Det.* 121-123) ; the birth of just Noah
   and his sons makes evident the abundance of the
   unjust (*Gig.* 3) ; being tenth from Adam (ten is
   a perfect number), righteous Noah's birth shows
   how his ancestor Seth was enlarged in virtue
   (*Post.* 173f), and how justice in the soul is perfect
   and the true goal (*Congr.* 90). In *Leg. All.* iii. 77,
   Abr. 27, Philo cites Gen. vi. 8 : " Noah found
   grace in the eyes of the Lord," even though he
   had as yet done nothing noble (*cf. Abr.* 47) : so
   God promotes goodly natures without giving
   reason (*cf. Quod Deus* 70-74) ; Noah's was an
   excellent nature, for he signifies 'rest' or 'righteous ' (see below). The deeper meaning of
   " finding grace " with God is that only God, not
   creation, has grace to bestow ; His grace is the
   origin of creation (*Leg. All.* iii. 78, *cf. Quod Deus*
   86, 104-108)

" These are the generations of Noah. Noah was a
   just man, perfect in his generation, Noah was
   well-pleasing to God " (vi. 9, LXX) : the offspring
   of a good mind are the virtues mentioned, that
   he was a man, just, perfect, well-pleasing to God

(*Quod Deus* 117f, *Abr.* 31-35); the righteous alone is a man (*Abr.* 32f); yet "perfect in his generation" indicates that he was not good absolutely but in comparison with the men of that time (*ib.* 36-39); Noah was pleasing to the Potencies, but Moses to God (*Quod Deus* 109, 116). This text supplies Philo with his regular epithet for Noah, "just" or "righteous," [a] and with "perfect," [b] and with the idea of Noah's virtues. [c] Other descriptions of Noah make him good (*Quod Deus* 70, *Mos.* ii. 15, *cf. Det.* 105, *Quod Deus* 107) and noble (*Abr.* 27, 35, 56, *Virt.* 201, *cf. Leg. All.* iii. 78) and wise (*Det.* 170f, *Abr.* 27, 31), holy and pious (*Virt.* 201), beloved of God (*Abr.* 27, 46, *Som.* ii. 225)

Noah begat sons (vi. 10), for the just man who follows the truly masculine reason (λόγος) begets males, true-born and excellent fruit (*Gig.* 4f)

The corruption of the earth, the flood, and Noah being spared (vi. 11ff) are variously interpreted. In *Det.* 170ff the deluge is the washing away of the soul's defilements, and Noah is the goodly reasoning faculty instructed to bring into the body or vessel containing the soul (the ark) "from among the clean beasts seven, male and female" (vii. 2) that it should find all parts of

---

[a] δίκαιος, *Leg. All.* iii. 77f, *Det.* 105-123, *Post.* 173f, *Gig.* 5, *Quod Deus* 85, 117f, 140, *Agr.* 2, 20, 181, *Plant.* 1. 140, *Sob.* 30, *Conf.* 105, *Mig.* 125, *Quis Her.* 260, *Congr.* 90, *Mut.* 189, *Som.* ii. 223f & n, *Abr.* 27, 33, 46, 56, *Praem.* 22f & n, *cf. Mos.* ii. 59.

[b] τέλειος, *Quod Deus* 117, 122, *Abr.* 34, 36ff, 47, *Praem.* 22 & n, *cf. Gig.* 5, see also VI. Gen. Introd. p. x.

[c] *Quod Deus* 117f, 122, 140, *Som.* ii. 225, *cf. Post.* 173; φιλάρετος, *Abr.* 27, 31, 34, 36ff, (48).

the irrational side clean for its use. In *Quod Deus* 73-76, 85, God in anger judges the earth, but mingles mercy with judgement, that the race might survive, and valued one just man above the multitude of unjust thoughts. In *Conf.* 105 Philo is discussing asphalt, and suggests that its safety (ἀσφάλεια) is of bodily rather than spiritual things ; so Noah, in the great ceaseless deluge of life, while still needing sense to behold realities, " coats the ark with asphalt " (vi. 14), that is, strengthens the bodily impressions ; but presently he will come forth from the body and use his understanding, free from it, to apprehend truth. In *Mig.* 125, where Philo is dealing with the blessing of Abraham, Noah illustrates his argument that the righteous man is a good influence in the race, as is the righteous mind in the soul, for he survived the engulfing of so many parts of the soul and begat wisdom's new race. In *Mos.* ii. 60-65 Philo tells the story of the Flood and the Ark to show how the historical part of Moses' law-book records the punishment of the wicked and the salvation of the good. In *Virt.* 201, on Nobility, and the inheriting of it, Noah's piety is emphasized by his being the only family to be preserved from the flood : yet his son Ham was degenerate. In *Praem.* 22f the individual Noah was rewarded for his justice with preservation from the deluge and made the founder of a new race.[a] This thought, that Noah was the last of the old race and first of the new, also occurs to Philo in *Abr.* 46, 56, *Mos.* ii. 60, 65, *cf. Mut.* 189. The covenant made with Noah

[a] Noah is here equated with Deucalion ; see [N].

(ix. 11) is briefly treated in *Som.* ii. 223-225 : the Pharaoh-mind had said, " I stood " ; but this stability belongs to God ; He imparts it to the Logos, which under the name of Covenant is said to be made to stand upon the just Noah. We learn that justice and God's covenant are identical, and that God gives the recipients of His gifts to themselves (see note *ad loc.*). It is the desire of the God-beloved to escape the waters of engrossing business and anchor in the calm and safety of virtue

" And Noah began to be a husbandman, and he planted a vineyard, and drank of the wine, and became drunken [LXX, " and was made naked "] within his house " (ix. 20f). Tilling the soil is a skilled trade and therefore proper to righteous Noah ; for the good man prunes away the growths of passions and vices in the soul (*Det.* 105, *Agr.* 1-10, 20) ; yet Noah only " began " : he had not the strength to complete his task (*Agr.* 125, 181). Noah's drunkenness leads to disquisitions on the subject (*Plant.* 140ff, *Ebr.* 4ff). His nakedness was of the foolish kind, a deprivation of virtue ; but " in his house " shows that the sin was limited in its harmful effect (*Leg. All.* ii. 60f, *cf. Ebr.* 4 and n). When Noah awoke to soberness, he blessed and cursed his sons (ix. 24ff) ; this indicates sobriety of the soul (*Sob.* 1-5), when it perceives the former doings of the young rebellious wickedness within it and curses them (*ib.* 30) ; and the blessing and cursing must have been the inspired utterances of a prophet (*Quis Her.* 260)

Noah symbolizes the good man, etc. (see above),

the righteous philosopher (*Leg. All.* iii. 77f, *Quod Deus* 107), the righteous reasoning in the soul (*Det.* 121, 170, *cf. Gig.* 5, *Quod Deus* 70-72, *Mig.* 125 & n), the incorruptible element (*Quod Deus* 123), the soul itself (*Leg. All.* ii. 60f). In *Abr.* 7-47 (see **VI.** Gen. Introd. p. x), an imperfectly wise Triad comprising Enos (Hope), Enoch (Repentance), and Noah (Justice) is contrasted with Abraham, Isaac, and Jacob ; the first three are like the studies of children in comparison with the exercises of grown athletes in the sacred contests (*ib.* 48) ; Philo again treats the Triad in *Praem.* 22f & n (see **VIII.** Gen. Introd. p. xxi)

I. *Leg. All.* ii. 60f, iii. 77f, **II.** *Det.* 105, 121-123, 170, *Post.* 173f, *Gig.* 1-5, **III.** *Quod Deus* 7-74, 86, 104-109, 116f, 122, 140, *Agr.* 1-10, 20, 125, 181, *Plant.* 1, 73, 140, *Ebr.* 4 & n, *Sob.* 1-5, 30-32, 44, 52n, (59), **IV.** *Conf.* 105 & n, *Mig.* 125 & n, *Quis Her.* 260, *Congr.* 90, **V.** *Mut.* 189, *Som.* ii. 223-225 & n, **VI.** Gen. Introd. p. x, *Abr.* 27, 31-39, 46-48, 56, *Mos.* ii. 59-65, **VIII.** Gen. Introd. p. xxi, *Virt.* 201f, *Praem.* 22f & n & [N], **IX.** *Quod Omn. Prob.* Introd. p. 4, 70[N]

Nod (lxx, Naid) : means ' tossing ' (σάλος), symbol of the vice that creates tumult (κλόνος) in the soul of the foolish man (**II.** *Cher.* 12, *Post.* 22 & n), or ' tumult,' the destination of Cain (*Post.* 1, 32)

Noeman : one of the degenerate descendants of Cain, the ' fatness ' of those whose goal is material comfort, **II.** *Post.* 120

Norbanus : **X.** *Leg.* 314f

Ocellus : **IX.** *Aet.* 12 & n & [N]
Odysseus : **IX.** *Vit. Cont.* 40f

INDEX OF NAMES

  The Passover represents the passage from the life
  of the passions to the practice of virtue (*Sac.* 63),
  sacrificed with haste that the mind may eagerly

397

INDEX OF NAMES

& [N], 100 & n & [N], **IX.** *Quod Omn. Prob.* 74

Petronius : **X.** *Leg.* 207-261, 333f

Pharaoh : Since Egypt (*q.v.*) represents the body, passions, etc., the king of Egypt (included here whether or not styled ' Pharaoh ') signifies much the same things. He is the mind which is king of the realm of the body (*Agr.* 57, *Conf.* 88, *Fug.* 124, *Jos.* 151), sovereign of the animal and composite (συγκρίτου ζῴου, *Sac.* 48), ruling the passions (*Leg. All.* iii. 13), the mind that fancies itself a king (*Mig.* 160, *Som.* ii. 215), the king of terror (*Mut.* 173). The same adjectives are used to describe Pharaoh as Egypt : he is a lover of pleasure and self, of the body and passion [a] ; he represents the foolish man,[b] the incontinent soul [c] ; he is proud (*Ebr.* 111, *Mos.* ii. 88), stubborn (*Som.* ii. 184, *cf. Mos.* ii. 89), impious (*Mut.* 19, *Som.* ii. 182 ; see below, on Exod. v. 2). But Philo's favourite description presupposes the derivation of ' Pharaoh ' from a word meaning ' to scatter,' [d] so that he is ' the scatterer of things noble.' [e] Frequent, too, is the term ' god-

---

[a] φιλήδων, *Leg. All.* iii. 212, *Mut.* 171f, *Jos.* 153; φίλαυτος, *Cher.* 74, *Som.* ii. 219 ; φιλοσώματος, *Abr.* 103 ; φιλοπαθής, *Ebr.* 208f, *Som.* ii. 277.

[b] ἄφρων, *Det.* 161f, *Mut.* 125, 128f, 171-175, *cf.* 89-91, *Som.* ii. 181 ; φαῦλος, *ib.* 237.

[c] *Ebr.* 210, *Som.* ii. 181f, 184, 200f, 211, *Abr.* 103, *Jos.* 153.

[d] ' Pharaoh ' is Egyptian and has no such meaning ; nor is there an obvious Hebrew word for ' scatter ' ; but Philo perhaps had in mind an intensive form of III. פרע, or even just the general sound of the word, akin to many that begin with ' para- ' and mean ' break out,' etc.; or perhaps the Greek equivalent, φάρω.

[e] ὁ σκεδαστὴς τῶν καλῶν *Leg. All.* iii. 236, 243, *cf.* 12f, *Sac.* 48, 69, *Det.* 95, *Quis Her.* 59f, *Som.* ii. 211.

less [a] ' ; it is an obvious term for the enemies
of God's people, but Philo justifies it in the case
of Egypt by their worship of sacred beasts, and
in the case of Pharaoh by Exod. v. 2, " I know
not the Lord." [b] God's words to Moses in vii. 1,
" I give thee as a god to Pharaoh," are also
much used.[c] Other relevant texts are Gen. xli.
17 (*Som.* ii. 215-219, instability), Exod. ii. 15
(*Leg. All.* iii. 12f, *Fug.* 47), ii. 23 (*ib.* 212, *Det.* 93-
95, Pharaoh's death and Israel's groaning), vii.
15 (*Conf.* 29f, *Som.* ii. 277f, wrong speaking of
pleasure-lovers, *i.e.* Epicureans), the passions,
viii. 9, 10 (*Sac.* 69-71, the folly of postponement),
meet the soul with xiv. 7, xv. 1, 4 (*Ebr.* 77-79 &
n, 111, the destruction of the wicked and boastful mind), xv. 9 (*Cher.* 74-83, God alone acts,
man's part is passivity) ; the wickedness of
making (brick) structures of evil-minded thoughts
(*Conf.* 88f) ; failure to seek and find (*Fug.* 124f,
147)

I. *Leg. All.* i. 40, iii. 12-14, 212, 236, 243, II. *Cher.*
74, *Sac.* 9 & [N], 48, 49-71, *Det.* 94f, 161f, *Post.*
115, III. *Agr.* 57-60, *Ebr.* 19, 77-79 & n, 111, 208-
210, 214ff, IV. *Conf.* 72, 88, *Mig.* 84, 159-162 &
n & 160[N], *Quis Her.* 20, 59f, V. *Fug.* 124f, 147,
Mut. 19-21, 89-91, 125, 128f & n, 171-175, 207-
209, *Som.* i. 77f, ii. 5, 159, 181-184, 195, 200f, 211,

---

[a] ἄθεος, *Leg. All.* iii. 12f, 212, *Ebr.* 19 ; ἀντίθεος, *Conf.* 88,
Congr. 118, *Som.* ii. 183, *cf.* 277.

[b] *Leg. All.* iii. 12f, 243, *Post.* 115, *Ebr.* 19, 77, *Som.* ii. 182,
Mos. i. 88.

[c] See *Sac.* 9[N] ; *Leg. All.* i. 40, *Sac.* 9, *Det.* 161f, *Mig.*
84, *Mut.* 19, 125, 128f, *Som.* ii. 189, *Quod Omn. Prob.* 43
& n.

---

[a] In Vol. VI only *Jos.* 151-153 contains allegorical matter
about Pharaoh. For the contrast between the *De Josepho*
and the *Allegorical Commentary* see **VI.** Gen. Introd. pp.
xiii f.

" Behold, I give unto him my covenant of peace
. . . even the covenant of an everlasting priesthood " (Num. xxv. 6-13).   Philo interprets this
as follows : Phinehas, the controller of the inlets
and outlets of the body (*Post.* 182), consecrated
intelligence (*ib.* 184), most war-like reason (*Conf.*
57), a hater of evil and zealous for good, came as
self-bidden champion (*Mut.* 108) ; he took a
spear or probe (σειρομάστης), that is, zeal for
virtue (*Leg. All.* iii. 242, *Conf.* 57) or the explor-
ing of the nature of existent things that discovers
virtue (*Post.* 182, *cf. Ebr.* 73), the sharp and two-
edged word (or ' reason,' λόγος) that explores
each thing (*Mut.* 108), and he pierced through
the Midianitish woman, the nature ' sifted out '
from the sacred company, namely folly (*Leg. All.*
iii.   242),   the   virtue-hating,   pleasure-loving
creature (*Post.* 182, *cf. Conf.* 57), passion (*Mut.*
108), the belief which ascribes causation to creation itself (*Ebr.* 73, *cf. Conf.* 57), and with her
the man, that is the ideas or reasonings based on
this belief (*Ebr.* 73) ; by thus thrusting through
her womb, the part that typifies her belief (*Ebr.*
73, *Conf.* 57), he destroyed the source of baseness
and voluptuousness (*Post.* 182), and prevented the
further growth of wickedness (*Leg. All.* iii. 242),
that the womb should bring to birth no plague of
God's sending (*Mut.* 108).   The twofold reward
of peace and priesthood (*Mos.* i. 304) are sister
virtues awarded to the soul for cutting out folly
(*Leg. All.* 242, *cf. Ebr.* 74), peace, because Phinehas had ended the war of lusts in the soul, and
priesthood, because it is akin to peace (the asso-
nance is never far from Philo's mind : *cf. Mut.*

108), and the consecrated intelligence delights to do God's will (*Post.* 183, *cf. Ebr.* 75) ; peace is awarded to warlike reason (*Conf.* 57)

A broader survey is this : Joseph and Phinehas represent two methods of dealing with pleasure —flight and fight (*Leg. All.* iii. 242) ; Onan and Phinehas are contrasted in their dealing with pleasure within themselves : Phinehas 'muzzled' his inward revolt. This war in the soul is the cause of all wars (*Post.* 182-185) ; like the Levites of the similar incident in Exod. xxxii, Phinehas is an example of those dutiful children who despise the female parent, convention, and follow the male parent, right reason, and he slays the philosophy which attributes causation to creation itself (*Ebr.* 73-76) ; there is a good ' symphony ' of men of peace (Gen. xlii. 11)—peace which is yet a warfare against the symphony of evil ; such was that of the captains who warred against Midian (led by Phinehas, Num. xxxi) ; most warlike of all is Phinehas himself, for his exploit (Num. xxv) : he wins the true peace ; but the captains share it in their turn (*Conf.* 55-57 & n) ; Midian is a double name, and it can stand for the exclusion by judgement of wrong elements, as it does in the story of Phinehas and the Midianite war that followed (*Mut.* 108f)

I. *Leg. All.* iii. 242, II. *Post.* 182-185, III. *Ebr.* 73-76, IV. *Conf.* 55-57 & n, V. *Mut.* 106-109, VI. *Mos.* i. 300-304 & n, 305f, 313, VII. *Spec. Leg.* i. 56 & n, VIII. *Virt.* 34 & [N]-42

Phocis : IX. *Prov.* 2. 33

Phoenicia, Phoenicians : VI. *Mos.* i. 163, 214, IX. *Hyp.* 6. 6, X. *Leg.* 222, 225f, 281

INDEX OF NAMES

[a] See further Index to Translators' Notes.

who meet pleasure with flight and fight ; Potiphar, eunuch and servant of Pharaoh, is the mind incapable of begetting wisdom because it serves the one who is disperser of noble things ; this interpretation explains how a eunuch can be said to have a wife. In **III.** *Quod Deus* 111-116 & [N] it is Potiphar himself who is identified with pleasure, the chief cateress of our compound nature ; Philo is contrasting Noah and Joseph, who " found grace " with the ruler of the prison : if we are prisoners of passion, we should at least avoid friendship with our gaoler. In **III.** *Ebr.* 210-217, 224 the subject is the relation of wine to greed, and Potiphar, eunuch and chief cook, shows that the ministers of pleasure are incapable of producing wisdom (*cf. Leg. All.* 236) or virtue. In **IV.** *Mig.* 19, 21 & [N] the discussion is on the survival of the higher qualities of the mixed or Joseph mind ; Potiphar's wife is pleasure, lusts, and passions. In **V.** *Mut.* 173, Philo, having said that joy is only for the good, says that Egyptian expressions of joy are either assumed or the hope of seducing the soul, as was done with Joseph ; Potiphar is the soul unable to beget anything that tends to discipline ; cook-like, he lives in an environment of dead ideas, hashed to pieces (see *Quis Her.* 242 [N]), arousing the appetites of the passions. His wife is bodily pleasure in **V.** *Som.* ii. 106 : but Joseph, like our own better judgement, refuses to acknowledge any claim but that of God. In *Jos.* 37-80 the same allegories are adapted to Philo's theme of Joseph as a statesman ; Potiphar represents the multitude that buys the statesman : as politicians, the multitude is occupied, like a cook, in choosing what will give pleasure, until the soul is enervated thereby ; eunuch-like, the multitude is unproductive of wisdom ; Potiphar's wife is desire, for the desire of the multitude makes love to the statesman, seducing him to succumb for its favour. Other references are insignificant —IV. *Conf.* 95, VI. *Jos.* 104, IX. *Flacc.* 72n

Potiphera : Priest of Heliopolis (Gen. xli. 45), V. *Som.* i. 78

Priene : IX. *Quod Omn. Prob.* 153

Protagoras : II. *Post.* 35, an offspring of Cain's madness

Proteus : III. *Ebr.* 36, X. *Leg.* 80

Psonthomphanech : V. *Mut.* 89 & n-91 ; see Joseph

Ptolemies : VI. *Jos.* 136, *Mos.* ii. 28-33, IX. *Quod Omn. Prob.* 125, X. *Leg.* 140

Puteoli (Dicaearchia) : IX. *Flacc.* 27 & n, X. *Leg.* 185

Pythagoreans : I. *Op.* 100 & n, *Leg. All.* i. 15, IX. *Quod Omn. Prob.* 2 & n, *Aet.* 12 & n

Raamses :- Egyptian city of Exod. i. 11, signifying sense-perception, for it means a ' moth's troubling,' since the mind is eaten out by each of the senses (II. *Post.* 54-57 & [N] & 56n, V. *Som.* i. 77)

Rachel : Rachel typifies sense-perception,[a] and she is usually depreciated in favour of Jacob, the Practiser, and Leah, virtue (see I. Gen. Introd. p. xii & n). Thus, as the younger daughter of Laban, though the more beautiful (Gen. xxix. 16), she is comeliness of the body, and mortal only, whereas Leah is immortal beauty of the soul (*Sob.* 12, *cf. Ebr.* 52). Again, " when the

[a] *Leg. All.* ii. 46, *Post.* 135, 177-179, *Ebr.* 54, *Sob.* 12, *Quis Her.* 50f, *Mut.* 96, *Som.* ii. 16.

Lord saw that Leah was hated, he opened her womb : but Rachel was barren " (xxix. 31) : when the soul is pregnant and bears excellent deeds, the erstwhile beloved objects of sense become barren (*Quis Her.* 50f, *cf. Post.* 135). And though Rachel demand children from Jacob (xxx. 1f), it is God only who is the source of creation, as Leah's case shows (*Leg. All.* iii. 180, *Post.* 135). Rachel later recanted, however (xxx. 24, *Post.* 179). Nearly all these points are included in *Leg. All.* ii. 46f

On the other hand, the story of the flight of Rachel and Leah with Jacob (xxxi. 14ff) classes them together as the faculties of the Practiser (*Fug.* 14-18, *cf. Cher.* 40 & [N], *Post.* 62, *Quis Her.* 43f, *Congr.* 24 & n-32), while Laban complains that Jacob has stolen his sound sense, namely his daughters (xxxi. 26f ; *Leg. All.* iii. 20-22), a stripping of the virtues (*Fug.* 15-18), a loss of the arts and branches of knowledge (*Cher.* 67-71). They, however, have rightly dissociated themselves from Laban and would refuse his kiss (xxxi. 28 ; *Quis Her.* 43f). In the search for the teraphim (xxxi. 34f), Rachel's words reveal that custom is followed more by women (weaker and effeminate souls), than by men, and they are the soul's confession that it cannot rise up against the external goods represented by Laban (*Ebr.* 54-59 & 56 [N])

After hard labour, Rachel died in giving birth to Benjamin, whom she wanted to call Benoni, ' son of my sorrow ' (xxxv. 16, 18f) ; here she is contrasted with Jacob, reason, and her words signify the secret misery of the soul that is mother of

407

vainglory; *cf. Ebr.* 52, for her bitter experience contrasts with public opinion of it; vainglory means the death of the soul (*Mut.* 92-96)

In *Congr.* 24 & n-32 we have Philo's only derivation of the name (but see *Fug.* 16 & [N]), and a different treatment: the Practiser of virtue has two wives; one is the smooth movement which proceeds to noble life without conflict (the λεία κίνησις of Stoic terminology): the other is Rachel, who is like a whetstone on which the mind sharpens its edge. Her name means ' vision of profanation,' because she judges the visible world to be profane; she belongs to the unreasoning element in the soul, training us through the senses (so her handmaid is Bilhah, ' swallowing,' a bodily function). The Practiser loves Rachel when he wrestles with the passions and opposes all objects of sense. Thus Leah helps by giving peaceful enjoyment of the good, Rachel by the fighting opposition to evil. See also Jacob, Laban, Leah

Rebecca : Rebecca is the symbol of Patience,[a] or

---

[a] ὑπομονή, *Leg. All.* iii. 88f (ὑπομονητικὴ ψυχή), *Sac.* 4, *Det.* 45, 51, *Plant.* 169f, (τῶν καλῶν), *Mig.* 208f, *Congr.* 36, 111-

Steadfastness in excellence, a queenly, virgin
virtue [a]; she is also to be connected with Reason
(*Post.* 77f) or Knowledge (*ib.* 77f, 138, *Fug.* 52,
195; see Isaac)

Abraham sent his servant to obtain a wife for
Isaac, and it was Rebecca who fulfilled his words
by offering water to the servant and for his
camels (Gen. xxiv. 15ff). In a sustained allegory,
Philo contrasts Rebecca with Hagar, the type of
School learning: Rebecca, virgin virtue, waters
her pupil from the well of divine wisdom (*cf.
Fug.* 194), not with gradual progress but with
perfection (*Post.* 132-153, and Introd. p. 325f).
She 'went down' to the well (xxiv. 16), a descent
from proud imposture; she 'came up' thereby
to virtue's height (*Fug.* 194f, *Post.* 136). In
Congr. 111-113 Philo illustrates the use of the
perfect number, Ten: the servant had ten
camels, he gave Rebecca bracelets of ten weights
of gold (xxiv. 10, 12)

Philo maintains that the lovers of wisdom, represented by Abraham, Isaac, Jacob, Moses, and
others, did not know women but were wedded
to virtues, Rebecca being Patience (*Cher.* 40f,
cf. *Congr.* 34-38, *Post.* 62, 132f). 'Taking a wife'
is to be understood in this way: good men
choose good, bad men choose evils; but some
are above that, so Isaac, though he "took Rebekah" (xxiv. 67), did so only in his mother's

113, *Fug.* 39, 194f, *Som.* i. 46, *cf. Fug.* 45 (ἐπιμονή, ἐπιμένω),
Cher. 41 (τῶν καλῶν), 47, *Det.* 30f (τοῖς καλοῖς), *Fug.* 24 (ὀρθο-
γνώμων).

[a] *Congr.* 36 and *Post.* 132f; ἀρετή, *Cher.* 40f, *Post.* 62,
77f, 132f, 136, *Congr.* 36, 111f.

tent (*Post.* 77f; Sarah is sovereign Virtue or Wisdom). Rebecca was barren, but Isaac prayed to the Lord and she conceived (xxv. 21) : virtue brings forth to her lover, but receives the divine seed from God (*Cher.* 47). She learned that she was to have twins (" Two nations are in thy womb . . ." xxv. 22f), the base and irrational nature, the good and rational (*Leg. All.* iii. 88). Hers being a pregnancy accompanied by wisdom, Rebecca received (opposed to ' having ') in her womb the knowledge of the two nations of the mind, virtue and vice, and distinguished between them, and she was happily delivered (*Congr.* 129f, *cf. Sac.* 4)

Abimelech saw Isaac " sporting with Rebekah his wife " (xxvi. 8)—a divine pursuit (*Cher.* 8 & n), the wise man making merry with her who waits patiently for all that is beautiful (*Plant.* 169f)

I. *Leg. All.* iii. 88f, II. *Cher.* 8 & n, 40f, 47, *Sac.* 4, *Det.* 30f, 45, 51, *Post.* 62, 77f, 132-153, III. *Plant.* 169f, IV. *Mig.* 208-211, *Congr.* 34-38, 111-113, 129, V. *Fug.* 23-25 & [N], (26-38), 39-52 & 45[N], 194f, *Som.* i. 46, VIII. *Virt.* 208f & n, 221n

Red Sea : VI. Gen. Introd. p. xv, *Mos.* i. 165, 169-181, ii. 1, 247-257, VII. *Spec. Leg.* ii. 145n, VIII. *Praem.* 78[N], IX. *Vit. Cont.* 85 ; *cf.* I. *Leg. All.* iii. 94, 172, III. *Ebr.* 79 & n, and see Passover

Reuben : Reuben is the symbol of good natural endowments, for ' seeing son ' he is called, in so far as he is a son not perfect, but in so far as he is a man with power to see and keenness of vision, well endowed by nature (*Som.* ii. 33). Philo keeps consistently to ' natural ability ' for Reuben, and develops the idea in accordance with various texts : thus in Num. iii. 12f the Levites are said to be a ransom for the first-born ; this means that Levi, ' sanctified reason,' is accepted by God before Reuben, natural ability (*Sac.* 118-121). " This our son is disobedient . . . " (Deut. xxi. 18-21) suggests other sons, not disobedient ; such are the reasonings of the naturally gifted, of which Reuben is a type (*Ebr.* 94). God employs subordinate ministers for the lower work of punishment, and so we find the six best tribe-leaders, Reuben amongst them, set over the blessing, and six others over the cursing (Deut. xxvii. 12f, *Fug.* 73). The blessing of Moses (mistakenly attributed to Jacob) prays that natural ability may live (Deut. xxxiii. 6, *Mut.* 210). Jacob's words in Gen. xlviii. 5, " Ephraim and Manasseh shall be as Reuben and Simeon to me," lead Philo to find an analogy between Reuben, the gifted nature, and Ephraim, memory, etc. (*Mut.* 97-102)

I. *Leg. All.* i. 81, II. *Sac.* 118-121, III *Ebr.* 94, V. *Fug.* 73, *Mut.* 97-102, 210, *Som.* ii. 33, VI. *Jos.* 13, 16-21, 173-176, 188, 217, *Mos.* ii. 175, 186n, VIII. Gen. Introd. p. xviii n, *Praem.* 75n

Reumah : Nahor, Abraham's kinsman, shared in his wisdom, yet his knowledge never went beyond the Chaldaean astrology ; he represents, therefore, any scheme of things that does not acknowledge God as Creator. He had a wife, Milcah, who symbolizes the Chaldaean astrology, queen of the sciences ; his concubine was Reumah, which means ' seeing something,' and symbolizes the sceptics, busying themselves with quibbling

143f). Before instructing Saul in kingship,
Samuel, appointed to the highest post in God's
service, withdraws him from the baggage (1
Sam. x. 22f, *Mig.* 196f). Samuel himself is
styled ' greatest of kings and prophets ' (*Ebr.*
143 & n). He represents an inspired temper
possessed by a God-sent frenzy (*Som.* i. 254 &
[N]). See also VIII. *Praem.* 4-6[N]

Sarah : Sarah stands for Virtue,[a] or Wisdom,[b] often
described as ' ruling ' or ' sovereign ' [c]; that is an
allusion to the interpretation of her names, made
in *Cher.* 3-10, *Congr.* 1-13, *Mut.* 61, 66n, 77-80,
130. Sarai, as her name was at the first, means
' my sovereignty,' and is a symbol of specific
virtue—the wisdom in me, the self-control in me,
etc.—which perishes with its possessor. When
the name was changed to Sarah (in Greek, by
the addition of another rho, *Mut.* 61, 77), that is,
' sovereignty,' she ceased to symbolize the particular and became the type of generic virtue,
greater than the species, the archetype, imperishable. She is thus the motherless principle
of things (ἀμήτωρ ἀρχή) : and this probably contains a play upon ἀρχή, ' rule,' ' sovereignty ';
certainly Philo alludes to the name when he uses
ἄρχουσα, ' ruling.' As wife of Abraham, the

[a] ἀρετή, *Leg. All.* ii. 82, iii. 218, 244, *Cher.* 3-7, 9 (τελεία),
41, *Sac.* 59, *Det.* 59-61, *Post.* 62, 132 (τελεία), 134, *Ebr.* 59
(φιλάρετος διάνοια), *Quis Her.* 62, 258, *Congr.* 2-12, 22f, 63,
71, 128, *cf.* 180, *Fug.* 128, *Mut.* 77, 80, 142, 148-150, 166f,
255, 261.
[b] σοφία, *Leg. All.* ii. 82, *Cher.* 9f, 45, 49f, *Det.* 124, *Congr.*
9, 13, 22, 79f, 129, *Mut.* 79f, 151-153, *Abr.* 100.
[c] ἄρχουσα, *Leg. All.* ii. 82, iii. 244, *Cher.* 3, 41 (ἄρχουσα καὶ
ἡγεμονίς), *Quis Her.* 258, (*cf.* ἀρχή, 62), *Abr.* 99.

wise man, the type of the virtue that comes by teaching, Sarah assists his advance from the inferior creeds of Chaldaea and Haran to the vision and knowledge of God, chiefly by advising him to have union with Hagar (see below). As Hagar's mistress, Sarah is repeatedly contrasted with her, the higher education compared with that of the Schools (*e.g. Leg. All.* iii. 244f, *Congr.* 71-80), the branches of knowledge compared with the lower arts (*Congr.* 139f). Besides virtue and wisdom, Sarah also signifies sound sense,[a] knowledge,[b] the fruitful mind (*Spec. Leg.* ii. 54, *cf. Mig.* 140), good (*Post.* 76f)

" Abram and Nahor took to themselves wives " (Gen. xi. 29) : among Cain's descendants was Lamech, who did the same ; such choices can be good or bad, according to the chooser, and Abram's was a deliberate choice of the good (*Post.* 76-78). Sarai was barren, and told Abram to obtain children by her handmaid Hagar (xvi. 1f) : she was barren, yet prolific, for from her sprang the populous Israel ; and virtue is barren of all that is bad, but a fruitful mother of the good (*Congr.* 3, *Mut.* 143). Yet as Sarai she represents wisdom in the individual, as yet unable to have children by her (" she was not bearing for him," xvi. 1) ; thus the incapacity is that of the immature soul (Abram), who must resort to the School learning (Hagar) (*Congr.* 1-23, *Leg. All.* iii. 244). " And Abram hearkened to the voice of Sarai " : the learner must obey virtue's com-

[a] φρόνησις, *Mig.* 126, *Congr.* 72, 154, 156, *cf.* 2, *Fug.* 207, *Mut.* 137, 151-153.
[b] ἐπιστήμη, *Congr.* 22, 139f, 154, 156.

mands (*cf. Leg. All.* iii. 244) ; yet only real lovers
of knowledge do hearken—which implies assent
and obedience as well as hearing (*Congr.* 63-70).
When Sarah gave him Hagar, she is again called
" Abram's wife " : this points the lesson that
the lover of learning engaged in the Encyclia
does not forget his faith plighted to his true wife,
philosophy (*ib.* 71-80). The words, " when she
saw that she had conceived " (xvi. 4f), are interpreted as " when Sarai saw," borne out by her
report to Abram in the next verse, and they
signify that the lower arts can only dimly see
their own products, whereas knowledge can
clearly apprehend them (*ib.* 139f). Abram said,
" Behold thy maid is in thy hands," which can
mean ' subject to thee,' but may also mean that
the school subjects require the bodily organs and
faculties, while the mistress wisdom reaches to
the soul (*ib.* 155 & [N]-158). Sarah then afflicted
Hagar ; but we are not here dealing with women's
jealousy, but with minds, that occupied with the
preliminary learning, and that striving for virtue's
palm, not ceasing till it is won (*ib.* 180). Hagar
fled ; but she could return because Sarai was
favourably disposed, a deduction made on the
basis of Hagar's flight being one of shame
(" humiliation " or " affliction," xvi. 11), not
fear (*Fug.* 1-6). The whole story is given in *Abr.*
247-254 as an instance of Sarah's wifely qualities
The change of name was made by God (xvii. 15).
It indicates a betterment of soul. While she was
Sarai, still specific virtue, Hagar will return to
her, lower to lower ; but later, when Sarai's name
and character have been changed, and Isaac has

been born, then the preliminary study and her sophist son will be banished for good (*Cher.* 4-8). The main lesson from this change of name is that generic virtue is higher than the specific, and imperishable (see above) ; but in passing, Philo states that we learn also that every virtue is a queen and a sovereign and a ruler of human life (*Mut.* 80). With Sarah's change of name came promises from God to Abraham. " I will give thee a child of her " : this means God is to be father of the child ; but he is also husband of the virtue-loving mind (proved by Gen. xxix. 31) (*Mut.* 130-132, *cf. Cher.* 49) ; " of her " can be taken in several ways : Philo prefers that which makes virtue the mother of the good (*Mut.* 141-144). The promise continues, " I will bless her and she shall be for nations, and kings of nations shall be from her." The first phrase indicates the subdivision of generic virtue ; but we may also learn that virtue is beneficial for nations, whether peoples or groups of ideas : and Philo praises virtue's part in life in terms that recall the praises of Wisdom (*e.g. Prov.* viii. 14ff). The last phrase shows that virtue's sons are all rulers, for the sage alone is king (*Mut.* 148-150, 151-153)

Omniscient God does not usually ask questions, which imply ignorance. But when he asked Abraham, " Where is Sarah thy wife ? " (xviii. 9), it was because it was necessary for Abraham to answer where his virtue was. Abraham replied that it was in the soul (" Behold, in the tent "), laid up like a treasure, yet not making him happy because happiness consists in the

exercise of virtue, impossible until the birth of
Isaac (*Det.* 57-61). The promise of a son was
renewed, but Sarah laughed, for " it had ceased
to be with Sarah after the manner of women
(ἐξέλειπεν δὲ Σάρρᾳ γίνεσθαι τὰ γυναίκια) "
(xviii. 11). This is a favourite text with Philo.
It means her passions were now calmed within
her (*Spec. Leg.* ii. 54 & n) ; the passions are
feminine and must be quitted for the masculine
noble affections (*Det.* 28, *Fug.* 128) ; the " customs of women " are the external things of
sense ; but Sarah fled from these to where the
men are quartered when she was about to conceive Isaac (*Ebr.* 59-64) ; his mother forsook the
human ways of custom and mere reasoning when
she was to bear Isaac, the self-taught nature
that finds without seeking (*Fug.* 167f) ; God is
husband of virginity, that is, wisdom, who is
Sarah : she was virgin, for she passed from the
emasculate passions to virtues (hence God only
speaks to her after v. 11) (*Cher.* 49f) ; her virginity was not of the ever-virgin type (Rebecca),
but she typifies those who pass from womanhood
to virginity (*Post.* 134). This text is closely connected with the birth of Isaac in *Leg. All.* iii. 217,
Cher. 8, *Post.* 134, *Ebr.* 59. In *Cher.* 8 it is
apparently applied to Isaac himself (see [N]).
When Sarah " laughed within herself " (xviii.
12) with incredulity (*Abr.* 111f), it was the joy
of virtue contrasted with sense-perception's
groaning (*Leg. All.* iii. 217f) ; even though Isaac
was not yet born, laughter was possible because
virtue is by nature cause for joy, while vice is
grievous (*Mut.* 166f). In *Abr.* 205f it is again

virtue's joy ; but Philo recognizes Sarah's incredulity by saying she doubted whether joy is
not more than humanity can expect ; so too
Spec. Leg. ii. 54f. In *Ebr.* 62 it is a mocking
laugh at the anxious cares of men, especially
their concern with the things of sense. Sarah
denied that she had laughed. Philo treats this
in *Abr.* 205f and *Spec. Leg.* ii. 54f : joy was in
mind's womb, so she smiled ; but she reflected
that joy is the property of God alone, and becoming afraid, she denied her soul's laughter.
God made her acknowledge it, thereby showing
her that joy is not altogether denied to the
creature : only it is a mixed joy, blended with
sorrow

The story of Abraham and Sarah deceiving Abimelech (Gen. xii) is given in *Abr.* 92-106. Abraham's
words in the parallel story of Gen. xx. (*v.* 12),
" She is my sister, daughter of my father but not
of my mother," are apt, for the virtue-loving
mind has no female parentage—the material
substance perceptible to the senses—but was
born of the Father and Cause of all things (*Ebr.*
61, *Quis Her.* 62). The same sort of interpretation is applied to the non-mention of Abraham
at Sarah's conception in Gen. xxi. 1 : " The Lord
visited Sarah." The lovers of wisdom wed virtues, not women, and these bear *to* their lovers
but *by* God ; an example is Sarah, who was alone
at her conception (*Cher.* 43-45 & [N]). She said,
" The Lord hath made laughter for me (E.V.,
" made me to laugh "), for whoever hears it
shall rejoice with me " (xxi. 6). This is (*a*) the
joy of virtue contrasted with sense-perception's

grief (*Leg. All.* iii. 219, *cf. Det.* 123 ; *cf.* also *Leg. All.* ii. 82, where it is used for an analogy), and (*b*) the truth that God is the Father (" The Lord hath made ") of the perfect (Isaac) nature (*Leg. All.* iii. 219), or of laughter, the offspring of wisdom (*Det.* 124),[a] and (*c*) the fact that few can receive this teaching (" whoever " suggests few) (*Mut.* 138f, *cf. Leg. All.* iii. 219). The next words of Sarah seem to mean to Philo that spiritually it is Isaac who suckles Sarah (*Mig.* 140 & [N]-142)

Sarah's death (xxiii. 2) calls forth from Philo a eulogy of her character (*Abr.* 245ff), and he describes in detail Abraham's grief and his purchase of a burial-ground (*ib.* 255-261). So eventually Abraham and Sarah were buried in Machpelah, the double cave that received the virtues in pairs (*Post.* 62)

I. Gen. Introd. p. xvi f, *Leg. All.* ii. 82, iii. 85, 217-219, 244f, II. *Cher.* 3-10, 40-52, *Sac.* 59f, *Det.* 28, 57-61, 123-125, *Post.* 62, 76-78, 130, 134, III. *Ebr.* 59-62 & n, IV. *Mig.* 126, 140 & [N]-142 & n, *Quis Her.* 62 & n, 258, *Congr.* 1-23, 63-82, 127-129, 139f, 151-158, 180, V. *Fug.* 16, 128, 166f, 207, *Mut.* 61 & [N], 66n, 77-80, 130, 137f, 141-143, 148-153, 166f & n, 176, 252, 261, 264, VI. *Abr.* 92-106 & 100-102[N], 108-113, 168, 206 & n, 254-261, VII. *Spec. Leg.* ii. 54 & n, 55

Sardanapalus : VIII. *Spec. Leg.* iv. 122
Sarmatians : X. *Leg.* 10
Saturn : IV. *Quis Her.* 224, X. *Leg.* 13

[a] God the Father of Sarah, *Ebr.* 61, *Quis Her.* 62 ; of Isaac, *Leg. All.* iii. 219, *Cher.* 43-45 & [N], 49, *Det.* 124, *Mig.* 140, *Mut.* 130-132, 137-141, 255.

419

INDEX OF NAMES

kind of first pattern of virtue begotten by the mind. In 173f the limit of Seth's attainment in knowledge is said to be the starting-point for that of righteous Noah, who is ten (the perfect number) places removed from Seth : Seth's virtue steadily grows in his descendants. Seth also occurs in II. *Cher.* 54, *Det.* 138, VI. *Abr.* 12n

Shechem : Jacob hid the " strange gods " under the terebinth in Shechem (Gen. xxxv. 4). These are bad men's gods, the passions or pleasures, and must be placed under guard in Shechem (' shoulder,' symbol of toil), for he that devotes toil to pleasures keeps them well guarded. Again, Shechem is the things of the body and of the senses when in Gen. xlviii. 22 Jacob is said to give a portion to Joseph, who toils at these things. They are secondary, so the wise man does not keep them but passes them on (I. *Leg. All.* iii. 23-26 & n). But Shechem is also used to signify toil *against* bodily pleasure, a struggle that is a great burden such as ' shoulder ' suggests (II. *Det.* 9, on Gen. xxxvii. 13). When Abraham " travelled through the country as far as Shechem " (xii. 6), it was the mind's quest for knowledge and mastery of the body and of created things, and Shechem signifies the toil involved (IV. *Mig.* 216, 221)—very necessary if the judgement faculties of the understanding are not to be raped by him who practises the opposite kind of toil, as does the Shechem of Gen. xxxiv. (*ib.* 223f & nn, *cf.* V. *Mut.* 193f)

Shem : Shem means simply ' name,' and so we must understand the whole genus, representing good, which alone is a thing of name and good report,

421

just as bad is nameless and of evil name. So Noah's prayer is unique and transcendent : it is the Lord whom he declares to be peculiarly the God of Shem (Gen. ix. 26, **III.** *Sob.* 51 & [N], 52 & n & [N], 53f). The words " let him dwell in the houses of Shem " may be a prayer that God Himself with His providential care may inhabit the mind ; and Shem was the root of those qualities seen in the Patriarchs and the twelve tribes, " the palace and priesthood of God " (Exod. xix. 6) (*ib.* 62-66). But perhaps it is Japhet who is to dwell in the houses of Shem : in that case it is a prayer that the mind that takes bodily and external things to be forms of the good should return to the one good which belongs to the soul (*ib.* 67f). In **V.** *Mut.* 189 Shem is used to prove the perfection of the number one hundred. Shem is also mentioned in **II.** *Post.* 173, **IV.** *Mig.* 125n, **VIII.** *Virt.* 221[N]

Sheshai : ' Outside me,' stands for external goods (**II.** *Post.* 60f)

Shinar : The Babel-builders " moved from the east (' rising ') and found a plain in the land of Shinar and dwelt there." This was where vice was located, the starting-point of folly : for Shinar means ' shaking out,' signifying the chaos and disintegration of the soul of the fool, from which all good is shaken out (**IV.** *Conf.* 1, 60, 68f)

Shittim : ' Thorns,' a symbol of passions pricking and wounding the soul (Num. xxv. 1, **V.** *Som.* i. 89-91)

Shur : Shur, where the angel of the Lord found Hagar (Gen. xvi. 7, **V.** *Fug.* 1, 203), means ' wall ' or ' straightening ' and symbolizes the way in which the soul is kept on the safe highway of discipline

Sicily : **I.** *Leg. All.* i. 62, **VI.** *Jos.* 132, **IX.** *Aet.* 139, *Prov.* 2. 26

Siddim : Gen. xiv. 3, A.V. LXX, " salt ravine " : the place of vices and passions (**IV.** *Conf.* 26)

Sidon : **IX.** *Aet.* 76 & n, **X.** *Leg.* 222, 337

Sihon : When Mind listens to Sense-perception, as Adam did to Eve, disaster follows ; the mind is set on fire. Philo illustrates this by allegorizing Num. xxi. 27-30 ; he interprets " a flame (hath gone forth) from the city of Sihon " as that an irrational impulse issues forth from the mind that corrupts the truth (Sihon=' corrupting '). Philo manages to read the destruction of the Sihon mind in the latter part of his text (**I.** *Leg. All.* iii. 225, 228, 233)

Silanus, M. : **X.** *Leg.* 62-65, 71f, 75

Simeon : " This our son is disobedient . . . " (Deut. xxi. 18) implies other sons who are not : among these are Reuben, Simeon, Levi, etc. Simeon is the docile scholar, for his name means ' hearing ' (**III.** *Ebr.* 94, **V.** *Som.* ii. 34, 37). In treating the Shechem of Gen. xii. 6, Philo discusses the incident of Gen. xxxiv, when Shechem, the toiler in folly, tried to ravish Dinah, the soul's judgement ; then the ' hearers ' and pupils of sound sense, Simeon and Levi, defeated him (**IV.** *Mig.* 224). These two champions were so much one in mind and purpose that Moses compresses Simeon into Levi in Deut. xxxiii. 8 (**V.** *Mut.* 200 & n). God uses subordinate ministers for punishment ; this is seen in his allocating blessing to the six best tribe-leaders (including

423

INDEX OF NAMES

Simeon), and setting the other six over the cursing (V. *Fug.* 73). Jacob's blessing in Gen. xlviii. 5, " Ephraim and Manasseh shall be as Reuben and Simeon to me," leads Philo to see a correspondence between Ephraim and Reuben, Manasseh and Simeon. The advance ' from forgetfulness ' (Manasseh) involves recollection (which M. symbolizes), and recollection is akin to learning (Simeon), in which it often plays a part. Reuben (natural excellence) is named before Simeon : so natural excellence, which resembles sight (Reuben='seeing son '), is better than learning, which resembles ' hearing ' (V. *Mut.* 97-102). Simeon is also mentioned in I. *Leg. All.* i. 81 and VI. *Jos.* 175-210

Sinai : IV. *Quis Her.* 251, VI. Gen. Introd. p. xv, *Mos.* i & ii, Introd. p. 275 & n, VII. Gen. Introd. p. ix, *Decal.* 32ff, VIII. *Praem.* 4-6[N]

Sisyphus : II. *Cher.* 78

Socrates : III. *Quod Deus* 146 & n, 147, *Plant.* 65f, V. *Som.* i. 55-58, IX. *Vit. Cont.* 57, *Prov.* 2. 21. In *Som.* i. 58 Socrates is equated with Terah : but whereas Socrates was a human propounding a philosophy of self-knowledge, Terah was self-knowledge itself

Sodom, Sodomites : Sodom means ' blindness ' and ' barrenness ' (*e.g. Som.* ii. 191f). Thus Gen. xiii. 12 indicates Lot's relapse into his old state of ignorance (ἀμαθία, *Mig.* 150 & [N]) ; the city of Sodom stands for the animal nature, blind of reason, nearly destroyed in the soul's warfare of Gen. xiv (*Congr.* 91f & n ; the events are described in *Abr.* 225ff) ; when Abraham refused the offer of the king of Sodom (" Give me the

424

men, and take the horses for thyself," xiv. 21,
LXX), it was the refusal to accept irrational
creatures in exchange for reasonable beings and
so make himself rich in the products of evil (*Leg.
All.* iii. 23f) ; Abraham was retaining God-given
property and ridding himself of the possessions
ignorantly claimed by the Sodom character
(*ib.* 195-197) ; Abraham interceded for Sodom,
but in spite of this it was destroyed : every wise
man is a ransom for the fool, unless his evil be a
sickness so violent that it overpowers the physician's treatment (*Sac.* 118, 121-123) ; when praying for the soul barren of good and blind of
reason, Abraham stopped at ten, the redemption
number (*Conf.* 109) ; Gen. xix. 4 tells how the
Sodomites, representing those barren of wisdom
and blind in understanding, surrounded the soul
to dishonour the sacred Thoughts that were its
guests (*ib.* 27f & n) ; they " wearied themselves
in seeking the door " (xix. 11), but this was a
seeking that had no finding (*Fug.* 143f) ; the
destruction of Sodom by fire (*Abr.* 1 & n, *Mos.* ii.
55f, *Aet.* 147[N], and, with an allegory attached,
Abr. 133ff) was judgement on the adversaries of
virtue (*Som.* i. 85, *cf. Leg. All.* 213) ; the raging
passion for wine is insatiable, and, allegorically,
drunkenness is a symbol for folly in general : all
of which is suggested by " the vine of Sodom,"
etc., in Deut. xxxii. 32f, for Sodom is barrenness
and blindness, and the fool's desires are barren
of true gladness (*Ebr.* 222-224, *Som.* ii. 191f)

I. *Leg. All.* iii. 23f, 195-197, 212f, II. *Sac.* 118, 121-
123, III. *Ebr.* 222-224, IV. *Conf.* 27f & n, 91f & n,
109, *Mig.* 150 & [N], V. *Fug.* 143f, *Som.* i. 85,

Jacob flees from " Laban the Syrian " (Gen. xxxi. 20f) because Syria means ' highlands,' and discretion is the better part of valour when the practising mind meets passion in an exalted state (*Leg. All.* iii. 16, 18). For the same reason,

when he fled to Laban in the first place, it was
to his mother's brother, not Laban " the Syrian "
(xxvii. 43), the mind empty of sound sense (*Fug.*
44f &[N], 49). " Syrian " stands for the loftiness
of arrogance when it is used of the concubine
married to Manasseh (*Congr.* 41-43)

Talmai : 'One hanging' from lifeless things, as does the
soul enamoured of external goods (II. *Post.* 60f)

Tamar : Tamar, ' palm,' is a symbol of victory ; but
Philo's interpretations are connected, not so
much with the name, as with the story of Judah
and Tamar in Gen. xxxviii, from which Tamar
emerges as a type of virtue, even of chastity.
" Judah took for Er a wife whose name was
Tamar " (*v.* 6) : the soul is a corpse-bearer ;
but it only realizes this when it becomes perfect
and worthy of reward—when it weds Tamar,
the sign of victory (I. *Leg. All.* iii. 74). She became widowed, and Judah bade her remain in
his house (*vv.* 11ff) : the soul was widowed of
passions and pleasures, remained in the house of
her Father and Saviour, received divine impregnation, conceived virtue, bore noble actions, and
so won the ' palm ' of victory (III. *Quod Deus*
136f). There the story of Tamar's deception of
Judah is only suggested in barest outline ; but
the details of it form increasingly elaborate
allegories. Thus, on *vv.* 14ff : virtue makes trial
of her scholars, and sits veiled at the cross-roads,
wanting inquiring minds to unveil her and behold
her virgin beauty ; it is the excellent Judah
soul who does so, and there follows a mutual
' conceiving ' or ' taking ' (IV. *Congr.* 124-126

& n). Invincible virtue, vexed at men's absurd
aims, is not found by Judah's messenger (seeking and not finding) ; a mind bent on purchasing
piety gave pledges, the human virtues of fidelity,
constancy, discipline ; but inquiries showed there
was no harlot-soul in the region of the excellent,
to the joy of the Judah mind, glad that his understanding (feminine, διάνοια ; but the allegory is
becoming confused : see 154n) is a lady of
chastity and no easy prey ; but his testing of the
Tamar character was excusable, for reality is
often concealed by semblance (V. *Fug.* 149-156
& 150[N]). When discussing divine parenthood,
Philo uses the Tamar story to illustrate his point :
the pledges are not the gifts of any mortal—
the archetypal pattern of the universe (seal), the
world's order and sequence of things (cord),
the divine discipline (staff)—these all reveal the
giver to be God ; (so the Tamar soul, or virtue,
is impregnated by God) and the Judah mind,
pleased at the divine inspiration that masters
her, says, " She is justified, since I gave her to
no mortal " : for he holds it impiety to defile
the divine with things profane (V. *Mut.* 134-136).
In V. *Som.* ii. 44 & n, 45, Judah's pledges to
Tamar (' the soul ') are contrasted with the insignia given to Joseph by Pharaoh.   In VIII.
Virt. 220-222, Tamar is said to have turned from
polytheism to worship the one great Cause, to
have kept her life stainless, and to be a pattern
and source of nobility (see 208[N], 221[N], and
VIII. Gen. Introd. pp. xvii, xviii & n)
Tantalus : IV. *Quis Her.* 269, VII. *Decal.* 149, VIII.
Spec. Leg. iv. 81

INDEX OF NAMES

INDEX OF NAMES

Zeus : **I.** *Op.* 100, **IX.** *Quod Omn. Prob.* 102, 127, 130, *Aet.* 81 & n, *Prov.* 2. 7, 2. 24, **X.** *Leg.* 188, 265, 346

Zillah : see Sella

Zilpah : The soul that learns by instruction (Abraham) needs the School learning (Hagar), but the Practiser (Jacob) has two wives and two concubines, of which Zilpah is one ; she is the handmaid of Leah (virtue) and signifies oratorical power : for her name means ' walking mouth ' (**IV.** *Congr.* 24 & n, 29 & [N], 30 & n, 33). In contrasting Noah and Joseph, the " generations " of Noah indicate a development of a good kind, whereas there is a regressive development from Jacob to Joseph, who is said to have been " young " and keeping sheep with the bastard sons of the concubines, Bilhah and Zilpah (Gen. xxxvii. 2, **III.** *Quod Deus* 119-121). In **VIII.** *Virt.* 223 & n-225 Philo describes the extraordinarily cordial relations of the wives with the concubines and their respective offspring with each other (!) as an example of nobility of character among women. Zilpah is also named in **I.** *Leg. All.* ii. 94

Zipporah : Zipporah, wife of Moses (Exod. ii. 21), means ' bird,' and so she represents virtue that wings its way from earth to heaven. Moses, therefore, like other virtuous souls, did not " know " a woman, but his mate was a virtue (**II.** *Cher.* 41) ; yet the virtues must generate, and so they are impregnated by God Himself, as was Zipporah (*ib.* 47). Moses did not *take* Zipporah to wife, but received her, as the perfect natures receive Reason from God Himself (**II.** *Post.* 77f). In **V.** *Mut.* 120 she is the winged, inspired, and prophetic nature

432

INDEX OF NAMES

The Hebrew midwife of Exod. i. 15 (E.V., Shiphrah) called Zipporah typifies the divine wisdom, which soars aloft like a bird (**IV.** *Quis Her.* 128)

INDEX TO TRANSLATORS' NOTES

An asterisk indicates words which are also included in the Index of Names to which reference should be made. They are only given here when they are discussed in the Notes without having been in the text of Philo at that point.

434

INDEX TO NOTES

INDEX TO NOTES

INDEX TO NOTES

437

INDEX TO NOTES

INDEX TO NOTES

INDEX TO NOTES

INDEX TO NOTES

INDEX TO NOTES

446

INDEX TO NOTES

INDEX TO NOTES

INDEX TO NOTES

451

[a] Only selected references are given.

INDEX TO NOTES

454

INDEX TO NOTES

INDEX TO NOTES

456

INDEX TO NOTES

INDEX TO NOTES

INDEX TO NOTES

INDEX TO NOTES

INDEX TO NOTES

Livilla : **X.** *Leg.* 87n
Loeb texts : **III.** *Quod Deus* 41n, **VI.** Gen. Introd. p. xvii n, **IX.** *Aet.* 13N, 121n, *Prov.* 2. 50N, **X.** *Leg.* Introd. p. xvii n
Longinus : **III.** *Ebr.* 198N, **VIII.** *Spec. Leg.* iv. 73N, **IX.** *Quod Omn. Prob.* 134N
Lucan : **I.** Gen. Introd. p. xix & n
Lucian : **III.** *Agr.* 73N, **IV.** *Conf.* 27N, **VI.** *Mos.* i. 22N, 285n, **VII.** *Spec. Leg.* ii. 91N, 183N, **IX.** *Vit. Cont.* 17N, *Flacc.* 85n, 131N, **X.** *Leg.* 338n
Lucius : **IX.** *Vit. Cont.* Introd. pp. 105, 106n, 107f, 17N, 65n
Lucretius : **I.** *Op.* 170fN, *Leg. All.* i. 60n, **II.** *Post.* 79N, **III.** *Ebr.* 173N
Lucullus : **VII.** *Spec. Leg.* iii. 17-18N
Lyons : **X.** *Leg.* Introd. p. xxx
Lysanias : **IX.** *Flacc.* 25N
Lysias : **VII.** *Spec. Leg.* i. 341n, **VIII.** *Virt.* 29N
Lysimachus * : **IX.** *Quod Omn. Prob.* 127N
Lystra : **VII.** *Spec. Leg.* i. 55N

Macaria : **VI.** *Abr.* 180n
Maccabees : **IX.** *Quod Omn. Prob.* Introd. p. 5n
Macedonia * : **II.** *Gig.* 7N, **VII.** *Spec. Leg.* i. 180N (calendar), iii. 164N (law), **IX.** *Aet.* 45n
McLean : see Brooke
Macro * : **IX.** *Flacc.* 11n, **X.** *Leg.* Introd. p. xxiv, 32n, 39n, 58n, 62n
Madvig : **IV.** *Quis Her.* 169n, **IX.** *Aet.* 36n
Maecenas * : **VIII.** *Spec. Leg.* iv. 237N,
Magi * : **VII.** *Spec. Leg.* iii. 13N, 100n & N, **IX.** *Quod Omn. Prob.* 74n & N
Malchus : **VIII.** *Praem.* 23N
Maltese dogs * : **VIII.** *Praem.* 89N

INDEX TO NOTES

INDEX TO NOTES

INDEX TO NOTES

INDEX TO NOTES

469

INDEX TO NOTES

470

INDEX TO NOTES

INDEX TO NOTES

INDEX TO NOTES

INDEX TO NOTES

INDEX TO NOTES

INDEX TO NOTES

INDEX TO NOTES

INDEX TO NOTES

INDEX TO NOTES

INDEX TO GREEK WORDS
IN THE TRANSLATORS' NOTES

487

INDEX TO GREEK WORDS

INDEX TO GREEK WORDS

489

INDEX TO GREEK WORDS

490

INDEX TO GREEK WORDS

INDEX TO GREEK WORDS

ἀτελῆ : III. *Agr.* 140fN
ἄτεχνος : III. *Plant.* 173N, VIII. *Spec. Leg.* iv. 40n & N, 149fN
ἀτυφία : VIII. *Virt.* 17N, IX. *Vit. Cont.* 39n
αὐθέκαστος : IX. *Flacc.* 15n
αὐλαία : IV. *Congr.* 116n
αὐλή : IV. *Congr.* 116n ? *ib.*
αὐτίκα : VI. *Mos.* ii. 203n
αὐτοκρατής : VII. *Spec. Leg.* i. Title n
αὐτομαθής : II. *Sac.* 5-7N
αὐτοχειρίᾳ : VII. *Spec. Leg.* iii. 91n, VIII. *Spec. Leg.* iv. 7n
αὐτόχθονος : II. *Cher.* 120n
ἀφανίζειν : VII. *Spec. Leg.* iii. 145n
ἀφάνταστος : IV. *Quis Her.* 137n
ἄφεσις : IV. *Mig.* 32N
ἀφή : IV. *Conf.* 52N
ἀφιδρυσθαι : V. *Fug.* 101N
ἀφ᾽ ἱερᾶς ἤρξατο : V. *Som.* ii. 119n & N, X. *Leg.* 22nn, 108n
ἀφορίζεσθαι -ισμός : V. *Som.* i. 101n & N
ἀφορμή : III. *Quod Deus* 44N
ἄχθος : VII. *Spec. Leg.* i. 74n
ἄχρι : IX. *Aet.* 4nn
ἄχρονος : III. *Ebr.* 48N

βαθεῖ ἤθει : VI. *Jos.* 168n & N, IX. *Quod Omn. Prob.* 144n
βαθύνειν : VIII. *Virt.* 158n
βαραθρώδης : IX. *Aet.* 141n
βαρβαρισμός : I. *Leg. All.* iii. 188n
βαρὺ ἦθος : VI. *Abr.* 210n, *Jos.* 220n
βασιλεῖον : III. *Sob.* 66n
βασιλικαὶ βίβλοι : IV. *Conf.* 149N

INDEX TO GREEK WORDS

βάσις : II. *Gig.* 22N
βάτος : V. *Fug.* 162n
βιάζεσθαι : III. *Ebr.* 143n, *Sob.* 6n
βουλευτήριον διανοίας : IX. *Flacc.* 102n
βούλησις : II. *Det.* 120N
βραβεύειν, -τής : VIII. *Spec. Leg.* iv. 64n & N, X. *Leg.* 2n
βρίθειν : VII. *Spec. Leg.* i. 34n

γάρ : VII. *Spec. Leg.* i. 6n, IX. *Aet.* 75n, *Flacc.* 48n
γαργαλισμός : I. *Leg. All.* iii. 160N
γαστέρα, τὰ ὑπὸ : I. *Som.* i. 122n
γαστριμαργία : III. *Ebr.* 206N, IX. *Aet.* 74n
γενάρχης : IV. *Congr.* 133n & N, IX. *Flacc.* 74n
γενεά : X. *Leg.* 230nn
γενεαλογικός : VI. *Mos.* ii. 47n & N
γενικώτερον : VIII. *Praem.* 67n
γεννᾶν : VII. *Decal.* 27n
γένος, -η : IV. *Mig.* 116n, *Quis Her.* 118n, V. *Som.* i. 28N
γέρας, γῆρας : III. *Sob.* 16n, IV. *Quis Her.* 291n
γλῶσσα : IV. *Conf.* 27N
γνήσιος : IX. *Quod Omn. Prob.* 87n, *Vit. Cont.* 72n, *Flacc.* 9n
γνωσιμαχεῖν, -ία : IV. *Congr.* 53N
γονορρυής : I. *Leg. All.* iii. 7N
γοῦν : III. *Agr.* 81N, V. *Fug.* 191N, VI. *Jos.* 249n, IX. *Prov.* 2. 8n
γραμμαί : IV. *Congr.* 77N
γράμματα : VII. *Spec. Leg.* ii. 230n
γραμματική : II. *Cher.* 105N, III. *Ebr.* 51N, IV. *Congr.* 77N, 148n & N, VI. *Jos.* 132n, VII. *Spec. Leg.* ii. 230n
γραμματιστής : VI. *Jos.* 132n

INDEX TO GREEK WORDS

γραμματοκύφων : **IX.** *Flacc.* 20n
γραμμή : **V.** *Som.* ii. 119n & N
γράφεσθαι : **II.** *Det.* 141N
γραφή : **VII.** *Spec. Leg.* i. 1n
γυμνάζειν : **II.** *Sac.* 85n
γυμνός : **II.** *Sac.* 85n, **IX.** *Quod Omn. Prob.* 43n
γύνανδρος : **IV.** *Quis Her.* 274N

δαίμονα, κατὰ : **IX.** *Hyp.* 6. 1n
δάκτυλος θεοῦ : **VI.** *Mos.* i. 112n
δανείζεσθαι : **VII.** *Spec. Leg.* ii. 183n
δέ : **IX.** *Hyp.* 7. 5n
δεῖν : **VIII.** *Virt.* 29N
δείξεις : **V.** *Mut.* 207N
δεισιδαιμονία : **V.** *Som.* i. 230n & N, *Mut.* 138N
δεξιότης : **V.** *Fug.* 31n & N, **VI.** *Abr.* 208n
δεξιῶς : **VI.** *Mos.* ii. 291n
δεύτερος πλοῦς : **V.** *Som.* i. 44N, **VI.** *Abr.* 123n
δημιουργός : **V.** *Som.* ii. 187n
δημοκρατία : **III.** *Det.* 176N, **IV.** *Conf.* 108n
δῆμος : **VII.** *Spec. Leg.* ii. 82n & N
διαβατήρια : **VII.** *Spec. Leg.* ii. 145n & N
διάγνωσις : **IX.** *Flacc.* 100n
διάθεσις : **II.** *Cher.* 62n, *Post.* 36n
διαιρετός : **III.** *Agr.* 134n & N
διακόσμησις : **VII.** *Spec. Leg.* i. 208n & N
διακύπτειν : **IX.** *Flacc.* 144n
διαλεκτική : **IV.** *Congr.* 18N
διαλεληθότες σοφοί : **III.** *Agr.* 161N
διάλογος : **III.** *Ebr.* 56N
διανέμειν : **VII.** *Spec. Leg.* ii. 183n, **VIII.** *Spec. Leg.* iv. 120n
διανίστασθαι : **IV.** *Mig.* 206n & N
διανόησις : **III.** *Quod Deus* 34N
494

INDEX TO GREEK WORDS

διάνοια : VII. *Decal.* 1N, IX. *Flacc.* 102n
διάπυρος : V. *Som.* i. 22n & N
διάστασις : I. *Op.* 120n
διάστημα : IX. *Aet.* 4n
διαφθείρειν : IV. *Mig.* 200n
διαφωνεῖν : III. *Ebr.* 114-118N, IV. *Conf.* 56n, V. *Mut.*
    109n, VIII. *Virt.* 44n & N
διδασκαλία : II. *Sac.* 5-7N, III. *Sob.* 38n
δίδυμος : IV. *Congr.* 18N, VII. *Spec. Leg.* iii. 179n
διεζευγμένα : III. *Agr.* 140fN
διεξοδικός : IV. *Congr.* 30n
διεστῶτα : II. *Det.* 49N
διϊσχυρίζειν : IX. *Hyp.* 6. 6n
δικαστήριον θεῖον : VIII. *Spec. Leg.* iv. 34n
δίκη : IV. *Quis Her.* 161n, VII. *Spec. Leg.* iii. 175n
διόρυγμα : VIII. *Spec. Leg.* iv. 7n & N
δὶς διὰ πασῶν : V. *Som.* ii. 27N
δίχα : IV. *Conf.* 159n, *Quis Her.* 161n, VIII. *Virt.* 226n,
    IX. *Quod Omn. Prob.* 124n
διχηλεῖν : VIII. *Spec. Leg.* iv. 106N
δόγματα : IV. *Congr.* 142n
δόκιμος : V. *Som.* i. 202n
δόξαι : VII. *Decal.* 4n
δύναμις : IV. *Conf.* 187n, VI. *Abr.* 131n, VII. *Spec. Leg.*
    i. 48n, ii. 212n, X. *Leg.* 126n
δυσθανατεῖν : VIII. *Virt.* 92n

ἑβδομάς, -η : IV. *Quis Her.* 170n & N, V. *Fug.* 173n,
    Mut. 144n, 260n, VI. *Mos.* i. 205n, VII. *Decal.*
    158n & N, *Spec. Leg.* ii. 176n & N, VIII. *Praem.*
    154n & N, IX. *Vit. Cont.* 65n & N
ἑβδοματικόν : VII. *Decal.* 162n
ἑβδόματος : VII. *Decal.* 96N
ἐγγράμματος : III. *Plant.* 10n & N

INDEX TO GREEK WORDS

496

INDEX TO GREEK WORDS

INDEX TO GREEK WORDS

498

ἐπίκρισις : II. *Sac.* 139n

ἐπιλάμπειν : VIII. *Praem.* 25n

ἐπιμελητής : VII. *Spec. Leg.* i. 131n

ἐπιμιξία : IX. *Vit. Cont.* 20n

ἐπινεανεύεσθαι : VIII. *Spec. Leg.* iv. 215n

Ἐπινομίς : VIII. *Spec. Leg.* iv. 160n & N

ἐπιορκεῖν : VII. *Spec. Leg.* ii. 26n

ἐπιπροσθεῖν : VII. *Decal.* 159n

ἐπίσημος : IV. *Mig.* 79N, V. *Fug.* 11-13N, *Som.* i. 202n

ἐπισπᾶσθαι : III. *Ebr.* 176N

ἐπιστήμη : I. *Leg. All.* i. 60n & N, II. *Post.* 141N, III. *Quod Deus* 92n, IV. *Congr.* 141N, V. *Som.* i. 47N, VI. *Mos.* ii. 97n, VII. *Decal.* 1N

ἐπισυμβαίνειν : IX. *Prov.* 2. 45n

ἐπισφραγίζεσθαι : VII. *Spec. Leg.* ii. 14n, 176n

ἐπίτασις : IV. *Quis Her.* 156N

ἐπιτίθεσθαι : VII. *Spec. Leg.* iii. 86n & N

ἐπιτρέπειν : VI. *Mos.* i. 320n

ἐπιφανής : X. *Leg.* 346n

ἐπιφημίζειν : IX. *Hyp.* 7. 3n

ἐπιφορεῖσθαι : II. *Post.* 149N

ἐπιφράττειν : VIII. *Spec. Leg.* iv. 88n

ἐπιχειρονομεῖν : VIII. *Spec. Leg.* iv. 215n

ἐπιχρᾶν : VIII. *Spec. Leg.* iv. 235n

ἔπη : IX. *Vit. Cont.* 80n

ἐπορθιάζειν : VI. *Abr.* 20n

ἔπος εἰπεῖν, ὡς : IV. *Quis Her.* 12n, VII. *Spec. Leg.* ii. 63n

ἐπουρίζειν : VI. *Abr.* 20n, *Mos.* i. 283n

ἑπτά : IV. *Conf.* 137N ; see also *s.v.* ἑβδομάς

ἐπώνυμος : VI. *Abr.* 10n

ἐρανίζειν : V. *Som.* i. 95n

ἔργα : IV. *Mig.* 167n & N, VII. *Decal.* 76n, *Spec. Leg.* ii. 170n

INDEX TO GREEK WORDS

INDEX TO GREEK WORDS

εὕρημα : **VIII.** *Virt.* 8n
εὐτελής : **IV.** *Quis Her.* 158n, **V.** *Som.* i. 6n
εὐτόνως : **II.** *Sac.* 80N
εὐφορεῖν : **VII.** *Spec. Leg.* iii. 23n
εὐχαί : **VII.** *Spec. Leg.* i. 83N
ἐφεδρεύειν : **IX.** *Flacc.* 5n
ἐφημερευταί : **IX.** *Vit. Cont.* 66n
ἐφιδρύσεις : **I.** *Leg. All.* iii. 188N, 189N
ἐφιστάναι : **IV.** *Conf.* 96n
ἔχειν κοινωνίαν : **VII.** *Spec. Leg.* ii. 110n

ζῆλος : **IX.** *Hyp.* 6. 4n
ζήλωσις : **IX.** *Quod Omn. Prob.* 82n
ζωγραφεῖν, -ος : **I.** *Leg. All.* i. 80n
ζωοτροφεῖν : **IV.** *Mig.* 210N
ζῶσι νόμοις : **V.** *Som.* ii. 55N

ἤ : **VIII.** *Spec. Leg.* iv. 34n
ἡβᾶν : **II.** *Cher.* 114N, **IV.** *Congr.* 162n
ἡβηδόν : **V.** *Fug.* 90n
ἡγεμονικόν : **VII.** *Spec. Leg.* i. 6N
ἡδονή : **II.** *Det.* 120N, **VII.** *Spec. Leg.* ii. 185N
ἠθικόν : **I.** *Leg. All.* i. 57N, **III.** *Ebr.* 48N
ἠθοποιός : **III.** *Ebr.* 48N
ἦθος : **II.** *Cher.* 105N, **IV.** *Congr.* 54 (read 53) N, **VI.** *Jos.*
    168n & N, *Mos.* ii. 256n, **VII.** *Decal.* 132n, **IX.** *Quod*
    Omn. Prob. 144n
ἡμέρα : **III.** *Ebr.* 149n & N
ἥμερος : **III.** *Ebr.* 149n & N, **VIII.** *Praem.* 8n, 60N
ἡμιμόχθηρος : **VIII.** *Spec. Leg.* iv. 63ffN
ἡνωμένα : **II.** *Det.* 49N, **IV.** *Mig.* 180N, **V.** *Som.* i. 128n
ἡσυχία : **V.** *Mut.* 242n & N
ἧττον : **VIII.** *Praem.* 135n

INDEX TO GREEK WORDS

ἱερομηνία : VI. *Mos.* ii. 23n, VII. *Decal.* 159n & N,
    Spec. Leg. i. 180n
ἱερόν : VII. *Spec. Leg.* iii. 171n & N
ἱερωμένος : VII. *Spec. Leg.* i. 96N
ἵνα : VIII. *Spec. Leg.* iv. 155n, 217n, IX. *Vit. Cont.* 16n
ἰσότης : VIII. *Spec. Leg.* iv. 231n & N, 237N
ἰσχύειν : IX. *Hyp.* 6. 6n

καθάπαξ : VI. *Abr.* 51N
καθαρός : VI. *Mos.* ii. 34n, 72n
καθάρσια : VII. *Spec. Leg.* i. 111n
καθήκειν, -οντα : I. *Leg. All.* i. 56n, III. *Quod Deus*
    100N, IV. *Mig.* 54N, *Quis Her.* 191n, VI *Mut.* 47N
καθιέντες πείρας : VIII. *Virt.* 34n & N
καθυποκρίνειν : IX. *Flacc.* 72n
καιρός : VII. *Spec. Leg.* ii. 56n & N, VIII. *Spec. Leg.*
    iv. 213n, IX. *Flacc.* 165n
κακία : IV. *Quis Her.* 241n, *Congr.* 54N
κακοτεχνία : V. *Mut.* 150N, VII. *Spec. Leg.* iii. 101n
κάκωσις : VIII. *Praem.* 146n, 160n
καλεῖν : I. *Leg. All.* ii. 16N, 44N
καλόν, τό : II. *Det.* 9N, VII. *Spec. Leg.* i. 318n & N,
    ii. 73N
καλός : IX. *Hyp.* 6. 2n, X. *Leg.* 234n, 338n
καλὸς καὶ ἀγαθός : I. *Op.* 136n
κάλυμμα : VI. *Mos.* ii. 87n
καλῶς : IV. *Mig.* 181n
κάμινος : III. *Ebr.* 73n
κανών : VIII. *Spec. Leg.* iv. 115n
καρποῦσθαι : VII. *Spec. Leg.* iii. 1n
κατά : IV. *Mig.* 39n, *Quis Her.* 241n
κατὰ δαίμονα : IX. *Hyp.* 6. 1n
κατὰ μέρος : VII. *Spec. Leg.* i. 108n, *cf.* **226n**
κατὰ πλάτος : VII. *Spec. Leg.* iii. 188n

INDEX TO GREEK WORDS

INDEX TO GREEK WORDS

κόρος : I. *Leg. All.* iii. 7N
κοσμοπολίτης : I. *Op.* 3N, 142N, IV. *Conf.* 106N,
    VI. *Jos.* 29n
κόσμος : I. *Op.* 3n, *Leg. All.* i. 1n, III. *Ebr.* 30n,
    VIII. *Spec. Leg.* iv. 210n, 237n
κουρίδιος : VIII. *Virt.* 222n
κράτος ἀρχῆς : VII. *Spec. Leg.* iii. 16n
κρίνον, κρινόμενον : III. *Ebr.* 172N
κρίσις : I. *Leg. All.* ii. 6N, iii. 116n, VII. *Spec. Leg.* ii.
    36n
κτᾶσθαι : III. *Ebr.* 31N
κτῆμα : VIII. *Spec. Leg.* iv. 22n
κυκλοφορητικός : IV. *Quis Her.* 283N
κυοφορεῖν : V. *Mut.* 252n
κύριον ὄνομα : V. *Mut.* 12fn & N, VI. *Mos.* ii. 38N,
    VIII. *Praem.* 111n & N
κύριος : VII. *Decal.* 176n
κωφός : VIII. *Spec. Leg.* iv. 197n

λαμπάδιον : I. *Op.* 148N, IV. *Quis Her.* 218N
λάχανα : IX. *Quod Omn. Prob.* 156n
λέγειν : VIII. *Praem.* 79n, IX. *Quod Omn. Prob.* 8n
λεῖος : II. *Post.* 79N, III. *Agr.* 142N, IV. *Congr.* 25n
λείπεσθαι : IX. *Flacc.* 124n
λείχων, λοχῶν : IV. *Mig.* 144n
λεκτόν : III. *Agr.* 139n
λῆμμα : V. *Mut.* 126n
ληπτόν, οὐ τῇ ἑτέρᾳ : IV. *Mig.* 220n & N, V. *Som.* i. 8n
λιθο-, λινογραφεῖν : IX. *Prov.* 2. 17n
λιπαίνειν : IX. *Vit. Cont.* 36n & N
λιποτάξιον : II. *Cher.* 32N
λογεῖον : VI. *Mos.* ii. 112n
λογικόν : I. *Leg. All.* i. 57N, 70N
λογικός : V. *Fug.* 177N, VII. *Spec. Leg.* iii. 83n, 103n

INDEX TO GREEK WORDS

506

INDEX TO GREEK WORDS

INDEX TO GREEK WORDS

INDEX TO GREEK WORDS

INDEX TO GREEK WORDS

INDEX TO GREEK WORDS

511

πλήττειν : III. *Quod Deus* 84N

πλοῦς : V. *Som.* i. 44N, VI. *Abr.* 123n, IX. *Flacc.* 31n

πλοῦτος : VII. *Spec. Leg.* i. 25n & N, VIII. *Virt.* 6n, IX. *Vit. Cont.* 17n

πλωτά : V. *Som.* ii. 143n

πνεῖν : VIII. *Spec. Leg.* iv. 50n, *Virt.* 171n, IX. *Flacc.* 124n

πνεῦμα : IV. *Quis Her.* 242n, V. *Fug.* 134N, VII. *Spec. Leg.* i. 6N, IX. *Quod Omn. Prob.* 26n

πνευματικός : IV. *Quis Her.* 242n, VIII. *Praem.* 48n, IX. *Quod Omn. Prob.* 26n

πνῖγος : VIII. *Praem.* 133n

ποιεῖσθαι : VIII. *Spec. Leg.* iv. 190n

ποίημα : II. *Sac.* 17N, IV. *Congr.* 61nn

ποιητικός : I. *Leg. All.* i. 57N, V. *Fug.* 26N

ποικίλος : V. *Som.* i. 202n

ποιός : II. *Cher.* 114N, V. *Fug.* 11-13N, *Mut.* 121nn & N, IX. *Aet.* 48nn & N

πολιτεία : X. *Leg.* Introd. p. xxvii n

πολιτικός : II. *Det.* 135N

πολῖτις : IV. *Conf.* 151N

πολὺ πρότερον : VII. *Spec. Leg.* i. 101n, IX. *Flacc.* 10n, X. *Leg.* 115n

πολύχηλος : VIII. *Spec. Leg.* iv. 109n & N

πολυψηφίαι : X. *Leg.* 149n

πόνος : II. *Sac.* 112n, IV. *Mig.* 224n

πόρνος, -εύειν : VII. *Spec. Leg.* iii. 37fN

πόρρωθεν : VII. *Spec. Leg.* iii. 63n, VIII. *Spec. Leg.* iv. 104N

ποσθένης : VII. *Spec. Leg.* i. 4n

πότιμοι λόγοι : VII. *Spec. Leg.* i. 321N

πράγματα : IV. *Conf.* 21n, *Quis Her.* 242N

πραγματολογεῖν : V. *Som.* i. 230n & N

πρακτικός : I. *Leg. All.* i. 57N

INDEX TO GREEK WORDS

πρόφασις : **V.** *Som.* i. 128n, **IX.** *Vit. Cont.* 66n
πρωτογενῆ : **IV.** *Quis Her.* 118n
πτοία : **VII.** *Decal.* 142-146N, **VIII.** *Praem.* 148n
πυκνός : **V.** *Som.* i. 22N
πυνθάνεσθαι : **III.** *Quod Deus* 92N
πυρίγονος : **II.** *Gig.* 7N
πυρφόρος : **VI.** *Mos.* i. 179n
πύσμα : **II.** *Det.* 57N, **III.** *Agr.* 140fN

ῥαψῳδία : **IX.** *Vit. Cont.* 17N
ῥεῦμα : **IX.** *Prov.* 2. 18n & N
ῥήματα : **IV.** *Mig.* 48fn & N, 80n
ῥητορική : **V.** *Som.* i. 205N
ῥοπή : **IX.** *Flacc.* 165n
ῥυείς, ῥύσις : **V.** *Fug.* 191N
ῥυθμοί : **V.** *Som.* i. 205N

σεβασμός : **IV.** *Conf.* 137N
σειρομάστης : **II.** *Post.* 182n, **III.** *Ebr.* 73n,**V.** *Mut.* 108n
σελήνην, κατὰ : **VII.** *Decal.* 96N
σιαγών, σείω : **VII.** *Spec. Leg.* i. 147n
σκηρίπτεσθαι : **VII.** *Spec. Leg.* ii. 23n
σοφός : **IV.** *Conf.* 137N
σπαθᾶν : **VIII.** *Spec. Leg.* iv. 217n
σπέρματα, -ικός : **IV.** *Quis Her.* 115N, **X.** *Leg.* 55n
σπονδή, -αί : **III.** *Ebr.* 208N, **VII.** *Spec. Leg.* iii. 96n, **IX.** *Vit. Cont.* 41n
στάσις : **V.** *Som.* i. 28N
στεῖρα, στερρά : **III.** *Quod Deus* 13n
στερέωμα : **IV.** *Conf.* 96n
στήλη : **V.** *Som.* i. 244N
στιβάς : **V.** *Som.* ii. 56n
στοιχεῖα : **IV.** *Quis Her.* 282n
στοχασμός : **IX.** *Aet.* 2n

514

INDEX TO GREEK WORDS

τέλεια : III. *Agr.* 140fN
τελεῖν, -εῖσθαι : V. *Som.* ii. 144n, VI. *Mos.* i. 62n
τελειότης : V. *Mut.* 12N
τελεσφόρος : VII. *Spec. Leg.* 319n
τελευταῖον : VI. *Jos.* 249n, VIII. *Spec. Leg.* iv. 23n
τέλος : IV. *Mig.* 139nn
τέμνειν : IV. *Quis Her.* 167n, V. *Mut.* 179n
τερθρεία : II. *Cher.* 42N
τέφρα : V. *Som.* i. 214n & N
τέχνη, -αι : II. *Sac.* 37N, *Post.* 130n, 141N, III. *Ebr.*
　　88N, IV. *Mig.* 167N, *Quis Her.* 156N, VI. *Mos.* ii.
　　211n, IX. *Vit. Cont.* 16n
τί : I. *Leg. All.* ii. 16N, iii. 175N
τιθέναι : see θεός, τίθημι
τιμή : III. *Quod Deus* 169n, VII. *Spec. Leg.* ii. 260n
τόκος : VIII. *Virt.* 82n
τονικῶς : II. *Post.* 30N
τόνος : II. *Sac.* 37N, 68N, 80N, IV. *Quis Her.* 242n,
　　VIII. *Praem.* 48n
τόπος : V. *Fug.* 75N, *Som.* i. 53n, 182n
τοῦτο : V. *Mut.* 129n ; *cf.* VII. *Spec. Leg.* i. 210n
τραγῳδία : V. *Mut.* 114n
τρανός : V. *Mut.* 108n
τρέπειν, -εσθαι : IX. *Quod Omn. Prob.* 123n, X. *Leg.*
　　119n
τρίκλινα : IX. *Vit. Cont.* 49n & N
τροπή, -αί : I. *Leg. All.* ii. 83-87N, VII. *Spec. Leg.* i.
　　34n
τροπός : III. *Agr.* 114N
τυγχάνοντα : V. *Mut.* 77N
τυπωδέστερον : VIII. *Praem.* 67n
τύπωσις : I. *Leg. All.* i. 30N, IV. *Mig.* 5N
τυφλός : VII. *Spec. Leg.* i. 25N
τυφοπλαστεῖν : X. *Leg.* 153n

INDEX TO GREEK WORDS

τῦφος : III. *Ebr.* 95N, IV. *Mig.* 160N, V. *Som.* ii. 140n,
    VIII. *Virt.* 17n & N, IX. *Vit. Cont.* 39nn
τύχη : VIII. *Spec. Leg.* iv. 153n

ὑγίεια : III. *Quod Deus* 57N
ὕλη : VIII. *Spec. Leg.* iv. 209n
ὑπάργυρος : IV. *Congr.* 159n & N
ὑπαρκτά : IV. *Mig.* 94n & N
ὑπάρχειν : X. *Leg.* 86n
ὑπάρχοντα : IV. *Mig.* 94n & N
ὑπερβατόν : V. *Mut.* 13n & N
ὑπηχεῖν : V. *Som.* i. 164N, VI. *Jos.* 110n, VII. *Spec.*
    Leg. ii. 80n, X. *Leg.* 245n
ὕπνος : I. *Leg. All.* iii. 183n
ὑπο- : IV. *Congr.* 159N
ὑπὸ γαστέρα, τὰ : V. *Som.* i. 122n
ὑπὸ πόδας χωρεῖν : VI. *Mos.* i. 270n
ὑπογάμιον : VII. *Spec. Leg.* iii. 72n & N
ὑπόδρομος, -δράμη : IV. *Conf.* 70N
ὑπόθεσις : VI. p. 611n
ὑπόκρισις : II. *Cher.* 105N, IV. *Mig.* 35N
ὑπομένειν : IX. *Quod Omn. Prob.* 122n
ὑπόμνησις : IX. *Vit. Cont.* 78N
ὑπομονή : V. *Mut.* 197N
ὑπόνοια : V. *Mut.* 62n & N
ὑποτίμησις : IX. *Hyp.* 7. 1n
ὑποτρέχειν : IV. *Conf.* 70N
ὑποτροπιάζειν : IX. *Flacc.* 153n
ὑπόχρυσος : IV. *Congr.* 159n & N
ὕφεσις : I. *Leg. All.* iii. 183n
ὑφιέναι : V. *Som.* ii. 140n & N

φαιδρύνειν : VII. *Spec. Leg.* i. 269n
φαίνειν : I. *Leg. All.* i. 82n

INDEX TO GREEK WORDS

518

INDEX TO GREEK WORDS

INDEX TO GREEK WORDS

Printed in Great Britain by R. & R. CLARK, LIMITED, *Edinburgh*

THE LOEB CLASSICAL LIBRARY

VOLUMES ALREADY PUBLISHED

LATIN AUTHORS

AMMIANUS MARCELLINUS. J. C. Rolfe. 3 Vols.

APULEIUS: THE GOLDEN ASS (METAMORPHOSES). W. Adlington (1566). Revised by S. Gaselee.

St. AUGUSTINE: CITY OF GOD. 7 Vols. Vol. I. G. E. McCracken. Vol. II. W. M. Green. Vol. III. D. Wiesen. Vol. IV. P. Levine. Vol. V. E. M. Sanford and W. M. Green. Vol. VI. W. C. Greene.

St. AUGUSTINE, CONFESSIONS OF. W. Watts (1631). 2 Vols.

St. AUGUSTINE: SELECT LETTERS. J. H. Baxter.

AUSONIUS. H. G. Evelyn White. 2 Vols.

BEDE. J. E. King. 2 Vols.

BOETHIUS; TRACTS AND DE CONSOLATIONE PHILOSOPHIAE. Rev. H. F. Stewart and E. K. Rand.

CAESAR: ALEXANDRIAN, AFRICAN AND SPANISH WARS. A. G. Way.

CAESAR: CIVIL WARS. A. G. Peskett.

CAESAR: GALLIC WAR. H. J. Edwards.

CATO AND VARRO: DE RE RUSTICA. H. B. Ash and W. D. Hooper.

CATULLUS. F. W. Cornish; TIBULLUS. J. B. Postgate; and PERVIGILIUM VENERIS. J. W. Mackail.

CELSUS: DE MEDICINA. W. G. Spencer. 3 Vols.

CICERO: BRUTUS AND ORATOR. G. L. Hendrickson and H. M. Hubbell.

CICERO: DE FINIBUS. H. Rackham.

CICERO: DE INVENTIONE, etc. H. M. Hubbell.

CICERO: DE NATURA DEORUM AND ACADEMICA. H. Rackham.

CICERO: DE OFFICIIS. Walter Miller.

CICERO: DE ORATORE, etc. 2 Vols. Vol. I: DE ORATORE, Books I and II. E. W. Sutton and H. Rackham. Vol. II: DE ORATORE, Book III; DE FATO; PARADOXA STOICORUM; DE PARTITIONE ORATORIA. H. Rackham.

CICERO: DE REPUBLICA, DE LEGIBUS, SOMNIUM SCIPIONIS. Clinton W. Keyes.

THE LOEB CLASSICAL LIBRARY

CICERO : DE SENECTUTE, DE AMICITIA, DE DIVINATIONE. W. A. Falconer.

CICERO : IN CATILINAM, PRO MURENA, PRO SULLA, PRO FLACCO. Louis E. Lord.

CICERO : LETTERS TO ATTICUS. E. O. Winstedt. 3 Vols.

CICERO : LETTERS TO HIS FRIENDS. W. Glynn Williams. 4 Vols.

CICERO : PHILIPPICS. W. C. A. Ker.

CICERO : PRO ARCHIA, POST REDITUM, DE DOMO, DE HARUSPICUM RESPONSIS, PRO PLANCIO. N. H. Watts.

CICERO : PRO CAECINA, PRO LEGE MANILIA, PRO CLUENTIO, PRO RABIRIO. H. Grose Hodge.

CICERO : PRO CAELIO, DE PROVINCIIS CONSULARIBUS, PRO BALBO. R. Gardner.

CICERO : PRO MILONE, IN PISONEM, PRO SCAURO, PRO FONTEIO, PRO RABIRIO POSTUMO, PRO MARCELLO, PRO LIGARIO, PRO REGE DEIOTARO. N. H. Watts.

CICERO : PRO QUINCTIO, PRO ROSCIO AMERINO, PRO ROSCIO COMOEDO, CONTRA RULLUM. J. H. Freese.

CICERO : PRO SESTIO, IN VATINIUM. R. Gardner.

[CICERO] : RHETORICA AD HERENNIUM. H. Caplan.

CICERO : TUSCULAN DISPUTATIONS. J. E. King.

CICERO : VERRINE ORATIONS. L. H. G. Greenwood. 2 Vols.

CLAUDIAN. M. Platnauer. 2 Vols.

COLUMELLA : DE RE RUSTICA, DE ARBORIBUS. H. B. Ash, E. S. Forster, E. Heffner. 3 Vols.

CURTIUS, Q.: HISTORY OF ALEXANDER. J. C. Rolfe. 2 Vols.

FLORUS. E. S. Forster; and CORNELIUS NEPOS. J. C. Rolfe.

FRONTINUS : STRATAGEMS AND AQUEDUCTS. C. E. Bennett and M. B. McElwain.

FRONTO : CORRESPONDENCE. C. R. Haines. 2 Vols.

GELLIUS. J. C. Rolfe. 3 Vols.

HORACE : ODES AND EPODES. C. E. Bennett.

HORACE : SATIRES, EPISTLES, ARS POETICA. H. R. Fairclough.

JEROME : SELECT LETTERS. F. A. Wright.

JUVENAL AND PERSIUS. G. G. Ramsay.

LIVY. B. O. Foster, F. G. Moore, Evan T. Sage, A. C. Schlesinger and R. M. Geer (General Index). 14 Vols.

LUCAN. J. D. Duff.

LUCRETIUS. W. H. D. Rouse.

MARTIAL. W. C. A. Ker. 2 Vols.

MINOR LATIN POETS : from PUBLILIUS SYRUS TO RUTILIUS NAMATIANUS, including GRATTIUS, CALPURNIUS SICULUS, NEMESIANUS, AVIANUS, with " Aetna," " Phoenix " and other poems. J. Wight Duff and Arnold M. Duff.

THE LOEB CLASSICAL LIBRARY

OVID: THE ART OF LOVE AND OTHER POEMS. J. H. Mozley.
OVID: FASTI. Sir James G. Frazer.
Ovid: HEROIDES AND AMORES. Grant Showerman.
OVID: METAMORPHOSES. F. J. Miller. 2 Vols.
OVID: TRISTIA AND EX PONTO. A. L. Wheeler.
PETRONIUS. M. Heseltine; SENECA: APOCOLOCYNTOSIS.
  W. H. D. Rouse.
PHAEDRUS AND BABRIUS (Greek). B. E. Perry.
PLAUTUS. Paul Nixon. 5 Vols.
PLINY: LETTERS, PANEGYRICUS. B. Radice. 2 Vols.
PLINY: NATURAL HISTORY. 10 Vols. Vols. I-V and IX.
  H. Rackham. Vols. VI-VIII. W. H. S. Jones. Vol. X.
  D. E. Eichholz.
PROPERTIUS. H. E. Butler.
PRUDENTIUS. H. J. Thomson. 2 Vols.
QUINTILIAN. H. E. Butler. 4 Vols.
REMAINS OF OLD LATIN. E. H. Warmington. 4 Vols.
  Vol. I (Ennius and Caecilius). Vol. II (Livius, Naevius,
  Pacuvius, Accius). Vol. III (Lucilius, Laws of the XII
  Tables). Vol. IV (Archaic Inscriptions).
SALLUST. J. C. Rolfe.
SCRIPTORES HISTORIAE AUGUSTAAE. D. Magie. 3 Vols.
SENECA: APOCOLOCYNTOSIS. Cf. PETRONIUS.
SENECA: EPISTULAE MORALES. R. M. Gummere. 3 Vols.
SENECA: MORAL ESSAYS. J. W. Basore. 3 Vols.
SENECA: NATURALES QUAESTIONES. T. H. Corcoran. 2 Vols.
SENECA: TRAGEDIES. F. J. Miller. 2 Vols.
SIDONIUS: POEMS AND LETTERS. W. B. Anderson. 2 Vols.
SILIUS ITALICUS. J. D. Duff. 2 Vols.
STATIUS. J. H. Mozley. 2 Vols.
SUETONIUS. J. C. Rolfe. 2 Vols.
TACITUS: AGRICOLA AND GERMANIA. Maurice Hutton: DIA-
  LOGUS. Sir Wm. Peterson.
TACITUS: HISTORIES AND ANNALS. C. H. Moore and J.
  Jackson. 4 Vols.
TERENCE. John Sargeaunt. 2 Vols.
TERTULLIAN: APOLOGIA AND DE SPECTACULIS. T. R. Glover;
  MINUCIUS FELIX. G. H. Rendall.
VALERIUS FLACCUS. J. H. Mozley.
VARRO: DE LINGUA LATINA. R. G. Kent. 2 Vols.
VELLEIUS PATERCULUS AND RES GESTAE DIVI AUGUSTI.
  F. W. Shipley.
VIRGIL. H. R. Fairclough. 2 Vols.
VITRUVIUS: DE ARCHITECTURA. F. Granger. 2 Vols.

3

THE LOEB CLASSICAL LIBRARY

ACHILLES TATIUS. S. Gaselee.

AELIAN: ON THE NATURE OF ANIMALS. A. F. Scholfield. 3 Vols.

AENEAS TACTICUS, ASCLEPIODOTUS AND ONASANDER. The Illinois Greek Club.

AESCHINES. C. D. Adams.

AESCHYLUS. H. Weir Smyth. 2 Vols.

ALCIPHRON, AELIAN AND PHILOSTRATUS: LETTERS. A. R. Benner and F. H. Fobes.

APOLLODORUS. Sir James G. Frazer. 2 Vols.

APOLLONIUS RHODIUS. R. C. Seaton.

THE APOSTOLIC FATHERS. Kirsopp Lake. 2 Vols.

APPIAN'S ROMAN HISTORY. Horace White. 4 Vols.

ARATUS. *Cf.* CALLIMACHUS.

ARISTOPHANES. Benjamin Bickley Rogers. 3 Vols. Verse trans.

ARISTOTLE: ART OF RHETORIC. J. H. Freese.

ARISTOTLE: ATHENIAN CONSTITUTION, EUDEMIAN ETHICS, VIRTUES AND VICES. H. Rackham.

ARISTOTLE: THE CATEGORIES. ON INTERPRETATION. H. P. Cooke; PRIOR ANALYTICS. H. Tredennick.

ARISTOTLE: GENERATION OF ANIMALS. A. L. Peck.

ARISTOTLE: HISTORIA ANIMALIUM. A. L. Peck. 3 Vols. Vols. I and II.

ARISTOTLE: METAPHYSICS. H. Tredennick. 2 Vols.

ARISTOTLE: METEOROLOGICA. H. D. P. Lee.

ARISTOTLE: MINOR WORKS. W. S. Hett. "On Colours," "On Things Heard," "Physiognomics," "On Plants," "On Marvellous Things Heard," "Mechanical Problems," "On Invisible Lines," "Situations and Names of Winds," "On Melissus, Xenophanes, and Gorgias."

ARISTOTLE: NICOMACHEAN ETHICS. H. Rackham.

ARISTOTLE: OECONOMICA AND MAGNA MORALIA. G. C. Armstrong. (With METAPHYSICS, Vol II.)

ARISTOTLE: ON THE HEAVENS. W. K. C. Guthrie.

ARISTOTLE: ON THE SOUL, PARVA NATURALIA, ON BREATH. W. S. Hett.

ARISTOTLE: PARTS OF ANIMALS. A. L. Peck; MOVEMENT AND PROGRESSION OF ANIMALS. E. S. Forster.

ARISTOTLE: PHYSICS. Rev. P. Wicksteed and F. M. Cornford. 2 Vols.

THE LOEB CLASSICAL LIBRARY

5

THE LOEB CLASSICAL LIBRARY

EURIPIDES. A. S. Way. 4 Vols. Verse trans.
EUSEBIUS: ECCLESIASTICAL HISTORY. Kirsopp Lake and J. E. L. Oulton. 2 Vols.
GALEN: ON THE NATURAL FACULTIES. A. J. Brock.
THE GREEK ANTHOLOGY. W. R. Paton. 5 Vols.
THE GREEK BUCOLIC POETS (THEOCRITUS, BION, MOSCHUS). J. M. Edmonds.
GREEK ELEGY AND IAMBUS WITH THE ANACREONTEA. J. M. Edmonds. 2 Vols.
GREEK MATHEMATICAL WORKS. Ivor Thomas. 2 Vols.
HERODES. *Cf.* THEOPHRASTUS: CHARACTERS.
HERODIAN: C. R. Whittaker. 2 Vols.
HERODOTUS. A. D. Godley. 4 Vols.
HESIOD AND THE HOMERIC HYMNS. H. G. Evelyn White.
HIPPOCRATES AND THE FRAGMENTS OF HERACLEITUS. W. H. S. Jones and E. T. Withington. 4 Vols.
HOMER: ILIAD. A. T. Murray. 2 Vols.
HOMER: ODYSSEY. A. T. Murray. 2 Vols.
ISAEUS. E. S. Forster.
ISOCRATES. George Norlin and LaRue Van Hook. 3 Vols.
[ST. JOHN DAMASCENE]: BARLAAM AND IOASAPH. Rev. G. R. Woodward, Harold Mattingly and D. M. Lang.
JOSEPHUS. 9 Vols. Vols. I-IV. H. St. J. Thackeray. Vol. V. H. St. J. Thackeray and Ralph Marcus. Vols VI and VII. Ralph Marcus. Vol. VIII. Ralph Marcus and Allen Wikgren. Vol. IX. L. H. Feldman.
JULIAN. Wilmer Cave Wright. 3 Vols.
LIBANIUS: SELECTED WORKS. A. F. Norman. 3 Vols. Vol. I.
LONGUS: DAPHNIS AND CHLOE. Thornley's translation revised by J. M. Edmonds; and PARTHENIUS. S. Gaselee.
LUCIAN. 8 Vols. Vols I-V. A. M. Harmon. Vol. VI. K. Kilburn. Vols. VII and VIII. M. D. Macleod.
LYCOPHRON. *Cf.* CALLIMACHUS.
LYRA GRAECA. J. M. Edmonds. 3 Vols.
LYSIAS. W. R. M. Lamb.
MANETHO. W. G. Waddell; PTOLEMY: TETRABIBLOS. F. E. Robbins.
MARCUS AURELIUS. C. R. Haines.
MENANDER. F. G. Allinson.
MINOR ATTIC ORATORS. 2 Vols. K. J. Maidment and J. O. Burtt.
NONNOS: DIONYSIACA. W. H. D. Rouse. 3 Vols.
OPPIAN, COLLUTHUS, TRYPHIODORUS. A. W. Mair.
PAPYRI. NON-LITERARY SELECTIONS. A. S. Hunt and C. C.

THE LOEB CLASSICAL LIBRARY

Edgar. 2 Vols. LITERARY SELECTIONS (Poetry). D. L. Page.

PARTHENIUS. *Cf.* LONGUS.

PAUSANIAS : DESCRIPTION OF GREECE. W. H. S. Jones. 4 Vols. and Companion Vol. arranged by R. E. Wycherley.

PHILO. 10 Vols. Vols. I-V. F. H. Colson and Rev. G. H. Whitaker. Vols. VI-X. F. H. Colson. General Index. Rev. J. W. Earp.

Two Supplementary Vols. Translation only from an Armenian Text. Ralph Marcus.

PHILOSTRATUS : THE LIFE OF APOLLONIUS OF TYANA. F. C. Conybeare. 2 Vols.

PHILOSTRATUS : IMAGINES ; CALLISTRATUS : DESCRIPTIONS. A. Fairbanks.

PHILOSTRATUS AND EUNAPIUS : LIVES OF THE SOPHISTS. Wilmer Cave Wright.

PINDAR. Sir J. E. Sandys.

PLATO : CHARMIDES, ALCIBIADES, HIPPARCHUS, THE LOVERS, THEAGES, MINOS AND EPINOMIS. W. R. M. Lamb.

PLATO : CRATYLUS, PARMENIDES, GREATER HIPPIAS, LESSER HIPPIAS. H. N. Fowler.

PLATO : EUTHYPHRO, APOLOGY, CRITO, PHAEDO, PHAEDRUS. H. N. Fowler.

PLATO : LACHES, PROTAGORAS, MENO, EUTHYDEMUS. W. R. M. Lamb.

PLATO : LAWS. Rev. R. G. Bury. 2 Vols.

PLATO : LYSIS, SYMPOSIUM, GORGIAS. W. R. M. Lamb.

PLATO : REPUBLIC. Paul Shorey. 2 Vols.

PLATO : STATESMAN. PHILEBUS. H. N. Fowler ; ION. W. R. M. Lamb.

PLATO : THEAETETUS AND SOPHIST. H. N. Fowler.

PLATO : TIMAEUS, CRITIAS, CLITOPHO, MENEXENUS, EPISTULAE. Rev. R. G. Bury.

PLOTINUS. A. H. Armstrong. 6 Vols. Vols. I-III.

PLUTARCH : MORALIA. 16 Vols. Vols. I-V. F. C. Babbitt. Vol. VI. W. C. Helmbold. Vol. VII. P. H. De Lacy and B. Einarson. Vol. VIII. P. A. Clement, H. B. Hoffleit. Vol. IX. E. L. Minar, Jr., F. H. Sandbach, W. C. Helmbold. Vol. X. H. N. Fowler. Vol. XI. L. Pearson, F. H. Sandbach. Vol. XII. H. Cherniss, W. C. Helmbold. Vol. XIV. P. H. De Lacy and B. Einarson. Vol. XV. F. H. Sandbach.

PLUTARCH : THE PARALLEL LIVES. B. Perrin. 11 Vols.

POLYBIUS. W. R. PATON. 6 Vols.

THE LOEB CLASSICAL LIBRARY

Procopius : History of the Wars. H. B. Dewing. 7 Vols.
Ptolemy : Tetrabiblos. *Cf.* Manetho.
Quintus Smyrnaeus. A. S. Way. Verse trans.
Sextus Empiricus. Rev. R. G. Bury. 4 Vols.
Sophocles. F. Storr. 2 Vols. Verse trans.
Strabo : Geography. Horace L. Jones. 8 Vols.
Theophrastus : Characters. J. M. Edmonds ; Herodes, etc. A. D. Knox.
Theophrastus : Enquiry into Plants. Sir Arthur Hort. 2 Vols.
Thucydides. C. F. Smith. 4 Vols.
Tryphiodorus. *Cf.* Oppian.
Xenophon : Anabasis. C. L. Brownson.
Xenophon : Cyropaedia. Walter Miller. 2 Vols.
Xenophon : Hellenica. C. L. Brownson.
Xenophon : Memorabilia and Oeconomicus. E. C. Marchant. Symposium and Apology. O. J. Todd.
Xenophon : Scripta Minora. E. C. Marchant and G. W. Bowersock.

VOLUMES IN PREPARATION

GREEK AUTHORS

Aristides : Orations. C. A. Behr.
Musaeus : Hero and Leander. T. Gelzer and C. H. Whitman.
Theophrastus : De Causis Plantarum. G. K. K. Link and B. Einarson.

LATIN AUTHORS

Asconius : Commentaries on Cicero's Orations. G. W. Bowersock.
Benedict : The Rule. P. Meyvaert.
Justin-Trogus. R. Moss.
Manilius. G. P. Goold.

DESCRIPTIVE PROSPECTUS ON APPLICATION

LONDON	CAMBRIDGE, MASS.
WILLIAM HEINEMANN LTD	HARVARD UNIV. PRESS